THE MYTH OF COMMUNITY

For
Rietje and Jaap Guijt
and
Shyama and Pushkar Nath Kaul

THE MYTH
OF COMMUNITY

*Gender issues
in participatory development*

edited by
IRENE GUIJT and MEERA KAUL SHAH

INTERMEDIATE TECHNOLOGY PUBLICATIONS 1998

Intermediate Technology Publications Ltd,
103–105 Southampton Row, London WC1B 4HH, UK

© the individual authors; this collection Intermediate Technology
Publications 1998

A CIP catalogue record for this book is available from the British
Library

ISBN 1 85339 421 1

Typeset by Dorwyn Ltd, Rowlands Castle, Hants
Printed in the UK by SRP Exeter

38747441

Contents

List of Figures

List of Tables

List of Boxes

Acknowledgements

A book is always a collective effort. We are grateful to the following people and organizations for making this publication possible:

○ for inspiration, encouragement and critical comments: Robert Chambers, Parmesh Shah, Jim Woodhill, Marlène Buchy, Andrea Cornwall and Alice Welbourn;
○ for vital logistical support: the International Institute for Environment and Development, particularly Ginni Tym, Hilary Pickford, Fiona Hinchcliffe, and Jo Abbot; Penny Admiral and Sue Ong at the Institute for Development Studies; and the Department of Forestry at the Australian National University, Canberra;
○ for essential funding: Swiss Agency for Development and Cooperation, Institute for Development studies, and Swedish International Development Cooperation Agency;
○ for the initial impetus: the participants at the 1993 IIED/IDS workshop on PRA and Gender;
○ for their support and patience in publication: Neal Burton and Jane Lanigan at Intermediate Technology Publications, London; and
○ for challenging accepted wisdom and documenting their insights: the authors and their colleagues.

Author Profiles

1. *Rhodante Ahlers* has a Master's degree in irrigation engineering with a specialization in gender and irrigation issues. She has undertaken research in this field in Bhutan, Ecuador and Cambodia. Rhodante's particular interest lies in unravelling the dimensions and simultaneity of the different variables shaping access to irrigation water, drawing primarily on feminist theory, political economy and critiques on racism in science. Currently, she is an associate expert working for the International Irrigation Management Institute doing research on gender issues and water markets in the north of Mexico.

2. *Meena Bilgi* has worked as a gender specialist for advice and training on gender and institutional strengthening of GOs and NGOs. She has a MPhil degree in Social Work and has extensive experience of integrating women in the mainstream of development processes, by working closely with women and grass-root level functionaries especially in the areas of natural resource management, health and energy.

3. *Robert Chambers* is widely recognized as one of the main driving forces behind the great surge of interest in the use of Participatory Rural Appraisal around the world. He has been a Fellow at the Institute of Development Studies since 1972 from where he has inspired government agencies, multilateral and non-governmental organizations, and community-based groups to seek more participatory styles of development. He is the author of many well known books, including the recent 'Whose Reality Counts? Putting the first last' (1997, IT) and 'Rural Development: Putting the Last First' (1983). He is co-editor of the influential 'Farmer First: farmer innovation and agricultural research' (1989, with Thrupp and Pacey, IT). He has encouraged many to 'fail forwards' as they 'hand over the stick' to local people.

4. *Andrea Cornwall* is a social anthropologist with special interests in gender, methodology and sexual and reproductive health. She is currently working as a researcher and trainer in participatory approaches to reproductive and community health, and is a Fellow at the Institute of Development Studies.

5. *Tessa Cousins* works for an NGO (AFRA) that focuses on land rights and land reform in KwaZuluNatal, South Africa. She manages a small unit of four people which supports the work of the organization with inputs on participatory methods, gender, training and organizational development and rural local government. She convenes a regional network on participatory approaches, thus assisting other organizations through training or design, or evaluation with a focus on participation, or on organizational development. She is especially keen to find approaches that enable the voices that are usually silent

to speak, within ourselves, groups and communities, to allow the creativity of people to be expressed and to work with the energy that this generates. Future work will deal more with land development and natural resource management, bringing her back to her roots as a farmer before her development career.

6. *Heaven Crawley* is a gender specialist and geographer, currently working on her PhD in Oxford on 'Engendering Refugee Law and Policy; the experiences of women seeking asylum in the UK'. Her work focuses on the experiences of refugee women in the UK, coming from Sub-Saharan Africa and the Middle East. She has written a legal handbook on behalf of the Refugee Women's Legal Group. She is critical of the public/private dichotomy within legal processes of asylum determination, how gender and culture are used by the state to justify particular policies towards refugee women, and the implications of this for their gendered and national identities during the resettlement process. Her three young children are also a major part of her life.

7. *Régine Debrabandere* is an agronomist by profession. She started her work overseas as a project co-ordinator of the Mutoko District Agricultural Development Project in Zimbabwe for the Belgian development NGO, COOPIBO. She was later involved in the start of the COOPIBO programme in Uganda as a programme adviser. Her main areas of interest are community forestry, tools for participatory development and organizational development of community-based farmer organizations. She is currently working in Belgium for the Flemish Association for Development Co-operation and Technical Support (VVOB), on programme support.

8. *Sarah Degnan Kambou* (PhD, MPH) is currently Technical Co-ordinator for CARE International's Refugee Reproductive Health Initiative and is based in Addis Ababa, Ethiopia. She has developed a participatory reproductive health needs assessment approach for application in refugee and internally displaced settings (field-tested in Northern Somalia, to be followed by Sudan and Rwanda). Before her current assignment, Sarah served as Health Sector Co-ordinator for CARE Zambia where she introduced participatory tools and techniques into CARE's health and population programme. Sarah has also worked extensively in Togo, Nepal, Indonesia, the Philippines, and the People's Republic of China. Her areas of specialization include reproductive health, urban health and adolescent health, and her present research interests focus on intra-household dynamics and the role of reproductive health within a livelihood security framework.

9. *Arnout Desmet* has a degree in tropical agriculture and development economics. He started work overseas in Zimbabwe as a project co-ordinator of UMP and Mudzi District agricultural development projects for the Belgian development NGO, COOPIBO. He later co-ordinated the programme for COOPIBO in Uganda as the country co-ordinator. He is currently working as a researcher at the Centre for Agricultural Economics in Developing Countries at the Catholic

University in Leuven, Belgium. His main areas of interest are the role and development of people's organizations, policy issues in relation to food security and economic reform, and planning, management and evaluation of rural development programmes.

10. *Christiane Frischmuth* has lived, travelled, studied and worked in Asia, Europe, Africa and the Americas. She holds degrees in international relations and rural development, and is currently involved in organizational development and institutional strengthening. Training, adult education, participatory extension systems and methods, and gender sensitization have been her focal points. She has worked primarily with government agencies and NGOs at village, district and national levels. Christiane is working in Malawi to make the existing extension systems more client-oriented, motivated, participatory and efficient. She also chairs the GTZ regional network working group on gender-oriented participatory extension.

11. *Reg Green*, who is a political economist, received a BA from Whiman College and an MA and PhD from Harvard. He is currently a fellow at the Institute of Development Studies in the UK and has been interested for 37 years in political economy and development policy, focusing on poverty, food security and regional integration, particularly in sub-Saharan Africa and the Philippines. His work has included research on vulnerability and structural adjustment policies, and the human and economic costs of war.

12. *Justin Greene-Roesel* is an analyst and demographer at the Wilson Centre for Public Research in Alexandria, Virginia. She received her doctorate in social anthropology from Cambridge University, with a dissertation on power and development in Guyana. She has also worked on development issues in Egypt (cultural resource management) and Ecuador (rural health care). She is currently working to support labour unions in planning and managing their activities better. She is also investigating demographic modelling that targets populations with demographic characteristics that make them especially likely to support pro-labour activities. Voluntary work involves helping found a legal aid centre for immigrant women in Washington DC.

13. *Irene Guijt* is a Visiting Fellow at the Department of Forestry at ANU and works as a Research Associate for the International Institute for Environment and Development in London. After obtaining BSc and MSc degrees in tropical land and water use engineering from Wageningen Agricultural University, she worked extensively on diverse aspects of participatory resource management in Brazil, eastern and west Africa, and south Asia. Her interests and publications relate to gender and environment policies and methodologies, the local-level valuation of wild resources, participatory monitoring, irrigation and ecological sustainability, and institutionalizing participatory planning. Current research involves organizational development for addressing intra-communal difference in community planning in Uganda, participatory monitoring of sustainable agriculture in Brazil, and farm forestry in Australia. She recently developed a new undergraduate

and graduate course in Participatory Resource Management in the School of Resource Management and Environmental Science (ANU).

14. *Ricardo Hernandez* is a researcher and freelance journalist with a BA in history and an MA in social history who has participated in various agricultural and forestry social research surveys. He has written magazine and news articles on the history of the Rosario Mine, the city of Cotui and social movements in the region, and has co-authored various publications on the social dimensions of farm forestry programmes.

15. *Rachel Hinton* is a lecturer at Edinburgh University and social scientist with the Department for International Development. Her doctoral research at Cambridge University focused on health and development among Bhutanese refugees in Nepal.

16. *Morag Humble* works as an independent consultant, trainer and writer on gender and development issues. She has an MA from Carleton University, where her thesis expanded on the issues presented in her chapter in this volume. Her current interests include using participatory approaches to improve the quality of sexual and reproductive health care programmes for women and adolescents. She is currently doing a Masters in Public Health from Harvard University.

17. *Meera Kaul Shah* has degrees in economics, rural management, and gender and development. She has been working in the development field for the last 17 years. She has worked for NGOs in India for about 10 years, including five years with Aga Khan Rural Support Programme (AKRSP), India, which supports local village institutions to manage their natural resources in a participatory way. While at AKRSP she helped pioneer, with others, PRA as a distinct shift from the more top-down RRA methodology. For the last seven years Meera has been freelancing as a development consultant, specializing as a trainer in participatory techniques and processes, participatory gender analysis, providing support for strengthening and developing sustainable local institutions. Although her main experience lies in participatory natural resources management, she has also been involved in developing field methodologies for participatory research for policy influencing, specially those related to participatory poverty assessment, urban violence, women's concerns and problems, and sexual and reproductive health. During this period she has provided support to various NGOs and government agencies in India, Zambia, Morocco, Ghana, Malawi, Tanzania, Ethiopia, Vietnam, Papua New Guinea and Jamaica.

18. *Sara Kindon* is a Lecturer in Human Geography and Geography and Development Studies in the School of Earth Sciences, Victoria University of Wellington, Aotearoa-New Zealand. Her areas of expertise include gender analysis, participatory methods, feminist research, and rural development in Indonesia. Her main interests lie in the intersections of gender, place and identity in rural communities, the practice of participatory geographic research, indigenous knowledge systems, and development issues in Southeast Asia and the South Pacific. Sara's current work includes exploring conceptions of 'trust' and

'social capital' as they are being used in relation to communities and socio-economic development in Aotearoa-New Zealand, and investigating gendered dimensions of small-scale eco-tourism operations in northern Bali, Indonesia.

19. *Tony Kisadha* has a BSc in Civil Engineering. He worked for three years in rural technology, water and sanitation and low-cost housing. Since 1990, he has been working with Redd Barna (Norwegian Save the Children) on child-centred community development. As part of this, he has been trained in several participatory methodologies, PRA, LFA and is now a proficient trainer himself. He is the Director of Programme Development in Redd Barna Uganda, in charge of strategic and annual planning, plans and budgets for the whole of Redd Barna Programme and for specific support projects to districts for Child Advocacy work. He is interested in pursuing networking issues among organizations using participatory methodologies under the Uganda Participatory Development Network. A special interest of his is on child participation integrated in the methodologies that deal with the community level. He has been instrumental in training Norwegian youth on the child-centred development approach being developed by Redd Barna Uganda.

20. *Caren Levy* is a Senior Lecturer at the Development Planning Unit, University College London and Director of the DPU Gender Policy and Planning Programme. She is a development planner specializing in planning methodology and organizational development, with expertise in gender, environment, and transport policy and planning. Her specific focus has been the institutionalization of social equity, with particular reference to gender, environment and poverty. She has undertaken operational research, training and advisory services in London and abroad in international organizations, including UNCHS/UNEP, EU, ODA (now DFID), SIDA, Ford Foundation, IBIS, and in-country, including Egypt, Mozambique, Namibia, Brazil, Chile and Sri Lanka.

21. *Julio Morrobel* is a forester, with an MA from CATIE (Centro Technico de Investigacion y Ensenanza de America Central). He is currently a professor of Forestry and Natural Resource Management at the ISA (Instituto Superior de Agricultura) in Santiago, Dominican Republic, and conducts research on the biological, economic and social feasibility of social and agroforestry programmes. He has co-authored several articles and papers on farm-forestry programmes and their relation to social and ecological change.

22. *Grace Mukasa* graduated from Makerere University with a BA and worked in the teaching service at secondary-school level both in Uganda and Kenya for five years. She joined Redd Barna Uganda in 1994 and worked initially as a Child Advocacy Project Officer. This entailed training and facilitating district and sub-county officials in participatory approaches (PRA, LFA, MLE and BCS), and networking with other child-centred NGOs. From 1995 on, she worked as a district supervisor. Since April 1997, she has been the Programme Officer at Redd Barna Uganda, engaged in developing partnerships

with other NGO and government agencies. Her interests are development work focusing on women and children.

23. *Ranjani K. Murthy* is an independent development consultant focusing on mainstreaming gender and other social relations within poverty, environment and human-rights programmes of NGOs and funding agencies. Her work is guided by the conviction that unless development interventions expand the agency and autonomy of women and other marginalized sections, they cannot succeed. Hence her strong interest in gender and community participation in development. She is presently working on a book titled 'Indian NGOs, Poverty Alleviation, and their Capacity Enhancement in the 1990s: an institutional and social-relations perspective'.

24. *Gladys Nkhama* has a BA in Demography and Economics and is currently Special Projects Coordinator with CARE based in Lusaka, Zambia. She has been instrumental in introducing participatory techniques into CARE's health and population sector. Gladys has been involved in different types of quantitative research with the Central Statistics Bureau of Zambia. Currently, she is working with CARE's Operations Research Unit whose interests include: female condom-demand study, enhancing contraceptive choice in Zambia (ECC study), a study on adolescent behaviour and sexual and reproductive health.

25. *Maria Protz* is a development communication specialist whose work and research interests are in the use of participatory media approaches for sustainable rural development. She is particularly interested in the ways in which rural women can use media to document their own indigenous agricultural knowledge so that it is properly included in the design and development of appropriate agricultural technologies. She lives and works in Jamaica where she is the director of Mekweseh Communications, in Jamaican patois 'Let's say something'.

26. *Dianne Rocheleau* is an Associate Professor of Geography at Clark University in Worcester. She is a political ecologist looking at the social and ecological dimensions of land use and landscape change. Her work has focused on the Dominican Republic, Kenya and the United States in both rural and urban ecosystems, particularly dealing with forestry and agroforestry and participatory research and planning methods. She has worked as a social and environmental researcher in Plan Sierra, the Dominican Republic, as a senior scientist at ICRAF in Nairobi, Kenya, a Ford Foundation Programme Officer for Rural Poverty and Resources in eastern and southern Africa (Nairobi, Kenya) and, since 1989, at Clark University. She is the co-author and editor of several books, the most recent of which is 'Feminist Political Ecology' (with B. Thomas-Slayter and E. Wangari, eds). Currently she is writing about tree biodiversity, agrarian change and emergent ecologies in the Dominican Republic and a book on a critical environmental history of the Akamba region in Kenya.

27. *Laurie Ross* has an MA in International Development and Social Change and a BA in Geography from Clark University and is currently pursuing a doctorate in Urban Planning at UMASS Boston.

She has worked as an interviewer, field supervisor and data analyst for the Better Homes Foundation, in a long-term survey of women receiving public assistance. She is also a founding partner in an urban planning consulting firm and has worked with community-development corporations to involve local residents, and especially youth, in planning of neighbourhood improvements and in design of parks and public space. Publications include several articles on research methods and case study research.

28. *Madhu Sarin* has almost 20 years experience with development work, initially with urban development and planning. Since 1980 her focus has been on decentralized rural natural resource management, particularly gender and equity concerns. Her recent book 'Joint Forest Management: The Haryana Experience' spans 16 years of participatory forest management in Haryana beginning with the well-known pilot experiment with social fencing in Sukhomajri. Amongst her current activities is the coordination of the sub-group on gender and equity concerns in JFM, within the national JFM network, through the Society for Promotion of Wastelands Development, New Delhi.

29. *Sonja Vlaar* obtained an MSc at Wageningen Agricultural University in the Netherlands and specialized in food security. From 1980–85 she worked in Mozambique and was involved in training and supervision of extension workers and the identification and formulation of projects. Back in the Netherlands, she managed the Dutch component of several NGO projects in the Andean and Central American region. From 1990–95 she was a consultant for SAWA, a Dutch consulting agency and focused mainly on institutional development of NGOs and gender issues. In 1995 she joined the Management for Development Foundation, where she conducts training programmes focusing on NGO organizational development. Recently she has been involved in organizational strengthening of NGOs in Angola, Guinea Bissau and Bulgaria.

30. *Alice Welbourn* is a social development trainer, writer, adviser and facilitator. She lived in Somalia and Kenya and worked on grass-roots development projects for 10 years, from 1980–90. Since then, she has led short training workshops in PRA, focusing on gender and the analysis of difference in communities in Eastern, Southern and West Africa, and has written about these in PLA Notes and elsewhere. Since 1993, she has worked on gender and HIV and currently leads the Stepping Stones Training and Adaptation Project. She lives with her family in the United Kingdom.

Foreword

ROBERT CHAMBERS

The Myth of Community fills a huge gap. With hindsight, the previous lack of a book like this appears little short of spectacular. During the past two decades, the two powerful but separate movements, of gender and of participation, have been transforming the rhetoric, and increasingly the reality, of local-level development. Each has generated much writing. Each has major implications for the other. Yet, astonishingly, to the best of my knowledge, this is the first book thoroughly to explore the overlaps, linkages, contradictions, and synergies between the two. It cannot be often that a vital gap cries out for so long to be filled; and that it is then filled so well, with such rich material and insight, and with so much of the excitement of significant discovery, as in this book.

Its importance can be understood against the background of the two movements.

First, gender and development has had an immense influence. In many ways – in rhetoric and syntax, in appointments and promotions, in organizational behaviour, in projects, programmes and policies, and above all in personal awareness and orientation – a tidal change has started and continues. At the personal level, many of us development professionals have been both threatened and liberated as we become more aware of the pervasive inequities of the socially constructed relations between women and men, and recognize the personal implications for ourselves. To be sure, there is far still to go; and whether we are women or men, we will always have much to learn and unlearn, and much to work to change. But in development thinking and action, the direction is clear. Gender awareness and equity are irreversibly on the agenda and increasingly pursued in practice.

For its part, participation has origins which go far back. It has, though, only recently come together in the mainstream of development discourse and action. Both donor agencies and governments now have policies to promote it. At the same time, methodologies for participatory development, among them PRA (originally participatory rural appraisal), have evolved and spread, presenting new opportunities and means for turning the rhetoric into reality. Participation, like gender, presents challenges and opportunities across a wide front. Not least these are institutional, to change organizations, and personal, to change individual behaviour and attitudes.

To explore and share experiences and ideas about gender and participation, Irene Guijt and Meera Shah convened a two-day workshop at the Institute of Development Studies (IDS) at the University of Sussex, UK in December 1993. It was one of a series on PRA organized jointly by IDS and the International Institute for Environment and Development, London. This book originates in the discussions and papers of that workshop. Papers have been updated and revised; others have been added; and the scope has been widened beyond PRA to include participatory approaches more broadly.

There is here a rich and diverse harvest for the reader. Across the board, the contributions offer insights. The direct personal experiences of the writers present an immediacy and realism which carries conviction. The realities described invite reflection. They provoke review and revision of one's sense of what is right and what is doable. Each reader will draw out her or his own themes and lessons. For me, four stand out.

First, there are many *biases* to be recognized and offset. Attitudes and behaviours which are dominating and discriminatory are common among those of us who are men: to become aware of these is a first and often difficult step. Even when the application of participatory methodologies is intended to minimize biases, women are often marginalized. Again and again, women are excluded by factors like time and place of meeting, composition of groups, conventions that only men speak in public, outsiders being only or mainly men, and men talking to men. In communities, it is easier for men than women to find the undisturbed blocks of time needed for PRA mapping, diagramming, discussions and analysis. The times best for women to meet, sometimes late after dark, are often inconvenient for outsiders. When outsiders rush, make short visits, do not stay the night, and come only once or twice, it is typically difficult for local women to participate, and issues of gender are likely to be marginalized or excluded. Again and again, the cases cited in this book are, in contrast, based on repeated, sustained and sensitive contact and interaction. Recognizing and offsetting these biases requires sensitivity, patience and commitment on the part of those who are outsiders to a community.

Second, local *contexts* are complex, diverse and dynamic. The reductionism of collective nouns misleads: 'community' hides many divisions and differences, with gender often hugely significant; 'women' as a focus distracts attention from gender relations between women and men, and from men themselves; and 'women' also conceals the many differences between females by age, class, marital status and social group. Nor are common beliefs valid everywhere: female-headed households are often the worst off, but not always. Moreover, social relations change, sometimes fast. It is not just the myth of community that this book dispels, but other myths of simple, stable and uniform social realities.

Third, *conflict* is sometimes necessary and positive for good change. For gender equity, much that needs to change concerns the power and priority of males over females. Several contributions to this book strikingly confront consensual participation as a myth, at least in the short term. They show that conflict can be an essential and creative factor in change for the better. Common examples are tackling issues of power and control over resources, and dealing with aggressive and violent behaviour. Domestic violence, drunken husbands, female infanticide, discrimination against females of all ages – these are phenomena difficult to confront without conflict. This does not mean a negative sum in well-being, that for females to gain, males must lose. To cease to dominate, oppress or be violent is itself a liberation. Responsible well-being is enhanced in shared responsibilities, in good relations in the family, in social harmony, and in personal peace of mind. The key is to facilitate changes in gender relations which lead to a positive sum, in which all come to feel better off, and so in which all gain.

Fourth, issues of *ethics* are repeatedly posed by both gender and participation: whether outsiders' interventions are based on universally valid values or a form of cultural domination; whether working with those who are weak and vulnerable leads to bad results for them, as when women are beaten by their husbands when the outsider leaves; whether gender-sensitive participation leads in practice to women and girls being better off or through a backlash worse off than before. There seem to be no easy answers. The imperative is to consult women and girls, and sometimes men, and seek their views on what it is right and practicable to do; it is to recognize the dilemmas of where values conflict, to puzzle and worry about them, and in a spirit of pluralism to act according to what seems best in each context, struggling to act well through self-aware judgement which respects the rights and realities of others.

Strikingly, these four themes all point to personal behaviour, attitudes, values and commitment. This is evident in many of the contributions. It applies to all of us who seek to intervene and influence the lives of others, whether through research, facilitation, sensitization or other development actions. In offsetting biases, this means working for gender equity, reducing dominance by men, and meeting, listening to and learn from women in places and at times they find convenient. In the local context it means being sensitive to social diversity and complexity in various dimensions of social difference, including, though not exclusively, gender. In conflict it means being alert and exercising good judgement in facilitating and managing process and mediating negotiation, resolving differences and nurturing relationships in which those who lose in one way gain in others. In ethical issues, it means consulting women, girls and others who are weak, and continual self-questioning, not to the point of paralysis, but reflecting on values, combining commitment with being open to self-doubt, and learning and changing oneself.

It is in this spirit that personal sensitivity pervades this book. The insights into gender relations and into participation are nuanced. The presentations are balanced, insightful and persuasive. The experience, evidence and analysis are often fascinating, recognizing and celebrating differences. The tensions and difficulties encountered with gender have generated concepts, methods and understandings which are subtle, and which ground participation in a deeper realism.

Now that we have this book, it deserves the widest distribution and readership. For those who specialize in gender, it opens up participation. For those who specialize in participation, it reinforces the gender dimension in full measure. For all other development professionals – whether academics, researchers or trainers, whether field practitioners, managers, consultants or policy-makers, and whether in government organizations, bilateral or multilateral donor agencies, or international or national

NGOs – it offers readable access to new development needs and opportunities.

The Myth of Community takes us – development professionals – a long step forward. After this, 'gender' and 'participation' can never be quite the same again. Let me hope that this book will be read, reread and reflected on, and that its insights will permeate and help to transform development theory and practice. The editors and authors would never claim to have made a final or definitive statement. They have, though, covered so much new ground so well and so convincingly that the good impact of their work should be deep and lasting. In our world, hundreds of millions are marginalized, oppressed and made miserable by domination and exclusion. Most of them are women. May those who read this book be inspired to act to reduce their marginalization, oppression and misery and to help relations between women and men change for the better. For gender equity and participation have, together, a huge potential for enhacing well-being for all.

1

Waking Up to Power, Conflict and Process

IRENE GUIJT and MEERA KAUL SHAH

For many, PRA seeks to empower lowers – women, minorities, the poor, the weak, and the vulnerable and to make power reversals real.
(Chambers, 1997:106)

Gender was hidden [in participatory research] in seemingly inclusive terms: 'the people', 'the oppressed', 'the campesinos', or simply 'the community'. It was only when comparing... projects that it became clear that 'the community' was all too often the male community.
(Maguire, 1996:29–30)

The cutting edge of development practice in the 1990s is described in terms of 'participation', 'community-driven action', and 'empowerment'. The broad aim of participatory development is to increase the involvement of socially and economically marginalized[1] people in decision-making over their own lives. The assumption is that participatory approaches empower local people with the skills and confidence to analyse their situation, reach consensus, make decisions and take action, so as to improve their circumstances. The ultimate goal is more equitable and sustainable development.

Yet in many cases where participation has been pursued something is going wrong. Despite the stated intentions of social inclusion, it has become clear that many participatory development initiatives do not deal well with the complexity of community differences, including age, economic, religious, caste, ethnic and, in particular, gender. Looking back, it is apparent that 'community' has often been viewed naively, or in practice dealt with, as an harmonious and internally equitable collective. Too often there has been an inadequate understanding of the internal dynamics and differences, that are so crucial to positive outcomes. This mythical notion of community cohesion continues to permeate much participatory work, hiding a bias that favours the opinions and priorities of those with more power and the ability to voice themselves publicly. In particular, there is a minimal consideration of gender issues and inadequate involvement of women. While a handful of women may sometimes be consulted, rarely does a thorough understanding of the complexity of gender relations help structure the process, the analysis and any resulting community plans. Some view a gender-neutral participatory approach, at times with pride, as non-intrusive and culturally sensitive. However, it is the theme of this book that the language and practice of 'participation' often obscures women's worlds, needs and contributions to development, making equitable participatory development an elusive goal.

It is bewildering that the fields of participatory development and gender have remained far apart, both in theory and practice, despite their shared goals of social inclusion[2] and societal transformation. More gender-responsive forms of participatory research and development would have many benefits. Misunderstanding or ignoring women's needs not only affects the women themselves but also, quite obviously, has a negative impact on the immediate family and the wider community. Greater involvement of women and attention to gender-differentiated needs holds the promise of much more effective and equitable processes of participatory development. The outcomes are more likely to be meaningful for all those involved. Furthermore, the process of inclusion, if constructed appropriately, can help raise women's confidence, open up space for their views, and ease oppressive gender relations (see Chapters 8,[3] 18, 20 and 21, this volume).

Community-based[4] action remains a powerful and essential vehicle for development, as long as it addresses gender and other dimensions of social difference explicitly. Making false claims to empowerment and inclusion when this is not the case will only undermine the current interest in participation for development (Chapter 6, this volume; Guijt and Cornwall, 1995).

This book urges those engaged in participatory development to understand gender differences in community and to integrate gender thinking into participatory practice. The chapters have been arranged into three parts:
(1) Theoretical Reflections; (2) Sharing Experiences in Research and Action, and (3) Institutional Processes.

This introductory chapter sets the context for the whole book and provides a rationale for each of the parts. It discusses first how participatory development has come to pay so little attention to community differences, focusing on the problem of simplistic notions of community, participation and empowerment. It then describes how development organizations are slowly waking up to the importance of these issues. The chapter summarizes the collective insights from the contributors to this volume in terms of the book's three parts:

(1) improving conceptual understanding about community, gender, participation and empowerment;
(2) developing improved methodologies that allow for better gender-based analysis and a more meaningful involvement of women; and
(3) creating institutional change that will result in organizational cultures and support structures that promote, enable and implement improved conceptual understanding and methodological development.

Parenthetical referencing to chapters only are to those in this volume.

Understanding the roots of gender naïvety in participatory development

To know how to improve current practice, it is essential to understand how the problems have emerged. This section examines the factors that have contributed to the gender naïvety of much participatory development. It is necessary to explain this from both an historical and conceptual perspective. The first two parts of this section reflect on the evolution of participatory development and gender studies and on the links, or more to the point, absence of links, between them. This sets a context for discussing the conceptual, definitional and ultimately practical confusion that has beset the use of the terms community, participation and empowerment.

Historical factors in the evolution of participatory development

Despite the recent explosion of interest in participatory development, it is not a new phenomenon. Early initiatives that stress empowerment and collective local action include among others, the New Deal in India in the 1930s (Eyben and Ladbury, 1995) and community-development programmes in Latin America in the 1950s (Huizer, 1979). While important precursors, they did not generate the frenetic levels of global interest that exist today. This has arisen mainly since the 1970s (see Box 1.1), when government and non-government agencies alike increasingly set out to structure processes to 'help amplify traditionally unacknowledged voices' (Slocum and Thomas-Slayter, 1995). These processes have often explicitly aimed to transfer some degree of control over natural and social resources to those previously without such power. They offer methods and strategies for increasing ownership by 'the community' over its own development.

Participatory research and development was pioneered mainly in the field, through trial and error. Some of the earlier efforts undoubtedly arose as challenges to the dominant power structures. Yet participatory processes have been increasingly approached as technical, management solutions to what are basically political issues, including the micro-politics of gender. Many of the individuals involved have not realized the implications of gender relations on development. If they have, they have been unable to implement their gender-sensitive intentions because of a methodological hiatus and/or organizational disinterest. They have often assumed that the presence of women at community gatherings, alongside men, means that women and their issues are being included. This assumption completely ignores the dynamics of gender relations – with significant implications for the validity of the participatory process. Conversely, attempts to work separately with women and women's projects have suffered the fate of not being reintegrated with the dominant decisionmaking structures within the community, resulting in little change to social relations (Chapters 3, 8, 11, 13, 18 and 21, this volume).

Many entrenched obstacles have hindered addressing even practical gender needs, not to mention the more structural changes needed to redress power imbalances in gender relations. Six factors stand out as particularly important:

(1) Development was driven largely by a poverty-alleviation agenda, and analysis of social difference was limited to those below and those above a theoretical 'poverty line'. Caste and economic differences fitted better in this view of development than gender issues, and efforts focused on creating space for 'the poor' and understanding their issues, for example through wealth ranking (Grandin, 1988).
(2) The professionals initially involved were mainly male, making communication with women culturally difficult in many areas. Also, as gender theories were not yet widespread in the 1970s, professionals were generally not exposed to gender analysis. The context in which participatory research emerged 'centred around male power, perceptions, problems and experiences' (de Koning and Martin, 1996).

3

Box 1.1:   Key phases in externally initiated, structured participatory processes in development

1. Need for alternatives

During the 1970s, despite some early experimentation with externally initiated forms of devolved local development, frustration rose over the ineffectiveness of the dominant externally imposed and 'expert' orientated forms of research and planning (Chambers, 1992). One of the main concerns was the lack of incorporation of local people's perspectives, priorities and skills in development interventions. This trend led to a search for alternative methods for data collection and planning. A second source of methodological rethinking started earlier, in the 1950s and 60s, driven by concerns about 'giving voice to the voiceless' and social transformation (Freire, 1972; Rahman, 1984). This helped to define basic principles to guide people's empowerment in their own development processes. While there was a strong focus on empowerment for poverty alleviation, gender issues were not mentioned explicitly and the poor were viewed largely as a homogeneous group.

2. The participation boom

The mid 1980s saw great activity, mainly amongst grassroots activists and NGOs, in seeking alternatives to outsider-driven development approaches. There was much experimenting with new research and planning approaches that incorporated the methods and the principles identified earlier on, creating a bewildering array of approaches and acronyms. The focus was on respecting and understanding insider/local knowledge, to balance the dominance of outsider/western scientific knowledge. Very few of the approaches explicitly addressed the social relations of gender or identified the need for gender-sensitive methods. Where gender issues were addressed it tended to be through specific projects or components of projects rather than as a core part of participatory planning processes. The 1980s witnessed the first feminist critiques of mainstream participation (Maguire, 1987) and growth of feminist research (Mies, 1983), but this critique was not taken on by mainstream development practice.

3. The participation imperative

The early 1990s witnessed frenzied levels of global interest in participatory methodologies, the new synonym for 'good' or 'sustainable' development. It also marked the beginning of what some critics have called the new methodological 'tyranny' (Bell, 1994). Funding bodies began demanding that 'participatory processes' become a condition for funding. This has continued unabated. The push for participation stimulated the production of countless guides, handbooks, courses and networks, many contributing in very positive ways to development thinking and practice. However, there was little consensus about what constituted good quality work, and failures and difficulties were common, provoking considerable and helpful criticism. Criticism about the lack of attention to gender issues (notably Welbourn, 1991) has resulted from the recent growing involvement of gender specialists and feminist thinking in participatory development.

4. The paradoxes of participation
The situation today reveals two paradoxes in participatory development. The first involves the standardization of approaches. This trend contradicts one of the original aims, to move away from the limitations of blueprint planning and implementation towards more flexible and context-specific methodologies. A second, related, paradox lies in the technical, rather than empowerment-oriented, use of 'participatory' methods. A manual and method-oriented mania has led many to claim successful participatory development, despite only a superficial understanding of the underlying empowerment principles that were at the root of much pioneering work. Yet the explicit focus on gender issues within participatory development is growing as part of the move back to empowerment-oriented and context-specific approaches.

Source: Adapted from Guijt, 1996a.

(3) Building rapport with women and negotiating changes with the men took courage and time, making gender-inclusiveness an unappealing task (Chapters 18 and 21). Unacceptability of what was considered, by some, to be a western and imposed feminist agenda created further resistance to the analysis of social relations of gender. Focusing on women's practical concerns was an escape route for field workers from the time-consuming and difficult process of negotiating more structural changes with women and men alike.

(4) The influence of little and poor quality documentation on participation in perpetuating poor practice should not be underestimated. Many early reports describe one-off training consultancies. Little attention was paid to the complex processes of social change, the depth of conceptual analysis required and the types of organizational follow-up that make or break these approaches. Too much was claimed of participation too early, without first undertaking intensive and lengthy engagements with communities (Shah and Kaul Shah, 1995). This situation continues.

(5) Many efforts focused, and continue to do so, on appraisal rather than community-based planning and implementation. The lack of efforts to engage communities in thorough planning processes, when more contentious decisions must be made that reveal stark differences in priorities, means participatory planning has been documented mainly as wishful thinking rather than on the basis of actual experiences. A common statement in the literature about the planning process is 'and then a community plan was identified'. The appraisal focus allowed participatory practice to skirt decision-making conflicts and ignore the need for conflict-resolution skills.

(6) Too much pressure from donors to incorporate gender concerns in projects has resulted in many organizations taking up gender issues in a mechanistic fashion. They are incorporated into many programmes

only to meet a requirement for resource mobilization. This has not allowed organizations to let gender issues evolve in an organic manner as part of pursuing participatory processes. It has also led to resistance from many indigenous organizations, as 'gender' is perceived to be an agenda imposed from outside.

Chambers' (1997) summary of the theoretical influences on PRA shed further light on the lack of gender awareness in its practice. He identifies five fields of particular importance to current practice: action-reflection research, agro-ecosystem analysis, applied anthropology, field research on farming systems, and rapid rural appraisal. Despite the rich and varied contributions of each of these fields, none, except anthropology,[5] were informed significantly by gender studies. Therefore, they could not contribute the much-needed gender awareness that is the focus of this book. More recent methodological inspiration has come from soft systems approaches to problem-solving, chaos theories, social sciences (particularly postmodernity) and business management (Chambers, 1997). Again, none of these are striking in their integration of or contribution to gender-aware perspectives on social change. While Chambers refers only to PRA, other participatory approaches (and there are many!)[6] share similar methodological roots. However, at last, gender studies, feminism and feminist participatory research is beginning to have its impact on participatory development, as testified by the contributions in this book. Yet, as is discussed below, criticisms can also be made of the failure of gender studies to address itself to participatory development issues.

The ambiguous contribution of gender studies

In the 1980s, feminist participatory research emerged, aiming to link scholarship and activism to change, rather than simply describe, social reality (Mies, 1983). Yet such feminist approaches have had only a marginal influence on mainstream development to date. The women in development (WID) and gender and development (GAD) fields were more influential, but also suffered limitations. The belated entry of gender studies into the field of participatory development needs to be understood as, in part, resulting from the nature of gender studies itself.

Firstly, the focus of gender studies has largely been conceptual with limited translation,[7] until recently, of ideas into practices applicable to sectors such as participatory development. As Humble (Chapter 3, this volume) argues: 'Gender and development is a concept in search of a methodology'. The relative unpopularity amongst gender specialists of spending time in the field at the grassroots level as opposed to attending international conferences such as Beijing, sits alongside a tendency to focus on publications and presentations. Where methodological development did occur, it was largely driven by outsiders' interest in information for others to plan more appropriately (for example, Feldstein and Jiggins, 1995; Feldstein and Poats, 1989), rather than local analysis and planning.

Secondly, inadequate attention has been paid to understanding and changing institutional contexts, with most efforts aimed at clarifying gender roles. While descriptions of who does what can help identify development needs, they fall short of dealing with the institutions and processes that underpin unequal power relations. Shaw (1995) writes: 'To be successful, mobilization that is initiated by participatory researchers must be actively supported in the face of opposition', yet time constraints and the academic requirements of many gender scholars have often precluded this type of involvement.

Thirdly, facilitators dealing with gender analysis often have a poor understanding of local women's organizations, and work insufficiently with local gender specialists.[8] They rarely consider the positive local experiences with organizing women (such as the influential video experiences of SEWA, India; Jumani, 1985). Even feminist participatory researchers have generally failed to break down the dominance of western researchers over their southern subjects, despite their explicit attempts to do so (Shaw, 1995). Mohanty (1991) has criticized western gender specialists for falling into a feminist trap of 'community averages' by conflating Third World women's realities into one type of oppressive experience.

Gender specialists are committed to changing oppressive gender relations. Their radical contributions lie at the very heart of the chapters in this volume. Yet all too often, gender has, in practice, meant only women. This has provoked resistance from many men and has made a ghetto of the gender agenda. Gender has remained the responsibility and domain of a few women specialists, who have only slowly started transforming the theoretical into the practical, in organizational cultures dominated by male management. Training agents of change, rather than local people, has been the main vehicle for this change, a necessary but inadequate condition (Rao *et al.*, 1991; Levy, 1992). Organizational policies on gender equity are also popular, but the limited translation to field practices remains a key constraint to meaningful implementation of new skills and policies.

Simplification of community

The use of 'community', the first of three conceptual problems, as the unit of analysis for much work that passes as participatory has a long history. Bryson and Mowbray (1981) describe how, well over a century ago, 'the ideal of a culturally and politically homogeneous, participatory local social system gained acceptability and currency'. Its widespread use today led one early commentator to describe it as: 'the aerosol word of the 1970s because of the hopeful way it is sprayed over deteriorating institutions' (Jones, 1977, cited in Bryson and Mowbray, 1981). It evokes images of meeting people's real needs and widespread participation at the grassroots level, thus creating a normative sense of 'a good thing'. The focus of much participatory work on 'community meetings' as the forum for decision-making, representing perceptions in terms of 'the community map' as if only one view exists, and striving for a single 'community action plan' (or 'village' equivalents) that will somehow meet the needs of the entire community, are signs of this ongoing simplification. Inequalities, oppressive social hierarchies and discrimination are often overlooked, and instead enthusiasm is generated for the cooperative and harmonious ideal promised by the imagery of 'community'.

Etzioni (1996) discusses five points of criticism about community as a unit of analysis and intervention (before refuting them):

o 'community' is poorly defined, leading to confusion and a lack of focus for action;
o the normative use of 'community' feeds political conservatism by conveniently ignoring 'the darker side of traditional communities';
o communities never existed in the way people romanticize them today;
o due to the focus on majority rule in community processes, minority groups may lose out; and
o a community focus may be culturally oppressive if members experience social pressure to abide by cultural norms and rules that are not truly shared.

Clearly, communities are neither homogeneous in composition and concerns, nor necessarily harmonious in their relations. Participatory approaches have ignored these simple social realities. Alice Welbourn has wryly described PRA[9] as suffering from 'HBS', the 'homogeneous blob syndrome' (IIED/IDS, 1993). As mentioned above, many approaches have been successful to varying degrees about discerning who is better-off and worse-off, partly facilitated by the method of wealth ranking (Grandin, 1988). As for gender issues, less commitment and a lack of easy methods has led many organizations and professionals to fall into the trap of community averages (Guijt and Kaul Shah, 1993). Any gender differences[10] that might appear in fieldwork usually disappear into the melting pot of an 'average community plan'.

Another, practical, problem appears when attempting to describe the boundaries of a community. As the general mobility of society worldwide intensifies, it becomes increasingly difficult to know who belongs where. Some countries do not have clear settlement patterns, like communities or villages, around which people organise their lives and with which they identify (Guijt and Sidersky, 1998). In others, out-migration (periodic or long-term) has stretched community boundaries and created 'part-time insiders'. Those who receive an education outside the community and return with a new way of thinking can find themselves neither one nor the other. Dynamic community boundaries and composition highlight the limited value of using the notion of a united community with one set of priority needs.

Nevertheless, while some critics may see the focus on 'community' as a strategy to further conservative politics and reduce government spending, 'community' is still important. Community-based or community-level development has, for example, helped and empowered people, improved services, enhanced self-confidence, harnessed energies for the collective good, influenced policy directions and led to more appropriate research. But it cannot be expected to be the only or even major vehicle for social change. Assumptions about homogeneity or harmony need to be replaced with greater recognition of conflicting interests within communities and the methodological implications of such differences. Professionals must be astute and self-critical enough to recognize when community interventions become 'part of the legitimation process which ultimately supports existing social relations' (Bryson and Mowbray, 1981), and hence further entrench community-level inequality and powerlessness.

Inadequate clarity about participation[11]

Common use of the term 'participation' conceals divergent views about its aims and practice. In many projects and programmes, participation is ill-defined and meaningless when it comes to implementation. It has often been used in a normative sense, whereby anything participatory is assumed to be synonymous with 'good' and 'empowering'. Participation has often been used to describe very rudimentary levels of consultation between agency staff and community members. Some critics have also likened it to a Trojan Horse that can hide manipulation and even coercion under a cloak of social palatability (Slocum and Thomas-Slayter, 1995).

Although developed in 1971, Arnstein's typology of participation, that was so influential in other fields, did not spark a critical debate in the development field where the concept was still embryonic. Discussions about participation since the early 1990s have been more successful at challenging simplified and normative uses of the term. One helpful distinction is that of participation as a means or an end (Goulet, 1989; Nelson and Wright, 1995). An instrumental approach views participation as a means to achieving better cost-effectiveness, living standards, etc., while an empowerment approach values the process of increasing participation as an important end in itself.

A recent spate of more elaborate typologies has helped to further break down misconceptions (Adnan *et al.* 1992; Biggs, 1989; Cornwall, 1995; Guijt, 1991; Hart, 1992; Oakley, 1991; Pretty, 1994; Selener, 1997; Stiefel and Wolfe, 1994). Generally, these typologies identify types of participation in terms of varying degrees of control over development decisions and resources between the supposed 'beneficiaries' (farmers, women, etc.) and the 'initiators' (project staff, planners, researchers, etc.).

Yet despite their conceptual contribution, these typologies still harbour the seeds of continued simplification in four ways (Guijt, 1998):

(1) Wrong assumption of a static picture. Classifying a certain intervention as a certain type of participation implies that this describes the entire life cycle of the initiative. Yet in most cases, women and men will participate in different ways at different moments. A common pattern is a high level of participation early on, with extensive community consultation, which is followed by a period of less participation when decisions are made. The implementation phase often sees high levels of participation again, when local labour is drawn in or 'contributed', etc. but the devolution of responsibility for financial management is often strikingly absent (Guijt, 1991).

(2) Simplifying difference in terms of 'insider and outsider'. Most typologies describe a sliding scale of shifting responsibility between insiders, or community members, and outsiders, or project/government

staff. The focus in the participation literature on differences between 'insider', or 'the community', and 'outsider', or 'development professional' simplifies a vastly more complex reality (Chambers, 1997; Cornwall *et al.*, 1993; Scoones and Thompson, 1993). Viewing all local people as insiders clearly perpetuates a simplification of intra-communal differences, and hides the reality of high levels of participation by some groups and none by others. It has detracted from discussions of differences among 'insiders' and among 'outsiders'.

(3) Normative assumption of an 'ideal' form of participation. Most typologies are presented as some kind of continuum, such as 'ladders'. They are also often couched in normative terms, moving from coercion to autonomy. Thus they imply that it is possible, desirable and necessary to move across this continuum to the most intense form of participation, a kind of participation 'nirvana' in which everyone gaily commits themselves to what can be quite conflictual and tedious processes of local analysis and planning. The feasibility of 100 per cent local participation is a myth. The local political context will strongly influence what is a feasible intensity and form of participation.

(4) Ignoring diversity. Clustering the myriad forms of participation into four or seven categories can hinder innovation, particularly if the typologies are being used in a prescriptive manner. Participation in a research context will be different from an action context. What is more important than finding one's place on a particular continuum, is describing how different players are participating and why those forms have been chosen.

The confusion about what is good and bad practice, what is and is not effective participation, continues. Academics accuse practitioners of raising false hopes of empowerment, who in turn retaliate by referring to 'ivory-tower purism', neither party clarifying sufficiently what, in fact, they mean (Guijt and Cornwall, 1995). Discussions of 'who' participates have been few and far between, other than in terms of the local versus external people. The moral superiority which accompanies the word 'participation' has allowed a way out of discussing and addressing the more controversial and radical notions of gender relations and women's oppression (Mayoux, 1995). While some experiences may mention women, men and maybe even gender issues explicitly, many others do not. After all, the reasoning goes: 'there is no need to look at gender issues separately; these are automatically taken care of through participation'.

Welbourn (1991) suggests that participatory development means the equal inclusion of all sections of a typical, stratified community: women, men, older, younger, better-off and worse-off. Yet this is easier said than done, and what is 'equal inclusion'? Each person experiences a unique combination of social, economic and physical constraints and opportunities that influence their willingness and capacity to participate in development processes. Understanding how these circumstances affect people's motivation to be involved in an externally-initiated participatory process needs far greater attention than it has been given to date.

The forgetting of power and empowerment

The ideal of empowering the marginalized has, in theory, been a driving force for many participatory projects (Nelson and Wright, 1995). The thinking was that by enabling the poor to analyse their own realities and thus influence development priorities, they would have a greater ability (more confidence and skills) to continue acting in their own interests. But closer examination reveals that many participatory approaches often focus on using consultation to relieve the symptoms of oppression, such as inadequate material well-being, rather than its causes. As de Koning (1995) describes: 'for PRA to live up to its aim, it must be part of this longer-term process [of challenging inequalities] and go beyond the moments of data collection, visual documentation and instant analysis'. The shift away from an empowerment focus to one which views empowerment more as 'management of power when in the hands of the powerful' (Leal, 1997) has contributed to one of the paradoxes of participatory development: mechanical solutions for political aims (see Box 1.1).

As discussed above, generalizing words like 'participation' and 'community' provides a smokescreen for professionals to avoid intra-communal struggles, notably the micro-politics of gender relations.[12] Many of the problems with participatory development arise when methods 'are treated uncritically as a one-off cheap option, facilitated by inexperienced researchers mainly as a tool for mobilization *without a clear strategy for negotiating conflicting interests* which arise between participants, and between participants and development agencies' (Mayoux, 1997, emphasis added). The emphasis on techniques of participation has detracted from a need to understand the causes of disempowerment.

Empowerment is complex and carries an inherent contradiction, namely the notion that 'some can act on others to give them power or enable them to realize their own potential' (Nelson and Wright, 1995). If power is essentially about the 'transformative capacity' of people or groups (Giddens, 1984), then empowerment involves increasing people's capacity to transform their lives. It is more than inviting people to partake in needs assessment or a decision-making process. Offering the marginalized opportunities for consultation, without following this through with analysis about causes of oppression and feasible action to redress the causes, is unlikely to be empowering (Chapter 2). For a process to be empowering, it also requires the development of iterative sequences that emphasize different discussions and skills at different points in time. To integrate other skills such as group organization, conflict resolution, management, and small-enterprise development requires appropriate support and institutional flexibility. The lack of resources needed for such follow-up has led some to comment on the disempowering nature of participation (Woodhill, 1996; Nelson and Wright, 1995).

The ease with which issues of power have been obscured and empowerment simplified has gone hand in hand with the language of 'facilitation'. External 'facilitators' have become part and parcel of most participatory approaches (Pretty *et al.*, 1995). Many of these facilitators and the organizations for which they work have assumed that it is possible to act in non-partisan ways. However, people's positions in a community, even if temporary, influence what information others are willing to share and analyse in the group processes that are so common to participatory approaches (Scoones and Thompson, 1994). As tensions, disputes and conflicts are inevitable in development processes, engaging in participatory development inevitably means taking sides or taking a mediating or negotiating role, all of which are political acts (Scoones, 1995). Ignoring the political nature of such actions is likely to be counter-productive and destructive to the development process (Shah and Kaul Shah, 1995).

Simplistic views on the speed of social change have also compromised the empowering potential of participatory development. If empowerment entails redressing power imbalances by increasing the 'transformative capacity' of the relatively marginalized, then time is needed (Thompson, 1995). It takes time for people and groups to decide what they want to see changed, and why, and then to act. It is difficult to anticipate which conflicts such processes of change may provoke or reveal. Real consensus is not reached in a two-week planning exercise (as described by some PRA practitioners, cf. Ford *et al.*, 1992; Schubert *et al.*, 1994). Given the entrenched nature of hierarchical structures and relationships, it is not possible to expect far-reaching changes with every intervention. This begs the question of what can be expected from externally-determined participatory research and planning processes when they are driven by speedy disbursement of funds (Chambers, 1997).

Bridging the gap between participation and gender

Against this history of conceptual simplicity, the 1990s have marked a steady growth in attempts to integrate theories of gender with the practices of participatory development. This has occurred in several contexts:

o training: to sensitize field workers to gender as a key factor in community differences and how this influences the development aspirations and opportunities of women and men (cf. Guijt *et al.*, 1992; Guijt, 1994, 1995b; Welbourn, 1991);

o research: to improve the quality of research in general and of gender analysis in particular (cf. Ashby, 1990; Commonwealth Secretariat, 1992; Cornwall, 1996; Feldstein and Jiggins, 1994; Kaul Shah and Bourararch, 1995; Lightfoot *et al.*, 1991; Rocheleau *et al.*, 1991; Thomas-Slayter *et al*, 1991; Tolley and Bentley, 1992);

o community development: to support the empowerment of women and/ or for gender-balanced development through local level analysis and planning (cf. Frischmuth, 1996; Grady *et al.*, 1991; Guijt *et al.*, 1995; Guijt, 1995a, 1996b; Kaul Shah, 1995; Kaul Shah and Shah, 1995; Mosse, 1994; MYRADA, 1992; Redd Barna, 1993; Srinavasan, 1990).

In 1993, the first workshop on 'PRA and Gender' was held at IDS,[13] in Brighton. It was also the first workshop held by IIED and IDS at which issues around conflict, power and the ethics of PRA were discussed at length, in sharp contrast to previous workshops that had dealt largely with the mechanics of methods. In 1994, gender awareness entered into discussions about the ethics and basic skills of PRA practitioners (Absalom *et al.*, 1994).

The gist of the discussions then and in this book is that equitable participatory development requires explicit attention to gender relations. This, in turn, can only be effective if based on a sound understanding of the dynamics of power, the nature of conflicts and conflict resolution, and the process of social change. Gender-responsive forms of participatory development can be effective at dealing with gender-based oppression. But the experiences here suggest this is possible only if attention is paid to three areas: conceptual clarity, appropriate methods and methodologies, and supportive organizations and institutions.

Conceptual clarity

Many concepts that underpin participatory approaches are plagued by non-committal use, vagueness and normative connotations. Think about the assumptions we make when using terms like 'empowerment', 'gender', 'participation', 'change' or 'conflict'. The confusion this has led to has provoked much justified criticism. Conceptual clarity lays the basis for practical application and organizational support. Discussion amongst those involved in a participatory initiative about the key concepts they use can increase awareness of the different interpretations that inevitably exist. This can reduce the making of false claims, the raising or dashing of expectations, and contradictions during the implementation that can jeopardize everyone's efforts.

(1) Clarify what gender means, in all its diverse local forms and as interpreted by researchers and professionals. Cornwall (Chapter 4, this volume) urges facilitators to be cautious in using simplistic and (western) stereotypical concepts of gender that alienate rather than bring men on board. Making assumptions about gender issues can be wrong, as Vlaar and Ahlers (Chapter 17, this volume) describe.

(2) Clarify what empowerment means to different people. Crawley (Chapter 2, this volume) throws out a challenge to proponents of participatory development 'Can [they] say, with certainty, that it has been the PRA process which has led to "empowerment"?' She argues that avoiding analysis of the source of oppression will perpetuate false claims to empowerment, and that indicators to judge empowerment will vary. Don't jeopardize vulnerable local groups/people in the interests of academic or professional gain (Chapter 6, this volume) by imposing a degree or form of empowerment that local women (or men) might not support.

(3) Be explicit about the likely depth and scope of participation, given the organization's mandate, local politics, time available, etc. Clarify whether participation is pursued more as a means or as an end in itself. What assumptions are being made about local women's and men's willingness to participate? The extent to which they will benefit from a concrete output will no doubt determine, at least in part, the extent to which they wish to engage in the process (Chapter 6, this volume).

(4) Identify what constitutes 'a community' locally. What term is most appropriate, acceptable, and feasible as a focus for analysis and action? What are the main differences that divide a particular community: is it gender or is it age, ethnicity, caste, religion, etc.? (Chapters 7, 10 and 17, this volume) As so much participatory work is based on group analysis, Cornwall (Chapter 4, this volume) urges for clear understanding of which differences matter locally and the dynamics of single-sex and mixed-sex groups.

(5) Accept the inevitability of dealing with conflict. Explore what participants consider to be positive forms of conflict or tension and which ones are considered antagonistic. Cousins (Chapter 5, this volume) draws attention to the centrality of conflict in social change and, therefore, the need to allow conflicts to emerge in a training context. 'Looking inside ourselves at what we ask of others' is essential to prepare for the emotional and confrontational moments of participatory development. When conflicts arise, assess whether they are latent (inherent to the local context) or emergent (resulting from the process and, therefore, avoidable). Take care not to expose or generate conflicts that increase the vulnerability of marginalized groups (Chapters 6 and 19, this volume).

(6) Clarify the role of outsiders in participatory development initiatives. Green (Chapter 6, this volume) warns practitioners of the ease with which well-meaning facilitation can become patronizing manipulation, and the limits of acting as 'a legitimate adjudicator'. Murthy's (Chapter 7, this volume) haunting account of a workshop on female infanticide in Bihar also highlights how the caste of the facilitators made it impossible to bridge the distance with the midwives. Humble (Chapter 3, this volume) urges for reflexivity as crucial for ensuring that external agents of change are self-critical. She also urges facilitators to vest authority to design how analysis is to take place with the women involved, which will enhance the chance that local priorities prevail over project priorities.

(7) Clarity includes more explicit statements about how participants view the process of organizational change and local institutional development. Equitable participatory development means including women alongside men, which in many cases requires examining gender relations and changing entrenched forms of social organization. This means being clear about what assumptions participants are making about the local social and political processes through which they think 'empowerment' takes place (Chapter 2, this volume).

Appropriate and consistent methodology

Part 2 of this book describes ten experiences that demonstrate the power of participatory approaches when they are consciously informed by equity and an understanding of gender relations. They offer many ideas on how methodologies can be made more inclusive of women and more focused on gender issues.

(1) Ensure gender-appropriate forums and spaces by asking women and men where they feel at ease. As opportunities for participation are

culturally defined, this will influence the nature, format and type of forum. Much participatory work relies on group-based analysis, so care needs to be taken in deciding how to work with groups, and understanding the composition and dynamics of groups even if single-sex (Chapter 10, this volume). Although men tend to dominate proceedings in mixed-group discussions, single-sex groups are not necessarily the best (Chapters 4, 11, 14 and 20, this volume). Women will not always be more at ease with strangers without their menfolk (Chapter 16, this volume) and organizing a women-only meeting can be difficult as their free time is not always synchronized (Chapters 7 and 9, this volume).

(2) Ensure gender-appropriate timing of opportunities for participation. Communication and social change take time (Chapters 8, 9, 11 and 14, this volume) and not everyone has it, least of all women. For women to sacrifice precious time, they need to be convinced that they will be better off for having been involved (Chapters 6 and 11, this volume). To gain men's support for women to spend time in meetings, seeking the approval of local leaders can be essential.

(3) Be clear which women are and are not involved. The authors of Chapters 7, 9 and 11 urge caution when setting up processes which favour a select group of women. It is easy to listen only to those who are more vocal due to a higher status and/or more experience with public speaking, and incorrect to assume that these are representative of larger groups (Chapter 16, this volume).

(4) Find methods that are inclusive and can analyse gender issues. Most methods are gender-neutral in terms of the issues they raise, with few gender-ameliorative or gender-transformative methods (Chapter 7, this volume). Seek research and planning methods that are culturally appropriate and go beyond gender neutrality, particularly those that can explore and alter the ideological basis of gender relations (Chapters 7, 9, 11, 13 and 18). This also means finding methods that can sensitize men and male staff in non-threatening ways (Chapters 4, 9 and 15). Bilgi (Chapter 8) offers a clever innovation: gaining men's support for change by asking them to analyse women's realities and how they think women's lives can be made less difficult.

(5) Seek methodological complementarity and effective sequences of methods. Not everything can be surveyed or visualized, such as psychological well-being and domestic violence (Chapter 7). If necessary seek other methods for expressing these, such as video or theatre (Chapters 12 and 15). Ensure that knowledge is built up systematically and sensitively by thinking carefully of the sequence of methods (Chapters 7, 11 and 16). Kindon (Chapter 14) offers us insights about how gender misconceptions in Bali were unravelled through a series of participatory techniques, as do Vlaar and Ahlers (Chapter 17) in Cambodia. Welbourn (Chapter 12) provides an inspiring and sobering reflection on the potential of community drama and PRA to deal with the pain and threat of HIV and AIDS in Uganda. Against the backdrop of the Dominican Republic, the authors of Chapter 16 used maps, life histories, and a questionnaire survey to understand the impact on women of changes in forested landscapes. But, as Protz (Chapter 15) cautions,

the power of any methodology, including that of moving pictures, to understand and challenge gender images and relations, only appears if based on an awareness of the potential pitfalls.

(6) Ensure that issues are of interest to women or that these issues can arise. Before starting, try and identify whether a particular topic is best investigated by asking women or men, the young or the old. This can also help if difficulties are encountered in getting the active participation of certain groups. Generally speaking, women are not as used as men to talking with outsiders, especially if these are men. They might experience inhibitions about certain topics and techniques (Chapters 7, 9 and 11). Discussing the questions that will be broached beforehand can help women to formulate their ideas and seek the support of others (Chapter 21). In Zambia, the use of participatory methods for exploring adolescent sexual health with girls and boys is described (Chapter 10).

(7) Support women to make use of the new opportunities for expression. Do not assume that women are able, willing or even interested in taking the space that has been created for them in participatory processes (Chapters 2, 7, 12 and 18). In participatory development, active effort may be needed to include and encourage the more inhibited to express their concerns in ways with which they feel comfortable. However, Kindon (Chapter 14) highlights how participatory methods themselves can actually break through societal misconceptions about women's supposed reluctance to engage in public discussions and social analysis.

(8) Understand the practical conditions that can make or break women's involvement. Even if women are willing to participate, they may be hindered by the need for child care, their husbands' permission, etc. (Chapters 7, 14, 18 and 20). Debrabandere and Desmet (Chapter 9) describe a planning process in Zimbabwe in which women's involvement was ensured through a series of practical considerations, unrelated to the participatory methodology itself.

(9) Learn to recognize and handle conflicts. What is the basis of gender-related conflicts, and what conflict resolution processes are beneficial for women and men alike? Even methods that appear gender-neutral can be the cause of household-level and community-level conflicts, as shown in the example of using video in the Caribbean (Chapter 15). Personal attitudes and feelings around the conflicts likely to emerge in fieldwork need to be explored in training if personal and community change is to take place (Chapters 4 and 5). Know where the limits of staff lie in terms of dealing with conflicts, and be aware that these are just as likely to occur within the organization as in the field (Chapter 19).

(10) Use methods not only to describe gender-differentiated needs but also to analyse and change the causes of needs. This requires being explicit about the social transformative goals of participatory processes (Chapters 2, 3, 4, 7, 10, 11, 12, 15 and 20). The successful use of methods for cause–effect analysis requires complementary skills in communication, facilitation, gender analysis and conflict negotiation.

Anyone can make a map or list priority needs but this does not mean that local learning or change takes place. Sarin (Chapter 11) describes how hasty PRA workshops in India intended to improve Joint Forest Management efforts focused on diagrams rather than more crucial and sensitive issues of personal and institutional processes. More positively, Protz (Chapter 15) describes how video reports proved to be effective for repeated and ever-deepening analysis of women's concerns, the causes and alternative solutions. Welbourn's (Chapter 12) experiences with drama and PRA methods are powerful for helping people change how they behave with respect to sensitive issues of sex and death.

Organizational support and institutional consistency

Past attempts at participatory research and planning show that any positive impacts will only be sustained if they are supported by consistent organizational procedures and wider institutional norms. Support is needed to encourage development practitioners to explore key concepts in non-threatening ways and to use participatory methods in critical and creative ways. Sufficient resources and time must be allocated and political commitment needs to be sincere if staff and local women and men are to remain motivated to work through analysis, conflict and change. Training in participatory approaches and in gender is essential but change requires more than just training. The final section of this introductory chapter, and Chapter 22, discuss the complexity of organizational and institutional change that is needed if positive experiences are to be sustained and spread.

(1) Participatory development needs enough time. While some methods associated with participatory approaches can be quick at stimulating discussion and initial analysis, the process of social change that unfolds is slow and difficult. Many organizations claim to seek gender-balanced, participatory development but they often lack long-term commitment. Redd Barna Uganda has taken three years, Siavonga Agricultural Development Programme in Zambia four years, and Aga Khan Rural Support Programme (AKRSP) in India eight years so far, and their methodologies are still evolving and improving. Fieldwork takes place over months, not days, and organizations need to make commitments that span years rather than months (Chapters 18, 20 and 21). This crucial need is often diametrically opposed to the speedy disbursement of funds or quick need for data that characterizes so many development initiatives.

(2) Training must be context-specific. A common response to new ideas is to train everyone in their use. However, gender-sensitive participatory training must be constructed to suit the structure and objectives of specific organizations. Also, care must be taken that training does not overemphasize methods and appraisal to the detriment of processes, principles and planning. Training programmes need to integrate the analysis of intra-communal difference into participatory practice

(Chapters 7, 11 and 20). As people's attitudes drive their actions, personal experiences are central to training (Chapters 5, 7 and 18). But it is also crucial to be realistic about what training can achieve (Chapter 22). It is only the beginning, and can only be effective in organizations that are willing and able to change in other ways.

(3) Assess and ensure the gender/participation capacity of organization and consistency. The challenge of integrating gender and participation means dealing with a closely knit 'web' of societal and organizational elements, not just innovative field methods or staff training (Chapter 22). Gender-aware participatory methodologies are needed for project planning, implementation, monitoring and evaluation. What staff and community incentives exist? Is money being set aside for research on gender needs and locally appropriate forms of participation? Other conditions range from allocation of sufficient resources to ensuring that women have ways to exert pressure on informal political processes (Chapter 22). Greene-Roesel and Hinton's (Chapter 19) comparison of three NGOs working in Bhutanese refugee camps highlights that the structure and procedures of organizations strongly influence the equitable and participatory nature of the outcomes.

(4) Stimulate continual critical reflection and innovation. Continual organizational self-reflection drove the process described in Chapter 18 in Zambia. This led women and men alike to change their attitudes, behaviour and values over a three-year period with the support of agricultural extension officers. Similarly, in India, Kaul Shah (Chapter 21) describes significant reflective moments in the life of AKRSP that have allowed it to make fundamental changes to its participatory approach and make the outcome more equitable. Bi-monthly review meetings of all field staff in Redd Barna Uganda and bi-annual external reviews are the basis of continual and thorough adaptation that now pervades the fieldwork (Chapter 20).

(5) Anticipate the consequences of equitable participation, and the organizational capacity to respond. An empowerment process can mean an initial focus on women's practical needs and then moving towards more structural discussions and changes (Chapters 6, 8, 18, 20 and 21). Staff must be prepared to deal with these consequences (and they will need enough time). Therefore, it is essential that organizations make a commitment to pursue whatever follow-up is required, and not just the activities that might have been proposed in initial project or programme plans. Organizational capacity is also strongly determined by its internal dynamics, as is highlighted by Greene-Roesel and Hinton (Chapter 19). They suggest that keeping track of how an organization functions internally (for example, where women are employed, and how participatory decisions are made) can be a significant indication of how gender-sensitive and participatory the work in the field is likely to be.

(6) Motivate those involved. Participation can be a hard slog. Incentives are needed for all those involved, community members and staff alike (Chapters 18 and 20). Ensuring that women are included on field teams, however few, can make a crucial difference to the topics

broached and the willingness of local women to participate, especially where socio-cultural circumstances limit access to village women by outside men (Chapters 5 and 20). A supportive system for team work and feedback, and a clear field-methodology were crucial in the Zambian experience (Chapter 18).

(7) Gender-focused and -disaggregated monitoring is essential. How do we know if women's and men's perspectives alike have been heard and incorporated into plans? Did it make a difference in the type of information gathered or the process of the discussion, if men or women or both were involved? How do we know if empowerment is occurring? A participatory evaluation was the turning-point for the Zambian work, not only because gender issues and equity were on the agenda but because women and men were consulted equally (Chapter 18). Kaul Shah (Chapter 21) describes how monitoring has become an essential organizational tool in AKRSP to ensure equitable development. For example, micro-planning is no longer considered complete until women are also involved. Chapter 19 describes how gender-disaggregated assessment of the nature of participation can prove valuable for assessing the extent to which the empowerment claims of much participatory work are, in fact, met.

Integrating participation and gender

Meeting the challenge of equitable participatory development means integrating gender awareness into practice, and not pursuing two approaches with two sets of principles and two series of methods. This much is clear: participation, a loose term to describe a wide variety of practices that aim for more inclusive development, does not automatically include those who were previously left out of such processes. It is only as inclusive as those who are driving the process choose it to be, or as those involved demand it to be. Furthermore, if gender relations are explicitly addressed through the use of participatory research or development, then conflicts are bound to emerge.

For those keen to improve the quality of their participatory work this book should provide a wealth of ideas. For those who might be tempted to say 'Why should we also be looking at gender? We're already following a participatory approach!' we hope they will reconsider.

References

Absalom *et al.* (1994) 'Sharing our Concerns and Looking to the Future', *PLA Notes* 22: 5–10.

Adnan, S., A. Barrett, S. M. Nurul Alam and A. Brustinow (1992) *People's Participation, NGOs and the Flood Action Plan*, Dhaka: Research and Advisory Services.

Arnstein, S.R. (1971) 'A Ladder of Citizens' Participation', *Journal of the American Institute of Planners*, Vol. 35 (July): 216–24.

Ashby, J. (1990) *Evaluating Technology with Farmers*, Colombia: CIAT.

Bell, S. (1994) 'Methods and Mindsets: towards an understanding of the tyranny of methodology', *Public Administration and Development*, Vol. 14: 323–38.

Biggs, S. (1989) *Resource-poor Farmer Participation in Research: a synthesis of experience from nine national agricultural research systems*, ISNAR, OFCOR Project Study No. 3, The Hague.

Bryson, L. and M. Mowbray (1981) ' "Community": the spray-on solution', *Australian Journal of Social Sciences*, 16 (4): 255–67.

Chambers, R. (1992) 'Rural Appraisal: rapid, relaxed and participatory', *IDS Discussion Paper* 311, Brighton: IDS.

Chambers, R. (1997) *Whose Reality Counts? Putting the first last*, London: Intermediate Technology Publications.

Commonwealth Secretariat (1992) *Women, Conservation and Agriculture*, London: Commonwealth Secretariat.

Cornwall, A. (1996) 'Towards Participatory Practice: participatory rural appraisal (PRA) and the participatory process', in Koning and Martin (eds), *Participatory Research in Health*, pp.94–103.

Cornwall, A., I. Guijt and A. Welbourn (1993) 'Acknowledging Process: challenges for agricultural research and extension methodology', *IDS Discussion Paper* 333, Brighton: IDS.

Etzioni, A. (1996) 'Positive Aspects of Community and the Dangers of Fragmentation', *Development and Change*, 27: 301–14.

Eyben, R. and S. Ladbury (1995) 'Popular Participation in Aid-assisted Projects: Why More in Theory than Practice?' in *Power and Participatory Development: theory and practice*, N. Nelson and S. Wright (eds), London: Intermediate Technology Publications.

Feldstein, H. and J. Jiggins (eds) (1994) *Tools for the Field: methodologies handbook for gender analysis in agriculture*, London: Intermediate Technology Publications.

Feldstein, H. and S. Poats (eds) (1989) *Working Together: gender analysis in agriculture*, Vols 1 and 2, Hartford, Conn: Kumarian Press.

Ford, R., C. Kabutha, N. Mageto, and K. Manneh (1992) *Sustaining Development through Community Mobilization: a case study of PRA in the Gambia*, Worchester, MA: Clark University.

Freire, P. (1972) *Pedagogy of the Oppressed*, London: Penguin Books.

Frischmuth, C. (1996) *The Siavonga Experience: integration of gender-oriented participatory approaches into the agricultural extension system – the gender-oriented participatory extension approach (GPEA) 1993–1995*, mimeo.

Giddens, A. (1984) *The Constitution of Society*, Cambridge: Polity Press.

Goulet, D. (1989) 'Participation in Development: new avenues', *World Development*, 17 (2): 165–78.

Grady, H. *et al.*, (1991) 'Assessing Women's Needs in Gaza Using Participatory Rapid Appraisal Techniques', *RRA Notes* 10: 12–19.

Grandin, B. (1988) *Wealth Ranking in Smallholder Communities: a field manual*, London: Intermediate Technology Publications.

Guijt, I. (1991) *Perspectives on Participation: views from Africa.* London: IIED.

Guijt, I. (1994) 'Making a Difference; Integrating Gender Analysis into PRA Training', *RRA Notes* 19: 49–55.

Guijt, I. (1995a) *Moving Slowly and Reaching Far: institutionalizing participatory planning for child-centred community development. An interim analysis for RBU*, Kampala: Redd Barna Uganda, London: IIED.

Guijt, I. (1995b) *Questions of Difference: PRA, gender and environment*, London: IIED, video.

Guijt, I. (1996a) 'Participation in Natural Resource Management: blemished past and hopeful future?' in *Making Forest Policy Work. Conference proceedings of the Oxford Summer Course Programme*, Kate Harris (ed.), Oxford: OFI.

Guijt, I. (1996b) *Participatory Planning in Redd Barna Uganda: reflections and guidelines*, Kampala: Redd Barna Uganda, and London: IIED.

Guijt, I. (1998) 'Assessing the Merits of Participation For Sustainable Agriculture: experiences from Brazil and central America', in J. Blauert and S. Zadek (eds),

Mediating Sustainability: practice to policy for sustainable agriculture and rural development in Latin America, Hartford, Conn: Kumarian Press.

Guijt, I. and A. Cornwall (1995) 'Critical Reflections on the Practice of PRA', *PLA Notes* 24: 2–7.

Guijt, I., A. Fuglesang and T. Kisadha (eds) (1995) *It is the Young Trees that Make a Thick Forest: a report on Redd Barna Uganda's learning experiences with PRA*, London: IIED, and Kampala: Redd Barna Uganda.

Guijt, I. and M. Kaul Shah (1993) 'The Trap of Community Averages: report on a PRA and gender workshop', *Agricultural Research and Extension Network Newsletter* 29: 24–7.

Guijt, I., M. Martin, T. Sarch and K. Manneh (1992) *From Inputs to Impact. Report of a PRA training workshop*, The Gambia: IIED/Action Aid.

Guijt, I. and P. Sidersky (1998) 'Matching Participatory Agricultural Development with the Social Landscape of northeast Brazil', in IIED (ed.) *Fertile Ground: the impacts of participatory watershed development*, London: Intermediate Technology Publications.

SHart, R. (1992) *Children's Participation: from tokenism to citizenship*, Florence: UNICEF.

Huizer, G. (1979) 'Research through action: some practical experiences with peasant organization,' in G. Huizer and B. Mannheim (eds) *The Politics of Anthropology*, The Hague: Mouton pp. 395–420.

IIED/IDS (1993) *PRA and Gender Workshop: summary of plenary discussions 6–7 December*, 1993. London: IIED and Brighton: IDS, mimeo.

Jones, M.A. (1977) *Organization and Social Planning in Australian Local Government*, Heinemann, Richmond, Vic. in L. Bryson and M. Mowbray, (1981) ' "Community": the spray-on solution', *Australian Journal of Social Sciences*, 16 (4): 255–67.

Jumani, J. (1985) *Coordinating Video Sewa – a personal account*, Ahmedabad, India: Self-Employed Women's Association.

Kaul Shah, M. and K. Bourararch (1995) *Participatory Assessment of Women's Problems and Concerns in Morocco*, report submitted to the World Bank, first draft.

Kaul Shah, M. and P. Shah (1995) 'Gender, Environment and Livelihood Security: an alternative viewpoint from India', *IDS Bulletin* 26 (1): 75–82.

Koning, K. de (1995) 'Participatory Appraisal and Education for Empowerment?', *PLA Notes* 24: 34–7.

Koning, K. de and M. Martin (eds) (1996) *Participatory Research in Health: issues and experiences*, London: Zed Books.

Leal, P. A. (1997) *Obscuring the Politics of Participatory Action*, Contribution to e-mail discussion on PRA, August.

Levy, C. (1992) 'Gender and the Environment: the challenge of cross-cutting issues in development policy and planning', *Environment and Urbanization* 4 (1): 134–149.

Lightfoot, C., R. Noble and R. Morales (1991) *Training Resource Book on a Participatory Method of Modelling Bioresource Flows*, Manila: ICLARM.

Maguire, P. (1987) *Doing Participatory Research: a feminist approach*, Amherst, Massachusetts: The Center for International Education.

Maguire, P. (1996) 'Proposing a More Feminist Participatory Research: knowing and being embraced openly', in: K. de Koning and M. Martin (eds), *Participatory Research in Health: issues and experiences*, London: Zed Books, pp.27–39.

Mayoux, L. (1995) 'Beyond Naivety: women, gender, inequality and participatory development', *Development and Change* (26): 235–58.

Mayoux, L. (1997) *Impact Assessment and Women's Empowerment in Microfinance Programmes: issues for a participatory learning and action approach*,

21

background paper submitted to CGAP virtual meeting on Impact Assessment Methodologies in Micro-Finance Programmes, April 7–19 1997.

Mies, M. (1983). 'Towards a Methodology for Feminist Research', in G. Bowles and R. Duelli Klein (eds), *Theories of Women's Studies*, London: Routledge and Kegan Paul.

Mohanty, C. (1991) 'Cartographies of struggle: Third World women and the politics of feminism', in C. Mohanty, A. Russo and G. Torres (eds), *Third World Women and the Politics of Feminism*, Bloomington and Indianapolis: Indiana University Press.

Moser, C. (1993) *Gender Planning and Development: theory, practice and training*, London and New York: Routledge.

Mosse, D. (1994) 'Authority, Gender and Knowledge: theoretical reflections on the practice of participatory rural appraisal', *Development and Change* 25 (3): 497–525.

MYRADA (1992) 'Analysis of Societal Roles and Problems from a Gender Perspective and Development of Gender-Sensitive Tools in PRA-PALM', *PRA-PALM Series 7*, Bangalore: MYRADA.

Nelson, N. and S. Wright. (eds) (1995) *Power and Participatory Development*, London: Intermediate Technology Publications.

Oakley, P. (1991) *Projects with People: the practice of participation in rural development*, Geneva: ILO.

Pretty, J. (1994) 'Alternative Systems of Inquiry for Sustainable Agriculture', *IDS Bulletin* 25(2): 37–48.

Pretty, J., I. Guijt, J. Thompson and I. Scoones (1995) *Participatory Learning and Action: a trainer's guide*, IIED Training Materials Series No 1, London: IIED.

Rahman, Md. A. (ed.) (1984) *Grass-roots Participation and Self-reliance: experiences in south and south-east Asia*, New Delhi: Oxford and IBH.

Rao, A. and H. Feldstein, K. Cloud and K. Staudt (1991) *Gender Training and Development Planning: learning from experience*. Conference report, New York: Population Council and Bergen: the Chr. Michelsen Institute.

Redd Barna (1993) *NOT ONLY the Well-off BUT ALSO the poor*, Report of a PRA, training workshop, 4–22 October, Zimbabwe: Redd Barna.

Rocheleau, D., K. Schofield and N. Mbuthi (1991) *People, Property, Poverty and Parks: a story of men, women, water and trees at Pwani*, ECOGEN/SARSA case study, Worchester, MA: Clark University.

Schubert, B. *et al.* (1994) *Facilitating the Introduction of a Participatory and Integrated Development Approach (PIDA) in Kilifi District Kenya*, Berlin: CATAD.

Scoones, I. (1995) 'PRA and Anthropology: challenges and dilemmas', *PLA Notes* 24: 17–20.

Scoones, I. and J. Thompson (eds) (1994) *Beyond Farmer First*, London: Intermediate Technology Publications.

Selener, D. (1997) *Participatory Action Research and Social Change*, Ithaca: Cornell University.

Shah, P. and M. Kaul Shah (1995) 'Participatory Methods: precipitating or avoiding conflict?' *PLA Notes* 24: 48–51.

Shaw, B. (1995) 'Contradictions between Action and Theory: feminist participatory research in Goa, India', *Antipode* 27 (1): 91–9.

locum, R. and B. Thomas-Slayter (1995) 'Participation, Empowerment and Sustainable Development', in Slocum, R., L. Wichart, D. Rocheleau and B. Thomas-Slayter, *Power, Process and Participation: tools for change*, London: Intermediate Technology Publications.

Srinavasan, L. (1990) *Tools for Community Participation. A manual for training trainers in participatory techniques*, New York, NY: PROWWESS/UNDP.

Stiefel M. and M. Wolfe (1994) *A Voice for the Excluded. Popular participation in development: utopia or necessity?* Geneva/London: UNRISD/Zed Books.

Thomas-Slayter, B., D. Rocheleau, D. Shields and M. Rojas (1991) *Introducing the ECOGEN Approach to Gender, Natural Resources Management and Sustainable Development*, Worchester, MA: Clark University.

Thompson, F. (1971) 'Suburban Living and the Concept of Community', *Australian and New Zealand Journal of Sociology*. 73: 23–37, cited in: L. Bryson and M. Mowbray (1981). '"Community": the spray-on solution', *Australian Journal of Social Sciences*, 16 (4), 255–67.

Thompson, J. (1995) 'Participatory Approaches in Government Bureaucracies: facilitating the process of institutional change', *World Development* 23(9): 1521–54.

Tolley, E. and M. Bentley (1992) 'Participatory Methods for Research on Women's Reproductive Health', *RRA Notes* 16: 63–8.

Welbourn, A. (1991) 'RRA and the Analysis of Difference', *Sustainable Agriculture Programme RRA Notes No. 14*: 14–23.

Welbourn, A. (1992) 'RRA, Gender and Health – Alternative Ways of Listening to Needs', IDS Bulletin 23(1): 8–18.

Woodhill, J. (1996) Natural Resources Decision-making: beyond the landcare paradox', *The Australasian Journal of Natural Resources, Law and Policy*, 3(1): 91–114.

Part 1
Theoretical Reflections

2

Living Up to the Empowerment Claim? The potential of PRA

Heaven Crawley

The application of participatory approaches has raised increasingly critical questions about their impact. Not least among these is the issue of whether participation is simply a more efficient 'means' of accessing information to achieve externally driven development aims, or whether it should be viewed as an 'end' in itself (Nelson and Wright, 1995). Many advocates and practitioners of one approach in particular, participatory rural appraisal (PRA), make a claim to 'empowerment' as the objective of their work. They clearly distinguish PRA from earlier methodologies, such as Rapid Rural Appraisal, arguing that '[i]nstead of imposing and extracting, PRA seeks to empower' (Chambers, 1992:46). Thus at the core of PRA is the belief that it enables a group of people to analyse their condition, giving them confidence to state and assert their priorities, to present proposals, to make demands and to take action, leading to sustainable and effective development proposals. This concept of participation as 'empowerment' is closely linked to the ideas of Paulo Freire (1972). He suggested that a process of 'awareness-training' and 'conscientization' occurs through the limited intervention of outsiders who interact with people by posing problems and generating discussions, thereby awakening them to structural causes (Bergall, 1993).

In this context, two central and related questions arise. The first concerns the extent to which PRA as a methodology and set of methods has the potential to be 'empowering' for those it involves. Despite the obvious nature of this question and the burgeoning use of PRA, there are surprisingly few theoretical or critical reflections on this issue (Mosse, 1993). The second, more specific, question is the basis of this article: does PRA have the potential to 'empower' women? By questioning the conceptualization of gender which is used to guide PRA-based processes, this article examines the extent to which PRA has been used to address issues of gender inequality, as opposed to simply describing the differences between the lives of women and men. It will be suggested that to assess the 'empowerment' claim of PRA requires clarity about the concept of 'empowerment' on which this article offers theoretical reflections.

The challenge

Despite efforts to create opportunities for wider participation, many have observed that PRA processes are unlikely to be equally accessible or open to all sections of a community (cf. Hinton, 1995; Mosse, 1993; Richards, 1995; Chapter 17, this volume). Moreover, women as a group (notwithstanding their many other differences) may experience 'double disempowerment': both as members of poor households and within the household by virtue of their gender (Friedmann, 1992; Griffen, 1989). Thus, while the experience of PRA may well be an empowering social process for poor communities, it also has the potential to create local conflict between groups with opposing interests in which asymmetric gender power relations may play a crucial role.

Part of the potential of PRA to empower women will depend upon the extent to which it: (i) is equally amenable for use by women and men; and (ii) is more successful than other methodologies at raising and addressing issues relevant to women. More critically, however, whilst some users of participatory rural appraisal have created the space where a discussion over power and the production of knowledge can be held, this debate has frequently skirted around central and contentious concerns of marginal groups and individuals. These have also taken for granted certain key concepts, in particular that of 'empowerment'. One consequence of this is the failure to address the local social and political processes through which 'empowerment' takes place. Most significant in the context of PRA is pervasive ignorance of gender as a critical aspect of power relations. For many involved in participatory research or action, gender is a footnote, rather than a place from which to begin the analysis. Concern with power and power relations is centred instead around the relationship between 'insiders' and 'outsiders', or between the North and the South.

Empowerment

Whilst concern for 'empowerment' is clearly not new in the development literature (cf. Freire, 1972), the easy use of the term in recent years disguises many different definitions. It is used to justify development propositions which are rooted in diverse ideological and political positions. In this sense it suffers from much the same fate as 'participation' which is used to describe processes ranging from cooption to self-mobilization (see Chapter 19, this volume). Perhaps most problematic, however, is that in many cases the language of empowerment creates an aura of moral superiority. This protects practitioners of PRA and other participatory approaches against criticism, and enables them to avoid critical self-reflection about the truth of their claims.

What then is meant by the term? If it implies 'adding to women's power' (Griffen, 1989) then some of the confusion arises, as Rowlands (1992) suggests, because the concept of power is itself much disputed.[1] As Kabeer (1990) notes, there are a number of different ways of analysing the issue of power as it relates to gender, with the result that theoretical debates about the nature of 'empowerment' are virtually endless.

In an obvious sense, empowerment is about people gaining the ability to undertake activities, to set their own agendas and change events. This interpretation is based on a traditional model of power and may simply involve giving people an active role in a decisionmaking process. A feminist interpretation goes beyond formal and institutional conceptions of power, however, to include the importance of understanding the dynamics of oppression and 'internalized oppression'.[2] These affect the ability of less powerful groups to participate in formal and informal decisionmaking and to exert influence. They also significantly affect how individuals or groups perceive themselves and their ability to influence the world around them. What is clear in the context of these debates is that empowerment is a concept that goes beyond the issue of participation. It is more than simply widening access to decisionmaking. As Gajanayake (1993) suggests, it implies enabling people to understand the reality of their situation, reflect on the factors shaping that situation and, most critically, take steps to affect changes to improve it.[3] As a result it must include processes that lead the individual or group to perceive itself as able to occupy a decisionmaking space. By implication, therefore, an empowerment focus involves the radical alteration of the structures which reproduce women's subordinate position as a gender.

To assess whether the use of PRA has the potential to be empowering for women requires, therefore, a definition of empowerment against which to judge this impact. We must be clear, however, about whose perceptions of empowerment we are using. What we define as empowerment may not be, and is highly unlikely to be, the same as that defined by others. Changes that can be empowering for some may not be recognized as such by others simply because they do not match our own aspirations and assumptions. A similar trap is to conclude that something is empowering when it is not for those involved.

These concerns raise a number of questions. How can we determine whether or not empowerment is happening for individuals or groups in the field? Whose criteria do we use to assess this? Given that empowerment is a process, how can we gather reliable information about change over time? Can any aspects of empowerment be evaluated quantitatively? Perhaps the greatest challenge, however, is to ascertain causality (Rowlands, 1992). How do we know which interventions or non-interventions have enabled or prevented empowerment? Can PRA practitioners say, with certainty, that it has been the PRA process which has led to empowerment?

To assist practitioners in answering these questions, it is first necessary to distinguish between 'methodology' and 'strategy' in a process of change (Bergall, 1993). This raises two broad issues in the context of 'empowerment': (i) how consciously is empowerment built into the methodology and methods of PRA?; and (ii) how consciously is it built into the strategy, or broad design, of the development programme and the manner in which it strives to achieve its aims?

This distinction is important because it forces an assessment of whether PRA attempts to identify and challenge structural causes of problems, or whether it attempts merely to integrate women into the existing system through an ameliorative process of gradual improvement. It suggests also that an approach cannot be described as 'empowering' if it overlooks the strategic needs of women. Such needs arise out of their relatively subordinate social position and require a radical transformation of interpersonal relations between women and men 'so that women have greater power over their own lives and men have less power over women's lives' (Kabeer, 1990:8).

To provide an analytical framework through which these issues can be considered, Mullender and Ward's (1991) model of 'empowerment' provides a useful starting-point. This model, which is based explicitly on an anti-oppressive perspective, suggests three simple questions to be addressed by those concerned that participatory approaches achieve their empowerment potential:

(1) What are the problems to be tackled?
(2) Why do the problems exist?
(3) How can we bring about change?

These questions, and the distinction between methodology and strategy, can help those who use participatory approaches to develop more conscious processes for empowerment.

PRA as an empowering methodology

A specific aim of the methodology of PRA is to catalyze a process that leads to new forms of awareness and self-confidence. PRA has clearly provided valuable opportunities to explore the ways in which the experiences, needs and perspectives of women and men differ (Adams *et al.*, 1993; Bilgi, 1992; Mosse, 1993; Welbourn, 1991, 1992, Chapter 12, this volume). It has also helped to represent these differences in innovative ways, so that, in contrast with conventional research and planning methodologies, PRA can be more responsive to women's input (Cornwall, 1992b; Krishnamurthy, 1994; Robinson, 1990; Tolley and Bentley, 1992; Chapter 7, this volume).

This is not an insignificant contribution, given that the first step in empowerment is women's ability to define their needs and realities. In other words, we need, as Mullender and Ward suggest, to identify what the problems are. Moreover, there is a general consensus within the literature that identifying shared interests increases women's individual and social motivation to work at changing existing circumstances (Bystydzienski, 1992; Hall, 1992; Kabeer, 1990).[4] Identification with other women strengthens their sense of connection to women as a distinct social group, producing a commonality that empowers personal and collective action (Warren, 1988). There is also an increased sense of self-confidence which comes, in part, from conquering a fear of acting outside culturally sanctioned (patriarchal) norms. If, as Hall (1992:87) suggests, 'the probability of realizing women's freedom is increased through their awareness of the plight and possibilities they share with other women', then the importance of this collective conscientization should not be underestimated.[5] Indeed Hall suggests that women's mutual support is a necessary condition for empowerment at the individual and collective level. If you understand your situation and the processes which are working to create it, you are more likely to act to change it.

Thus identifying what the problems are precedes all other steps to empowerment, to which the use of PRA methods and techniques have undoubtedly contributed. Yet this in itself does not make PRA an inherently empowering methodology. Two areas of concern help to highlight this.

First, because the language surrounding 'participation' is often gender neutral, in that it frequently fails to make explicit reference to either women or men, it masks complex and varied levels of participation by particular social groups and subsets within those groups. This may, in fact, create biases against women due to gendered power-relations at the local level. One common example is that, while women might be physically present at group meetings and thus are 'participating', they often effectively withdraw from discussion and allow the men to speak. The very structure of PRA sessions assumes and encourages the expression of consensus rather than difference (Mosse, 1993; Pottier and Orone, 1995). The result of this is that 'the interactive context of PRA emphasizes mediation between 'outsiders' and 'insiders', 'experts' and 'locals' but is not so good at identifying and handling differences of perception within communities' (Mosse, 1993:12). Thus public expression of community consensus, or of women, should not be mistaken for the absence of distinct, and perhaps conflicting, interests.

Second, a related point, and one which is critical in the empowerment context, is that PRA is not automatically gender sensitive. Indeed the reality of much PRA-based fieldwork bears witness to a marked lack of understanding about gender as an important axis of social diversity within communities (Cornwall, 1992a; Guijt, 1994; Welbourn, 1991). In the context of PRA, and indeed many participatory methodologies, gender has tended to be synonymous with an interest in, and concern about, women's livelihoods and perspectives. Moreover, the extent to which these perspectives are encouraged to emerge appears to depend greatly on the personal interests of the facilitators involved. This brings with it the risk that participatory methodologies involving women, and this includes PRA, will be used to gain access to information about a very particular, pre-determined set of gendered issues, for example, relating to health and nutrition (cf. Cornwall, 1992b; Tolley and Bentley, 1992; Welbourn, 1992). Although these issues may well be of concern to the women, or men, who have identified them, they may also result from more directive forms of facilitation (see Chapters 3 and 7, this volume). PRA used in this way does not challenge, and may reinforce, the publicly endorsed definition of women's roles. It will not necessarily be a means of changing gender relations or of enhancing women's status.

PRA as an empowering strategy

The preceding section has suggested that being open to the possibility of change is a prerequisite for change to occur, and that participatory approaches which bring women together in groups can form an important stage in this conscientization process. Supposing then, that existing gender-biases in PRA methods can be addressed, the second issue is whether or not it can form the basis for action. Using the methodology of PRA to ensure the implementation of projects which do not marginalize women is one thing, but using it fundamentally to challenge and change power relations between men and women is quite another. Being aware of a situation of unequal power relations, as could be realized with gender-responsive PRA methods, does not automatically guarantee change through a gender-responsive development strategy. Indeed, facilitators need to recognize that women already know and understand many of the issues surrounding their realities but are often unable to make changes in their lives.

When assessing PRA as an empowering strategy therefore, it is important to distinguish between a 'situation of empowerment' and an 'empowering situation'. While the methods of PRA may create opportunities for empowerment, they are not automatically empowering.[6] As Hall (1992:91) suggests: 'Women's mutual support is a necessary, but not sufficient, condition of their empowerment'. Take, for example, those cases in which PRA methods are used in women-only meetings to identify problems in access to resources, perhaps as land or income, and to decisionmaking structures related to these resources. Although women may feel 'empowered' after participating in the discussions, this is unlikely to enable them simply to take more control. Moreover, there is a danger of producing a backlash which can further disempower, for example in discussions around domestic violence or alcohol abuse (see Chapter 7, this volume). As Kabeer (1990:11) suggests, therefore, 'empowering women must begin with the individual consciousness—but to bring about social change it must move from changing our personal ways of thinking and doing to changing external relations'.

Women's involvement in the collection and representation of information through PRA is only the first stage in a strategy for participatory planning (see Chapters 18 and 20, this volume). Empowerment only occurs when the disempowered become able to take collective social action to alleviate particular socio-economic and political conditions, and claim power. For this to happen, PRA must question and address gender relations. This involves the second and third of Mullender and Ward's questions: why does women's relative lack of power exist in a given situation, and how can that situation be changed.

In this context, it is significant that the literature of PRA does not define power and tends to avoid terms like oppression and subordination except with reference to the relationship between North and South. Yet Mullender and Ward (and others including Freire), insist that empowerment must be used in conjunction with an understanding of oppression, given that it is about working to remove the existence and effects of inequality. Thus, '*an understanding of oppression and power* is what draws empowerment away from the meaninglessness which otherwise afflicts and devalues the term' (Mullender and Ward, 1991:7, emphasis added).

The need to understand the relationship between oppression, power and change is central to the argument presented in this chapter. Unless advocates and practitioners are clear about their understanding of power and oppression, the claim that PRA is an empowering strategy is effectively meaningless. For work to be empowering, it must challenge oppression based on any form of social differentiation on which notions of superiority and inferiority have been built historically and maintained by exercising power over others. To challenge oppression, we need to examine what it involves, both as a state of affairs and as a process through which that state of affairs is created and maintained. Statements of the intention to 'empower' can be found in much of the documentation relevant to PRA, but unless accompanied by a commitment to understanding and challenging oppression, both in words and actions, it allows us simply to rewrite our professional accounts without fundamentally changing how our advocacy and practice is experienced by participants.

Due to the failure to analyse and challenge oppression, the ideal of empowerment to which many practitioners profess is often not being carried through into practice. In its current use, PRA appears an appropriate methodology to find out what the issues relevant to women are. In some circumstances, an analysis of women's problems and priorities has helped women and men identify how particular initiatives could meet some of women's practical needs (see Chapters 8 and 18, this volume). PRA to date has, however, generally failed to tackle the *why* question. This is central to Mullender and Ward's model of an empowering, participatory approach as opposed to one that is participatory only. As they suggest, '[a]sking the question *why* puts oppression firmly on the agenda' and on challenging it. Such an analysis is, they argue, 'a distinctive feature of practice which seeks to achieve empowerment' (1991: 91). Only by asking why women are, in some situations, systematically marginalized can power relations be confronted and the necessary changes for them to gain greater power and control be identified.

Looking for conflict

Two other features of PRA highlight its inadequacy, to date, in realizing its claim as an empowering strategy.

Perhaps most significant is the fact that conflict and confrontation are conspicuous by their absence from the documentation of PRA. Women's interests as revealed through the documented use of PRA instead often revolve around health care, child care, nutrition, domestic work and acceptable home-based income-generating activities (Mosse, 1993). Whilst some have been a mechanism for discussing wider issues, for example health projects leading to reproductive-rights discussion (Cornwall, 1992b; Tolley and Bentley, 1992; Welbourn, 1992), the tendency is one of generalization and consensus-seeking. This reflects, in part, a lack of techniques to deal with conflict including an incapacity of PRA methods to represent adequately issues of power. Welbourn (1991), for example, has noted that many aspects of social relations central to women's lives cannot be represented spatially.[7] More fundamental, however, is the underlying inadequate conceptualization of power and the practical implication of this for participatory approaches which seek to empower.

PRA statements about empowerment underestimate the potential for conflict, which is found in either local cleavages, including asymmetric gender relations, or in differing interests between local groups and a larger polity. Welbourn (1993) describes how many PRA practitioners have tended to assume that conflict is politics and as a result have tried to avoid it. Yet if, as was suggested in the preceding analysis, empowerment is a relative concept, it cannot take place without the relative disempowerment of another group, and power is usually not given up voluntarily, rather it must be taken. This suggests that where participatory approaches do not give rise to situations of conflict,[8] they are failing to challenge existing power relations and therefore cannot claim to empower. This conclusion has implications for those in the field. A recognition that empowerment will almost inevitably lead to confrontation, of some sort at some point, about issues of power and autonomy, demands the use of strategies and techniques with which to address conflict.

A related feature concerns the wider issue of how participatory approaches have been embraced and accepted by the mainstream. In a recent and substantial rhetorical shift, participatory approaches are becoming the new orthodoxy within organizations such as the World Bank and the UN (World Bank, 1996; UNDP, 1996). These are calling for more participation in their development projects, and in research and evaluation. This may well indicate a positive change within the dominant development paradigm. It could, however, also reflect the fact that participatory approaches do not, in their current use, threaten significantly the status quo and existing power relations.

Many institutions have viewed PRA and related approaches as a mechanism for cost recovery in projects initiated externally to local communities, for reducing initial outlay, and for improving the accuracy and acceptability of research. Whilst functional efficiency is an important objective, it is not the same as empowerment. As most participatory approaches fail to define empowerment, or even power, they have no agenda which challenges gender power-relations and do not ask too many 'why' questions. As a result they are taken on board by mainstream organizations able to accept the rhetoric, without changing their approach to gender issues.

This chapter suggests that despite the importance of empowerment as a guiding concept, its current usage in the context of much PRA work is inconsistent and ill-defined, with little thought given to the practical implications of its pursuit. For participatory approaches such as PRA to be empowering, they must adopt a far more explicit and critical agenda, even if that means rejection by the mainstream.

Can PRA be empowering for women?

There is nothing inherently empowering for women about participatory rural appraisal as a methodology or a strategy. PRA current practice may achieve a 'pre-empowerment' stage which is helpful in identifying issues critical to women but it does not necessarily aim to change the gendered power relations which give rise to these situations. Given that '[t]here is nothing inherently radical or conservative in any method. It is the purposes of those using them that breathe into them one or other of the characteristics' (Ragg 1977:145, cited in Mullender and Ward, 1991:81), the onus of responsibility for living up to the empowerment claim of PRA falls upon practitioners.

Although changing a methodology can significantly increase our ability to interpret complex issues, it cannot by itself resolve these issues or empower (see Chapter 22, this volume). More discussion and feedback may provide the basis for the empowerment of women in their struggle for change but it is not an inherent outcome of participation. Powerlessness not only impedes the powerless from articulating their demands, it also often makes acting on those demands unimaginable.

Participatory rural appraisal can make claims to empowerment, which includes empowering women, only if it explicitly challenges oppressive gender power relations and, as part of these, women's marginalized and subordinated positions in society. Only an approach based on these anti-oppressive principles can deal with the roots rather than just the symptoms of the issues faced by women.

Most PRA misses out an essential step between appraisal and action through its failure to recognize that empowerment involves an analysis of power and oppression. Although an assessment of what the issues facing women are is valuable, particularly in the context of Freire's (1972) call for collective consciousness-raising, it does not necessarily help participants to generalize from their particular situation to wider societal processes. Without this, there can be no awareness of the forces of oppression or the potential for powerless groups to take action to confront them. Furthermore, by failing systematically to address issues of social difference, including those of gender, in training and practice, participatory approaches are in danger of reinforcing the development biases they aim to avoid, instead serving to maintain the status quo.

Empowerment is, as Bergall (1993) suggests, a very important qualitative dimension of participatory approaches. Given that PRA does not automatically empower, the challenge is one of how to increase the power associated with participation. Can the methodology and strategy of PRA be modified so as to become more empowering for those women involved? Mullender and Ward suggest that the answer lies in asking questions about why subordination and powerlessness occur. Gendered relations of power must be a fundamental premise upon which the approach is based. This means:

o acknowledging that women's subordination stems from socially constructed gender power relations, which interlock with caste, class, race, ethnicity and religious identities;
o recognizing the centrality of gender in the shaping of consciousness, skills and institutions, as well as in the distribution of power and privilege; and

o aiming not only to make visible the experiences of women but also to alter fundamentally oppressive aspects of gender relations.

Potential but no panacea

PRA represents a potential but not a panacea for research and development that is empowering. The fulfilment of that potential is dependent, to a significant extent, upon trainers and practitioners. If PRA is to be empowering for local people, it must also be empowering for women. In order to empower women, it will need to address gendered power-relations. This demands that the individuals facilitating its use adopt a gender framework and make this explicit to those involved. As Griffen suggests, 'we need to make deeper inroads into the system of society – the way it is organized, the way in which women are equally represented' (1989:125). In practical terms, a first step involves incorporating the empowerment framework of Mullender and Ward by working with women and men to seek answers to these questions:

o what are the issues of concern to women, as voiced by women?
o why do these issues exist, including women's own analysis of their underlying causes? and
o how can women be organized in order that they are heard and that they can gain power?

As Griffen (1989) suggests, this checklist can help to decide whether our activities contribute to empowering women and the different ways in which participatory approaches could be improved to empower women more. If the advocates and practitioners of participatory rural appraisal choose not to ask the critical question of 'why?', then any claims to empowerment should be questioned. If they do, then the potential of PRA to empower women has yet to be fulfilled.

References

Adams, A. *et al.* (1993) 'Participatory Methods to Assess Change in Health and Women's Lives', mimeo.

Bergall, T. (1993) *Methods for Active Participation: experiences in rural development from East and Central Africa*, Nairobi: OUP.

Bilgi, M. (1992) 'Entering Women's World Through Men's Eyes – a Participatory Rural Appraisal at Boripitha, Netrang', mimeo.

Bystydzienski, J. (1992) *Women Transforming Politics; worldwide strategies for empowerment*, Bloomington and Indianapolis: Indiana University Press.

Chambers, R. (1992) 'Rural Appraisal; Rapid, Relaxed and Participatory', *IDS Discussion Paper*, No. 31, Brighton: IDS.

Cornwall, A. (1992a) 'Engendering Ethnocentricity? PRA and the Analysis of Gender', mimeo.

Cornwall, A. (1992b) 'Body-mapping in RRA/PRA', *RRA Notes* 16: 69–76.

Devaraj, S. (1993) 'Participatory Rural Appraisal: an initiation in Tamil Nadu', mimeo.

Deutchman, I. (1991) 'The Politics of Empowerment', *Women and Politics* 11(2), 1–18.

Friedmann, J. (1992) *Empowerment: the politics of an alternative development*, Oxford: Basil Blackwell.

Freire, P. (1972) *The Pedagogy of the Oppressed*, London: Penguin.

Gajanayake, S. and J. (1993) *Community Empowerment: a participatory training manual on community project development*, Office of International Training and Consultation, Illinois, USA.

Grady, H. *et al.* (1991) 'Assessing Women's Needs in Gaza Using Participatory Rapid Appraisal Techniques', *RRA Notes* 10: 12–19.

Griffen, V (ed.). (1989) *Women, Development and Empowerment: a Pacific feminist perspective*, Kuala Lumpur: Asian and Pacific Development Centre.

Guijt, I. (1994) 'Making a Difference: integrating gender analysis into PRA training', *RRA Notes* 19: 49–55.

Hall, C.M. (1992) *Women and Empowerment: strategies for increasing autonomy*, Washington: Hemisphere Publishing Corporation.

Hinton, R. (1995) 'Trades in Different Worlds: listening to refugee voices', *PLA Notes* 24: 21–26.

Kabeer, N. (1990) 'Gender, Development and Training: raising awareness in development planning', GADU Newspack No.14.

Kabeer, N. (1995) *Reversed Realities: gender hierarchies in development thought*, London: Verso.

Krishnamurthy, R. (1994) 'Gender and Participatory Experiences: implications and experiences', mimeo.

Lukes, S. (1986) *Power*, Oxford: Basil Blackwell.

Mosse, D. (1993) Authority, Gender and Knowledge: theoretical reflections on the practice of participatory rural appraisal', *ODI Agricultural Administration (Research and Extension) Network Papers*, No. 44.

Mullender, A and D. Ward (1991) *Self-Directed Groupwork: users take action for empowerment*, London: Whiting and Birch.

Nelson, N. and S. Wright (1995) *Power and Participatory Development*, London: Intermediate Technology Publications.

Pottier, J. and P. Orone (1995) 'Consensus or Cover up? The limitations of group meetings', *PLA Notes* 24: 38–42.

Richards, P. (1995) 'Participatory Rural Appraisal: A quick and dirty critique', *PLA Notes* 24: 13–16.

Robinson, E. (1990) 'Women's PRA, Hindupur, Andhra Pradesh, India', mimeo.

Rowlands, J. (1992) 'What is Empowerment? The Challenge of Researching Women, Empowerment and Development in Honduras', paper presented to the GAPP Conference on Participatory Development, Goldsmiths College, London 9–10 July 1992.

Tolley, E. and M. Bentley (1992) 'Participatory Methods for Research on Women's Reproductive Health', in *RRA Notes* 16: 63–8.

UNDP (1996) Learning Network on Empowerment and Participation (LEAP), Programme Proposal, New York: UNDP.

Warren, C. (1988) *Gender Issues in Field Research*, California: Sage Publications.

Welbourn, A. (1991) 'RRA and the Analysis of Difference', *RRA Notes*: 14: 14–23.

Welbourn, A. (1992) 'Rapid Rural Appraisal, Gender and Health – alternative ways of listening to needs', *IDS Bulletin* 23(1): 8–18.

Welbourn, A. (1993) 'PRA, Gender and Conflict Resolution: some problems and possibilities', paper presented at the PRA and Gender Workshop, Institute of Development Studies, 6–7 December.

World Bank (1996) *The Participation Sourcebook*, Washington DC: World Bank.

3

Assessing PRA for Implementing Gender and Development

MORAG HUMBLE

Since consideration of women's participation in development activities became more serious at the end of the 1970s, two major streams of theory and practice have been developed (Rathgeber, 1990). The dominant approach, 'women in development' (WID), assumes that women have been left out of development and need to be integrated by others in order to benefit from it. The mechanism for this is generally special, women-only projects which focus on what are considered 'traditional' women's roles related to domestic activities. In the early 1980s, the WID orientation of donor agencies and NGOs was so strong that few questions were asked about whether the interventions or their objectives were, in fact, beneficial to or desired by women.

The alternative approach, 'gender and development' (GAD), is more critical of development. GAD theory asserts that women have always participated in development but from an unequal position and without acknowledgement. GAD supporters argue that the crucial constraints for women's advancement are the social structures and processes which create and maintain male superiority and female subordination. GAD theory recognizes that women's lives are strongly shaped by men, hence efforts to promote women's empowerment must involve men and women alike. Gender equity is only possible by addressing gender relations and rethinking development practice.

Chapter 3 starts by outlining the core principles of GAD theory. It then reviews the characteristics needed of a methodology to implement GAD in order to make development empowering for men and women alike. Participatory rural appraisal (PRA) is suggested as a methodology with an empowerment agenda similar to GAD theory. An examination of two cases where PRA was applied to address gender issues in the field provides the basis for an initial assessment of its potential to serve as a GAD methodology. The conclusion highlights areas of concern for practitioners of both GAD and PRA. Ensuring gender-responsive use of PRA requires particular attention to:

○ prolonged critical investigations, not rapid descriptions;
○ non-directive facilitation;
○ sensitive handling of inevitable conflicts; and
○ raising expectations only when ensuring follow-up support.

GAD theory

GAD theory focuses on women's empowerment at two levels: at a personal level its concern is women's self-confidence and sense of personal potency;

at a higher political level women's capacity to make public decisions and control resources is the focus. Any methodology developed to implement GAD must, therefore, centre also on women's empowerment. To do this, it must address not only women's immediate, practical needs for their own and their families' survival, but their longer-term, strategic needs for greater gender equality.

Women's daily activities tend to focus on their practical gender needs, which come from their roles as mothers, wives and daughters in the existing gender division of labour. While these require immediate attention, gains are bound to be short-term unless the underlying problem of women's subordination is addressed. Addressing these more strategic needs is, however, considered by many to be confrontational, and is often avoided.

The structure of gender relations in most societies appears to be 'natural' and unchangeable, despite being socially constructed over time. As a result, the majority of women and men alike accept the division of labour and power, and women may not recognize their subordinate position.[1] Nor do they necessarily give priority to longer-term needs, even if they are recognized. Because societies are also stratified by race, class and other lines, women may more readily recognize interests they share with men of their own social group (such as overcoming poverty and responding to common practical needs) than any they share with women of another group. In addition, women may resist social change in their current position if they feel it may threaten their short-term practical interests or threaten their safety without immediate protection or compensation (see Molyneux, 1985: 234). If the pursuit of women's strategic gender interests is to be managed without jeopardizing women's present condition, then the women concerned must be engaged in the analysis and in determining the direction and pace of change.

GAD theorists have made a valuable contribution by highlighting the complexity of gender relations in different socio-economic contexts. However, they have not shown how these complexities can be used by development workers to translate theory into action. Most development agencies still adopt a 'WID' approach to women's participation. Having rejected most development approaches as 'gender blind', GAD still remains a theory in need of a methodology for implementation.

Characteristics of a GAD methodology

To abide by the rigorous empowerment orientation of GAD theory, any methodology used to implement it must conform to three essential characteristics: it must be critical, participatory and reflexive. Each of these three characteristics is necessary for the others to function properly and for the emancipatory objectives of GAD to be realized (see Humble, 1994).

First, a critical methodology tries to uncover and address the causes of inequality. From a gender perspective, critical practice involves undertaking a detailed analysis of local communities in order to determine the local structures of gender relations and gender division of labour. Critical practice involves going beyond the simple identification of needs to ask how they arose and why they are not being addressed. In addition, a critical methodology must be oriented towards action. By exposing the basis of previously concealed power relations, critical practice helps to encourage people to see themselves as subjects capable of changing their own lives.[2]

Second, it follows, therefore, that a critical methodology must also be participatory, facilitating women's own identification and analysis of their practical and strategic needs. 'Participation' is a much-debated concept in development (see Chapters 1 and 2, this volume), with definitions differing essentially in terms of the relative amounts of control exercised by outsiders or local people. GAD requires the most rigorous forms of participation in which local people, particularly women, set the agenda and initiate their own action. Outsiders can be involved in the process as facilitators and catalysts, but not as decisionmakers.

Men must, however, also be participants in a gender-sensitive approach to development, as any attempt to change gender relations has to involve both sexes. If women's control over resources and decisionmaking is to increase, those who are currently in control will have to allow for this redistribution, either consciously or not.

An inherent tension exists between these two elements of the participatory requirement in GAD. On the one hand, men must be involved in a gender approach to development, while on the other, women must be able to define their own needs, goals and strategies, and decide on the direction of their own development. Since women's and men's priorities are likely to differ at some point in project planning or implementation, a GAD methodology should include mechanisms for managing and diffusing conflict. Part of the key to conflict resolution is being able to anticipate areas of contention, which should be uncovered by critical analysis. Approaching women's strategic interests through their practical needs is often considered a way of avoiding conflict, at least initially. Men can often be persuaded to help meet women's practical needs if they see benefits accrue to their families.

A GAD methodology must be able to balance and mediate between men's and women's participation and priorities without losing the focus on strategic activities and empowerment. It must also aim to change, fundamentally, people's perspectives, attitudes and behaviour, and thus demands a certain degree of introspection. Constant monitoring of the development process is required to ensure that all component activities or steps contribute to and promote the empowerment and equity of participants. In other words, the means must be consistent with the ends.

This points to the third requirement for GAD implementation: reflexivity. A reflexive methodology progresses through an iterative cycle of analysis – planning, action, self-evaluation, and back to planning – reshaping itself through reflection and adaptation. Participants involved in the process learn from each cycle, allowing them to adjust activities on a regular basis. This reflexivity does not, however, pertain only to the activities of local communities affected by development initiatives. In a GAD context, reflexivity also challenges the attitudes and practices of northern development professionals and agencies. It forces them to examine their own organizations and personal relationships, to create the same gender equity and empowerment as is the objective of the external work.[3]

Congruence between PRA and GAD

While there is no automatic priority awarded to addressing women's needs and decision-making in PRA as would be expected in a GAD approach, a strong compatibility appears to exist in theory between the core elements and intentions of PRA and the requirements of GAD methodology as described above:

o PRA is critical by design: it attempts to raise 'people's self-awareness, suggests viable solutions, and helps people analyse complex issues and problems' (Theis and Grady, 1991: 32). Its methods are intended to reveal a range of physical, social and economic conditions and structures which constrain or stimulate local development and empowerment. It encourages planners, usually outsiders, to seek a deeper understanding of the specifics of local conditions rather than generalizing across regions. PRA methods such as activity charts and seasonal calendars, social mapping and problem ranking could be used to discuss the structure of gender relations and the specificity of local gender divisions of labour.[4] The same mapping exercise done by separate groups of women and men can highlight their different practical needs, and women's strategic need for more equitable gender relations.[5]

o As suggested by its name, PRA is participatory in intention. It aims to place control over development processes in the hands of the intended beneficiaries. Local people become active in their own development, and they prioritize needs and interventions (see Chambers, 1992). PRA's relatively rapid and visual methods appear to make it particularly suitable for use with women, who are more often illiterate than their menfolk, and face considerable time constraints.

o Reflexivity and process-orientation are key principles of PRA. PRA-based planning is context-specific and adapts to new circumstances and information. Participants are encouraged to review and revise plans on an ongoing basis. Sequencing exercises and cross-checking information ensures that additional dimensions of understanding are added with each step (see Theis and Grady, 1991). External professionals are also challenged to listen and learn from local people. They are required to revise their assumptions about the abilities and creativity of rural people, and about the unity or common interest of communities or even households.[6] Ideally, external experts will be encouraged to examine how such assumptions operate to maintain hierarchical structures within their own agencies, and to reassess their perspective of development processes (see Thompson, 1994).

A quick look at the theory of PRA seems, therefore, to indicate that potentially it fulfils the needs of a GAD methodology: it pursues a critical, societal objective of change; it seeks to do this with, and not for, intended beneficiaries; and it espouses self-reflection and learning in both theory and practice. An examination of two concrete examples of PRA will, however, shed a more critical light on the potential of a PRA–GAD merger.

The use of PRA explicitly to implement GAD theory in the field is relatively new, dating from about 1990. Examples from two initiatives, the Aga Khan Rural Support Programme (AKRSP) in India (see Chapters 8 and 21, this volume) and the Bali Sustainable Development Project (BSDP) in Indonesia (see Chapter 14, this volume), highlight some of the potentials and problems for practitioners to consider.

The Aga Khan Rural Support Programme, India[7]

The Aga Khan Rural Support Programme (AKRSP) in Gujarat, India, has been a centre for PRA innovation and practice since the late 1980s. The organization adopted a gender approach with two strategies: (i) of working with women in separate groups to improve their skills, increase their confidence and help them identify their own needs and priorities; and (ii), working to sensitize men and change their attitudes. Groups of women participate in wealth ranking, social mapping, making daily and seasonal-activity profiles, and problem ranking. Exercises to chart women's daily activities have also been undertaken with separate men's groups, followed by discussions on women's needs.

Activity profiles and social mapping have proved particularly useful for uncovering the specifics of the local gender division of labour and attitudes towards women's and men's work. When combined with problem-ranking exercises, the process highlights women's practical needs for labour-saving technologies, and better access to water and fuel resources, in order to reduce the drudgery of their everyday tasks.

In terms of broader strategic interests, these community-based reflections reveal the fairly obvious point that women need to be relieved of drudgery or a more equitable division of labour. The brevity of many PRA exercises may limit the range of strategic interests that can be uncovered without more probing and analysis. However, AKRSP's strategy on gender issues is to use women's practical needs as an entry point to empowerment, and short exercises and discussions take place in the context of a longer process of community development. With the provision of appropriate technology and the expansion of opportunities for women to secure independent incomes, more space can be created, allowing them to consider, articulate and act upon their strategic interests.

In women-focused PRA work, AKRSP facilitators create an environment in which women lead the analysis of the information that they themselves gather. While women's confidence in their own analytical ability is strengthened, some questions can still be raised about the degree of direction which AKRSP imposes on these processes. The subjects of pressure cookers and biogas plants are regularly introduced by the facilitators. This prompting does not necessarily mean that women do not feel strongly about such developments. There is little written record, however, of whether women ever prioritized other needs, such as for health care or literacy classes.[8]

The introduction of women-focused PRA work with men further increased the participatory content of AKRSP's gender programme. Through these discussions, men are encouraged to examine their own perceptions of women's contribution to community and household well-being, and to revalue women's work. Follow-up evidence from AKRSP suggests that men are now playing a role in helping women develop new skills and income-earning opportunities, and are even learning from the experience of local women's groups.

The ability of PRA to manage conflict between men's and women's needs and interests is an important element of ensuring a balance between the two aspects of participation in GAD. By focusing on women's practical gender needs, AKRSP avoided some male–female confrontation. The continued segregation of women's and men's groups and the lack of information about mixed-sex interactions makes it difficult, however, to gauge the conflict-resolving potential of PRA as used by AKRSP.

Assessing reflexivity in AKRSP's PRA process requires detailed information on follow-up activities held with the same participants, which is not readily available. The original PRA exercises, sometimes lasting only half a day, are too short to show the integration of learning from one stage to another. Exercises with men gave them little time to adjust their long-held but evidently incorrect assumptions about women's work. There is no record of attempts being made to encourage men to reflect on the implications of their conclusions, or to try to plan how they may be able to reduce women's workload, such as by taking on new (previously female) responsibilities, accepting new technologies or prioritizing the building of a new village well.

There are, however, clear signs of reflexivity in the impact that the gender activities have had on the AKRSP programme as a whole, resulting in greater participation of women in the project's training and employment activities, and increasingly in management roles. Concepts such as practical and strategic needs are now being used in work with marginalized castes and other groups, as well as with women.

The Bali Sustainable Development Project[9]

The Bali Sustainable Development Project (BSDP) was a collaborative study between universities in Canada and Indonesia, one component of an environmental management initiative supported by the Canadian International Development Agency (CIDA). BSDP aimed to develop a Sustainable Development Strategy for Bali, covering a range of social, economic and environmental issues. Conventional, extractive research methods were used in combination with participatory methods. One component of the project focused on examining gender roles and needs at the community level, and was organized explicitly to test PRA as a methodological approach to GAD (see Chapter 14, this volume). A variety of PRA techniques was used during the gender-focused research, such as daily activity profiles, trend analysis, problem ranking, resource mapping and planning exercises. Some were undertaken in sex-segregated groups and others in mixed meetings.

The various exercises stimulated women's critical thinking about their own lives and needs. Practical and strategic needs alike were identified in women's discussion groups, the latter including the need for more decision-making power and better treatment from men. Daily activity charts uncovered the disparities of the local gender division of labour among female and male farmers, labourers and entrepreneurs, showing that gender relations were not as equitable in Bali as had been believed.

Women's participation was strongest in single-sex meetings, where there was adequate space and time for them to discuss and define their needs and priorities. However, planning exercises only took place in mixed groups, where men tended to dominate. If women had been able to plan together beforehand, they might have had the additional confidence needed to defend their positions in front of men.[10]

The facilitator's commitment to GAD ensured that men also participated in discussions about gender roles, needs and relations. As with the AKRSP experience described above, men's first response to learning about women's different needs was to refute their significance. There were also positive signs of a change in male attitudes, however. Traditionally, women and men operated in separate spheres, rarely conferring or making decisions together. After having discussions with women for the first time and seeing their different priorities and needs, some men expressed a desire to have more meetings together to discuss community development.

It is obviously difficult to evaluate reflexivity in a research project with a discrete end such as BSDP. Information on whether men and women continued their discussion and planning meetings separately or together, which could have shown a learning process in operation, is not available. While the problem-ranking and planning exercises developed some strategies for addressing discrete community needs, BSDP as a project did not have a mandate to meet those needs. Participants reaped personal benefit from being involved in the PRA-based work, which also raised expectations that were not met.

The GAD research yielded a number of recommendations about gender training and strengthening the participation of women in the Sustainable Development Strategy. These were incorporated into the final report for the Indonesian government. However, the gender-focused research started towards the end of the overall research process and limited the influence its findings could have had over the entire project. Evidence of any change in attitudes or practice on the part of the external professionals (Indonesian and Canadian) will have to wait for a possible second phase of the project.

The limits and potential of PRA for GAD

In theory, PRA sounds like a development approach firmly rooted in an empowerment objective. This suggests it could be an appropriate methodology for realizing GAD's objectives. However, a cursory look at these two examples of PRA in practice, one in a development context and another research-based, reveal some serious cracks in the surface. Four concerns are identified here: the tension between rapid and critical investigation; the problem of directed participation; theneed for mechanisms to manage gender conflict; and the issue of expectations.

Rapid versus critical investigation

There is a potential conflict between PRA's image of and use as a rapid approach and GAD's requirement for critical analysis. One of the appeals of PRA is its time and cost-efficient way of generating information for project planning, particularly when compared to other approaches like rural surveys or the residential style of social anthropology. The shift from rapid rural appraisal to participatory rural appraisal was intended to involve local people more in the process of analysis, to increase rapport between outsiders and insiders and make the process more relaxed, but not necessarily to slow it down or draw it out significantly (see Chambers, 1992). Yet it is one thing to ask people to consider the constraints and opportunities in their natural environment and to plan activities which could increase their agricultural yields or reduce soil loss from their lands. It is quite another to ask them to evaluate the strengths and limitations of age-old forms of social organization and to plan to change them. More time may be required for discussion and analysis in a PRA on gender issues, both for the structures and ideology of gender oppression to be revealed, and for women to develop confidence and awareness of themselves as critical social actors capable of promoting change.

While uncovering gender needs and interests is a time-consuming process, most poor women have heavy daily work burdens which leave them with little time. A partial solution is to spread the analysis of data, prioritization of needs and planning of activities over time, allowing participants space and time to reflect on one step or exercise before moving on to another (see Chapter 20, this volume). This strategy was used by both AKRSP and BDSP, although the BSDP's limited time frame did not allow for the continuation of the discussion groups. In AKRSP's case, the space which was created for women's ongoing dialogue and action appears to have empowered them to meet some of their practical gender needs, while also enhancing their confidence and status and enabling their greater participation in village affairs. A strong advantage of AKRSP is its indigenous character and location close to the communities it supports. For foreign development agencies, universities or other non-local actors engaging in PRA work on gender issues, taking a slower pace or longer time frame presents greater difficulties.

PRA's principles of 'optimal ignorance' and 'appropriate imprecision',[11] lie at the root of this tension with critical analysis. Pursuing 'optimal ignorance' can provide an easy excuse to limit the depth of analysis, restricting attention to women's practical needs and ignoring their strategic interests. The critical potential of PRA methods would be lost if the optimal level of understanding was assumed to be reached upon completion of a map or ranking exercise. Identification of the structures of social and gender relations in a community must be followed by an examination of why they are that way (see Chapter 2, this volume). Generally, those who decide on the 'optimal' or 'appropriate' levels of ignorance are external facilitators. If PRA is to become a GAD technique, the authority to determine the appropriate depth, direction and pace of analysis must be vested in the women participants themselves.

Directed participation

It was noted in the first part of this chapter that GAD requires an empowering conception of participation, where local people set their own agenda and carry it out, facilitated by, but largely independent of, outsiders. In many examples of PRA, including both cases reviewed above, the participation is more directed. Outsiders and local people work in cooperation, but the former still exercise some control over priorities and decisions. Facilitators can influence the agenda or priorities of local actors in many ways, such as by choosing the exercises to be undertaken, introducing topics for discussion (such as fuel-saving technologies in the AKRSP project), or using prepared pictures to stimulate discussion around the identification of needs (a practice followed in the BSDP project).

The balance between facilitation and covert direction is a fine one, and can be understood in the context of the dynamic between bottom-up participation and agency planning, with the latter's associated time constraints and reporting requirements. AKRSP acknowledges this, noting that encouraging genuine participation is 'a time-consuming task. Often there is a tension between trying to achieve targets and trying to involve communities. Often communities have different priorities to those we feel are important' (AKRSP, 1994: ix). While this dilemma is not exclusive to PRA as a methodology, it does affect it. There is always a danger of PRA being implemented without due attention to the principles of facilitating (not leading), and hence of the participation becoming instrumental.

Managing conflict

Development interventions aim to change – a process which is never neutral. GAD's focus on power relations between women and men recognizes the inevitability of conflict that will arise while using participatory approaches to promote women's strategic interests (see Chapter 5, this volume). Exercises that rank problems and identify community-based solutions can be used in some instances to moderate conflict between priorities, but their utility in dealing with the larger questions of power imbalances between women and men has yet to be proven. Overall, conflict management with PRA is an area in which considerably more research, experimentation and, above all, training is needed.

The consequences of drawing attention to areas of gender conflict in communities need to be considered carefully. There may be a backlash against women which threatens their economic or even physical security. Even where women want to change inequitable gender relations, they have little desire to see their situation become more precarious in the short term. While sharing of information is one of the key principles of PRA, the existence of gender conflict and the need to respect confidentiality and secure safety may require constraints on this between women's and men's groups. The judge of 'appropriate' risks and changes in all cases needs to be the women themselves.

Raising expectations

The issue of raised expectations permeates all of the above, and should be a particular concern for groups using participatory methods for research. If villagers undertake exercises with an external facilitator to identify and prioritize their needs, and make plans on the basis of this analysis, their expectations that additional financial and other assistance will be provided to help implement these plans are going to be raised. Likewise, if women become determined to act for their strategic goals and the desired changes are not forthcoming, frustration which could be disempowering may result.

Possible solutions include ensuring clear and limited objectives of PRA work, helping villagers to plan for only those activities that can be sustained locally without outside assistance, putting villagers in touch with agencies that could provide additional assistance, or building in follow-up work on implementation to all research proposals.

Implementing gender and development theory requires a long-term commitment to change, and an unwavering focus on women's strategic empowerment, through a critical, participatory and reflexive methodology. PRA, while not automatically gender-aware, can facilitate the analysis of gender relations and the prioritization of strategies for change. Maintaining self-critical awareness and responsibility, moving slowly and probing deeply with women and men alike will help PRA to live up to its full potential as a GAD methodology. Incorporating GAD theory into the training of PRA facilitators is an important first step.

References

AKRSP (1994) (Aga Khan Rural Support Programme) *Annual Progress Reports 1991, 1992, 1993*, Ahmedabad: AKRSP.

Chambers, Robert (1992) 'Rural Appraisal: rapid, relaxed and participatory', *IDS Discussion Paper* 311, Brighton: IDS.

Flora, Cornelia Butler (1994) 'Using Focus Groups with Rural Women', in Hilary Sims Feldstein and Janice Jiggins (eds) *Tools for the Field: methodologies handbook for gender analysis in agriculture*, Hartford, Conn: Kumarian Press, pp. 62–7.

Held, David (1980) *Critical Theory: Horkheimer to Habermas*, Hutchinson: London.

Humble, Morag (1994) 'Implementing Gender and Development Theory: assessing participatory rural appraisal as a GAD technique', MA thesis, Ottawa: Carleton University.

Kabeer, Naila (1994) *Reversed Realities: gender hierarchies in development thought*. London: Verso.

Molyneux, Maxine (1985) 'Mobilization without Emancipation? Women's interests, the state and revolution in Nicaragua', *Feminist Studies* 11(2): 227–54.

Rathgeber, Eva (1990) 'WID, WAD, GAD: trends in research and practice', *Journal of Developing Areas* 24 (July): 489–502.

Theis, Joachim and Heather M. Grady (1991) *Participatory Rapid Appraisal for Community Development: a training manual based on experiences in the Middle East and North Africa*, London: Save the Children and IIED.

Thompson, John (1994) 'From Participatory Appraisal to Participatory Practice: viewing training as part of a broader process of institutional development', *RRA Notes* 19: 56–60.

Welbourn, Alice (1991) 'RRA and the Analysis of Difference', *RRA Notes* 14: 14–23.

Young, Kate (1993) *Planning Development with Women: making a world of difference*, London: Macmillan.

4

Gender, Participation and the Politics of Difference

ANDREA CORNWALL

A group of men return from a gender-analysis exercise in a rural African village. They show their trainer diagrams representing analyses carried out by groups of women and men in the community. The diagrams highlight the hardships faced by adolescent men. The team have not done it properly, the trainer tells them. This is not gender analysis, she says, they have got it all wrong.

Usually gender prejudice is seen as a peculiarly male problem. Yet, as this example shows, women's gender prejudices can be just as blinding. When gender analysis reveals that young men may actually be the ones at the bottom of the heap, challenges are posed to received wisdom about gender. It is with these challenges, and their implications for participatory learning and action, that this chapter is concerned.

All too often in development, 'gender' is taken to mean 'women', and women are treated as an identifiable single category, thought of in a narrow range of stereotypical ways. 'Men', equally thought of as a single category, lurk in the background, imagined as powerful and oppositional figures. 'Gender', then, becomes something women are or should be concerned about. Men become 'the problem'. Much of the time, 'gender analysis' does not extend to analysing men's positions, views and reactions *as men*. Those men who would become involved in bringing about change can feel excluded from gender work by virtue of their sex. Those who retain their prejudices can feel affronted by a perceived totalizing assault on masculinity, become defensive and angry, and resist. Rather than addressing issues that should be everyone's issues, 'gender' becomes a battleground on which other struggles are waged.

Disregarding the complexity of difference doesn't help anyone, least of all those whose livelihoods are at stake in development interventions. Making assumptions about people based on their sex does not get us anywhere in working with them. Think of our sons, brothers, fathers, friends: are they not also men? What of those young men in that African village, caught between gerontocracy and a gender division of labour in which they lost out whichever way they turned? There are men, like these young men, who are as powerless as the archetypical 'woman' who appears in versions of 'gender-aware' thinking that would cast them as long-suffering victims. There are men who are marginalized and subjected to the brutality of prejudice because they step outside expected norms, failing to do 'what a man's gotta do'.

Thinking of the men we know, we need to ask ourselves: can I put them all in a category, label them as such and make assumptions about them based on the fact that they all have a penis? And although it may sit uneasily with a feminist outlook, there are women who are just as 'patriarchal' as the patriarchs themselves. These are women who use whatever strategies they can to enhance their position and power, acting at times as if they were powerful men and alongside certain kinds of men at others (cf. Kandiyoti, 1988). Women like these disappear quietly in representations of woman-as-oppressed.

Differences make an impact in complex, culturally distinct ways. Breaking away from stereotyped assumptions about 'women' or 'men' calls for an approach to gender that takes an account of other differences and that works from categories that are meaningful to the communities with whom development workers work. Participatory rural appraisal, with its emphasis on locally determined criteria, local materials and local concerns, would seem to offer appropriate tools to explore difference. And yet PRA facilitators are often unable to let go of their own received wisdoms about gender and really begin from locally perceived realities.

It is my argument in this chapter that for 'gender-aware PRA' to be genuinely aware of gender and to be really participatory, it is crucial that facilitators take a step back and reflect on their own preconceived ideas and prejudices. By working with the differences that affect local people's lives and livelihoods, rather than with blanket notions of difference that fail to do justice to the complexities of most people's lived realities, they can then take a step forward to work effectively for change.

Participatory approaches and the politics of difference

Despite diverse origins, the growing range of participatory approaches share a common emphasis on enabling local people to play an active role in their own development (Chambers, 1997). The rhetoric of participation, by now so familiar in the most unexpected of places, is rich with expressions like 'empowerment' (see Chapter 2, this volume). The message of participatory development is ultimately about power and about change. PRA becomes 'participatory', in a political sense, only when allied with the explicit aim of bringing about changes that transform current inequalities. While PRA methods open up the possibility of dialogue, their use does not in itself constitute the making of a participatory process (Cornwall, 1996). PRA offers a tool kit of techniques that can be used to embrace divergent political agendas. In practice, PRA can serve, as well as confront, established interests. Among the range of participatory toolkits currently available, few systematically address issues of gender difference and fewer still contain the tools that are needed to make sense of the complexities of difference.[1] There tends, rather, to be naive optimism inherent in many of these approaches that glosses over the realities of conflict and inequality.

There is nothing inherent in the PRA approach that addresses gender as an issue, yet PRA is rooted deeply in a philosophy of respect in which contributions from every member of a community are solicited and valued

(Chambers, 1992, 1997). The PRA principles would appear to suggest that gender would automatically be taken into consideration as one among a range of differences. The reflective PRA practitioner is considered to be one who acknowledges and builds into her/his practice an awareness of what feminist theorists have termed the 'politics of location': the recognition that all who speak do so from a particular place and from particular experience (Mohanty, 1987). Yet contradictions and prejudices abound in practice. Those who would guard against changes in attitudes to women and men may fervently embrace participatory approaches, approaches that are in principle concerned equally with equity and change. Those who would enable people to explore and describe their own realities may allow their own prejudices to steer them towards and away from certain kinds of people, ideas or conclusions. Where those who initiate and facilitate PRA activities situate themselves in terms of their personal and institutional agendas clearly plays an important part in the approach that individual facilitators take on issues of power and difference.

Where these issues concern participatory work is in the ways that women's and men's interests are represented, i.e. how they emerge (or not) as part of the PRA process, how they are spoken about and whose voices speak out for them. The community action plans that emerge from PRA can so easily become the action plans of the powerful minority, who have co-opted the process to their own advantage. In much of the PRA literature, the 'insider'/'outsider' relationship is virtually the only one discussed in terms of power. The internal dynamics of 'communities', the relationships between those who take part in a PRA exercise, those who stand up to present or make a case and those who watch from the sidelines, are rarely given sufficient consideration. There is no reason to assume that just because women are present they represent women-in-general, nor that because women do not speak that they do not have any decisionmaking power. Matters are more complex than this, and the men who are involved in such events should not just be regarded as a lumpen category, 'men'. They too are often particular kinds of men and other kinds of men may well be marginalized or excluded from these settings.

The question of 'whose reality counts?' (Chambers, 1997) takes on wider significance when decisions are made on what paths of action to pursue. For some issues, treating 'women' and 'men' as single-interest groups remains politically expedient. Where there are gross inequities in opportunities for access to services such as credit, access to fertiliser or involvement in extension activities, for example, woman-centred development efforts can make a difference. Yet merely addressing 'women's issues' can result in a failure to recognize complex interdependencies between women and men, undermining the livelihoods of people whose realities are far more complex than simplifying models might allow (Goetz, 1989; Kabeer, 1994).

The participatory research movement has tended to be 'gender-blind' (Maguire, 1987), thus failing to live up to the ideals that are espoused. Yet the use of a 'gender perspective' that focuses primarily on women-in-general does not offer sustainable solutions to the issues of equity and empowerment that both participatory and feminist research focus on.

Human relationships are more complex than this: the underlying issues can so easily be overlooked or misunderstood when viewed through the lens offered by the simplistic models used in most variants of 'gender analysis'. Many development workers resist delving into social complexities, drawing attention to the practical realities of development and the need for a simple framework that can ensure the inclusion of women in development initiatives. But the implications of imposing simplistic, often Eurocentric, notions of gender in development interventions can be far-reaching. Strategies are needed to make gender issues everybody's issues. The discussion below draws attention to some of the key areas in which caution is merited and makes practical suggestions for developing an approach to gender in PRA which takes account of the complexity of difference.

Engendering disquiet? Beyond Eurocentric notions of gender

Euro-American feminists writing in the 1970s made much of a series of key distinctions that informed the basis for feminist theorizing until they began to be undermined in the 1980s. Three of these distinctions were particularly important in shaping feminist approaches to questions of gender difference: sex/gender, nature/culture and public/private (see Ortner, 1974 and Rosaldo, 1974). It is these distinctions which have been carried forward into the GAD approach, which stresses a definition of gender as a social and cultural construct: gender corresponds to 'culture', where sexual difference is ascribed to 'nature'. Accordingly, as gender constructs vary cross-culturally, the ways in which we think about what being a man or a woman means is not fixed but is part of the ways in which people of our historical, social and cultural context have come to think, and therefore is amenable to being changed. This is a very attractive way of seeing difference. The problem with it, however, is that we cannot just wish away our bodies (see Gatens, 1983), nor can we detach 'gender' from the range of other differences that have an effect on how others respond to us and how we think of ourselves.

In the 1980s, it became apparent that the Euro-American feminists who spoke about Universal Woman were taking a bit too much for granted. Many of them spoke as white, middle-class, heterosexual women. Black, lesbian and working-class women, women who, among others, experienced the effects of other differences and suffered other discriminations, began to speak out (see, for example, Moraga and Anzaldua, 1981). They were joined by women from the South, for whom the feminism purveyed by Euro-American writers had a distinctly Northern tinge (Mohanty, 1987). Out of the internal debates, and struggles, within the feminist scene emerged a rainbow of difference: multiple feminisms (de Lauretis, 1986).

Taking a closer look at the ways in which gender is thought about in the models that are used in GAD work, it is possible to identify certain assumptions that are based on a Eurocentric conception of gender difference and on concerns which were relevant to middle-class Euro-American feminists, but do not necessarily correspond with the ways in which African, Asian and Latin American women and men think, speak about and live gender difference. Feminist anthropology has provided ample evidence to show that western understandings of gender, and of biology, are not universal, but particular and culturally specific (Moore, 1988, 1993; Strathern, 1988). The constructs 'men' and 'women' have tended to be used in much gender and development work to describe mutually exclusive groups which are assumed to have distinct interests and concerns yet, in practice, 'gender analysis' often tells us very little about *gender* as it is locally constructed. 'Gender' is instead elided with western notions of sexual difference. In some cultural contexts, and in some settings within them, this corresponds with the local effects of gender difference. But in others, this kind of blanket categorization can be quite misleading.

The categories 'women' and 'men' simplify what is a much more complex picture. Over people's life courses and in different contexts within a single setting, what being a 'man' or 'woman' means in terms of opportunities and constraints can be very different. This has implications that make the use of single, static categories of 'men' and 'women' problematic. I go on to consider some of the issues at stake.

Gender is not the only difference

The most obvious problem is that gender is not the only difference, nor is it always the main difference that affects people's options or choices. Defining women-in-general as an identifiable interest group obscures the effects of other cross-cutting differences. Qualifying the category 'woman' by subdividing women into smaller groups of older, poorer, minority women and so on can clarify some of the effects of these differences (see Welbourn, 1991). Yet other dimensions of difference may be more significant to these women in particular contexts. Rich and poorer women not only have a range of concerns and priorities; their experiences of being a woman are also different. In some settings and for some purposes, their identification as 'women' may be less of an issue than their relative prosperity. In others, these differences matter less than others. The implications of being a woman or a man changes over people's lives. Not only do men and women of different generations have different priorities and concerns, they also have a variety of views and expectations as a result of their life experiences. The effects of difference, then, are specific both to the cultural setting and the context and cannot be generalized about with any accuracy.

Differences within, differences between

Differences within the notional interest group 'women' may be just as much of an obstacle to collective action as differences between women and men. These differences may also be played out in terms of what might be regarded as gender difference, where certain women strike 'bargains with patriarchy' (Kandiyoti, 1988). These 'patriarchal bargains' identify the interests of such women with certain (but not all) men. If development interventions focus on 'women' and 'men' as groups, processes of negotiation, of contestation or collaboration between and among women and men are neglected.

The terminology of practical and strategic needs used in gender planning (Moser, 1993) leads to gross assumptions about what women-in-general want or need. Yet there is no reason to presume that women in similar situations have common interests. It is important also to recognize that it may be precisely in these situations where their interests are similar that other, inter-personal, differences matter most. Before making assumptions about people's interests and concerns, it is vital to situate individuals within their own social networks.

Structural factors alone may give some insights into the dynamics of difference, yet an analysis based purely on structural differences would lack the explanatory force to make sense of the inter-personal politics of difference. The construction of oppositional categories ranged along broadly defined markers of difference tells us very little about how women or men actually get on with each other. The end product, in many cases, is gross assumptions about commonality. These need both to be situated in actual practices and to be challenged in terms of their adequacy on a descriptive or analytic basis.

Multiple models

In any cultural setting, there are multiple models of gender. Some arise from cultural stereotypes of particular kinds of ways of being male or female. Think, for example, of the masculinity of a male soldier. Others emerge as alternatives to or reactions against expected norms – such as the 'tomboy' girl who declines dolls and frills or the 'New Man' who redefines masculinity to allow himself space to express his feelings. Different models of gender offer a range of possibilities for defining identities and judging activities. They can also be used to limit and control the behaviour of others. Those who step outside the kind of behaviour that is valued within mainstream culture may find themselves labelled and discriminated against. Idealized models of gender, then, need to be seen not as fixed descriptions of what people are, but as ways of describing and judging what they do (Cornwall and Lindisfarne, 1994; Strathern, 1988).

As there are many ways of being a man or a woman, the single categories 'women' and 'men' that are often used in development work mask the dynamics of power between gendered individuals. Not all men have power. Some are men who, like the young African men in the example above, are disadvantaged as not-quite-yet-adult males capable of men's and women's work alike. Others are those who fail to conform with dominant models of masculinity and are treated with disdain by other men and.women. Others still may be under pressure to demonstrate the public face of acceptable masculinity and yet behave quite differently in private. And not all those who have power are men. Certain ways of being a woman are also associated with power. Think, for example, of the power of mothers over their sons, or images of women as goddesses. Yet in many cultures associations are made between masculinity and power (Cornwall and Lindisfarne, 1994), where women who appear powerful are either cast as quasi-men or labelled as anti-social.

'Gender' is often used as a catch-all category that encompasses all contexts in which an individual acts and interacts with others. Dominant models of gender are taken to represent fixed, essential differences between women and men. Yet differences between women and men emerge and become significant in different ways in different contexts. Their use forms part of dynamic relations of power between people. During the course of a day, people move from one setting to another and interact with different people. In each of these settings and interactions, the implications of gender difference and the ways in which people behave and judge others can change. Women who assert themselves and speak out can be labelled as 'aggressive' or 'domineering' simply for behaving like the men around them in some contexts, while such behaviour would be expected in others. And the messages that women and men hear about who or what they are expected to be vary in different settings: what 'gender' means, then, depends to some extent on the context and the kind of activities people are engaged in.

Strathern (1988) reports New Guinea men saying about their community: 'We are all men'. They did not mean that there were no women. Rather, they used the terms for the male gender to emphasise culturally valued attributes. In south-western Nigeria, people might say of an older woman that 'she has become a man' to indicate that she is now in a position to wield influence. Gender, then, becomes a metaphor. So if 'gender' in effect provides ways of talking about power, then it would seem important to take a closer look at relationships between actual men and women.

Broadening the scope of 'gender relations'

Given the complexity of relationships between and among women and men, what does the term 'gender relations' refer to? At face value, 'gender relations' would seem to refer to any relation in which gender makes a difference (cf. Peters, 1995). Yet it is frequently the case that 'gender relations' become a short-hand for relationships that are regarded as inherently oppositional and that describe particular relations between women and men. These are, for the most part, relations which are premised on situations in which women are subject to men and, often, those which are or could potentially be sexual relationships (Tcherzekoff, 1993).

Relations of dominance and subordination are clearly not exclusive to those that exist between some men and some women, nor are 'gender relations' necessarily those in which all women, by virtue of their femaleness, are at a disadvantage. Relations, for example, between mothers and sons or between a female employer and her male employees could also be considered 'gender relations' and be elaborated in culturally constructed models of women-as-mother or women-as-businesswoman. They do not, however, easily fit the mould of 'gender analysis'.

Shifting the focus to look at other male–female relations raises potent questions about what 'gender' is actually taken to mean. Relational ties between and among women and men create complex, sometimes competing, arenas for their interests and involvement beyond the narrow confines of heterosexual relationships. Contests can arise between women within relational contexts defined by marriage – as in the case of the kinds of tensions that can exist between mothers-in-law and daughters-in-law or between co-wives – as well as in those beyond the domestic domain, such as in informal associations or in the market. But people move within different domains. Their position in one setting does not necessarily place them in a similar position *vis-a-vis* others in another.

Making a difference: implications for practice

These issues raise a number of challenges for participatory approaches to development. If participatory development is explicitly concerned with the effects of inequality, it is crucial that gendered inequalities are addressed. Unless gender analysis addresses some of the complexities outlined here, it will remain a superficial process of categorization that makes little sense in terms of people's lived experience, and without the active participation of men in the process of change, 'gender' will continue to be regarded as a 'women's issue'. To make a difference, context-specific analyses and strategies are required.

Working with personal experience

The feminist slogan 'the personal is the political' continues to have important implications for training. In the realm of gender training, greater emphasis is placed on understanding structures of resource allocation, control and looking at rules and norms (Moser, 1993; Kabeer, 1994) than on understanding and working with the inter-personal dynamics and experiential aspects of gender identity. By neglecting these dimensions, opportunities for bringing about personal change are lost.

Working with trainees' own experiences through a process that introduces an analysis of gender on an experiential rather than intellectual level can create opportunities for them to make sense of their own experience and reflect on what they have come to take for granted (see Chapter 5, this volume). The first step would be to establish what people understand by the term 'gender', whether such a term exists in local languages and what it has come to mean to those involved in development work. Brainstorming the range of meanings that the word 'gender' has for people can reveal a spectrum of concerns, each of which can be taken up and explored further. Going on to unpack the categories 'men' and 'women', by looking at associations with these words and then at the many different ways of being a man or a woman can help to highlight some of the complexities and contradictions in ways of thinking about gender. This can serve as a starting-point to explore relations of power between and among women and men. Blanket statements about 'women' or 'men' cease to make sense in the light of people's own experiences and their analysis of their own cultural settings. By raising trainees' awareness of the complexity of difference, the tendency to make sweeping generalizations can be challenged effectively.

Men and gender in development

Much of the resistance experienced by those who attempt to introduce a gender perspective comes from men, who feel that 'gender' has nothing to do with them. In practice, it is true, 'gender analysis' fails to address the diversity and complexity of male experiences and interests. Bringing male development workers into the process requires strategies for both description and analysis that enable gender issues to be raised in a non-threatening way.

While those who suffer racial, sexual or other forms of discrimination can catalogue experiences from their adult lives, there are male adults who may be completely unaware of the implications of difference. But everyone, at some stage in their lives, has had the experience of being made to feel powerless. These experiences can be used as a starting-point to explore the ways in which difference becomes hierarchy and leads to inequality. By using examples of power relations between men to raise these issues and by naming them as questions of gender, men can become involved in becoming aware of what is at stake. From this, analysis can move on to relations between certain kinds of women and men. The goal of these activities, raising awareness of gender discrimination, would remain essentially unchanged, but the process would reframe these issues in terms of power, rather than as 'women's issues'.

Making gender everybody's issue

Working with an implicit agenda to explore gender difference can allay the kinds of anxieties and anger provoked in men when 'gender' is explicitly raised. Instead, it makes sense to focus first on exploring different representations just to look at the differences that come up. Once these representations are analysed, it becomes clear that there may be significant differences and these can then be used as pointers for further exploration. All through the process, the intention is made clear: an understanding of the dynamics of resource allocation and use requires that issues of difference are examined; good research and effective action requires that we pay attention to these different perspectives and the relations of power that create hierarchy out of difference.

Exploring local models of difference

As I have argued here, many of the shortcomings of gender analysis as it is currently practised involve operating on the basis of over-simplistic assumptions. To challenge these assumptions, we need to start instead from the ways in which local people experience gender and other differences. Instead of assuming, and therefore 'discovering', gender difference, some basic questions need to be asked at the outset. What are the differences that have an effect locally? How do these differences intersect to create inequalities? This would lead into looking in more detail at the range of local models of gender. Which of these models are culturally valued and which are regarded as negative? How are these notions of gender used to evaluate what people do? What are the contradictions between the ways people talk about gender difference and what they actually do?

Normative notions of gender that can emerge in PRA exercises can be interrogated by seeking examples where women or men fail to live up to expectations. What do people do that transgresses ideas about what they ought to be or do as women or as men? This can open up discussions of the consequences of these failures and the pressures on men and women to comply with dominant notions of gender. Such an approach would take gender not as a given, but as a dynamic relation that is subject to change and to contest: a relation of power set in a wider social context.

Situating difference

Rather than presume that gender difference makes a difference in all settings, the next step would be to investigate the contexts in which ways of thinking about gender emerge. For example, notions of gender used in the mosque may be very different to those used in the market or on the farm. How do these notions affect what men and women do? If 'being a man' is associated with certain behaviours or attitudes in particular spaces, how do these translate to other spaces? Exploring these dynamics is clearly important in terms of setting agendas for action. It also raises issues in terms of the sites chosen for PRA activities.

Localizing strategies

The complexities described here call for strategies that go beyond dividing women/men up into notionally homogeneous interest groups according to wealth, age and so on. Preliminary work on establishing which differences matter locally needs to be done before such groups can be identified. As much PRA work relies on group-based analysis, care needs to be taken in deciding how to work with groups. Carefully composed focus groups or opportunistically gathered groups in particular spaces, women at the well or men in a bottle store, may bring together people with similar concerns. But before assuming that they are going to want to share their views and experiences openly with others, it is important to have a cultural understanding of the dynamics and composition of single-sex groups. Creating artificial groupings according to presumed differences can produce misleading conclusions and, in addition, may offer little in the way of prospects for future work as such groups would probably not exist otherwise.

In any cultural context, groups form according to different, but potentially overlapping, common interests. For example, in south-west Nigeria, women may meet as members of a market association, as a prayer group or as members of a lineage group. All these groups have different dynamics and aims, specific to the experiences of the members and the context. In these contexts differences between women emerge in different ways. There may be aspects of women's lives and livelihoods which are especially important to conceal from fellow traders, worshippers or from family members, that might be shared with others. Exploring the social networks of particular individuals in these groups can offer valuable insights into how women and men get together, for which purposes and how collective action might be catalyzed through group work.

Embracing complexity

Analysis of gender differences, I have argued, involves more than simply describing differences between 'women' and 'men'. Exploring cultural models of difference and the ways in which these are used to create inequalities can make space for sensitization about prejudice and discrimination as an integral part of the participatory process. Challenging biases about gender in the initial stages of PRA by coming in with an explicit 'gender perspective' may be less effective than a gradual process of uncovering biases and addressing them, moving towards a realization that prejudice against women cannot be separated from other prejudices.

The strategic use of essentialisms such as 'women' and 'men' may form part of raising awareness but the analysis should not end there. Where we must be careful is in the danger of confusing strategic categories with the much more complex situations we work in. Without a more exploratory and rigorous approach to questions of difference, gender-aware participatory development work can easily repeat the mistakes of previous approaches. In doing so, well-intentioned activities can merely replicate local hierarchies and do little to challenge, let alone change, the condition of those who are most disempowered by them. Challenging assumptions about gender – the kinds of assumptions made about and by those using western feminist approaches, as well as those made by local-level project workers – requires an approach to gender difference that is set firmly within the framework of participatory action and that makes gender everybody's issue.

References

Buenavista, Gladys and Cornelia Flora Butler, (1993) *Surviving Natural Resource Decline. Exploring Gender, Class and Social Capital in Agbanga, Philippines*, An ECOGEN case study, Blacksburg VA: Virgina Polytechnic Institute and State University.
Chambers, Robert (1992) 'Rural Appraisal: relaxed, rapid and participatory', *IDS Discussion Paper*, No. 227, Brighton: IDS.
Chambers, Robert (1997) *Whose Reality Counts? Putting the First Last*, London: Intermediate Technology Publications.
Cornwall, Andrea (1996) 'PRA and the Participatory Process', in Korrie de Koning and Marian Martin (eds), *Participatory Research in Health: Issues and Experiences*, London: Zed Publications.
Cornwall, Andrea and Nancy Lindisfarne (eds) (1994) *Dislocating Masculinities: comparative ethnographies*, London: Routledge.
Gatens, Moira (1983) 'A Critique of the Sex/Gender Distinction', in J. Allen and P. Patten (eds), *Beyond Marx? Interventions After Marx*, Sydney: Intervention Press.
Goetz, Anne-Marie (1989) 'Misbehaving Policy: a feminist analysis of assumptions informing a project for women fish-smokers in Guinea', paper presented to the Canadian Association of Africa Scholars Annual Meeting, Kingston, Ontario: Queen's University.
Guijt, Irene (1995) *Questions of Difference: PRA, Gender and environment* (video). London: ILED.
Kabeer, Naila (1994) *Reversed Realities: gender hierarchies in development thought*, London and New York: Verso.

Gender, Participation and the Politics of Difference

Kandiyoti, Deniz (1988) 'Bargaining with Patriarchy', *Gender and Society* 2(3): 274–90.

de Lauretis, Teresa (1986) 'Feminist Studies/Critical Studies: issues, terms and contexts', in *Feminist Studies/Critical Studies*, Bloomington: Indiana University Press.

Maguire, Patricia (1987) 'Doing Participatory Research: a feminist approach.' Amherst, MA: Center for International Education, School of Education, University of Massachusetts.

Mohanty, Chandra Talpade (1987) 'Under Western Eyes: feminist scholarship and colonial discourses', *Feminist Review*, 30: 61–88.

Moore, Henrietta (1988) *Feminism and Anthropology*, London: Polity Press

Moore, Henrietta (1993) 'The Differences Within and the Differences Between', in Teresa del Valle (ed.), *Gendered Anthropology*, London: Routledge.

Moraga, Cherrie and Gloria Anzaldua (1981) *This Bridge Called My Back: writings by radical women of color*, Watertown, MA: Persephone.

Moser, Caroline (1993) *Gender Planning and Development. Theory, practice and training.* London and New York: Routledge.

Ortner, Sherry (1974) 'Is Female to Male as Nature is to Culture', in Michelle Zimbalist Rosaldo and Louise Lamphere (eds), *Woman, Culture and Society*, Stanford: Stanford University Press.

Peters, Pauline (1995) 'Uses and Abuses of the Concept of "Female-headed Households" in Research on Agrarian Transformation and Policy', in Deborah Fahy Bryceson, (ed.) *Women Wielding the Hoe: lessons from rural Africa for feminist theory and development practice*, Oxford: Berg.

Rocheleau, Dianna, Karen Schofield and Njoki Mbuthi (1991) *People, Property, Poverty and Parks: A Story of Men, Women, Water and Trees at Pwani.* ECOGEN/SARSA case study, Worchester, MA: Clark University.

Rosaldo, Michelle Zimbalist (1974) 'Women, Culture and Society: a theoretical overview', in M. Rosaldo and Louise Lamphere, (eds) *Women, Culture and Society*, Stanford: Stanford University Press.

Strathern, Marilyn (1988) *The Gender of the Gift*, Berkeley, CA: University of California Press.

Srinivasan, Lyra and Deepa Narayan. 1994. *Participatory Development Tool Kit.* Washington: World Bank.

Tcherzekoff, Sergei (1993) 'The Illusion of Dualism in Samoa', in Teresa del Valle (ed.) *Gendered Anthropology*, London: Routledge.

Thomas-Slayter, Barbara, Dianne Rocheleau, Dale Shields and Maria Rojas (1991) *Introducing the ECOGEN Approach to Gender, Natural Resources Management and Sustainable Development*, Worchester, MA: Clark University.

Welbourn, Alice (1991) 'RRA and the Analysis of Difference', *RRA Notes*, No. 14, pp. 14–23.

5

Giving Space to Conflict in Training

TESSA COUSINS

I have a cartoon on my wall which shows a small boy boasting to his friend that he has taught Spot, his dog, to whistle. After listening a while, the disappointed friend turns to the boy, saying he can't hear Spot whistling. The boy replies 'Well, I never said he had learnt!'

Teaching does not mean that learning takes place. In my experience, teaching the theory of gender relations in workshops on participatory development is not the same as internalizing gender-awareness and carrying it out. Conflict plays an important role in internalizing awareness of social differences, such as those of gender, in a workshop setting. But internalization is a highly personal process, which is shaped by the different identities and diverse experiences that people bring to a workshop. While diversity is commonly asserted to equal strength, to use an ecological metaphor, most of us are afraid of its potential destructiveness. To be able to hold space for multiple realities and for conflict and power to be processed, we, as facilitators, need ways to understand and deal with differences.

But there are also limits to the responsibility we can take to encourage participants to learn about issues such as gender differences. Leaps of insight in training situations often feel almost like mysterious processes. Arthur Mindell (1993) uses the term 'metaskill' to describe this elusive quality that leads to leaps of insight and 'pennies dropping':

> When I learn to hammer in a nail, I have learned a skill. The way in which I use the hammer is a metaskill . . . the decisive factor for the facilitator is not in the skills or methods she uses but the attitudes she has towards the group. . . We all know how to teach skills but metaskills are more complex, for how does one teach and learn attitudes, beliefs, and feelings about people?. . . Discovering and developing metaskills require a mixture of talent, inner development, and *outer role models* as well as other factors I have not yet identified [emphasis added]. (p. 49).

This chapter shares some reflections on my personal process of accepting the role of conflict in training for participatory development. In particular, I have gained much by viewing the workshop setting as an 'outer role model' in which participants can build their skills for subsequent fieldwork. This means dealing with conflicts, including those resulting from gender and racial differences, as an integral part of workshops on participatory development.

Participation, learning and facilitation

Cornwall *et al.* (1992) point out that power relations are central to development, that participatory processes are likely to allow conflict to become visible, and that the challenge to us is to learn to deal with it. The value of conflict and the inevitability of dealing with issues of difference, such as gender and race, becomes clear when considering the principles of participatory development. For me, it means working with communities knowing that:

○ people have much experience and knowledge;
○ people are creative; and that
○ there are diverse groups within communities, with different experiences, interests, perceptions, priorities and with different amounts of power in relation to each other.

These principles underpin a wide range of approaches, including that known as participatory rural appraisal (PRA) and SARAR,[1] on which most of my experience is based.

Participatory work aims, in essence, to enable people to experience themselves differently and to mobilize their resources and energy for group action aimed at change, within the community and in its relations to the wider world. This means pursuing a combination of structural changes to power relations (transforming of political and material society) and of attitudes to self (experiencing self as powerful and creative). Therefore, my central role as a facilitator lies in attempting to enable people to name their realities, their criteria and their feelings.[2] This personal learning, then, leads to action at a collective level.

But an enabling role is not one that most facilitators have been taught or seen modelled. Be it in schools, families, training institutions, politics, or the church, our experience is one of hierarchies. We have been taught that there are those who 'know and have'. Such people give skills, knowledge, the 'truth', or resources, to those who do not 'know or have'. Embracing a participatory approach to development means asking ourselves to occupy a different position. We become people who have only something, not lots, to offer and have much to receive, instead of knowing it all. As facilitators, our specific contribution lies in stimulating a process of reflection that can lead trainees to a new perception of reality. They will, in turn, be encouraging similar reflections by communities with which they interact.

The workshop as a community

PRA trainers are increasingly emphasizing the behaviour rather than the tools of participation (Chambers, 1995; South-South workshop, 1996). In any participatory methodology training context, be it PRA, SARAR or similar approaches, we want trainees not only to learn about the approaches and methods but to be committed to them. This requires them to reflect critically on their own behaviour and be prepared to change it. The challenge for us is how we can 'train' people to be more self-conscious, to let go of a sense of power, to listen and learn from 'lowers' (Chambers, 1995) with respect.

Modelling is one of the most powerful ways to facilitate learning (see Box 5.1). Thus, an effective facilitator can view his/her group of participants as a 'community', a micro-version of development, organizational, and national politics. It, too, is a context filled with differences, unequal power relations, and conflicts. The quality of the training experience offered to the 'workshop community' is one that will hopefully be replicated in subsequent fieldwork.

Box 5.1: Looking inside at what we ask of others

My organization invited a black, male, process-oriented facilitator to help us deal with how we could work better with gender. His approach views organizations involved in social change, like ours, as operating mainly at the thinking, talking and action levels. This means that its staff do not acknowledge underlying beliefs, feelings, needs and fears. To be accepted, we learn the correct 'organizational language'. Thus misunderstandings are inevitable as beliefs are not understood. In this context, gender is an abstract, depersonalized concept, surrounded by the right language and distanced from our lives. To avoid hidden emotions sabotaging our work in the long term, we will need to personalize it and think of ourselves, our mothers and fathers, sisters and brothers, daughters and sons.

Before exploring more personalized forms of gender with us, the facilitator worked on building interpersonal trust. This made us able to share personal fears and doubts in profound ways. It left us deeply moved and able to see gender as working with women and men amongst ourselves and in the communities.

Soon after, our gender worker ran a community workshop which was to focus on women's rights. Instead, the discussion revolved around gender roles, using a daily routine exercise (see Chapter 8, this volume). Women challenged men and men challenged each other in ways we had not seen before in a community that had been extremely conservative on gender issues. For example, one older man challenged a younger one about helping his wife: 'Of course he should be able to change and feed the baby if his wife was out collecting water. If she was busy, wasn't it the baby that counted?' The fieldworker had enabled a more constructive debate, by moving away from imposing her own sense of right and wrong about women's rights to opening up discussion about gender relations.

Differences in conflicts

Conflicts are different in terms of which issues emerge and how they emerge. Conflicts are rarely one dimensional. Gender issues are situated around other differences, such as of race or professional status: 'Each difference makes a difference to the way we experience ourselves and each other' (Cousins *et al.*, 1994), and therefore to the nature of conflict. Recurrent issues of difference in the South African context are:

○ race – black vs. white;
○ gender – men vs. women;

o professional – researchers vs. field workers and managers vs. field staff;
o nationality – nationals vs. expatriates; and
o locals vs. outsiders.

How issues of conflict emerge seems to depend on several factors, not least of which the dynamic between facilitators and participants. Who are facilitators and what do they personify in terms of power for participants? There is an inherent power relation between trainers and trainees which can amplify a particular issue of difference. In one workshop setting, as a team of three white women facilitators, we provided an easy target on which participants could focus their inner conflicts and rage both about racial oppression and gender stereotypes. A mixed facilitation team means less polarization as participants cannot project their anger so easily onto dominant traits of the facilitators. In this situation, it is more likely that differences which exist within the group will emerge, and also, of course, within the facilitation team.

Group composition in terms of race, gender and discipline is also critical. I work with agriculture and environment, fields dominated by men. If I were to work in health and nutrition, dealing with gender, race and conflict would be different. Whenever possible, I try to select a mixed group of participants. However, this has its limit as there are far fewer female than male staff in NGOs and government agencies. More importantly, engineering the composition of the group will not take away conflict; it will simply change its nature.

I have come to be less anxious about trying to engineer the composition of participants but try to be ready to work with whatever emerges. Most conflicts reflect current issues in the immediate social and political environment of participants and facilitators. And there is no better way to learn than by making sense of these personal experiences.

Gender in training

Dealing with gender issues in communities requires more than just meeting with women in separate groups. Being gender-sensitive, working on gender relations, and empowering women through PRA means bringing the different perspectives together, facilitating analysis, and discussing and negotiating around these differences. It means following up and supporting further action arising from the exercise. It means accepting that sharp conflict may emerge and being ready to work with it.

If that is the field reality, then what does it mean for the training context? Gender-sensitization in workshops takes many forms. But it is essentially one of two basic types: one that evokes the emotional, dealing with the personal and gender-related conflict, and one that remains intellectual, working with the descriptive and the rational.

To engage with gender equality for reasons beyond those of political correctness means that participants and facilitators alike will need to understand what it means in their own lives and work. I have increasingly developed a workshop style that deals openly with emotions, as my own belief in the value of and confidence with working at that level has increased. Gender, when internalized, forces painful self-reflections and provokes conflicts in workshop and fieldwork settings alike. How conflict is dealt with in the training context sets the tone for subsequent fieldwork. Allowing the space for participants to examine these conflicts is essential if they are to mirror this 'good practice' in the field.

Opening up to conflict

On my journey towards valuing conflict in training, a workshop in 1993 proved particularly catalytic. I was one of three white women facilitators,[3] coordinating a workshop on participatory methods for working with women. The participants were all field staff from NGOs of a national network which deals with land tenure. At the time of the workshop, only one of the NGOs worked with rural women's groups and the network members were keen to increase work with women. Most of the workshop participants were men. During the workshop the men were increasingly resisting and undermining the training process, expressing suspicion of the 'gender agenda'. We battled along with our programme until eventually suggesting that participants stop to discuss their concerns among themselves.

In their feedback session to us, it emerged that there was a high degree of racial anger about what took place within their respective organizations. This had manifested itself in resistance to attending the workshop in the first place. Most managers of the NGOs in the network were white and had a stated commitment to gender issues. They had organized the training for fieldworkers, most of whom were black. The fieldworkers felt they were 'sent' by their managers without being in a position to refuse, or to question the notion of 'taking on gender' within their organizations.

In dealing with these race-based emotions, we strayed from the original focus of the workshop. While we as facilitators initially felt bewildered about and hurt by the hostility we faced, later self-evaluation sessions helped us realise how much we had learnt from it. We also saw clearly that we had missed a valuable opportunity for everyone: we had been unable to open ourselves and the group up to look at the dynamics of race and gender which led us to bury the gender theme of the workshop.

Shortly afterwards, I was part of a team which organized the first PRA training in South Africa.[4] Based on the first experience, I was preparing myself to work with conflict more proactively. The lead trainer, however, expressed the view that conflict was to be avoided, and indeed, at the time, conflicts did not arise between the workshop participants. It was a very 'feel-good' workshop, much to my relief! Months later, however, claims of racism were still being made. The accusation was only voiced much later in a small group discussion with the original lead trainer, but never during the workshop in which it could have been dealt with. Attempts to clarify it were unsuccessful, so it moved into the realm of gossip and rumour, and remained a source of dissension amongst South African PRA people for the next two years.

What caught my interest was that a parallel situation had arisen in the community where the PRA fieldwork had taken place. One field team[5] had been troubled by a 'difficult' landowner. Consistent with the conflict-avoidance approach of that workshop, it had distracted him from other discussions with the community members by taking him on a transect walk. Today, that community is on the verge of severe conflict, with the 'difficult' person at the heart of the issue. The deep-rooted conflict between landowners and tenants had been side-stepped. Taking the man out of the community-level discussions had led us to ignore the issue and to lose an opportunity to open it up.

About a year later, I was one of several facilitators of a participatory land-use planning exercise which included a PRA component. During the last minute planning of the fieldwork, several participants expressed their resistance to spending nights in the field. We allowed their views to be heard. When it was clear that most people felt good about the night stops but had openly discussed existing concerns, we went ahead with the original plan. The fieldwork included discussions about the contentious local issue of limiting cattle numbers. One fieldworker in particular dealt with this in a markedly different way than before the workshop, when he would force a group vote whenever there was no immediate agreement amongst community members. Now he encouraged the group to come up with different ideas, and to formulate and present proposals. He allowed much hot debate until a clear consensus emerged. He had learned not to fear conflict, but to let decisions emerge.

Living with conflict

It should be noted that this personal sequence of learning experiences took place in South Africa, with its unique history and mix of cultures that have shaped a far from conflict-free nation. All South Africans have personal experience of this in some form. Race has obviously been the site of most oppression and struggle in South Africa. It was a clear moral position during the apartheid era, but with the new-found freedom of expression of the post-apartheid times, came accusations of subtle racism between colleagues who had previously worked and struggled together, provoking anger and pain on all sides. These seriously challenged most NGOs particularly before and just after the 1994 elections. The more democratic and open the organization, the more we witnessed this expression of hurt, anger and demand for acknowledgment of non-whites.

The issue of racial freedom was mixed in with the rising acknowledgment that we needed to 'take gender seriously'. In the years preceding the 1994 general elections of South Africa, women involved in the political struggle were determined that gender oppression be taken seriously and not seen as secondary to race. Subsequently, gender equality has gained much attention and the term is liberally sprinkled into our new constitution and all new policies. At the same time, development practice had been increasingly under scrutiny for its gender sensitivity. The question facing all of us was how to work with this effectively. The pressure of political correctness had us all build gender equality into our mission statements and into methodology-focused workshops, in the hope that this would lead to changing field practice.

The two aspects of gender and race link in some messy and unclear ways. For example, white feminists have been prominent in raising the profile of the importance of gender inequalities in South Africa. Thus many people are now 'adamant that gender is a "white woman's issue", an imperialist import being imposed upon them by funders' (Cousins *et al.*, 1994).

Looking at it from the other side are gender trainers. They often feel that 'race' jumps up to claim centre stage whenever 'gender' is raised, yelling loudly for attention and the correction of racial abuses. In South Africa, many workshops consist predominantly of black men, with a sprinkling of black women, white men and white women. In such groups, I have often found that black men put pressure on the black women to profess solidarity to the overriding importance of the issue of race.

Yet race can obscure very real gender issues that women want to raise. This was apparent in the first workshop I described above. Early on we had split participants into gender-separate groups for an exercise. The men objected vehemently before and after the exercise and insisted this should not be repeated. Yet some of the women told us privately they would like more such group work but were under pressure to maintain racial solidarity and felt unable to raise it openly in the group.

I, for one, have not found one consistent pattern of how gender and race interact. I see only that both race and gender provoke fierce debates, which are shaped by everyone's unique experiences. I used to feel that my own lack of clarity on gender-race dynamics placed me in a weak position as a trainer when trying to 'integrate gender' into workshops. I now feel stronger about taking my uncertainty into intense workshop situations and opening up to the unique ways in which it will arise and with which it will be dealt. I listen to my feelings and aim to create space for and hear those of others, without needing to prove everyone's 'correctness'. This encourages everyone to learn about the complex interactions of difference in their own way.

In community interactions, too, we do not always understand how class, race, gender etc. intersect. Nor do we need to, as our role is to facilitate a process of naming and discussing different realities and experiences, rather than presenting people with pre-cooked analyses and answers. This, of course, relates particularly to those of us working with participatory development.

Facilitating the processing of conflict

Perhaps the greatest value of that painful first workshop was that it provoked me to reflect intensively on conflict in the training context. I have a passionate commitment to participatory ways of working, and to promoting gender equality in my work and life. Both of these social goals and processes are embedded in conflict. Yet I recognized that I was a conflict avoider myself. So how was I going to understand and work with this dangerous, powerful dynamic?

At that time I discovered the work of Arnold Mindell (1993), who has written extensively about conflict and ways to understand and work with it. He describes how emotions that are commonly considered negative, such as anger, jealousy and fear, become like poisonous garbage if we put a lid on them and try to ignore or deny them. However, if we process them, they can enrich us all. He urges facilitators to welcome conflicts and learn how to work with them. We will then, he argues, find that groups can gain deep insights and move to new levels of understanding and relationship.

Mindell's process-oriented viewpoint posits that we are confronted by exactly those problems that are the perfect ones to grow with. What seem like painful or difficult events can become useful if we follow them with compassion and awareness. He talks of 'deep democracy', which recognises that group conflicts are connected to the spirit of the times. As individuals in group conflicts, we personally give voice to issues needing to be named and resolved more broadly in our society, a micro-reflection of a larger reality.

Dealing with the processing of such macro-conflicts in the micro context of workshops has two dimensions: (i) although conflicts have immense learning value, there is no need to stimulate them unnecessarily but rather to guide how they emerge consciously; (ii) once conflicts do arise, they need appropriate facilitation.

Guiding conflicts

The challenge is how to achieve the right mix of working with rich and conflictual experiences while providing enough structure and safety that enables people to explore, risk and learn. Conflict can feel unmanageable and may appear to 'derail' our carefully constructed learning process. Some conflicts may well distract from other, more fundamental issues, so it is important to allow them to emerge in a contained manner.

To allow conflicts to emerge 'safely', I have structured my training sessions in several ways. For example, I prefer to use role plays early on in workshops. When people talk only about issues, as when discussing written case studies, they often focus on how a situation should work and how one should respond. In role plays, the 'roles' stimulate people to play out situations in emotionally more vivid and realistic ways. Yet because they are only roles, participants feel relatively safe about expressing feelings and ideas that are those of their fictional person. After one role play, one group said that they had deviated considerably from their planned viewpoint during the role play. They had planned to resolve a conflict between community people, game rangers and the rangers' managers. But they were surprised by the strength of anger expressed by the community and game rangers alike, and their planned 'resolution' could not take place!

I devote considerable time to exercises which allow people to express and process their emotions instead of letting them fester into full-blown conflicts. This often means arguing with the organisers for more time for the whole workshop event. But in any context, at the beginning of the workshop, I ask participants to divide randomly into groups that will coordinate daily reflection sessions in turn. These sessions open and close each day, allowing people to raise issues and, if necessary, discuss them. I also put up a flip chart which functions as a 'parking lot' for issues raised. Contentious or important points are written down and not lost but simply postponed until the immediate task at hand is completed. I then make time for discussion, with the group prioritizing the issues once a few have collected.

Activities that encourage humour and mutual affirmation amongst participants can help defuse some of the minor conflicts. I like a game called 'Secret Admirer' that can be played throughout the training. Everyone has a secret person, designated at random by the facilitator, and must find ways to affirm each of them throughout the workshop, without, of course, revealing their identity as 'secret admirer'! Stimulating people to express positive feelings for others helps to offset some of the inevitable tensions of workshop settings.

In another workshop, we asked people to identify local sayings about men and women. The cultural diversity and similarities were interesting, evoking strong emotions from group members but also many laughs! It highlighted quickly the cultural specificity of gender roles and images, and allowed people to relate it to themselves and their community work. We immediately moved on to discuss the criteria that are important for forming field teams. Because of what had just taken place, gender immediately became a criterion.

But we then had a long and difficult discussion about whether to form single-sex or mixed field teams. Most of the women wanted a women-only group, yet most men objected fiercely to this. We agreed finally to form one women-only team, one mixed-gender team and one men-only team. Everyone looked forward to comparing the results from the different teams to see if and how they affected the community processes. Unfortunately, the effectiveness of this approach was not tested as a tragedy on the first day of fieldwork truncated the rest of the workshop. The point here is that the light-hearted game evoked the importance of gender differences, and the different opinions were immediately channelled into a decision-making process that allowed the group to reflect on it in more detail.

Emerging conflicts

When conflicts do arise and clamour for attention, we are best able to work with the compassion that this requires when we have confronted the issue at hand ourselves. I once experienced a black male facilitator deal with a racial issue with great confidence. He named the unnamed without judgement, and guided discussions with calmness and respect. But when a gender issue arose shortly afterwards, the same person became clumsy and dismissive. Although he tried to deny it and smooth it away, his composure was gone and people responded with anger. He quickly handed over his role of facilitator.

The message to me is two-fold. First, we need to be conscious of our strengths and use the facilitating team and participants appropriately. We can do this only if we know our own strengths and weaknesses. Second, we can note our weaknesses as signals that these issues are ones we need to work on personally, and, of course, then do so!

I am still learning about facilitating when conflicts emerge. But knowing my weakness of being a conflict avoider, I have been able actively to cultivate my personal attitude and approach to different conflict issues.

I try not to see conflict as 'getting in the way' of the training. I avoid allowing the conflict to become personalized onto so-called 'difficult people', but rather to value the people who are willing to carry that role.[6] This is, in effect, putting into action the third principle of participatory development I mention above, about accepting multiple realities and not one truth. And some opinions, after all, are bound to be very different from mine!

From Mindell (1993), I have learned the importance of 'holding the space' for all the voices and facilitating conversations between them. Thus, as a facilitator in communities or training groups, I try not to take sides with a particular viewpoint, which would not allow the group to process it. This does not mean that I, or any other facilitator, do not have values or convictions. I fully acknowledge the existence (and undesirability) of power imbalances and the political nature of our interventions. But I know that no single intervention on my part will resolve the power relations and conflicts we face, be it class and gender in communities, or status, race and gender amongst trainees. Change happens over time, and a community-based PRA exercise or a training for field staff is only one step in potential transformation.

I see now that safety in training comes primarily from my own attitude of not being afraid. I have watched myself become less afraid and less insistent on smoothing over or dismissing difficulties. This has mean getting personal, both in the professional and home context. For example, when working with other facilitators we set aside some time each day to discuss what happened, how each of us felt, what was exciting, what was difficult personally, and what we are learning. This helps transform difficulties into valuable lessons, and to allow conflicts between facilitators to emerge and be processed. I have also actively sought therapy. This helped me see more clearly how the personal plays itself out in the professional setting, a deep insight that continues to shape my facilitation style.

Our contribution to the learning process will have more impact if we recognise its limitations and potential. We can then feel less anxious about both raising and resolving conflict. This will unleash the tremendous learning potential that comes from enabling a squashed and hidden issue to surface and be talked about. Two recent experiences give me confidence to persist in my search for ways to allow conflicts to emerge under guidance and to facilitate participants to process them.

Where there are few women participants, one option that is both challenging and empowering is to have women work together as one field team as women often work together more easily. I often offer them the option, knowing full well that it will provoke heated emotions! When I did this last, my (male) co-facilitators and many male participants were annoyed with me for bringing it up. This made for a difficult decision-making process. Most of the women jumped at the idea, with only one feeling uncomfortable. This type of suggestion is a risky strategy for facilitators to pursue, as it is not clear where the process will go or what the result will be. But for me the decision itself is not important, as long as the group has an opportunity to engage with the issue openly. Such interactions certainly lead to heightened awareness of gender in the field work!

Expression of gender awareness in the field seems to depend a lot on who is in the team. Just one sensitive person can make an enormous difference but only if they are given the space by others. During one training in Namibia, the conflict that dominated group dynamics was that of the relative value and power of expatriate development professionals and local people. This issue had been written clearly on the 'parking lot' page and was prioritized as the discussion topic. A Namibian facilitated the emotive discussion which cleared the air considerably. Later on, during the fieldwork, a white expatriate woman suggested doing a gender-differentiated Venn diagram (see Figure 5.1). Her team, fortunately, was open to her idea. The gender-differentiated discussions that arose in the rest of the fieldwork powerfully reinforced the value of a gender-aware perspective in participatory development. In other situations, where conflict was not dealt with prior to the fieldwork, such activities have been blocked, especially if suggested by white, let alone expatriate, women.

Conclusions

Our world is not conflict free. Do we think that fieldwork will be conflict free? Why do so many of us aim for conflict-free training? Avoiding conflict means avoiding engagement in a developmental process. Conflicting issues are real and will arise in any situation where a group of people spend enough time together. A participatory training or intervention is inevitably intense, and the methodology itself will encourage the emergence of differences. These training sessions are potentially a valuable place for us to confront and process important issues and to equip us to help others to process theirs. The attitudinal and behavioural shifts, the personal transformation that this often calls for, will come from experience in the training room as much as in the field.

The challenge is for us, as facilitators, to be consistent in our practice. Communicating the attitudinal and behavioural aspects of participatory approaches means modelling them in every aspect of our learning event. Learning to work with conflict and to model it in the training sessions means preparing participants to deal better with the inevitable community-based conflicts. If we do this, then differences, attitudes and emotions will be expressed within the group and conflict will be welcomed as part of the development process. Participatory approaches have the potential to allow conflicts to emerge rather than stay submerged and fester. Working with this effectively is critical if our intervention is to be meaningful and empowering.

References

Chambers, R. (1995) 'NGOs and Development: the primacy of the personal', *IDS Working Paper* 14, Brighton: IDS.
Cornwall, A., I. Guijt and A. Welbourn (1992). 'Acknowledging Process: challenges for agricultural research and extension methodology', *IDS Discussion Paper*, No. 333, Brighton: IDS.

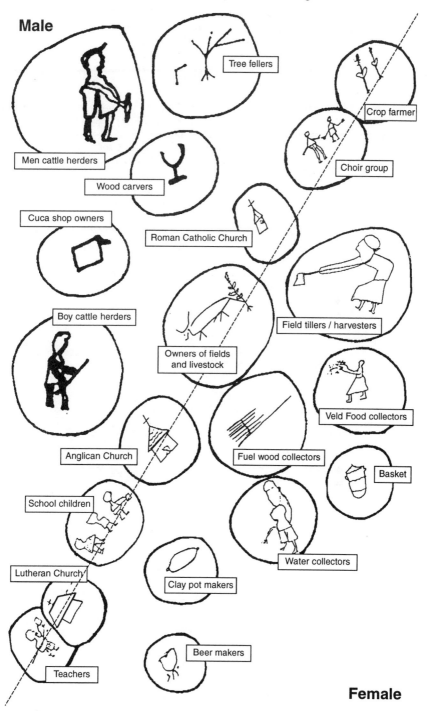

Male

Men cattle herders

Tree fellers

Crop farmer

Wood carvers

Choir group

Cuca shop owners

Roman Catholic Church

Boy cattle herders

Field tillers / harvesters

Owners of fields and livestock

Veld Food collectors

Anglican Church

Fuel wood collectors

Basket

School children

Lutheran Church

Clay pot makers

Water collectors

Teachers

Beer makers

Female

Figure 5.1: Institutional analysis in Okambuga, 24 April 1994

Cousins, T., M. Friedmann and C. Crawford-Cousins (1994) 'Holding the Space: explorations of power and control in training and development', *Avocado Series*, 6/94, Durban: Olive Publications.

Mindell, A. (1993) *The Leader as Martial Artist. An introduction to deep democracy.* New York: Harper Collins.

South-South Workshop (1996) ABC of PRA: *Attitudes, Behaviour, Change,* ActionAid India and Bangalore: SPEECH.

Srinavasan, L. (1990) *Tools for Community Participation. A manual for training trainers in participatory techniques.* New York: PROWESS/UNDP Technical Series Involving Women in Water and Sanitation.

Srinavasan, L. (1992) *Options for Educators. A Monograph for Decision Makers on Alternative Participatory Strategies*, New York: PACT/CDS.

6

Problematics and Pointers about Participatory Research and Gender

REGINALD HERBOLD GREEN

'I participate. You participate. He participates. We participate.
They rule'.
Gaullist Declension of 'To Participate'

'Women's work is never done. Women's voice is rarely heard'.
Adage

'The African farmer, she . . .'
UNICEF Deputy Director on Household Provisioning

Participatory research has attracted growing attention and enthusiasm since the late 1960s. In the 1990s it has become a fashion, a rather dangerous thing judging by the history of both development theory and social policy. In the process, rather too much is claimed for it (resulting quite often in less being achieved) and real problematics glossed over. A curious conflation is made between the technique, the product and the highly personal goals of many of the users and promoters of participatory research. These facilitators often have aims which are, in some sense, radical or revolutionary. By no stretch of the imagination, therefore, can they be considered neutral.

This chapter seeks not to discredit participatory research nor to suggest it is irrelevant to empower women to be able to define and pursue less unequal and less constricted roles for themselves. Instead it aims to raise certain problematics in procedure, product and the inherently interventionist roles of facilitators. It seeks also to examine certain key gender-related issues in sub-Saharan Africa for which participatory research (and decentralized policy articulation and operation) is potentially important.

Seven problematics

Participation in research, appraisal or process

Participation has different meanings, depending on the objective of its use. Participatory research may be a means to a thesis, a job, a consultancy to a non-participatory client, etc. As long as the participating community is not given false expectations, there is nothing inherently wrong with this. There may even be a good deal to be say for such approaches to research.

Similarly, participatory appraisal by, for example, aid agencies or foreign non-governmental organizations (NGOs), is frequently a specific input into a basically non-participatory process. This, too, has valid uses, even if the participation is limited to data and perception collection. The people who are consulted often are closer to being subjects than those who are not consulted, and who therefore remain 'objects' of research. Mystifying the basic top-down (or outside-in) nature of the process and persuading the 'objects' of the process that they are 'subjects', as is common, is not, however, valid.

A participatory process includes participatory research and appraisal as components in a flow of knowledge-generation and use: design–decision through implementation–monitoring–review and modification. Except in this context, participatory research cannot claim to be empowering in the Freireian sense (Freire, 1972) beyond a modest potential contribution to self and other understanding. That is not to say it is invalid, but simply that to claim too much is both discrediting and confusing.

Product matters

Poor and marginalized people usually view processes primarily as a means to secure something that can improve their circumstances. A process that does not yield a product is too expensive for them to pursue. A productless process is a very western, upper-middle class, intellectual and psychological amenity good. Equally, however, process matters. Processes that treat people as ends, not merely means, are empowering and are more likely to produce recipient-friendly products. Process and product interact.

Specific, material results matter and link with power

African rural women farmers, many of whom are poor, are concerned about their workloads and their budgets (of time, receipts, expenditure obligations) because poor people have to be. They may want a research-action process about the water situation in their household and garden plots. This would help them produce better supplies, more reliably, at lower labour costs, and more sustainably. This is a functional approach to participatory research but is not 'anti-participatory' if many community members desire it, nor is it as unrelated to power as might be supposed, especially by critics of practical-oriented gender actions. In most of Africa, men build (including wells, small water systems, and homes) while women operate and maintain. Teaching men how to maintain wells and water schemes and, therefore, setting up male management committees does not tend to work well.

Directing training activities to women and encouraging them to form a majority on management committees is usually feasible, once the idea is raised. If that happens, assuming that the men perceive the importance of water for the household and garden-plot food for the table, the general status of women *vis-à-vis* men in community public affairs is likely to be enhanced. For the women as much as the men, it is the functional, material gain, and not abstract empowerment, which is the entry point. Clearly, some labour divisions are problematic and inequitable. Understanding what they are is, therefore, the first step to working with or altering them.

Conflict, conflict of interest, tension, contradictions and head-on clashes differ from each other

Any systemic change, and most functional ones, entail conflicts of interest. To suppose that all members of a geographic community have common interests is a disempowering illusion. Not all differences in interest are antagonistic contradictions, however, that lead inevitably to open confrontation. Negotiated compromises based on perceived overlapping interests are possible, especially if the divergence of other interests is accepted and not ignored. A process of inclusion and empowerment (gender or other) is usually best if started with positive-sum games, in which compromises leave most parties demonstrably better off. The outsider can, if trained and informed, be a useful catalyst and mediator but rarely a legitimate adjudicator. Seeking deliberately to heighten contradictions is even more rarely a valid external role. Contrary to Trotsky's perception, worse is not usually better later on, and is even more rarely perceived as such by poor African women.

A participatory process must be understood and controlled by participants

Much participatory research involves highly complex structuring of, for example, sub-groups and role playing, etc. These may be quite different from the cultural context into which they are inserted. Most participants may be unable to understand, internalize or control such forms of participation. The danger of manipulation is only too clear from the proud explanations of some participatory researchers of the elaborate processes they imposed to secure 'participation'. Neither is the problem gender-neutral. The weakest and the least familiar with western cultural processes and procedures will be the most excluded or manipulated. In practice these are women, particularly, but not only, in rural Africa.

Any outsider intervenes

Whether an engineer or a facilitator, a catalyst causes events which would not have happened in her/his absence. This is the case even if the catalyst her/himself is largely unaffected by such events, as is the typical visiting researcher, consultant or expert involved in participatory research, who can fly away and live to research another day, another way, another place. That does not mean intervention as such is bad. If the result is empowering, including and/or providing clear functional gains for a large majority, then it is justified, whether by a hydrologist indicating where and how water can be secured or by a facilitator triggering reflection on alternative water-supply maintenance, management, allocation and cost-sharing approaches. Guidelines for positive-outcome intervention include: transparency (motives up-front); self-consciousness and self-reflection; ethical standards (including anticipating the effect on participants) (Absalom *et al.*, 1994).

The assertion that participatory research is or should be 'subversive' is a dangerous one.[1] Subversion can mean many things, e.g. being hired by a foreign government in association with an élitist foundation to produce a recipient-acceptable livelihood project to demobilize a marginalized community about to be deprived of its present livelihood by the funders of the foundation.[2] As a synonym for 'promoting revolution', subversion is dangerously likely to reflect (however unintentionally) a romantic, outside view of change as a clean, tidy morality play. That is a perception those close to the blood, tears, agonies and failures of even successful revolutions rarely share. The role of any outsider in any revolution, except as a servant of the insiders leading it and under their discipline, is highly problematic. Certainly it neither is, nor should be, a normal part of participatory research or any other catalytic/facilitation process.

Approaches must be context-specific

Any technique, approach or structure tends to have different meanings in differing geographical, cultural and temporal contexts. For example, the original purpose of brothers' obligation to marry siblings' widows was to insure the widow and children against loss of access to land, house and the family safety net. Hardly unique to Africa, it has become far less positive in present contexts. Similarly, land reform through homes and home plots has been an integral component of attempting to empower the poor in West Bengal, but also of attempting to demobilize Filipinos in West Negros (the Philippines). The full meaning of processes, procedures, policies and structures is context-limited and context-enhanced. This is as true of participatory research as of anything else. To assume otherwise is both misplaced romanticism and dangerous, especially to those who have to live with actual outcomes and rarely have the 'back to the drawing board' option of facilitators and researchers, particularly expatriates.

Gender in sub-Saharan Africa

In Africa, participatory research related to gender issues is especially problematic. In sub-Saharan Africa, most facilitators today neither identify gender issues nor pose issues in gender terms, even when common sense would seem to point out the functional value, nor do most participants, even women, think or speak in gender terms without external prompting.

Rural African women, and even many middle- to senior-level female civil servants, tend to be less vocal than men in large, mixed groups and on unfamiliar topics. They are also less likely to be familiar with complicated procedures and techniques, such as the Northern/Western ones dominating participatory research.[3] Participatory approaches may in this way lessen indirect, traditional women's input, rather than enhance it if care is not taken when proposing group structures and procedures.

Women In Development (WID) approaches have, if anything, accentuated such problems in Africa. They often represent the wholesale importation of Northern/Western procedures and practices designed to appease donors or mollify foreign NGOs. To date, there has been little African internalization of these approaches, even by many African female staff.

In practice, WID approaches take gender issues out of the mainstream and make ghettos of them in small, underfunded, near-powerless units.

When one sees a lone female cabinet minister in charge of a women/ community development/youth ministry, with two-thirds of the budget allocated to the second two issues under a male junior minister, the irresistible image is one of tossing a few rag dolls to the girls. Gender sensitivity in departments dealing with agriculture, water, education and health[4] is paramount. Only if the big battalions with adequate resources and political/ institutional clout see gender as important are real material products, relevant to poor women, likely to emerge.

Some guideposts toward fruitful research

With intense and growing rural and peri-urban absolute poverty, and with 20–25 per cent of households headed by women, the case for decentralization in data provision, goal-setting, articulation of strategic frameworks and operation/adjustment ought to be evident. Top-down procedures usually lack data to formulate adequate strategies, the capacity to articulate them, the mobilizing power to involve intended beneficiaries in self-determined operations, or any serious user-feedback to revise plans. With the specific roles of sub-Saharan women in production and reproduction, decentralization which lacks gender consciousness and substantive female input at all stages is inherently flawed. For those urging more gender-sensitive participatory research, this argument is perhaps the best entry point and the one most likely to gain broad support. Seven areas require urgent attention for the purposes of data collection, action on women's welfare (as perceived by themselves) and functional perspectives. These are set out in Box 6.1.

In each area, 'women' are unlikely to be a homogeneous category. Juvenile, adult-married, adult-single, divorced, widowed, aged-women's status, rights and opportunities may diverge sharply even in a single community, and certainly between communities. These topics can be researched in many ways but appear particularly likely to benefit from participatory research for two reasons: (i) contexts and perceptions of the impact of ongoing changes and the potential for desirable ones are central to dynamics and results; (ii) standard empirical survey techniques, even when feasible, often give a limited understanding of products, processes and preferences.

Participatory research in Africa or African participatory research?

Neither procedures nor products can safely be extracted from context, unless the aim is to produce an analogue to dehydrated water. Participatory research and gender issues are ill-served by those seeking to export basically unaltered packages of ideas from studies in their urban, home lower-income areas, let alone their home universities. More importantly, poor rural African women are even less well-served.

What are the priorities and what is useful for poor rural Africa women are questions on which they, not any outsider (including those African university graduates addicted to intellectual importation and unadapted replication) are the experts. If one is serious in making these women the subjects of participatory development, the 'how' and 'what' of participation is primarily for them to decide.

Box 6.1: Priority areas for research

o What are workloads and tasks for women, girls, boys, men? How, and why, are they shifting? In what way would new proposals help whom? How could any existing work overload of women and girls be reduced, and how would that extra time be spent? What resources, from whom, would be required?

o What labour obligations (women to men, men to women, intra-generational) exist and how are these evolving?[5] Are women compensated for extra work on 'men's' crops? And if so, how: by cross-hiring among households additional male inputs into women's activities, husband-to-wife cash payments?[6] What actions can avoid increasing women's total workload and/or deterioration of household food and nutritional security?

o How are household budgets divided in terms of income sources and expenditure obligations (as few African rural households have a single, integrated budget)? To what extent has increased market involvement shifted obligations regarding food (exotic items?), child care (school fees?) and other household provisioning (fuel, water?) from women to men? What extended family budgetary processes exist? Are urban–rural transfers significant? To whom? How can women's incomes be augmented and provisioning obligations made less onerous?

o What has been the historic pattern of access to land (household or individual basis)? How were women's rights to land to meet provisioning obligations ensured? If allocated to households, how was it provided to widowed, divorced and unmarried women? Why has evolution of these historic, secure household land-use right systems usually affected women adversely? What steps, beyond recognition of female-headed households and granting equal access, can redress the increasingly inequitable position of women?

o Are water and fuel supply purely women's/girl's obligations? Are construction and maintenance/operation tasks male and/or female? What are the implications for voluntary male input into reducing women's subsequent workload (for water-source/tree-management structures, and improved water, wood, tree access)?

o How real is the apparent gender sensitivity of health services? How much of whose time would be saved by universal primary health care? How much would it reduce poor household vulnerability? Can community, especially women's, participation in design, provision and management (not just funding) be increased? If so, how?

o Why are women farmers largely invisible to agricultural extension services (even when they do, in fact, address them!)? How does this impede functional efficiency of extension services and, especially, of female-headed households? Are new crops/techniques assessed in terms of gender impact? Do small stock,

> crops and trees particularly relevant to women receive adequate attention? Why not (e.g. because nobody knows which they are)? How can nutrition (and especially child feeding) linked to agriculture and health services be an entry point for participatory female-led initiatives (including income generation) as it has become in a majority of Tanzanian districts?

This is, in fairness, not a challenge unique to participatory research nor to gender issues. Over the last decade and a half, sub-Saharan Africa has, with exceptions, come to respond to foreign intellectual, social, political and economic agendas, and not to propose its own. Although there may be some bargaining, the underlying strategies and agendas are set by outsiders. Practitioners of participatory research should be among those most able to see that this pattern denigrates, fragments and erodes self-respect. Reversing this pattern of responding to outside agendas goes far beyond developing gender-sensitive approaches to participatory research. Participatory research by and for African women, not merely participatory research in Africa on African women, is almost certainly what most African women would choose were the choice put to them in terms they could understand. Donors, NGOs and, admittedly, African officials and academics rarely trouble to put the choice, or even to be fully aware of the problem.

References

Absalom, E. *et al.* (1994) 'Sharing our Concerns and Looking to the Future', *PLA Notes* 22.
Freire, P. (1972) *Pedagogy of the Oppressed*, Harmondsworth: Penguin.

7

Learning About Participation from Gender Relations of Female Infanticide

RANJANI K. MURTHY[1]

The 1980s saw the emergence of social relations of gender as a distinct category of social analysis. In the development context, the case for examining gender relations has been argued mainly from two perspectives: one which addresses women's subordinate position in society and one which seeks to enhance the efficiency and effectiveness of development efforts.

Gender relations are socially constructed power relations between men and women, and unravelling them is not an easy task. They are shaped by a range of other social relations, notably those of race, class, caste, ethnicity and religion. A woman's age, her relative position in the family, her marital status and sexual preference also influence her particular position, and this will change over time. This complexity is difficult to capture with conventional research methodologies like surveys, making a strong case for the use of participatory approaches. However, the process and methods of participatory approaches, like participatory rural appraisal (PRA), are often not gender-sensitive.

This chapter looks at participatory methodologies for examining gender relations which have the potential to transform the oppressive subordinate position of women in society. I draw on lessons learnt from a participatory workshop with local midwives involved in female-infanticide in northern India. We aimed to understand gender inequalities leading to this practice in Bihar (Express News Service, 1992; Priya and Tyab, 1996; Vydianathan and Mathew, 1992) and identify possible solutions. This case study is selected not as an example of an ideal methodology, but rather because it offers several important lessons. If participatory approaches are to help examine and transform gender relations, the underlying assumptions and methods require careful consideration. The goals, objectives and levels of participation need precise definition, and social relations must be taken into account within the process followed and methods used.

Limitations of surveys for unravelling gender relations

Questionnaire-based surveys are the most common methodology to gather information on gender relations. Pre-determined, standardized and closed questions are normally directed at individuals. While such surveys may be appropriate to gather information on individual traits like age, weight and personal preferences, they are inadequate for understanding gender and other social relations. The construction of gender relations makes standard methodologies[2] relatively ineffective.

First, gender relations are not properties of particular individuals but are determined by social structures. Therefore, this requires not just discussions with individuals, but with separate and mixed groups of men and women. Questions must be open-ended and discussions allowed to develop flexibly.

Second, questionnaire-based surveys assume that women have a clear understanding of their oppression and are able to articulate their experience. Such surveys may seek to understand practical gender needs and strategic gender interests. Practical gender needs may be easier to assess than strategic gender interests. Discussing strategic interests presupposes a level of consciousness amongst women about these interests and about strategies to bring about change. In reality, their subordinate position may not be apparent to them due to ideologies, structures and practices of societal institutions which condone gender-based oppression to such an extent that they are the norm. Given the socialization of women, a process of raising women's collective consciousness may be necessary in research methodologies focusing on understanding gender relations.

A third limitation is that questionnaires are based on the assumption that it is possible to verbalize all aspects of the experience of being located in a subordinate societal position. While the material aspects of being relatively powerless are amenable to verbal expression, the intangible aspects of powerlessness are difficult to express. This is particularly the case for women who are socialized into a culture of relative silence, such as in India. Thus non-verbal forms of expression can help to understand better women's experience of gender-related oppression.

A more practical concern about the appropriateness of questionnaire surveys relates to how they are conducted. When surveys about gender relations have been carried out by men, they have at worst excluded women, especially those subject to heavy norms on seclusion, and at best led to superficial discussions with women. The problem is compounded when the male interviewers are strangers to the women and topics fall within what is considered the private domain, e.g. fertility, sexuality or male violence. If men are interviewed, given the unequal power relations between men and women, the picture which emerges may be far removed from women's reality.

Class and caste differences and social relations of gender also influence interviews by women with women in both practical and conceptual ways. Most female interviewers are middle class. Their responsibilities with regard to domestic work and child care, and norms on mobility, determine when interviews take place. These are often held during the day, which may be inconvenient for poorer women. Discussions are also inhibited due to norms on local women's interaction with strangers and the demands made on their time by social responsibilities. The hierarchy between 'interviewer' and 'interviewee' is interlinked with hierarchies based on caste, class, religion, marital status and age. These influence what information is shared and how it is analysed, and may not capture the complexity of gender relations. What then are alternative approaches to examining gender relations?

A participatory approach for understanding female infanticide

ADITHI, an NGO working in the eastern Indian state of Bihar, conducted a study on the reasons for a low sex-ratio, 820 females per 1000 males, in four administrative blocks in four districts (Srinivasan et al, 1995). They found that female infanticide was the second largest contributing factor, after neglect of girl children leading to death in early childhood. The study also revealed that, while female infanticide was practised most by upper castes, it had also spread to other castes. *Dais*, traditional midwives who are all women, are paid to kill female infants. Although local parents were unwilling to discuss the practice, the *dais* expressed their concerns about the economic and social pressures that force them to engage with it.

The questionnaire-based survey did not provide an in-depth understanding of the issues surrounding female infanticide. It had also not helped identify strategies to tackle the problem. So ADITHI, with Bal Mahila Kalyan (BMK) another local NGO, organized a two-day workshop with 28 *dais* in one of the districts, Katihar, in May 1995. Some of the *dais* had attended a state-level meeting organized earlier by ADITHI on female infanticide.

The workshop was facilitated by three people: one staff member each from ADITHI and BMK, and myself, as an external consultant. A male journalist also attended the workshop to help publicize the issue. The workshop was followed by a one-day meeting with BMK staff to identify how to carry forward the solutions recommended by the *dais*.

The workshop aimed to:

o explore forms of gender discrimination as differentiated by caste and religion;
o understand the local history and extent of female infanticide (and variations with caste, class, religion and relative position occupied by the infant); and
o identify possible strategies to draw public attention to the prevalence of female infanticide and to combat it.

Your next life as male or a female?

We started the workshop by discussing the question: 'If you can have the choice, would you like to be born as a male or a female in your next life?' Each *dais* indicated her preference alongside a diagram of a boy and a girl, and explained her motivation. Of the 23 *dais* present (five joined us a bit later), 18 preferred to be born as a male and only five wanted to be born again as a female.

Their reasons varied considerably and several stated more than one. The benefits associated with being a man included:

o *Emotional/social benefits* (13 responses): the possibility of residing close to one's parents and looking after them in their old age, not being a financial burden on one's parents (dowry etc.), not facing harassment, and having the option to marry again if one's life partner dies;
o *Material benefits* (12 responses): rights to property, higher wages, control over income, reduced work burden, better access to food and education, and financial security in old age;

- ○ *Biological benefits* (2 responses): not having to go through the pain of childbirth (note that this derives from the social norms on compulsory motherhood); and
- ○ *Religious benefits* (1 response): within the Hindu religion, the higher place accorded to men in religion and the power to light the funeral pyre of one's parents on death.

Of the five *dais* who wanted to be born again as a female, two felt that women play an important role in producing life and sustaining generations. One of them said, 'If all of us became males, how will life continue? We play an important role in society'. Two *dais* felt that women have a closer and, therefore, more fulfilling relationship with their children. Another two cited that women do not need to go out and strain themselves as much as men. Thus on the issue of the gender-based division of labour, it appears that some of the *dais* had struck bargains with patriarchy (cf. Kandiyoti, 1988), enjoying some of the privileges which the system has to offer, although at the cost of access and control over resources. On the positive side, it was encouraging to note that some also felt that women play a key role in society.

We used a pictorial representation to synthesize this discussion. The *dais* who felt comfortable with drawing made pictures to show why most of them prefer not to be born again as females (Figure 7.1). This exercise allowed us to discuss more specific forms of gender discrimination in Katihar district, as a gentle introduction into later exercises dealing with female infanticide.

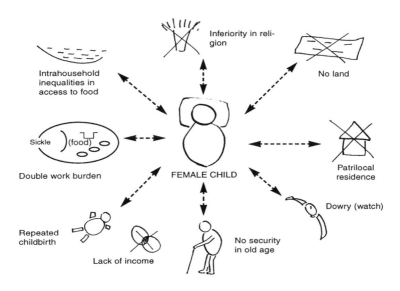

Figure 7.1: The *dais'* experience of gender discrimination

The influence of caste and religion on gender inequalities

Our discussion then focused on the extent to which gender-based discrimination was prevalent amongst different castes. To facilitate this, we used a matrix-scoring exercise (Figure 7.2). After much debate, the *dais* reached agreement on the pictorial forms of representing different caste groups. The subsequent discussion raised many key issues that shed light on the problematics of female infanticide.

The *dais* explained that gender-based discrimination was not only prevalent in upper caste Hindu communities, but in fact took more extreme forms when compared to the *dalit* communities, the lowest caste cluster from which the *dais* are drawn. The upper castes indeed scored the highest, followed by the backward castes (see Figure 7.2). They said there are fewer gender inequalities in the very poor *dalit* communities, and in Muslim communities, although the situation is far from equal.

There are three caste groups in Katihar District: upper/forward castes; backward castes; and *dalits*. Irrespective of caste, Hindu women have no customary rights to land. Patrilocal residence after marriage was common across all castes, so parents cannot derive any economic benefit or social support from their daughters after marriage. The practice of dowry is widely prevalent, though the extent varies with caste. Hindu religion

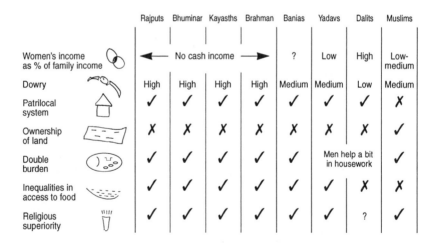

		Rajputs	Bhuminar	Kayasths	Brahman	Banias	Yadavs	Dalits	Muslims
Women's income as % of family income		←——— No cash income ———→				?	Low	High	Low-medium
Dowry		High	High	High	High	Medium	Medium	Low	Medium
Patrilocal system		✓	✓	✓	✓	✓	✓	✓	✗
Ownership of land		✗	✗	✗	✗	✗	✗	✗	✓
Double burden		✓	✓	✓	✓	✓	Men help a bit in housework		✓
Inequalities in access to food		✓	✓	✓	✓	✓	✓	✗	✗
Religious superiority		✓	✓	✓	✓	✓	✓	?	✓

Figure 7.2. Matrix of caste-differentiated gender discrimination

accords women lower status than men. It is a common belief that parents can only attain salvation after death if their sons light the funeral pyre.

Other forms of gender discrimination are caste-specific. Women from the upper/forward caste live in severe seclusion and do not work outside their home, irrespective of their economic condition. They experience a much higher incidence and rate of dowry than amongst other castes. Domestic work and child care are solely their responsibility. Women from backward castes engage in income-generating activities. They either receive money themselves or can claim a share of their husbands' resources. However, their economic contribution to the household is usually significantly lower than their husbands. Women from *dalit* communities play an important economic role in the household, at times contributing more than their husbands. Husbands help out in housework and child care, although these remain the primary responsibility of women.

The *dais* noted that, on the whole, the costs of a female child to the parents and the community were highest for the upper caste. As one went down the castes, the costs decreased and economic benefits to the parents and the community increased. In all castes, the costs of daughters to parents were higher than those of sons, and the benefits lower.

It was a surprise for some of the facilitators to hear that the status of Muslim women was generally better than upper caste Hindi women. The *dais* pointed out that Muslim women earn an income with home-based work and help in agriculture. Some Muslim women own land, and daughters are married out within the village or in nearby villages. This makes it easier for them and their husbands to manage land owned by the women.

However, like their Hindu counterparts, Muslim women certainly encounter inequalities. Their earnings are substantially lower than their husbands'. They carry the burden of domestic work and child care, and do not have full control over their earnings. The practice of dowry is widespread. Religion accords women a lower status, though sons do not represent a higher spiritual status as in the Hindu communities. The socio-economic costs associated with daughters are higher than the benefits which accrue to Muslim parents, and certainly when compared with sons.

The practice and causes of female infanticide

More discussion followed on how gender differentials in the economic, social and religious costs and benefits of sons and daughters cause, on a daily basis, inequalities in access to food and education. More extreme forms of discrimination include practices like female infanticide. The vulnerability of girls to infanticide varies across castes. In upper/forward castes, the first daughter is much less vulnerable than those which follow, while in the backward castes, vulnerability increases with the birth of the fourth daughter. According to the *dais*, neither *dalit* nor Muslim households practice female infanticide.[3] Muslims believe that Islamic principles do not condone killing a female infant, and that the practice incurs the wrath of God. When discussing the history of female infanticide, the *dais* used important events to mark time. The practice started around 15 years ago in the upper castes, and spread much later to backward castes.

To understand how female infanticide takes place, we then asked the *dais* to develop and perform a role play. They chose to enact the process which transpires before killing the female infant. The father was portrayed as asking the *dai* to kill the female infant for Rs1000 (US$30) and threatening the *dai* with harming her entire family if she did not comply. A rope was used to strangle the female infant. In the end, the *dai* was paid only Rs100. The mother was a silent observer throughout the play.

When we asked the *dais* how mothers reacted in such cases, they pointed out that no mother would willingly kill her own child, even if it was a female. According to them, mothers do not have any power in the household. In the post-role play session, the *dais* expressed that they did not like to heed requests to kill female infants. They feel forced to do so because of low remuneration for delivery (lower if the infant is a girl), the extreme poverty of their families, dependency on upper caste households for agricultural employment and credit, and the power which some of the men from these castes wield in their community.

It was clear that we needed a more private discussion to understand the context and different forms in which female infanticide occurs. During one of the breaks we spoke with four *dais* who had delivered 14 children (of whom eight were girls) between them in the past month. Four of the girls had been killed and all the boys were alive. Two girls were killed by the parents and the other two by the *dais*. A variety of methods was used to kill female infants. Strangulation, giving a large quantity of salt, mixing poisonous seeds with milk, and leaving the infant in a covered clay pot were common methods. The *dais* were often promised Rs600–Rs1000 before killing the infants but paid much less.

Further discussion with the *dais* was stopped short when the (male) reporter asked for the names and addresses of the *dais* and the concerned parents. They feared the information would be abused. This drew our attention to some methodological issues (see next section).

Causes of gender-based inequalities and discrimination

Initially, we thought that some of the workshop issues were best raised through simple group discussion, without diagramming or theatrical exercizes. We asked the *dais* what they saw as the underlying causes behind the various advantages faced by men and disadvantages faced by women cited earlier. Some said that men performed difficult tasks and hence deserved more income, a few said that women's inferior status was ordained by God, while others pointed out that societal structures were the underlying causes. We analysed each of these perspectives.

o Is women's work easier than that of men? The more vocal amongst the *dais* felt this was not true. One of the facilitators pointed out that the *dais* have many skills. In health centres, clinics and hospitals such work fetches considerable income. Similarly, cooking earns money when done (predominantly by men) outside the household, but not inside. Transplanting and weeding, commonly performed by women, are as strenuous as ploughing, a man's task. This discussion focused on the lower value attached by society on women's work.

○ Is women's social inferiority ordained by God? The more vocal amongst the *dais* argued that this was not true. They said that it is caused by the predominantly male religious leaders who interpret religion. They pointed out that local communities revere many Hindu goddesses: Lakshmi as the goddess of wealth, Saraswati as the goddess of education, and Durga or Kali as the goddess of strength and power.

○ Are social structures at fault? Again the more vocal *dais* felt that the problem lay in the social structures. One of the facilitators pointed out that society includes different institutions: family, community (including religion), market and the state. The ideologies, practices, structure and distribution of resources in these areas leads to gender and other forms of discrimination. Given that these are societal problems, and not biological or God-ordained, she observed that gender inequalities can be changed over a period of time.

This discussion in particular gave us food for thought about participatory methodologies to understand gender relations (see below). We felt that the participation of the *dais* had not been optimal and were critical of our own performance. Perhaps asking this question directly was not appropriate. The language we had used clearly did not match that of the *dais*, and we had let our own opinions guide the discussion too much.

Strategies to stop female infanticide

The final discussions with the *dais*, on strategies to combat the practice of female infanticide, was constrained by several factors. Not all *dais* participated equally. Some were more vocal than others and several had to leave early. Nevertheless they suggested several innovative strategies which ADITHI and BMK discussed further after the workshop:

(1) Make public and visible the prevalence of female infanticide.

While it might sound illogical to make visible a practice that one aims to prevent, recognition of the problem was seen as a first important step in tackling it. *Dais* observed that the prevalence of female infanticide was not officially accepted by the government. Therefore no government survey had ever been conducted on the extent of female infanticide and its caste, class, and spatial distribution, and the variation with the relative position occupied by the infant. One of the constraints was that not all births and deaths were registered officially, and even when registered the relative position of infants was not recorded.[4]

We decided that BMK would pursue the idea of a joint survey (government and NGOs) on demographic changes across different caste and religious groups, and over time. The incidence of female infanticide would not be probed directly through the survey. Instead, wherever female infants were noted to have died, data would be gathered on the position of the infants *vis-à-vis* other girl children in the family. Parents, *dais* and progressive village members would be interviewed to gather such information. The results of the survey would feed into a workshop on female infanticide with government, bank officials, NGOs, *dais* and village leaders in which joint strategies would be discussed.

As BMK is headed by a bank manager who was well respected by government officials and village leaders, this survey was indeed carried out. A campaign for the compulsory registration of births and deaths would also be launched, and care would be taken that *dais*, who although the official culprits are also victims of the system, would not be victimized.

(2) Create a watchdog committee at the village level.

The *dais* suggested setting up watchdog committees at the village level, whose responsibility would be to:

○ keep track of demographic changes as discussed above, and ensure registration of all births and deaths;
○ raise awareness on the issue of female infanticide and other forms of gender discrimination; and
○ apply social and moral pressure to prevent female infanticide, and failing this to take legal recourse.

The committee would consist of *dais*, representatives from different communities, school teachers, religious leaders, government officials and local staff of NGOs sensitive to the issue of female infanticide and gender discrimination. Membership would be gender-balanced. The *dais* did not want to lead these committees as they did not want to incur the wrath of the community.

After the workshop, BMK staff and the facilitating team had a heated debate about whether enough gender-sensitive people exist in some of the groups mentioned, whether one should use religion to apply moral pressure (by campaigning that it is a sin to commit female infanticide), and whether police and legal action would be useful if social and moral pressures failed. A majority felt that benevolent patriarchs can be found (who may be against female infanticide, but not against other patriarchal norms and practices) and should be used strategically, as should religious institutions which, on the whole, uphold patriarchy. Similarly, while the state perpetuates patriarchal values in many ways, we felt that its official commitment to gender justice can and should be used optimally.

(3) Promote anti-poverty programmes with *dais* and women from vulnerable groups.

The poverty of *dais* is an important factor that makes them participants in the criminal act of female infanticide. The *dais* suggested the following anti-poverty programmes: fight for higher wages for services rendered, equal remuneration for delivery of boys and girls, mobilization of government provision of Rs100 per month (if it still exists) for *dais*, and initiation of non-traditional income generation programmes as supplementary income. They were also interested in upgrading their health-related skills, so that they could offer a wider range of services and earn more.

However, in the post-workshop meeting, the facilitating team felt that increasing the income of *dais* was not a very sustainable and effective solution. Parents/relatives could still hire others to commit the crime or kill the female infants themselves. Efforts to enhance the economic status of *dais* need to be complemented by efforts to increase the control of women from upper-caste communities over resources. Lack of economic independence is, after all, one of the reasons for gender-differentiated costs and benefits of daughters and sons.

(4) Promote welfare programmes directed at the girl child.

Some *dais* suggested establishing orphanages for girls, where parents could leave their unwanted daughters. One of the facilitators cited her experience from Tamil Nadu with this suggestion. The government there had introduced a similar scheme. Girls, irrespective of age, had been abandoned by their parents, the centres were not well run, and food and education were inadequate, but the *dais* persisted, pointing out that these problems could be reduced if NGOs or federations of watchdog committees helped run the orphanages. Despite realizing that this strategy does not address the root of the problem, they argued that it can provide immediate relief and save the lives of female infants.

(5) Raise awareness and empower women, using *dais* as change agents.

A strategy identified more by the staff of BMK, the facilitators and the *dais* well exposed to other groups was the training of interested and committed *dais* to act as change agents. These *dais* could enhance general awareness about gender discrimination in society and work specifically with women. Such programmes could be carried out by NGOs in Katihar District, and would be directed at all communities, not only at economically weaker sections as is normally the case with NGO-based work. *Dais* interested in acting as change agents could meet on a monthly basis, during which they could learn more about gender and development, strengthen their leadership skills, and develop concrete action plans together.

Other awareness-raising strategies identified included: establishing gender-sensitive cultural groups; development of audio-visual aids on gender and development; and organizing a march of parents with their daughters of whom they are proud and happy. But empowerment of women may demand strategies beyond sporadic events. The formation of women's groups and the strengthening of their economic and social base were considered essential by the *dais*, BMK staff and the facilitating team.

Lessons on participatory approaches to examining gender relations

The workshop on female infanticide achieved its overall objectives to a significant extent. We understood more about different forms of gender discrimination and female infanticide, and had identified a number of concrete strategies. When compared to the limitations of questionnaire surveys, our process had helped to look at gender relations in the group context. We helped the *dais* articulate their experiences of gender-based oppression, using innovative methods such as drama and diagrams. But the extent to which strategies were implemented and female infanticide reduced still needs to be assessed rigorously.

The workshop also had its limitations, teaching us several lessons about participation and the transformation of gender relations.

Be explicit about gender transformative goals

Participatory approaches used to examine gender relations can have different goals: to increase project efficiency, to improve women's condition, or to empower women and transform the consciousness of women and men alike. The latter goal must be integrated consciously in the process. In our workshop, we were not neutral about the broader goals of the exercise and attempted to weave the gender transformative component through the choice of appropriate methods and methodologies (see below).

Clarity and consensus on the objectives

The objectives of gender-sensitive participatory development exercises can vary:

○ enhancing the effectiveness of research on gender relations;
○ strengthening community awareness on gender issues;
○ enhancing the effectiveness of community-level problem solving;
○ strengthening the effectiveness of project planning, implementation, monitoring and evaluation; and
○ increasing the understanding of gender issues within organizations.

As each objective will demand a different process, clarity and consensus about aims at the outset is essential. Our workshop focused on the first three objectives. The BMK and ADITHI staff, and myself were clear about this from the start. The journalist, however, had conflicting objectives. On the one hand, he was committed to educating the press and the public in an accountable manner, yet he was also under pressure to gather sensational news to increase circulation of his newspaper. This affected the discussions. Also, although the *dais* were generally clear about the objectives, their personal interests in improving their economic position coloured the discussion on anti-poverty measures to combat female infanticide. Facilitators need to be clear about the objectives and must ensure that these guide the process throughout.

Clarity about participants

Participatory approaches that aim to examine and address gender relations must, in principle, hear the voices and perceptions of the women themselves. In many cases it is important to draw men into the process also, in separate groups. The two groups can, if necessary and feasible, be brought together.

In our workshop, we consciously decided to focus first on *dais*, as the questionnaire survey had revealed that they were most likely to be interested in and able to discuss the issue of female infanticide. However, lasting solutions to the violence of female infanticide will mean consciously seeking other perspectives on the topic and on gender relations. This will be essential for developing a comprehensive strategy that can help to understand and confront those who perpetuate the crime.

Significance of degree of participation

The physical presence of the right people does not automatically ensure their participation, as participation has many faces. People can participate by being physically present, listening actively, contributing to the design of the process and co-facilitating or initiating the work. If the goal is to support the transformation of gender relations and the empowerment of women, more intense levels of participation must be pursued.

Reflecting critically on our workshop, the *dais* did not participate enough as equal partners. Some of the discussions, notably on causes of women's subordinate position, were dominated by us as facilitators. Facilitators of participatory processes may in future need to review continually the level of participation they are encouraging and achieving, and to develop skills to enhance this.

Groundwork to enable effective participation

As already mentioned, not all *dais* participated in the workshop to the same extent. Those who had been involved in state-level meetings on female infanticide were more vocal than others, contributed to the design of the workshop and had even put pressure on ADITHI to come to Katihar District. They were also more aware of gender issues, and were in a better position to identify empowering strategies to combat female infanticide. A few of the *dais* came to the workshop knowing neither its objectives nor what was expected of them, which reduced their participation. They were often just passive listeners.

In participatory processes that focus on transforming gender relations, more active forms of participation, particularly of women, may require preparatory efforts. Such efforts could include building the confidence of women, raising awareness on gender issues and clarifying objectives prior to the participatory exercise.

Creating a 'private' space

If participatory approaches are going to be effective in examining gender relations, it is essential to hear the viewpoints of those occupying subordinate positions: the women themselves. In India, one of the barriers to hearing their voices and their concerns in large public gatherings is the strict demarcation of the public and private domains. The former is seen as the domain of men and the latter as that of women. It is important to create more private spaces for carrying out participatory exercises with women on gender relations, especially on sensitive topics like female infanticide, male violence and reproductive rights.

In our workshop, we made a conscious decision to invite the *dais* to a location away from their villages, at the office of BMK. We asked them to come without their husbands and adult sons, so that they could express themselves more freely. This strategy may not, however, work in activities with upper-caste women who may be subject to more strict norms on purdah.[5] Private spaces may need to be created in the village. Another factor which will probably hinder the creation of private space is the presence of male facilitators, particularly if topics are considered personal and in areas where norms restricting women's interaction with men are strong.

Considering women's socially and biologically differentiated needs

Most women in India, as elsewhere, juggle a range of responsibilities: cooking, child care, care of the elderly, cleaning, and specific agricultural/ livelihood operations. It is important to consider these when deciding on the dates for the exercise, the daily schedule and the type of support services provided at the workshop venue. Women may need to bring infants along. Toys to keep them occupied and food to cater to their hunger may also be required for promoting the women's effective participation.

As many of the *dais* are agricultural labourers, our workshop was scheduled in May, a season with few agricultural activities. We aimed first to close each day at 5 pm but changed this to 3 pm. We encouraged the *dais* to bring their infants and provided supplementary milk.

Dealing with hierarchies between facilitators and the participants

No matter how 'participatory' the exercise, there is always a hierarchical difference between facilitators and participants. This may be based on race, class, caste, spatial location (urban–rural), knowledge, job title, language, etc. We found it important to be conscious of this hierarchy and to deal with it.

We made an effort early on in our workshop to stress our common identity as women, sat on the ground together, ate together and sang songs. I did not, however, speak the local language, and belong to the middle class and upper caste, while ADITHI staff and BMK staff occupied a position of authority *vis-à-vis* the *dais*, so some distance remained between us and the *dais*. This affected the factual validity of some of the discussions (see below). Hence facilitators need to be constantly aware of how differences between their background and that of community women participants influence the outcome of discussions. Including gender-sensitive community members on the facilitating team and building their facilitation skills may help bridge this hierarchy and ensure the validity of information gathered.

Need for appropriate participatory methods to unravel gender relations

Participatory methods are not automatically gender sensitive. Gender is present or absent in different ways. Some methods are gender blind, as they do not refer to men and women but rather to households, families or communities. For example, wealth ranking uses the economic status of households as the focus of discussion, and is blind to gender inequalities within households. Other methods are gender ameliorative. They provide gender-differentiated information which may be useful for planning interventions to meet the practical gender needs of women. Strategic gender interests are, however, usually ignored. Gender-differentiated matrix scoring of, for example, preference of tree species can provide information about meeting women's requirements for fuel, fodder, fruit and income, but this does not provide information about how to transform women's control over those resources.

A limited number of methods are gender transformative, that is they generate information on women's strategic gender interests. The process of generating this information is transformative. For example, body and sexuality mapping, fertility monitoring and violence mapping are methods which provoke discussions about the strategic gender interests of women. Participating in such exercises itself has proven to be empowering for the women involved (EDA, 1996; Murthy, 1993, 1996).

If participatory development is to be effective in dealing with gender relations, then more effort must be invested in developing innovative gender-transformative methods. Methods which try to alter the ideological underpinning of gender relations are likely to be particularly effective. We tried to develop and use such methods during our workshop, with varying degrees of success. We were more successful in discussing different forms of gender discrimination and the practice of female infanticide, but less effective when discussing the root causes of women's subordination and strategies for combating female infanticide.

Another concern is the need for methods to understand how social relations of caste, class, ethnicity, religion and age influence gender relations. We were fairly successful with this in the workshop and were greatly helped with the pictorial representations (see Figure 7.2). It is important also to remember that not all themes can be explored directly and immediately. More methods are needed that can help raise sensitive topics indirectly and the sequence of issues must be thought through carefully. For example, we made a conscious decision to start with gender-based discrimination in general and different forms of discrimination. Only after this did we feel ready to tackle the topic of female infanticide, but even this was to some extent pursued in a separate, smaller discussion.

Being aware of the limitations of participatory approaches

While participatory approaches may, in some cases, provide more accurate information than surveys, they are not foolproof. Lack of rapport between the facilitators and the community can lead to inaccurate information. Community members may give information which they think the facilitators want to hear, rather than the truth. Fear of community backlash or state repression may also hamper the discussions.

We were not able to achieve complete trust. In one example, two *dais* had told ADITHI staff before the workshop that they had killed female infants, yet during the workshop they claimed that the parents were responsible. Another example occurred during role play, in which mothers were portrayed as passive onlookers in the process leading to female infanticide, with no power to raise objections. Later studies revealed, however, that this process is more complicated. Some mothers condone the practice as mothers of only or too many daughters are accorded lesser status than mothers of only sons or those with more sons than daughters. Also, given the lower status of women throughout Bihar, some mothers want to avoid their daughters having a miserable life. Creating a certain degree of trust and transparency is, therefore, essential to ensure accurate information sharing. Validating information with other methods is important.

Concluding remarks

The effectiveness of participatory approaches in unravelling gender relations and contributing to the process of transforming them depends on several factors. Goals and methods must be explicitly gender transformative. Objectives must be clear and shared. The participants must be chosen with care, and the degree of participation matched to the objectives. Attention must be paid to women's need for private space and they must be supported in fulfilling their socially- and biologically-differentiated responsibilities during the process. Conscious efforts must be made to reduce hierarchies between facilitators and the participants.

If the methods and methodology used in the context of participatory development are gender transformative they may be more effective than surveys in capturing and transforming gender relations, but they are likely to be ineffective if they are gender blind or only gender ameliorative. Finally, participatory approaches and survey methods are not mutually exclusive. Effective participatory approaches may need to supplement their analysis with quantitative data gathered through surveys, participant observation or in-depth one-to-one discussions.

References

EDA (Economic Development Associates) (1996) A Report on a Workshop on Capacity Building of the Share Cropper Women of Mahila Vigyan Kendra, New Delhi: EDA.

Express News Service (1992) 'Cradles for Unwanted Attracting Bigger Kids', *Indian Express*, 26 November.

Kandiyoti, D. (1988) 'Bargaining with Patriarchy', *Gender and Society*, Vol. 2, No. 3.

Murthy, R.K. (1993) 'Participatory Research on Credit Needs of Women. Lessons from Nari Nidhi', Bihar: ADITHI, mimeo.

Murthy, R.K. (1996) 'Report on the Workshop "Raising Awareness Amongst Men and Women on Gender Issues and Division of Responsibilities and Benefits in Inland Fisheries" ', Bihar: ADITHI, mimeo.

Priya, D. and S. Tyab (1996) 'Birthday Deathday', *Humanscape*, January.

Srinivasan, V., Vijay Parinita, Alice Sankar, Medha and Anila Kumari (1995) *Female Infanticide in Bihar*, Bihar: ADITHI.

Vydhianathan, S. and T. Mathew (1992) 'No Babies for TN Cradles', *Indian Express*, 2 December.

Part 2

Sharing Experiences in Research and Action

8

Entering Women's World through Men's Eyes

MEENA BILGI

Aga Khan Rural Support Programme-India (AKRSP) is a development organization working in three districts of Gujarat state (see Chapter 21, this volume). Each district is distinct: Bharuch, a tribal area, Junadagh, a coastal area with salinity ingress, and Surendranagar, a drought-prone area. Therefore, while the work focuses on natural resource management and human-resource development, the focus and process of programme activities vary according to differing local conditions.

AKRSP's mission is to support the empowerment of rural communities and groups, particularly the underprivileged, including women. In all three districts, AKRSP has used participatory rural appraisal and planning (PRAP) as a process of local-level analysis, planning and action to increase local control over development and to improve well-being by better environmental management. An essential part of this work is the formation of village groups called village institutions (VI) or women's organizations. These groups form around small concrete projects, which local people have planned, and are supported technically and organizationally by AKRSP.

Since its establishment in 1983, equity has always been one of the core quality parameters of AKRSP's work (see Chapter 21). The focus of the equity discussion and activities centred on marginalized castes and classes, two areas of social difference that deeply split Indian society. Until 1990, AKRSP had no formal policy stand on gender and did not use the concept of 'gender' to inform its activities. However, field staff worked hard at working with women on issues of their concern.

Since 1987, the organization shifted towards addressing some of women's concerns through programme activities specifically reserved for them. From 1990 on, gender components were integrated more systematically into each programme. Notably, AKRSP appointed me as the Programme Executive for Gender, and more focused field studies were conducted with groups of women on their situation, aspirations and needs. This process of developing and implementing a more integrated and comprehensive gender-sensitive approach met with resistance at different levels, partly due to village men's attitudes towards women. This chapter describes one way in which AKRSP staff tried to deal with this resistance. It outlines how men's understanding of the drudgery and hardship of women's tasks increased by asking them to describe a women's day.

Men's resistance to women's concerns

In various PRAP-based studies carried out by AKRSP staff, many women had expressed their heavy workload. A day of 17 to 19 hours was not at all uncommon for most rural women (see Box 8.1). When they analysed their time, women felt that there was scope for reducing their daily workload by introducing time-saving devices, such as biogas, pressure cookers, flour mills and threshers. For example, they can save at least 2 to 3 hours a day in processing food with a village flour mill. However, buying assets like flour mills is generally a decision made by men, since they control the cash.

Box 8.1: Time division of women in Jambar of Netrang, Bharuch District

Waking up	4 am
Personal care (brushing hair and washing)	30 minutes
Cleaning the house, cattle shed, etc	60 minutes
Tea	10–15 minutes
Morning cooking	60–90 minutes
Milking the cow, cleaning, giving water/fodder	60 minutes
Collecting morning water	60–90 minutes
Washing utensils	20 minutes
Making cow-dung cakes	30 minutes
Agricultural work	6 hours
Child care	20–30 minutes
Cooking evening meal	60 minutes
Collecting evening water	60–90 minutes
Cleaning evening utensils	20 minutes
Converting milk into ghee	20 minutes
Bringing fodder	15–20 minutes
Washing clothes	60 minutes

Many of the men with whom we then discussed the possibility of buying such devices did not see the point, and thereby resisted the women's wishes. The men felt that women's workload was not excessive and that hard work had many benefits. For them three to four hours of grinding, pounding, husking, etc. was not drudgery and no issue of concern. If women had more time, they argued, they would loiter all day. This, they said, would lead only to more gossip and back-biting. Others said that, although women might work longer hours, women's work was softer than men's. Yet others resisted these devices as they felt that the flour from such mills and food from pressure cookers would be tasteless.

At AKRSP, we realised that we would be unable to support women's expressed wish for time-saving devices until men's resistance to the idea could be reduced. We needed to understand men's views on women's issues better, in particular concerning women's workload. To this end, we set out to use one method in a focused manner to discuss women's issues with groups of men. This was not a PRAP process, but the beginning of understanding men's views about women's work burdens and how it would be possible to sensitize the men about women's concerns. What follows is an account of the outcome of these discussions in one village, Boripitha in Bharuch District, in 1992.

Seeing women's work

Before setting out for Boripitha, we[1] had decided that developing a daily activity profile would probably allow us to probe the issue of women's workload and possible options for addressing excessive work. It is important to understand that a longer PRAP process had already been taking place there for about two years. Boripitha had been actively involved with AKRSP staff before these focused discussions took place, and the 18 men who met with us were involved with the AKRSP-supported activities.

When we met the men, I started by explaining AKRSP's intentions of working with women and that we wanted to know more about women's activities from the men's point of view. I asked them if they could describe the time that women spend on each of their activities during the day. As with most village-based discussions using PRA methods, we suggested that they do the collective analysis on the ground using diagrams. This would allow all the men to see the issues being discussed more easily, contribute better and reach a shared conclusion.

One man, Ramsingbhai, picked up a stick and drew a box on the ground. Another villager, Phoolsingbhai, suggested that he draw a broom to symbolise the cleaning that women do immediately after getting up in the morning. The picture was made more visible by highlighting it with wheat flour that was fetched from a nearby house by a curious boy who had joined us. I started probing by asking how much time the men think that women spend on cleaning, and they decided that this was about 30 minutes. One literate man wanted to show the time by writing numbers but I suggested that maybe leaves and pebbles would be better as not everyone could read numbers. They decided that one full leaf would represent one hour.

The discussion proceeded, with the men identifying tasks and times for each task. They mentioned water collection, grinding wheat and cooking breakfast in quick succession. I probed each activity further by asking if some activities required the women to carry out other related activities:

Meena: What do women use for cooking?
Dharamsingbhai: Fuel wood or cow dung.
Ramsingbhai: Oh, we forgot to mention the time spent by women on fuel wood collection.

As the women collect fuel wood and care for cattle even before cleaning the house, they went back to the first box and added two others. In this way, the questions and discussion led to the steady development of the profile of women's activities (see Figure 8.1).

Defensive men in disbelief

When the men felt satisfied that they had identified all the activities, they counted the number of leaves to see how many hours of work the women do each day. They were astonished to realise that all these activities totalled 19 hours a day.

> Margabhai (to Meena):   You mean to say that women work 19 hours a day?
> Meena: I am not saying anything. It is all your information.
> Margabhai: How can that be? If women worked for 19 hours, they would not be able get up in the morning, they would become ill.

When we asked what they wanted to do after reaching what was, for them, an unbelievable outcome, the men said they wanted to redo the exercise. They started to take off five minutes here and ten minutes there, and seemed quite baffled by this discussion. Finally, when they calculated the number of hours worked by women again, they found that they had only reduced the total by one hour!

And then they became defensive. The men said that women's work was less difficult and arduous than their own work. For example, it was very tiring to plough or to let the cattle graze under the hot sun. They claimed that cooking, washing and the other activities did not involve as much work for the women.

Realizing the difficulties

We then probed further by referring back to the different tasks and asking them to imagine what women experienced as they undertook each of the tasks. For example, we asked what they think happens to the women as they go to the forest to collect wood or cook food. They were silent and we repeated the question, asking if they thought it was an easy task or not. One man started by mentioning that women have to walk long distances often with bare feet.

> Poolsingbhai: Even in summer, she walks barefoot in the heat. My wife once got boils on her feet.
> Another man said: Sometimes the forest guards behave very badly. Once when my wife tied the bundle of wood and was about to leave, a guard snatched her sickle.
> Ramsingbhai: They don't even get water to drink. It is especially difficult in the summer. When my wife arrives at home, she is very thirsty.

We probed further and other men mentioned various difficulties that their wives and daughters face when collecting firewood. One man's daughter had sustained a head injury from carrying heavy wood. Others

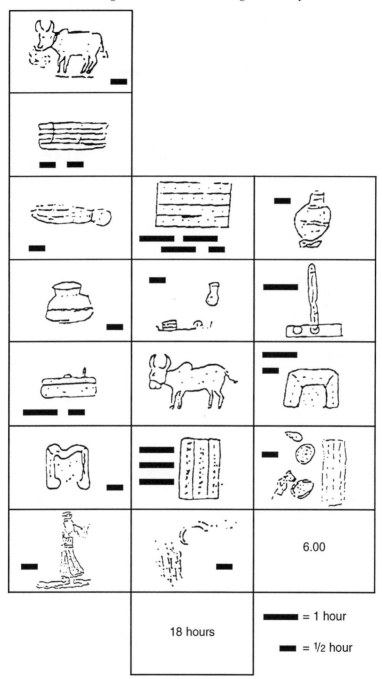

Figure 8.1: Diagram of women's daily activities, according to the men in Boripitha (redrawn from original for purposes of publication)

mentioned a death from a snake bite, and many of the men recalled injuries from other insect bites, including scorpions. Many women have had swollen feet and hands and some had even been hospitalized. This has meant spending money on expensive treatment.

Then we asked them to compare such incidents to their own activities, like ploughing, and they agreed that they do not experience such difficulties. And when we asked if these incidents were easy for women, they agreed that they were not.

> Meena: And you said their work is softer. Do you think that?
> (After a silence)   They do have hardships but our work is still harder
> Ramsingbhai: But their work is also not very easy. We agree with that.

We moved on to discuss other activities, like water collection and agricultural labour. The men identified other problems, such as standing in the queue, getting into fights, walking long distances especially if the borehole is out of order, walking at least 3 or 4 times a day with pots on their heads, and the labourious task of pulling water from the well which affects women's stomachs.

The ardour of agricultural labour was discussed, with the pain of bending for long periods, insect bites especially in the rainy season, cutting themselves with the sickle while harvesting, etc. Other tasks and difficulties were discussed, like the cuts and roughness of hands from washing, and the smoke that gets into women's lungs and eyes while cooking.

The men were quite engrossed as they described the problems that women face in their daily lives and gave many examples. They seemed to realize, as if for the first time, just how much work is being carried out by women and how strenuous that work actually is. In effect, they were being sensitized to women's situations.

From information to sensitization

We went to Boripitha aiming simply to collect information about how men view women's tasks. We never thought that the whole process would also sensitize the men we met about the hardships that women face in their daily activities. We have had similar experiences in other villages in Junadagh and Bharuch districts. There, too, the men were initially defensive and then slowly realized that women's work was not as easy as they used to think.

However, the process was not entirely straightforward. Part of the success of these sensitization discussions was undoubtedly because they took place in villages where AKRSP had already been working with men's groups. A longer PRAP process had taken place and had led to the formation of the village institution. Therefore, we already had good rapport with the men, making it possible to enter into such sensitive discussions. We think that undertaking this type of discussion in villages where AKRSP had only recently become established would have been much more difficult.

We also experienced some practical problems, such as keeping the men together for the seven or eight hours that were necessary for this discussion. More important, however, was the need for patience. Although this account of the discussion makes it sound like an easy process, we had to do a considerable amount of probing by asking: 'And what else?' and 'So what does this mean?'. We asked each question in several ways and, of course, had to fit our own pace to that with which the men felt comfortable. The men took a considerable amount of time to answer, as if they were thinking about these issues for the first time. At the end of this discussion, most (but not all) of the men seemed to realize that women's work is indeed harder than their own and certainly harder than they had originally thought.

Slow change

These discussions in themselves did not cause men to change miraculously overnight. We had to follow up these initial discussions with other meetings with men on three issues related to women: (1) information about the improved technologies which could reduce the drudgery and workload of women, (2) the need to form separate women's groups, and (3) the need for men to support women's groups.

These experiences also helped AKRSP to make several policy changes to involve men more in the process of women's development:

o women were encouraged to join the men at village meetings;
o men were encouraged to help women's groups maintain accounts and registers;
o women's groups were encouraged to keep their savings separate from the men's savings;
o men were encouraged to allow women to leave the village for training trips; and
o men were encouraged to accompany women on exposure trips to successful women's organization, an idea that they had resisted in the past. Seeing women's capabilities in one situation would help them believe in the potential of the women in their own community.

All these efforts helped men to develop a better understanding of the strengths and capabilities of women to contribute to community development. Men are now accepting that women can be effective as leaders and programme extension volunteers.[2] Men are encouraging women to become members of the committees that run the village institutions. The same men who were reluctant to allow women to invest in time-saving devices are now asking for the new technologies. Joint exposure trips are helping women gain men's support and are leading to less interference by men in women's affairs.

Our experiences with the use of one method as part of a longer PRAP process in communities shows that participatory methods have the potential to initiate a process of gender sensitization.

9

Brides have a Price: Gender dimensions of objective-oriented project planning in Zimbabwe

RÉGINE DEBRABANDERE and ARNOUT DESMET

The application of a participatory planning method is commonly assumed to guarantee, automatically, a gender-sensitive outcome. However, our experiences with objective-oriented project planning indicate that other factors are certainly as important as the participatory methodology itself to guarantee that gender issues are taken seriously.

The process and results of a planning workshop with farmers in Mutoko District, Zimbabwe, suggest that women were able to set their priorities and influenced the problem ranking and project planning in the presence of their male counterparts. Chapter 9 discusses the methodology and gender-related results of the workshop. An analysis of these experiences enabled us to identify critical factors that contributed to women's involvement and strength in the decision-making process.

The planning workshop

The Mutoko (Communal Lands) Agricultural Development Project (Mutoko ADP) started in 1988 in Mutoko District as a collaboration between the Mutoko Rural District Council, Agritex[1] and COOPIBO, a Belgian non-governmental organization. It aims to improve the living conditions of farming households in the Mutoko communal lands through support and the strengthening of farmer organization, improvement of the interaction between farmers and service institutions, and assistance to farmers in the identification, evaluation, adoption and adaption of sound agricultural practices.

After an expansion of the project area, Mutoko ADP felt the need to revise the problem analysis and initial planning that had been carried out five years before. Therefore, 15 members of the project implementation team (PIT) participated in a six-day analysis and planning workshop in March 1994. For this workshop, we used a methodology based mainly on objective-oriented project planning (OOPP) but adapted to the needs and context of work with communal farmers. The workshop process was divided in two stages: analysis and planning. Under ideal circumstances, there is a stage between the analysis and planning stage of the OOPP process, when participants return to their communities to seek feedback. They assess the relevance of the prioritized problem areas with a larger cross-section of their community before returning for the planning stage. In the specific case of the Mutoko workshop, this feedback was only organized after both the analysis and the workshop. The analysis stage involved problem identification, problem clustering, problem ranking and selection, and further analysis of the key problem. The planning stage consisted of transforming problems into objectives, and identifying strategies and specific activities to achieve the defined objectives. Gender-specific issues were relevant at each stage and needed to be considered carefully by the facilitators.

Analysis of constraints to agriculture

The workshop started with an individual brainstorming session on the problems affecting the agricultural practices of farmers in Mutoko. Everyone was asked to write his/her problem statements on small cards. As each person had only a limited number of cards, everyone first made a personal priority ranking to select the key problems affecting their agriculture. Women and men wrote on different coloured cards which allowed everyone to determine gender-specific information during the problem analysis process.

In the feedback, the women's cards highlighted certain constraints that affect them more than men, such as the small size of fields, the drying-up of shallow wells in the garden, the lack of women leaders in the village, the lack of income-generating activities for women, and the lack of efficient ways to use cattle (*mombe dzoumai*) given to the mother-in-law. This last issue, in particular, provoked lively plenary discussions between men and women since it touched on culture and traditional gender roles in Zimbabwean society.

Women also commented more on social problems and gender issues in their communities, such as inadequate leadership and leadership struggles, poor organization of farmers, and the oppression of women at household and community level. Women discussed many other cultural and traditional constraints, generating much debate between themselves and the men. It was clear that in a setting conducive to open discussion and with men willing to react to women's contributions, the result was exciting and challenging for both groups.

The problem cards were used to construct a 'problem tree' (see, for example, Figure 9.1). Starting with one card and probing continuously about the causes and effects of each problem, the group gradually built a problem tree which depicted the causal relationships between different problem statements. A card was only positioned in the tree after women and men reached a consensus. During this process, each participant was asked at least once to present a large section of the problem tree, or the entire tree, in front of the others. Besides ensuring regular revision of the tree and the causal linkages, this had another significant advantage. Presenting the analysis up to that point enabled each participant to become familiar with the logic behind the problem tree. The understanding generated by this repetition was extremely important for men, as well as women, to engage actively with the discussion and contribute to the entire analytical process.

When the problem tree was completed, the participants were asked to identify groups of related problems into 'problem fields'. Each field was named and drawn onto the problem tree. This is a very difficult but crucial step in the process. The clustering of problems should be based on common

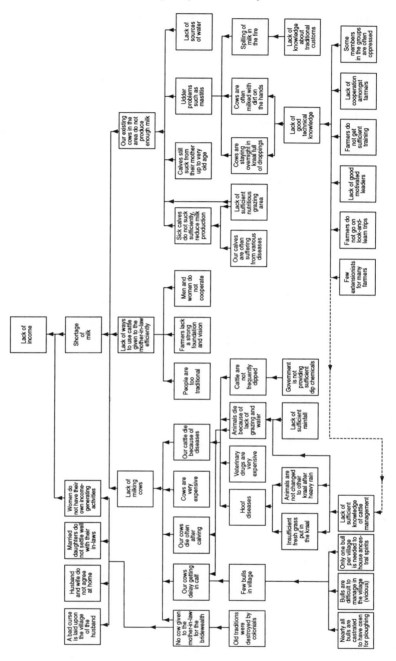

Figure 9.1: Problem tree of lack of milk for sale and home consumption, Mutoko, Zimbabwe

sense and the practical value for the planning stage. The facilitator's role is to prevent problem fields from becoming too broadly or too narrowly defined. In the Mutoko workshop, the participants identified eight problem clusters: soil degradation and depletion of soil fertility; lack of draught power; lack of vegetables for sale and home consumption; lack of milk for sale and home consumption; lack of cooperation amongst farmers; problems in transport and marketing of produce; no strong foundation in or vision on farming; and the high cost of agricultural inputs.

Participants formed small groups to discuss which criteria should be used to rank the identified problem clusters. Some criteria proposed by the participants clearly reflected their gender roles. Women focused more on social and equity aspects within their society, such as:

o the elderly and the young alike should be affected by this problem;
o solutions to the problem must help farmers to put forward their grievances in an appropriate forum;
o a problem must be solved by the majority of the people and leave no one behind;
o solutions to the problem should help women to be self-sufficient and sustain their families; and
o solutions to the problem should have a strong chance of being sustainable in the future.

Using these and other criteria, the farmers prioritized 'lack of milk for home consumption and sale' as the most important problem area for further planning. This priority was strongly influenced by the importance that women attribute to their problems in using the *mombe dzoumai* for the development of their families and themselves. In Shona culture, on the marriage of a daughter the mother receives her *mombe dzoumai* from the new son-in-law. A woman will often dedicate this cow to the spirit of her mother or her mother's mother. If the beast has not been given on marriage, any trouble in the new family is likely to be interpreted as a demand for the cow by one of these spirits. Various problems mentioned in the problem tree were linked to this, such as a bad curse on the husband's village or married daughters not settling in well with their in-laws. Therefore, every son-in-law will make sure that he pays that cow to his mother-in-law as soon as possible.

A woman can acquire some property of her own by selling the handicrafts she makes or the produce from her own fields. But if a woman can build up a small herd from the *mombe dzoumai* and use it efficiently for milk production, this would be a more solid basis for the accumulation of independent wealth for herself and her family. Action undertaken in connection with this problem field could address women's practical needs as well as their strategic interests. The selection of this priority will also improve the situation of their husbands and families.

Looking at women's participation in this stage of the workshop, the key problem cluster which formed the basis of the subsequent project planning would probably not even have been mentioned had women not been present. They had also been encouraged by the facilitators to set their priorities and express their insights, strongly influencing the planning of project activities. By lobbying during the workshop and reaching consensus amongst themselves, the women managed to place their priority at the top of the project team's agenda.

After reaching agreement on the selected problem field for action, a more detailed problem tree on 'lack of milk for sale and home consumption' was constructed (see Figure 9.1). This enabled the team in particular to develop a better understanding of the root causes of the different problems raised and to identify the appropriate intervention options to tackle this problem field.

Planning stage

In the planning stage, we selected the upper-level problem statements in the detailed problem tree (Figure 9.1) and transformed them into concrete objectives and outcomes. This led to the following result identifying three objectives, with the ultimate goal of raising incomes:

We gain more income
↑
Production of sufficient milk for sale and home consumption
↑   ↑   ↑

| (i) We have more milking cows | (ii) We have proper ways to use cows | (iii) The cows that we have given to mother-in-law now produce sufficient milk |

The participants elaborated which strategies and specific activities would help them to achieve the specific objectives. The first objective, increase the number of milking cows, focused on three strategies:

(i)   reducing cattle death and increased calving rate through permanent water supply;
(ii)   improving grazing and additional feeding in dry periods, and training of men and women in heat detection of cows; and
(iii) good care of cows-in-calf and optimal weaning periods.

The second objective, improving the productive use of cows for income-generation, concentrated on various milk collection, processing and marketing strategies. Participants felt the need for more information and it was decided to organize look-and-learn visits to small-scale dairy development schemes to collect the required information. The third objective, increasing milk production of existing cows, focused on activities to improve cattle health: proper drinking facilities; improved grazing and additional feeding; the training of farmers in prevention and curing of udder problems (e.g. mastitis); and an inventory of the traditional treatment of such problems and other cattle diseases.

Of particular interest was the discussion on mastitis. Farmers explained that mastitis is very common, especially during the rainy season, and mentioned several simple treatments. One of the female participants described a traditional remedy based on the roots of a local plant, *shoramombe*. During the lunch break, she guided other participants to a place where this plant was found to dig up some roots and showed them how to prepare the treatment. When asked why this knowledge was not widespread, farmers replied that this information is often kept secret by a few people who will charge money to cure your cattle. Others do not trust the treatment and are afraid it might kill their herds. The farmers said that if such traditional knowledge is made public in a forum like this workshop, it will be easier to disseminate that information to others. Since women are the most experienced proprietors of this traditional knowledge, it was important that all participants suggested the need to make an inventory of and share this information. This improves the status mainly of elder women and will enhance their commitment to and involvement in the programme.

Women also played a key role during the planning stage in defining the concrete activities. They insisted that all activities, such as look-and-learn trips and training, should involve an equal number of men and women. On the basis of these suggestions, a detailed operational planning matrix was elaborated to guide project activities during the following five years. Figure 9.2 represents the analysis and planning process of the Mutoko workshop.

Critical factors enhancing women's participation

It is a culturally accepted practice in Zimbabwe to organize mixed community or group meetings which are attended by men and women. This does not guarantee equal participation, however, since men generally tend to dominate in the discussions at these meetings. To enhance the active participation of women and men alike, it is important to consider a number of critical factors that will support women's involvement within the context of mixed meetings: those that relate to the OOPP methodology, those that relate to the profile of the participants and the facilitators, and the topic.

Elements linked to the OOPP methodology

OOPP is based on an assumption of literacy. Writing and playing around with cards, as well as brainstorming on flip charts, requires a certain degree of literacy. All participants in Mutoko were literate. However, this can be a

Brainstorming on problems/constraints
↓
Construction of a general problem tree
↓
Identification of problem fields in general problem tree
↓
Setting criteria for ranking of problem fields
↓
Ranking of problem fields
↓
Selection of key problem field 'Lack of milk for sale and home consumption'
↓
Construction of a detailed problem tree for the key problem field
↓
Turning higher-level problems into objectives
↓
Brainstorming about solutions/activities
↓
Elaborating an operational planning matrix

Figure 9.2: Steps in the planning workshop in Mutoko

major bottleneck when planning work with women, and men, in other rural areas and requires a reassessment of the literacy assumption. In a similar planning workshop held in 1995 in Pallisa (Uganda), we tried to overcome this by asking all groups to draw the problem 'statements' and ideas for activities. For this purpose, four sub-groups were formed: elder men, elder women, younger men and younger women.

The unusual character of this exercise was exciting for all participants and led to active engagement in all four groups. The younger men tried to excel in the quality of their drawings, spending much time on each, thus slowing down the discussion in that group. The elder women and men understood much better that the idea behind the drawing was more important than the quality of the artwork. Generally, participants were able to depict and re-member even small nuances of meaning. Since this visualization greatly stimulated what would otherwise have been the marginal participation of the women and allowed them to incorporate their views into the analysis, we used it more often in work with farmers in Uganda.

Another bottleneck in working with rural women is the time commit-ment. To carry out a proper OOPP-based analysis and realistic planning with ample time for cross-checks and reiteration, one needs at least five to six full days. Careful selection of the period and scheduling is crucial to allow a significant number of women to be involved. It might help to split up the process into several shorter periods, for example three meetings of two days each, with a short interval between the meetings.

Selection of participants

The active participation of women and men is clearly influenced by the relative numbers of both groups. However, the profile and background of participants also has a strong influence on the quality of their participation, and thus on the final outcome.

○ Numbers
Women and men participated in more or less equal numbers during this planning workshop. This is extremely important. During a recent farmer-based analysis of agricultural mechanisation in Arua, Uganda, women were in a minority. The problems they identified all related to their heavy work-load: fetching firewood and water, and the processing of millet and sorghum. These problems did not feature at all in the men's groups. When presented in a plenary discussion, women had to struggle hard to defend their ideas. A straightforward ranking of problems, based on one vote per participant, would have further undervalued women's inputs because of their numeric minority.

To overcome the effects of numeric gender imbalances, ranking of prob-lem fields can be carried out with a broader section of the community at a later stage or after feedback to the participants' groups. However, although important, a numeric gender balance is not a sufficient condition to ensure full participation of all the women present. The profile and background of the participants has a stronger influence on the quality of participation, and in particular, their level of confidence.

○ Confidence

Most women in the Mutoko workshop were very self-confident. A large number of women representatives in the project implementation team were widows, divorced or with husbands working elsewhere. Because of this independent status, they could participate more assertively in public meetings and were decision-makers at home. This helped them to gain more confidence, develop as leaders in their community, and they were therefore elected to represent their fellow villagers in the PIT.

The Mutoko ADP's policy of positive action towards female participation in exchange visits, leadership training and workshops helped tremendously. All participants in the Mutoko workshop had attended leadership training organized by a local NGO, Silveira House. Its approach, known as Training for Transformation, integrates Paulo Freirean principles and practices, focusing on group methods essential for participatory adult education, organizational development leading to people's self-reliance and liberation, and social analysis. One of the women joined a Rwanda–Zimbabwe farmer exchange visit and gained tremendous confidence from this experience.

During the workshop in Pallisa, Uganda, we recognized a similar self-confidence amongst women participants, based on their joint achievements and successes in the initiation and organization of a community-based primary health-care system. In cases where participants do not display such self-assurance, however, it may be more appropriate to work initially with separate groups of men and women, particularly during the situation analysis.

○ Socio-economic status

All participants at the Mutoko workshop were PIT members. They are elected at community meetings for a specific task: e.g. farmer representative, savings-club representative, area chairperson. As such all participants, including the women, had a clear and defined mandate and position in the workshop. Despite this, however, personal agendas surfaced clearly during discussion. Generally, PIT members are among the better-off farmers within their community and have access to more resources than the average household. Furthermore, the domestic position of the majority of women PIT members is not representative for the average woman in their village. PIT members are highly independent and often have access to external remittances. Despite having been selected by their fellow villagers to represent the collective view, it is likely that their particular household position biased the analysis and planning to some extent.

Adjusting biases

The working experience of the facilitators in the area and their knowledge of social differences within the local communities can, in part, help to overcome these biases, by asking critical questions and challenging the participants about the representativeness of their statements. Ideally, feedback, and therefore an adjustment stage, is part of the OOPP process, with a community-wide assessment of key problem fields between the analysis and planning stages. Another approach involves the use of wealth ranking. During a workshop with representatives of community groups in Kabarole, Uganda, we conducted a wealth-ranking exercise before starting the problem analysis and planning. By constantly referring to the characteristics and resource-base of the poorer socio-economic categories identified, participants can be encouraged to adjust their suggestions to reflect such differences better in the discussions about problems and possible activities.

Since the PIT meets on a monthly basis, all participants know each other well and have been working together for many years. Mutual trust and respect had gradually developed amongst women and men. The participating males were open to discussion, and often confirmed and approved the contributions from the women. This was the basis for the relaxed atmosphere which persisted throughout the workshop. The absence of government extensionists, local politicians or local-government officials also contributed to this openness. In situations where mutual trust and respect are uncertain, working with small groups of men and women separately, in both the analysis and the planning stages, might prove to be a more effective process.

Although women of all ages were present, there were no women with small children. In other workshops, where this was the case, the project arranged for baby-minders to care for the babies and bring them to their mother for breast-feeding only. This is an important detail to ensure that even young mothers can concentrate and participate in discussions.

Facilitators' skills

In Mutoko, an expatriate man and a Zimbabwean woman, both well-known by the participants, facilitated the workshop. Due to a long working relationship between facilitators and participants, there was a general atmosphere of mutual trust. Issues about local traditions and the Shona culture were discussed openly. The facilitators encouraged participants to mention all the traditional beliefs and cultural elements which risk being concealed if farmers think it is of little interest to outsiders, yet which might play a key role in solving certain problems. As a cultural outsider with less insight into Shona tradition, the expatriate facilitator could more easily probe into the reasons underpinning certain beliefs and their consequences. This was more difficult for the Zimbabwean facilitator, who was expected to know her culture and not question accepted practices.

Although this is obvious and necessary in all participatory processes, it is essential that facilitators understand group dynamics and gender-specific communication issues, in order to balance the involvement of women and men. The seating arrangements, ways of addressing the group and communication, finding a balanced mix of guidance and free discussion, time management, repetition and reiteration, use of energizers and breaks, need careful attention to create an atmosphere in which men and women feel motivated and able to contribute.

Relevance of the issue

Women have no time to waste. If they do not see immediate relevance in a meeting or workshop, they will be inclined to lose attention, leave or stop attending. If, on the contrary, the issues discussed are of real importance to them, they will pay full attention and be prepared to invest much time and efforts in the exercise. In this case, particularly when it was decided that 'their' problem field would be selected for further planning, women in Mutoko felt responsible for the proper planning of the activities.

The same enthusiasm and participation was recognised in Pallisa, Uganda, when planning with women and men about household-level food security, only months after an acute famine had ravaged their families and community. Since women were affected most during this famine, they took the lead in the analysis and discussions.

Appropriate expectations

The expectations of the participants were clear and easy to match with the specific objectives and the programme of the workshop. It is important that participants do not attend an OOPP planning workshop or any other participatory exercise with the wrong expectations. If these expectations are not fulfilled, discouragement can be intense and future work jeopardized. In this case, several participants were familiar with the OOPP methodology and informed their friends beforehand about the actual objectives. Every participant was also aware that her/his full concentration and participation was required to come up with a relevant plan for the future.

Challenges ahead

We have indicated a number of elements that could contribute to a balanced gender involvement in project planning. Planning, however, is only a first step. Implementation is the next big move. We can reasonably expect that women, if fully involved in analysis and planning, will also take up their responsibility and claim their part in the implementation. However, some activities could easily be hijacked or diverted to serve other needs if the initial analysis and planning are not continuously guarded by the PIT and Mutoko ADP staff.

The planning started from a woman's concern about the ineffective use of the *mombe dzoumai* to generate personal income and satisfy women's practical needs, but also to improve their status in the community. A gender-specific impact assessment as part of a participatory monitoring process with carefully selected indicators is necessary to assess the impact. During evaluations of such planning workshops, participants frequently express their pride in what has been achieved after several days of intense work and discussion. Although farmers, especially women, are understandably unsure beforehand about allocating such a long time to a planning workshop, the effort and the results are generally considered worthwhile and enlightening.

Although the OOPP methodology has proven an effective approach for participatory planning with farmers, some conditions need to be fulfilled to guarantee full involvement of both genders. The preparation of the workshop is critical, in particular the selection of the participants and the choice of facilitators. The relevance of the topic discussed and the open conducive atmosphere also influence gender-balanced involvement.

Continuous creativity and experimentation is required to adapt the OOPP methodology to the needs, expectations, capacity and cultural context of every group of rural people. Potential constraints, such as illiteracy, communication norms and barriers between men and women, and time, must be addressed through new innovations and the exchange of experiences.

10

For a Pencil: Sex and adolescence in peri-urban Lusaka[1]

SARAH DEGNAN KAMBOU, MEERA KAUL SHAH and
GLADYS NKHAMA

During a discussion about contraceptive methods with adolescent
boys residing in a peri-urban shanty-town of Lusaka, a young man
revealed that an Indian friend had supplied him with a packet of pills.
He explained that these pills killed sexual appetite: 'You need to take
only two pills a month, and there is no desire left for sex. It is very
effective. You don't have to worry about condoms or making a girl
pregnant'. When asked to show a packet of these pills, the young man
spread his hands, and said: 'No, it is finished now. The pills my friend
gave lasted for three months. I don't know where I can get more'.
(Field notes: Meera Kaul Shah, Chawama PLA Study, August 1996)

Where are there adolescents who do not struggle with their emerging
sexuality, who do not agonize over emotional entanglements, who are not
confused by rumour and deceived by promises of miracle drugs? The answer is nowhere. Be it North America or Southern Africa, an adolescent is
principally concerned about achieving status within adolescent society, determined as it is by a sub-cultural value system that is complex, evolution-
ary, and normally unarticulated. Adolescents the world over face similar
issues related to sexuality and reproductive health, and must learn, often
through trial and error, to navigate adolescence safely.

In the not too-distant past, many African societies provided for adolescent instruction by assigning elders the task of initiating youth. As in so
many other areas of social life, rapid urbanization has displaced traditional
systems of initiation. Many reports on health status conclude that the time
has come to reassign the responsibility of informing youth on the basics of
sexuality and human reproduction. High or increasing rates of pregnancy,
abortion and sexually-transmitted infection among adolescents are issues
that plague global society. And society, adult society that is, has thus far
been limited in its ability to address the needs of adolescents. The health-
care delivery system is equally inept at dealing with adolescent sexuality.
This is due partly to a lack of understanding about and communication with
contemporary adolescent society, to the paternalism which often characterizes provider-client interaction, and to the anxiety of individuals who cannot separate their personal parental role from their role of health
professional when counselling young clients.

Chapter 10 discusses selected findings and the approach of a participatory study conducted with adolescents in a peri-urban compound of

Lusaka, Zambia. The study focused on adolescent sexual and reproductive health, with the aim of initiating a community-generated response to the perceived needs of adolescents.

The setting

Adolescent sexuality in Zambia

Zambia, a land-locked country in southern Africa, has nearly nine million inhabitants, with approximately 36 per cent between 10 and 19 years old (Central Statistical Office, 1990). Steady migration from rural areas to industrial centres has created a highly urbanized national profile with 42 per cent now living in cities. One in every seven Zambians lives in the capital, Lusaka, and more than 700 000 Lusakans live in peri-urban shanty-towns called compounds. Under the World Bank/IMF structural adjustment programme initiated in 1991, adolescents feature as one of several social sub-groups that have been adversely affected by deteriorating economic and social conditions within the country (World Bank, 1994). The shrinking formal sector has increased competition for 'piecework', or casual labour, within the informal sector, thus producing an acute lack of livelihood opportunities for the youth. Vocational training programmes are few, and recreational facilities inaccessible for the majority of the population.

Within Zambia, more is known about the sexual behaviour of adolescent girls than about that of adolescent boys. This is probably because most studies have been carried out by female researchers who have had greater access to female respondents. Zambians commonly believe that adolescents initiate sex during their mid-teens, in contrast with older generations who delayed sexual activity until engagement and marriage in their late teens and early twenties. As in many impoverished societies, the 'sugar daddy' phenomenon is present in Zambia, with school girls from poorer families selling sex to older men for the payment of school fees, toiletries and other essentials. However, sex as an economic transaction is extending beyond cross-generational relationships, and is also emerging as a pattern among age-mates.

Statistics on adolescent sexual behaviour and reproductive health

Zambia's total fertility rate is 6.5 for women aged 15–49 years (Gaisie *et al.*, 1993). For young women between 15 and 19 this is 156 per 1000. Adolescent fertility rates are higher in rural areas than in urban areas. Nineteen is the median age at first birth for women aged between 20 and 49 years. Only 1.5 per cent of 15–19 year olds use modern contraception, and currently 22 per cent of all births are to mothers of this age group (ibid).

As elsewhere in the world, adolescent girls do not attend ante-natal clinic early in their pregnancy, hence reducing the benefits of antenatal screening and preventive care. Although the official maternal mortality rate in Zambia is 220 per 100 000 live births, the United Nations Fund for Population Activities recently revised its projection of the national rate to

914 per 100 000 (pers.comm.). The UN agencies estimate that, on a global scale, 30 per cent of maternal deaths are due to self-induced abortion. Given the presumably large number of unplanned pregnancies among adolescents, it is not surprising that 25 per cent of maternal deaths due to self-induced abortion in Zambia occur among adolescent girls aged 18 years and younger (FLMZ, 1995).

In a country such as Zambia, where the risk of contracting HIV/AIDS through heterosexual sex is high, adolescent girls face a great risk of infection. Although often knowledgeable about the infection, they are ill-equipped to negotiate safe sexual practices with partners. One government study estimated that the infection rate of girls is six times higher than that of boys. Another government study estimated that 40 per cent of primary and secondary pupils enrolled in school between 1988 and 1991 were infected with a sexually transmitted disease.

Such alarming statistics have dire consequences, not only in terms of personal tragedies but also for overall national development strategies. They justify quick and focused action to decrease the vulnerability of adolescents, particularly girls, to the impacts of sexual health-related problems. For this purpose CARE Zambia undertook a study to understand more about adolescent sexuality and formulate a community-based project towards redressing this situation.

Studying adolescent sexuality in Chawama

Although quantitative data on adolescent sexual and reproductive health are available in Zambia, there are few qualitative studies that provide information on adolescents' perceptions. Giving adolescents an opportunity to analyse their behaviour, its causes and consequences provides the basis for designing a project which is relevant for and culturally acceptable to them. CARE Zambia[2] undertook the study described here in March 1996 as part of its initiative to develop a new programme in adolescent health. Since then, CARE's health staff have conducted two additional participatory studies with adolescents in other peri-urban centres. Seed funding has been acquired, and adolescent sexual and reproductive health activities are already underway.[3]

To understand better the situation of adolescents living in peri-urban compounds, a study based on participatory learning and action (PLA) was carried out in Chawama Compound from March 11–15. Chawama is a peri-urban compound with about 100 000 residents. It lacks basic infrastructure and is plagued by crime and social violence. The residents share one health clinic amongst about 200 000 people, which is staffed by 46 health workers. There are four primary schools, four basic schools and no secondary schools.[4] Most of the families living within Chawama can be classified as 'core poor'.[5]

Our fieldwork objectives were the following:

o to learn about male and female adolescent knowledge, attitudes and behaviour regarding sexual and reproductive health; sexually transmitted infections (STI) and pregnancy; their sources of information;

o to learn about adolescent gender and generational relations, e.g. how age-mates and cross-generational couples interact sexually and prevent STI or pregnancy; and, where adolescents go for help and support during crises, and

o to identify the obstacles for adolescents to use reproductive health services at public clinics, and determine potential points for interventions.

Methodology

To enable the adolescents and other community members to carry out their own analysis as part of the fieldwork team and to ensure a participatory process, we opted for a methodology based on participatory learning and action (PLA).[6] Participants use a variety of visual and verbal methods to appraise their own situation and to draw conclusions based on careful analysis of the information that has been generated. These methods have been described at length in the literature (RRA Notes, 1988–; PLA Notes 1995–; Pretty *et al.*, 1995). During the Chawama study we used various methods: transect walks, area mapping, body mapping, matrix ranking and scoring, Venn diagramming, trend analysis, cartooning and focus-group discussions. The PLA process is open-ended, yet focused. The research questions guide the fieldwork, but do not dominate it. As participants become familiar with the methodology and the methods, and more intent on exploring the research issues at hand, other topics emerge and may be pursued in the same PLA study or subsequently. Our team of facilitators consisted of 14 women and 8 men: 4 nurses from Chawama Clinic, 6 members of the Chawama Neighbourhood Health Committee (NHC) and 11 CARE staff members. The team divided into four sub-teams, two of women and two of men, to ensure that adolescents felt free to talk with facilitators of the same gender.[7] Each team comprised a mix of clinical staff, NHC members and CARE staff.

To ensure that the study represented as many adolescents as possible in the compound, the teams sub-divided Chawama into four sections and covered one section each. Teams consciously sought the opinions on adolescent sexual behaviour of different age groups: school-going and non-school-going adolescents, and older people. During the five-day fieldwork period, facilitators met with more than 300 adolescents. Several adolescent groups actually followed the study teams throughout the week to continue discussions. Visual exercises were conducted using either locally available materials, such as pebbles, bottle caps or dry beans, or flip-chart paper and markers. Outputs were always transferred onto paper by the facilitators after each exercise.[8] These outputs were normally presented during daily review sessions when teams shared experiences, cross-checked information, sorted data for analysis and set the next day's agenda. Daily reports were kept in a team field-journal, including sketches of all the original visual outputs, which were labelled and stored for future reference.

After the fieldwork was complete, a meeting was held at Chawama Clinic with all the staff and members of the Neighbourhood Health Committee. The fieldwork team presented the major findings from the four sections of Chawama and shared the personal insights they had gained from the discussions with the adolescents. It was agreed that the next step would be to formulate a development intervention with the adolescents, clinic staff, NHC and other interested community members. Now that funding has been received, this is being implemented.

Opening our eyes to adolescent sexuality

Community definition of adolescence

One of the first issues on the research agenda in Chawama was to learn how the community defined 'adolescence', the core unit of analysis of the study, and what local equivalent terms existed. To do this, we probed to understand how the community perceives different stages of growth in an individual. In general, the progression was defined as follows:

a) child → boy → older boy → man
b) child → girl → older girl → woman.

'Child' refers to infants and toddlers, 'boy' and 'girl' are used loosely to refer to the stage from pre-pubescence up to the late teens, i.e. 9 to 18 years. *Mutsikana* is used to refer to girls aged 10 to 20 years, who are subsequently called *bakulu* (older girl) during their twenties and thirties. A female is called *amai* (woman) only when she is thirty or older. By this time, she is also expected to have at least one child. Having a baby before thirty does not, however, qualify a *bakulu* to be called *amai*.

Before starting the fieldwork, the facilitators presumed that adolescence started with sexual activity and encompassed 13 to 19 year-olds. However, the discussions revealed that sexual activity starts before puberty in some cases, thus forcing us to revisit our definition of 'adolescent' to include children as young as eight years old.[9]

Adolescent sex and urban livelihood security

In some respects, livelihoods in urban areas are more precarious than those in rural areas where households have greater access to resources, such as land, that enable food production. Chambers and Conway provide a useful definition of livelihoods:

> A livelihood comprises the capabilities, assets (stores, resources, claims and access) and activities required for a means of living: a livelihood is sustainable which can cope with and recover from stress and shocks, maintain or enhance its capabilities and assets, and provide sustainable livelihood opportunities for the next generation; and which contributes net benefits to other livelihoods at the local and global levels and in the short and long term.
>
> (Chambers and Conway, 1992: 7–8)

In Chawama, earning a 'living', as defined by Chambers and Conway, is difficult, and shocks such as illness, retrenchment, currency devaluation and food shortages force already fragile households through cycles of acute poverty, which become chronic situations for some.[10] In many Zambian households, adolescent boys and girls are expected to make financial contributions to the family or to earn their own pocket money. However, there are few youth-employment opportunities in the country, especially in periurban areas, where the local economy is predominantly informal, with residents earning income through small business activity, e.g. street vending, and 'piecework'.

The effect of economic pressure on adolescent sexual behaviour was apparent during the study:

> Throughout the fieldwork in Chawama, adolescents talked about mothers who train their daughters to find rich boyfriends, or men who would be able to pay well for sexual favours. Adolescents described these households as 'poor', and observed that selling sex may have been the only option available to the family. A story was told of how a mother did not directly instruct her daughter to sell sex but simply told her to go out and come back with food: 'In such a situation, the mother is aware that the girl has no money, and will not be able to buy any food. It is understood by both that the daughter will have to sell her body in order to come back with some food.' (Field notes, Meera Kaul Shah, Chawama PLA Study, August 1996)

It is possible, therefore, to use a livelihoods framework to analyse the experience of adolescents seeking to contribute to household income. Boys generally vend[11] or do 'piecework'. Girls may also vend or run errands, but according to male and female adolescents alike, poorer and better-off girls alike engage in sex for money (Table 10.1). Although the analysis in Table 9.1 was carried out by a group of 30 boys, it was confirmed by all groups contacted during the study. Within contemporary adolescent society in Chawama, sex is clearly 'an asset' for adolescent girls, a means by which to generate economic gain.

Whereas a boy will take the initiative to propose sex, a girl may, in principle, accept or refuse him. During the study, several girls stated categorically that they would refuse to have sex with a boy if he did not pay them in cash or in kind. All girls mentioned that having sex with a boy meant that she would expect something in return.

Table 10.1: Pair-wise ranking[12] of reasons for early initiation of sexual activity in girls (carried out by 30 boys)

	peer pressure	*children*	*money*	*enjoyment*
enjoyment	enjoyment	enjoyment	money	—
money	money	money	—	—
children	children	—	—	—
peer pressure	—	—	—	—
Frequency mentioned	0	1	3	2

Source: Shah and Nkhama (1996)

115

In the words of a group of school-going girls, out-of-school girls 'take sex seriously', going out with male vendors and insisting on small payments for sexual favours. (Shah and Nkhama, Chawama PLA Study, August 1996)

Girls from poor families are far more sexually active and have sex with a larger number of partners than girls from better-off families,[13] although both groups seem to initiate it at the same age.[14] Girls from households with insecure livelihoods may actually be encouraged by their mothers to sell sex. Also, throughout the world, there is considerable peer pressure within adolescent society. Boys seek to establish their manhood, while girls compete in terms of looks and dress. In Zambia, out-of-school girls report that they need money for basic items such as clothes, cosmetics and sanitary pads. School-going girls engage in sex for pocket money to buy sweets, biscuits and body lotion. Whereas adult Zambian society may not view cosmetics and body lotion as essential commodities that would merit engaging in sex for a few hundred kwacha, in peri-urban adolescent society, quite obviously they are and they do.

Bartering for sex

Given that adolescent society considers sex as an asset, it is not surprising that adolescent boys who do not have money readily available seek to barter other valued commodities and services in exchange for sex, as the following anecdote illustrates:

A group of girls aged nine to fifteen years explained that boys in school frequently ask their female schoolmates for sexual favours: 'Sometimes they want only to touch some parts of our body, and sometimes they also pinch us. They also ask us to have sex. When they ask us to have sex, we have to agree'. When asked why they felt that they had to agree to have sex, one small girl explained: 'Because if the girl refuses, the boy will not help her with homework, and may refuse to lend her a pencil when she wants one'. (Field notes: Meera Kaul Shah, Chawama PLA Report, August 1996)

Accommodation is also bartered for sex. During the study, adolescents described a range of living arrangements within Chawama. In as much as adolescents would prefer to live with both parents, few are able to do so. With the death of one or both parents, or through separation of parents, children end up residing with relatives or a series of relatives or neighbours. Given crowded housing conditions, some adolescents may engage in sex with a relative or neighbour to secure a roof over their head. This particular finding illustrates the fragility of adolescent livelihood security, and explains how some adolescents may find themselves in a situation where they need to consider making use of any and all assets in order to fulfil the most basic of human needs.

Other examples of bartering for sex comes from a similar study conducted subsequently in M'tendere Compound, Lusaka. There, girls chose drivers (mini-bus, taxi and truck) and bus conductors as sex partners as they have ready cash and are able to pay well. Drivers are also able to offer girls free rides. Similarly, a girl can agree to have sex with a school teacher in return for 'leakage' of exam questions, and with a doctor if he is willing to provide free medicine. These examples highlight the role that sex plays as a currency in Zambia, and pose serious challenges for development interventions that aim to improve livelihood security.

Pregnancy as a consequence of adolescent sexual activity

Adolescent boys and girls alike are fully aware of the consequences of unprotected sexual activity. While teenage boys are more preoccupied with avoiding STIs, girls worry about pregnancy. Causal-flow diagrams produced by adolescents during the Chawama study focused on the negative consequences of adolescent pregnancy. The progression of events overwhelmingly linked social marginalization and rejection with psychological suffering (i.e. misery), clandestine abortion, illness and eventual death. Further probing revealed that adolescents are concerned about services to help prevent STIs and unwanted pregnancy. While they are partially knowledgeable about prevention, they lack easy access to preventive services such as the health centre, and other points of sale/distribution of condoms and other barrier methods.

Methodological reflections

The value of PLA for exploring adolescent society

Except where noted, the findings reported above were selected from much invaluable data collected during a five-day field exercise in Chawama Compound. The material generated through participatory exploration was revealing. For those who are able and willing to listen, it resonates with realism. Several of the findings are disconcerting and challenge adult Zambian society to review its vision of reality. For many, the findings would be far easier to reject or deny than to try to understand and use to redirect health and community programmes.

Such was the case when the report was shared with senior social scientists who participated in an introductory workshop on PLA which we facilitated.[15] Whereas several participants were able to understand the findings, many remained unconvinced of their value and validity. Men and women who had dedicated their professional lives to researching Zambian society had difficulty accepting the findings, thus calling the methodology into question. The workshop participants used classical elements of social science research to try to disqualify the findings on the basis of methodological error: sample size, instrument validation, interviewer bias, analytical methods, etc.[16] Given the introductory nature of the workshop, we asked the participants to suspend their disbelief temporarily and allow themselves to experience the methodology before making a final judgement. Accordingly, they participated in a two-and-a-half-day PLA-based field exercise on the topic of adolescent sexual and reproductive health in Dambwa Compound in Livingstone. Most of the initial sceptics returned from the field convinced of the value of the methodology, and recognizing the Chawama report as insightful and valuable to policy and programme formulation. Several have since incorporated PLA into their on-going research or are preparing to replicate the adolescent study in their own communities.

With sensitive and serious issues like adolescent sexual behaviour and reproductive health, it is understandable that people, even trained observers of social behaviour, question findings that are upsetting and alarming. We, as adults, have too much at stake: our own memories of adolescence, our concerns for our children, friends and relatives, perhaps even a fear of encroaching social disorder ('what is this world coming to?'). Simply presenting the findings is generally not enough if a thoughtful, coordinated response is desired. Fortunately, participatory learning and action allows individuals to explore an issue as a team, and in the process builds a shared understanding of the problem and a predisposition to respond together. Hence, it is critical to include key stakeholders from the community, so that they may communicate their experience to those unable to participate. In the Chawama PLA, this was clearly the role of team members who represented the Chawama Clinic and the Neighbourhood Health Committee. They were proxies for the entire community, and served as its 'eyes and ears'.

For some health professionals, participating in a study like ours has helped them to modify their views on their own roles and responsibilities in providing health services to adolescents. Once the initial shock had worn off, some adopted a more practical attitude towards adolescents. Others, despite participating in such an experiential exercise, are not yet ready to adapt their behaviour. At the conclusion of the Dambwa PLA, an experienced mid-wife recounted her personal reaction after the first day of fieldwork:

> I went home that evening and sat on the edge of my bed staring into space. All of my children came into the bedroom. I have five, all of them teenagers! And they were saying, 'Mommy, Mommy, tell us what is wrong'. From the look on my face, maybe they thought someone had died. I looked at my children and thought: 'Who is doing what?!' I looked at my girl who has almost finished her secondary school. And I thought is it going to be you? Who? I couldn't say anything to them. I finally asked them to leave the room, and went to sleep. They still don't know what was troubling me that night. (Field notes: Sarah Degnan Kambou, Dambwa PLA, August 1996)

While exposure to reality is necessary for promoting understanding and encouraging behaviour change, it is not sufficient for a comprehensive understanding or dramatic behaviour change. Participatory learning and action is, however, a useful methodology for initiating the process.

PLA and the adolescent participant

While much of the data in the Chawama study could have been collected through focus-group discussions with adolescent respondents, the dynamism and vitality of a 'participatory learning and action' process would have been lost. PLA is a dynamic, accessible methodology which seeks to make participants comfortable with themselves and each other, with their definition of the problem at hand and their proposal of solutions. PLA methods encourage reflection and expression, promote dialogue and cooperation, and, when executed well, reduce conflict and tension.

Adolescents proved to be effective participants in the PLA study:

All of the groups of boys and girls we met in Chawama showed a lot of interest in the subject [sexual behaviour and reproductive health]. Some groups asked us to visit them again to continue, which we were occasionally able to do. However, a couple of groups of 8 to 15 year old girls insisted on continuing discussions throughout the week. We would find them waiting at the gates of the clinic every morning at 8:30, even though we had never asked them to come there to meet us.

We were overwhelmed by the enthusiastic response from the younger people in Chawama, and even asked the girls why they kept coming back. The reply was: 'Because we want to learn'. Of course, we had not been 'teaching' them anything, except on the few occasions when they asked pointed questions at the end of a session which we felt obliged to answer. Most of the time it was them talking, drawing and preparing visuals to analyse their own perceptions and behaviour regarding sex and reproductive health. (Field notes: Meera Kaul Shah, Chawama PLA Study, August 1996)

For the adolescent participants, PLA was clearly captivating. They enjoyed mapping as much as any other community member, taking pride in pointing out and explaining their own landmarks to visitors.[17] Cartooning provided an opportunity for adolescents to express their concerns or doubts through a non-critical and non-intimidating medium. Scoring and ranking exercises were tackled with vigour, and discussions grew into debates. The fact that so many adolescents returned on a voluntary basis indicated their interest.

Given the sensitivity of the topic, we felt it was not wise to use mixed groups in the PLA exercises. The facilitators noted that boys were more free than girls in participating in the discussions and activities, particularly in discussing knowledge and past experience. Girls would generally speak in the third person, e.g. 'I have a friend who . . . ', while boys spoke directly about their own behaviour. It was also sometimes necessary to divide them into age groups. Younger adolescents of both sexes remained shy in front of their elders, yet would communicate more freely amongst age-mates.

From a researcher's perspective, perhaps the strength of PLA is its fluidity. When we heard something interesting from the girls, we checked it when we next met the boys. When we began to suspect cross-generational differences in behaviour, then we arranged to meet a group of older people. When adolescents asserted that there was a high local level of STI, we checked it with the clinic. Through a process of triangulation, each piece of information was verified and common interest in the topic grew.

Next steps

As a result of the exploratory PLA-based studies in Chawama and other compounds of Lusaka, CARE and its partners were able to gain and share unusual insight into adolescent society. Consequently, we were able to attract funding from several donors for a pilot project on adolescent sexual and reproductive health in peri-urban Zambia. The project design relies on PLA to establish and maintain a responsive and collaborative strategy. PLA is being used alongside surveys to collect qualitative and quantitative data. The project emphasizes partnership and communication: between groups of individuals such as adolescents and adults, and community-based organizations and institutions, such as the clinic and Neighbourhood Health Committee. Adolescents figure centrally in the project, with essential support from health professionals, other local-development workers and the community at large.

We are continually learning how to use PLA to understand adolescent sexuality. As of this writing, school-going and non-schoolgoing adolescents from the community have been even more closely involved in the design phase. They are being recruited and trained to conduct peer interviews for the baseline survey. This strategy has been adopted to increase the accuracy of personal information about adolescent sexual behaviour and practices. Not only will we be able to assess the project's impacts more accurately, but those involved in the survey will develop a keen awareness of the problems and pressures affecting their peers.

CARE anticipates that many of those involved as interviewers will also come forward to volunteer as community counsellors during its implementation phase. Due to the gender dynamics of adolescent society, it is expected that male and female community counsellors will be trained so that male counsellors can deal directly with male peers, and female counsellors with female peers. After some experience with this strategy, and if the adolescents are receptive, it may be worthwhile to consider any additional benefits cross-gender counselling may have. In preliminary feedback sessions with adolescents in Chawama, assistance was requested to form peer support groups. Initially, same-sex groups will be organized, but if interest is expressed, mixed groups will also be formed. Finally, given the different profiles of adolescent males and females, gender-specific personal empowerment and life-skills curricula will be developed to meet the unique needs of each group.

References

Central Statistical Office, Census of Population (1990) *Housing and Agriculture: Preliminary Report*. Lusaka, Republic of Zambia: Central Statistical Office.
Chambers, R. and G. Conway (1992) 'Sustainable Rural Livelihoods: practical concepts for the 21st century', *IDS Discussion Paper* 296, Brighton: IDS.
FLMZ (Family Life Movement of Zambia) (1995) *A Literature Review on Adolescent Sexual and Reproductive Health*, Lusaka: FLMZ.
Gaisie, Kwesi, Anne R. Cross and Geoffrey Nsemukila (1993) *Zambia Demographic and Health Survey*, Lusaka: University of Zambia; Lusaka: Central Statistical Office; Columbia, USA: Macro International Inc.
PLA Notes (1995–), London: IIED.
Pretty, J., I. Guijt, J. Thompson and I. Scoones (1995) *Participatory Learning and Action: a trainer's guide*, London: IIED.
RRA Notes (1988–95), London: IIED.
Shah, Meera Kaul and Gladys Nkhama (1996) *Listening to Young Voices: participatory appraisal on adolescent sexual and reproductive health in peri-urban Lusaka*, Lusaka: CARE International in Zambia.
UNDP (1995) *Prospects for Sustainable Human Development in Zambia: more choices for our children*, Lusaka: The United Nations Development Programme.
World Bank (1994) *Zambia Poverty Assessment*, Vol 1–5., Washington, DC: World Bank.

11

Community Forest Management: Whose participation . . .?

MADHU SARIN

One of the key objectives of the National Forest Policy of India is 'meeting the requirements of fuelwood, fodder, minor forest products and small timber of the rural populations'. To achieve this objective, the policy suggests, 'creating a massive people's movement, with the involvement of women' (GOI, 1988). These policy statements are being matched in deeds by a recent shift in India from totally state-controlled to Joint Forest Management (JFM).[1] JFM holds great promise as a participatory form of forest-related development.

State-owned forests account for 23 per cent of India's land area and represent the country's largest land-based common property resource. Vast sections of the 68 million tribal population of the country, and the women and men of other disadvantaged communities living in or near forest areas, continue to depend on forests for many of their livelihood and subsistence needs. Therefore the shift to joint resource management can potentially benefit millions of the poor. It offers immense opportunities for empowering the women and men of the most forest-dependent and marginalized communities to gain equal access to and control over the use and management of common-pool forest resources. In so doing, it can, in theory, improve their well-being.

However, JFM's promise is not bearing fruit for everyone yet. In practice, forest management still focuses mainly on forest protection to regenerate timber. This has led to a differential impact of JFM between men and women. Better-off village men tend to define the priorities and make the decisions, with women pressurized to follow men's rules, being told what trees they can and cannot touch.

Chapter 11 highlights the need for and difficulties of participatory approaches in the context of JFM that allow for the concerns of different groups to be understood, respected and addressed. Those people whose forest-dependence is greatest would need an especially prominent place in the decision-making process, which is, at present, not the case.

Gender in forestry

Be it in the non-tribal mountain areas or the tribal forested belt of central India, women have been, and continue to be, major gatherers and users of a much more diverse range of forest products than men. According to socially and culturally determined gender roles, some products are collected exclusively by women (primarily non-timber forest products (NTFPs) both for subsistence and income). Other products are collected exclusively by men (primarily timber for house construction and agri-cultural implements, as well as for sale) and some are collected by women and men alike. There are also wide variations in gender roles between different communities, with women and men of some communities collect-ing certain forest products which the women and men of other commu-nities do not collect.

In the socio-cultural hierarchy of castes, tribes and occupational groups, there are also strong associations of superiority and inferiority with the collection and use of different forest products. Thus in north Haryana, women of the Gujjar community consider it beneath their dignity to pro-cess a local fibrous grass (*Eulaliopsis binata*) into rope, as that is the tradi-tional vocation of the lower-status Banjara community. Similarly, the Panchmahals district of Gujarat, gum of the *Dhawra* (*Annogeisus latifolia*) tree is collected primarily by the women of the tribal Naik community. Although the gum is nutritious and fetches a good price in the market, women of other local communities, tribal and non-tribal classes alike feel ashamed to collect Dhawra gum as the Naiks have the lowest social status. On the other hand, while women of most other local communities collect and sell the leaves of the *Timru* tree (used for rolling Indian cigarettes), the Naik women do not. Thus, women are by no means an homogeneous category and may have widely different forest management priorities, often for the same species, depending upon which species are of greater value to which group.

From the women's point of view, access to NTFPs has another important dimension. Among most tribal societies, women's income from the sale or processing of NTFPs that they collect from common lands is respected as *their* income which *they* control. In comparison, despite the hard work they invest in private land owned by men, all income from private lands belongs to the male landowners. Such socially diverse needs and greatly differing norms of use and control are influenced by and, in turn, influence the impact of JFM.

The joint forest management framework

The transition to JFM essentially involves developing partnerships be-tween state forest departments and local institutions of forest-right holders/users. This partnership is based on sharing benefits and responsibilities for the management of defined forest areas. While the forest departments retain ownership over the land and its overall control, the major respon-sibility of local institutions is to regulate access to the forest. Regulation is supposed to protect fresh planting or existing rootstock through natural regeneration. The local institution enforces rules for regulating access and penalizing violators, primarily through social sanctions. In return for hon-ouring its responsibilities, the local institution as a whole and/or its individ-ual members are assured access to specified non-timber forest products (leaves, flowers, fruit, medicinal plants, mushrooms, grasses, fallen twigs and branches, etc.) and a certain percentage of the mature timber (in cash or in kind) when ready for harvesting.

As local institutions enter into formal partnerships with state agencies, their rules represent a new regime of property rights for common-property forest resources. This overlaps with the existing regime of legal usufruct rights to forest products, as specified in forest settlements with existing users when the state took control of forest lands at the turn of the century.

Although the JFM mandates of many state governments provide for local need-based, or 'participatory', micro-planning, so far very little of this has been done in practice. The primary emphasis of JFM continues to be forest protection, rather than management based on disaggregation of local needs by caste, class and gender.

Access to a share of the income from timber harvests under JFM agreements is linked to membership of the local institution, particularly where distribution of income among individual members has been provided for. In this respect, women's independent right to local institution membership becomes important for ensuring them equal entitlements (Sarin, 1995b).

Multiple actors are involved in implementing JFM. They include the staff of large state bureaucracies (the forest departments), diverse government and non-government training and research institutions, a wide array of non-government organizations (NGOs) and, above all, the women and men who are members of the participating local institutions. Due to JFM's commitment to 'people's participation', all the actors are searching for tangible methods for facilitating such participation. With its remarkably rapid spread and acquisition of legitimacy in recent years, participatory rural appraisal (PRA) is being increasingly adopted by several agencies as a basket of methods useful for negotiating JFM agreements with local village institutions.

Concerns about PRA for JFM

The near boom in the adoption of PRA for JFM, however, is the cause of three major concerns.

The first is caused by the rapidly growing demand for PRA training with limited availability of sensitive and experienced trainers. A major casualty of this is inadequate attention to the perspectives, behaviour and attitudes of those facilitating PRA which must accompany its meaningful application (Absalom *et al.*, 1994). Many PRA orientation workshops given in the context of JFM last for only 0.5 to 3 days. Due to time constraints, many trainers inevitably emphasize visible outputs (transect diagrams, ranking matrices, time lines, seasonal calendars, maps) more than the sensitive issues of inter-personal, social and institutional processes that determine how they are produced. This shortcoming is further aggravated by the fact that the majority of trainees, particularly from state forest departments, have no, or only a very limited, social-science background. Thus, although an ever-increasing number of people are now 'talking' PRA and its jargon, many continue 'grabbing the stick'[2] from villagers' hands and putting colours on maps themselves. They find it difficult to shift towards a role of facilitating a process that leads villagers to speak, construct, analyse and decide.

Second, with a primary focus on completing exercises in a public arena, few fieldworkers learn to 'see' who participated in public and who was absent. They do not analyse why this was the case and what constraints prevented some from contributing or being present (Pottier and Orone, 1995). Due to such widespread adoption of PRA and the absence of clear, agreed standards surrounding its use, it is becoming difficult to distinguish between those genuinely committed to participatory and equitable development and those who have simply joined the bandwagon to 'stay in business'.

The third concern is the almost total absence of any socio-economic and gender analysis in the use of PRA. This gender-ignorance in a methodology used to negotiate forest-use agreements can have a potentially large negative impact by reducing the access of most forest-dependent women (and men) to forest resources under JFM. Like any other methodology, PRA is not 'automatically' gender- or class-sensitive. This account details some areas of concern and how PRA could be more gender-sensitive when used in the context of JFM.

The example of Panchmahals District and SARTHI[3]

SARTHI, an NGO, has been working in the Panchmahals District of Gujarat for 15 years. During this period, it has developed a good understanding of the gender-differentiated impact of common 'development' interventions. From the mid 1980s, staff have worked on empowering women to gain greater control over management of local resources through organised action for wasteland development (Sarin, 1993). In continuation of this approach, when the Gujarat Forest Department passed its JFM order in 1991, SARTHI started exploring the possibility of women's groups taking up JFM. While looking for suitable forest areas, SARTHI's staff discovered that, in many of the villages where they were working, villagers had started protecting degraded forests through autonomous organized action. This phenomenon of self-initiated forest protection by members of forest-dependent communities is evident in several Indian states.

Impressed by these community initiatives, SARTHI revised its objective to explore the feasibility of the self-initiated groups gaining formal access to forest produce through participation in JFM. Early interaction with leaders of the groups made it evident that these were exclusively male initiatives conforming to the dominant cultural tradition and therefore cannot be considered as 'community' activities. Exploring the feasibility of transforming these all-male community institutions to include women became an additional objective for SARTHI in line with its commitment to organizing local women. The experience discussed below is not of formal JFM groups but of self-initiated forest protection groups now keen to participate in JFM. It highlights the additional constraints faced by women in having a voice in community affairs under traditional, exclusively male, 'community' initiatives. SARTHI decided to explore the potential of PRA for improving their work with the women and men of these self-initiated forestry groups.[4]

The PRA training was conducted in two tribal villages in the Panchmahals District of Gujarat. The two villages belong to a cluster of villages which started regenerating the degraded forests in their vicinity, entirely on their own initiative, from the mid-1980s. Elite male leaders of these villages were successful in motivating most village men to start regenerating the forests through collective protection. The cost for everyone of failing to be involved in the collective action was potentially high, as even the surviving rootstock was likely to be lost for good.

Simple but strict access controls have been introduced. There is a ban on entry into the forest with any tools, and only fallen twigs and branches, and hand-plucked leaves (of *Timru* and of other fodder species) may be collected. Each village has appointed two to three full time watchmen. Every family contributes 10 to 15kgs of grain annually to pay the watchmen. After three to five years of such closure, the male village leaders have started permitting supervised harvesting of one or two shrubs for firewood by representatives of member households during one to five pre-announced days per year.

The men's major motivation for forest protection had been to regenerate timber for house building and agricultural implements, which has become acutely scarce. During preliminary discussions with the male leaders, they seemed to have given little consideration to the impact of their strict access rules on firewood availability for women. In a separate meeting, women from three of the forest-protecting villages said that they must now travel much further to unprotected forests to collect firewood. This has led to substantial increases of labour and time. It has also increased the women's vulnerability to humiliation by residents of other villages. The women also implied that they had not dared question the men's strict access regulations as they feared being rebuked or beaten at home.

PRA to explore women's access to forests

The SARTHI management decided that its staff needed to be sensitized to the gender-differentiated impact of the new access regulations for forests which had previously been accessible to all. They identified PRA training as an ideal opportunity for staff to probe women's and men's views and experiences with the access rules. This would provide an opportunity to facilitate discussions to explore more gender-sensitive forestry-management options. Reflections on the potential and constraints of PRA methods in facilitating gender-sensitive analysis for JFM during and after a PRA training programme for the staff of SARTHI are discussed below. A colleague (C. Sharma) and I participated in the training with the specific objective of ensuring that it was gender-sensitive, in line with the NGO's overall commitment to women's empowerment. Our primary role was to be participant observers in order to facilitate reflection by the trainees on their gender sensitivity in the field during the feedback and review sessions held each evening. We also helped plan and structure the training exercises to ensure that gender differences were not overlooked.

We experienced several problems with the PRA exercises. The first was related to the scattered settlement pattern of the villages. Individual houses are scattered in agricultural fields spread over vast geographical areas. Although the villagers refer to *phalias* (hamlets) of different sub-tribes, there are no physically compact hamlets. It is quite difficult to assemble village women and men for group-based PRA exercises. Although each group of trainees managed to gather a few women and men for their respective PRA exercises, it was difficult to know which interest subgroups had participated and which had remained absent. Although SARTHI had been working in both the villages for some years on some projects, even its staff members did not have a comprehensive picture of their socio-economic structures. Given the differences of issues between socio-economic groups and gender, such a physical setting makes it doubly difficult to gain a holistic understanding of gender differences within the village as a whole and between women of different sub-groups in particular. The chances of the poorest women being left out of the PRA process are even higher than normal as these are the least likely to walk long distances to participate in 'participatory exercises'.

A second methodological problem concerned the degree of appropriateness of some of the highly visual PRA methods. Three separate groups of trainees attempted preparing seasonal calendars of firewood and fodder availability with small groups of village women to understand the impact of the forest protection rules on them. Not one could be completed! It took so much time and effort to explain the objective of the exercise to the women and how to depict the information visually in an alien idiom, that half of them had left to attend to their multiple chores and the rest were tired and bored before the calendars could be completed. Not surprisingly, one of the women's groups was more interested in knowing more about us and whether we could help increase food security from their rainfed agriculture. At the end of the discussions, both sides were left with a sense of frustration.

The trainees' lack of familiarity with using seasonal calendars, combined with poor facilitation, may have caused this problem. However, the women's relatively limited exposure to such communication techniques as compared to the men, who are more used to public interactions, compounded the situation. A valuable opportunity for interacting through other, more familiar participatory methods had been missed, including the simplest one of informal discussion. The use of an alien and structured form of expression had not helped to make the women feel motivated to share their views. However, even informal discussions must also be used with care as the third example shows.

During a subsequent village meeting attended by about 30 women and 30 men,[5] the team tried to probe into the impact of forest protection on firewood availability with the women. Although in less public fora the women had talked about the resulting acute scarcity of firewood, in the larger gathering they would not say so directly. When SARTHI staff asked if they had adequate cooking fuel, the women first replied that they were permitted to cut bushes from the forest for 3 to 5 days every year. When further asked if that provided adequate firewood for the entire year, they replied that they dug up the roots of dead trees if they faced a shortage. On continuing being asked whether they were permitted to take tools into the forest to dig out the roots, one of the forest watchmen suddenly erupted. He asked the women why they were complaining about firewood scarcity

126

when they were permitted to dig out roots with tools. He shouted that once, when he'd stopped a woman from cutting firewood from the forest, she had asked him if she was expected to burn her hands as fuel to cook food with!

The women present were visibly upset by the watchman's outburst, feeling that he had humiliated them unnecessarily in front of so many outsiders when they had so scrupulously avoided saying openly that forest closure by the men had increased their hardship. Some of them moved to one side of the gathering in quiet protest.

Reflections and follow-up

During the evening feedback session, the trainees discussed the incident at length, trying to understand its gender-related lessons. Had it represented a disruption of an otherwise good 'participatory' process due to their obsessive preoccupation with gender concerns? Or was it an unanticipated consequence of bringing the women centre-stage by raising an issue affecting them intimately and not treating them (as usual) like passive puppets capable only of listening to discussions between the men?

We also asked the trainees to reflect on their own behaviour and body language during the village meeting. One problem had been that during most of the fairly long meeting, only the male trainees and trainer had taken an active role. Second, despite the presence of equal numbers of village women and men, the men had looked only at, and talked only to, the village men. The participants pondered about how the relationship between the male and female SARTHI staff was projected onto the villagers as a facet of gender relations through the distribution of roles and responsibilities. Could they be effective in promoting village women's active participation in village affairs when female staff members themselves remained passive and accepted being ignored by their male colleagues?

What had really surfaced through the watchman's outburst was the underlying gender-based conflict caused by the strict rules of forest closure. These rules were formulated by men without either involving the women in framing them or proposing any viable alternatives for how the women could carry out their gendered responsibility of meeting household firewood requirements following forest closure.

After the PRA training

After the PRA training ended, SARTHI staff continued their work in both the villages. Although they were positive about learning the PRA methods, they have not subsequently used them, other than socio-economic and resource maps in other villages. The majority of SARTHI's staff feel more comfortable with small-group discussions and informal day-to-day interaction with women and men.

SARTHI has also encouraged the village leaders to document the history and processes by which their forest-protection efforts evolved. In addition, a post-graduate student and SARTHI staff conducted a house-hold survey in two villages and among different interest groups for several months. This was followed by discussion with the women of different sub-communities, both individually and in small homogeneous groups, in the privacy of their homes and neighbourhoods.

It was through these processes, spread over several months after the PRA training, that it slowly became clear that the women had by no means passively accepted total forest closure by the men. On several occasions, some women had abused and even physically assaulted the forest watch-men when they tried to stop the women from cutting firewood. The history of their groups' evolution, written by the male leaders of one of the vil-lages, also highlighted the immense problems their watchmen had faced in preventing women from violating the rules set by the men (Sarin and SARTHI, 1995).

It has also become evident that there are considerable conflicts of inter-est over forest-management priorities between the women of different socio-economic groups. While the better-off Baria women cut down the regenerating *Dhawra* tree as firewood on permitted firewood harvesting days with their men looking the other way, the Naik women see this as a 'kick on their stomachs' as *Dhawra* gum is a valuable source of income for them (Sarin 1995a; Sharma, 1995).

An understanding of the above dynamics and conflicting interests be-tween different groups within the villages could not be identified during the structured PRA exercises in the training workshop in the villages. Neither members of the most marginalized local Naik community nor the women of the poorest households suffering the most negative impact of total forest closure, will normally articulate their problems in public 'participatory' fora. Nor can chapati diagrams, wealth ranking or social maps capture fully the complexity of such underlying conflicts and power dynamics within and between communities. It has taken SARTHI's staff months of continuous interaction with the villagers, building upon their existing rapport and relationship of trust with village women and men through other ongoing programmes, that the above understanding has emerged. PRA works only if used in the context of such a long-term commitment.

There is growing evidence that at least for the most regularly and recur-rently collected forest produce by women, i.e. firewood, the absence of gender analysis in JFM, both with and without the use of PRA, has com-pelled the most disadvantaged women of large numbers of both community-initiated and formally promoted JFM groups to go searching for firewood elsewhere and/or switch to much worse or ecologically un-desirable fuels. To be labelled 'offenders' and forest destroyers into the bargain, while suffering an increase in labour and the time required for performing an almost daily chore, is making a parody of participatory forest management. Thorough social analysis is essential for ensuring not only that participatory management is equitable by gender and class/tribe, but necessary if emerging local institutions are to be founded on principles of participatory democracy and gender equality. Only then will sustainable forest management under both self-organized community forest protection and under formal JFM become a reality.

Conclusion

Given the complexity and diversity of forest dependencies by caste, class, tribe and gender, each change to access and/or control put in place by a local institution is likely to have a different impact on different sub-groups of forest users. To ensure that the interests of the most forest-dependent women and men are protected, they must be involved in formulating the rules and be given opportunities to articulate their priorities in collective decisionmaking processes.

However, facilitation of such change requires a clear commitment on the part of the facilitating agency, whether an NGO, the forest department or any other party, to reach out to the most disadvantaged. To develop effective strategies for empowering the disempowered also means pursuing a rigorous analysis of the dynamics of domination and subordination between different sub-groups. Participatory appraisal processes and methods for facilitating such analysis need to be sensitive to the differences in needs, priorities and interests by caste, class and tribe and, within and between each group, by gender and age. They also need to recognize that, although women of different communities do not constitute a homogeneous group, as a group they are located in a subordinate position by virtue of the structure of patriarchal gender relations.

To ensure that half the population and its specific problems do not remain invisible, development practitioners need to incorporate gender and class analysis of communities' needs into all participatory approaches. In the villages mentioned above, due to SARTHI's facilitation today, many male leaders and growing numbers of women are beginning to explore forest management alternatives incorporating more gender-sensitive access regulations which will regenerate their forests without penalizing the most disadvantaged women and other marginalized groups. In this process, while some PRA methods may be helpful, what is more important is the outside facilitators' clarity of perspective which guides the analysis of the information generated through participatory methods. A gender-sensitive perspective entails an understanding of the multiple, socially-constructed constraints inhibiting women's participation in participatory decisionmaking. It requires greater respect for village women's time due to their triple roles and locating PRA activities into available time slots. It also requires sensitivity to the cultural constraints which inhibit women from talking openly in front of large numbers of men in public fora. At the same time, communication methods and tools are required which build upon women's own idioms instead of imposing new, alien ones.

Most of all, a gender- and equity-sensitive perspective requires a commitment to empowering women to diagnose their own situations and problems. This forms a basis for developing strategies for dealing with them and improving their relative status *vis-à-vis* men. Today, due to the absence of a gender perspective in JFM, most efforts to involve women have focused on using them as instruments for achieving the goal of improved forest protection. This has been attempted by seeking their cooperation for forest protection or 'sensitizing' or 'educating' them about the importance of forest conservation without analysing why they are compelled to resort to

129

unsustainable forest extraction. The focus needs to shift to how participatory forest management can provide women with sustainable alternatives for meeting their forest-product needs, both in the short and long term, by recognizing them as equally capable and responsible members of communities. If this is not possible, then joint forest management, with all stakeholders, will continue to be fiction and not fact.

References

Absalom *et al.* (1994) 'Sharing Our Concerns, Looking to the Future', *PLA Notes* 22: 5–10.

GOI (Government of India) (1988) 'National Forestry Policy Resolution', in SPWD (1993) Joint Forest Management Update, New Delhi.

Pottier, J. and P. Orone (1995) 'Consensus or Cover-up? The limitations of group meetings', *PLA Notes* 24.

Sarin, M. (1993) 'Wasteland Development and the Empowerment of Women: the SARTHI experience', New York: SEEDS.

Sarin, M. (1995a) 'Delving Beneath the Surface: latent gender-based conflicts in community forestry institutions', paper written for the FTPP, Rome: FAO.

Sarin, M. (1995b) 'Regenerating India's Forests: reconciling gender equity with Joint Forest Management', *IDS Bulletin*, Vol. 26, No. 1.

Sarin, M. and SARTHI (1995) 'Process Documentation by a Self-initiated Forest Protection Group in Gujarat', *Wasteland News*, Feb–April, New Delhi: SPWD.

Sharma, C. (1995) 'Community Initiatives in Forest Management: issues of class and gender; a case study of Panchmahals district, Gujarat', Trivandrum: Centre for Development Studies, December.

12

Gender, Participation and HIV: A positive force for change[1]

ALICE WELBOURN

As a trainer in PRA in different parts of sub-Saharan Africa during the early 1990s, I became increasingly challenged by a number of questions:

o PRA training revealed to many development workers the need to learn more about people's realities, instead of deciding what they needed on the basis of assumed local realities. It helped them to recognize the different needs of gender and age groups within a community, strengthening doubts about the 'we know best' approach and the ability of external technical fixes to provide answers to development (Welbourn, 1991). It also enabled women and men in these communities to discover these things.

But, I asked myself, did this help any of the staff or communities to do anything with this knowledge?

o The women in these communities often described how their problems related to household costs, school and hospital fees. They felt that men's contribution was inadequate but could not complain for fear of being beaten or thrown out.

So, if I cannot change anything with and for the women, was I not simply increasing their burden by asking them to describe these problems?

o Women and men alike were airing their concerns about HIV increasingly but felt incapable of addressing this new problem alone.

What was I, as a development worker, going to do about HIV and AIDS?

In 1992, I learnt that a close friend was HIV-positive. To be confronted for the first time with this knowledge about 'someone like me', in any case whom I had known and loved well for many years as a close friend, is often a turning-point in many people's feelings about the virus, which has so deeply and irrevocably touched many people's lives. Therefore, in 1993, I moved out of mainstream PRA training work to explore how what PRA has taught me could be put to use to deal with these three questions.

HIV: the context

Over the past ten years, there has been a huge amount of commitment, time and energy devoted by many people from all walks of life to HIV prevention, education, care and support work. Many people have given up their former jobs as teachers, health workers and so on to focus on HIV. Much essential and ground-breaking work has been done on pre- and post-test counselling, on breaking down the stigma around HIV, on care and support for sick people and their (mostly female) carers. Many counsellors have learnt to help clients talk openly about sex, about death, about their fears for their partners and children, and about how to live positively with the virus or to protect themselves from the virus. Although this moral support has been invaluable, many female clients still find it impossible to bring their partners to counselling or to introduce the use of condoms into their sex lives. Also, the sheer numbers of people who need counselling means that these individual client services are greatly overstretched.

Information versus prevention

Providing information about HIV is not the same as preventing it. Understandably so, there has, therefore, been less progress in preventing the spread of the virus than informing about it. To date, much of what passes as 'prevention' work has been very top-down in nature, focusing on providing people with information about the virus and what it can do to them, invoking people to behave in a particular way, while threatening them with death if they refuse. The British government approach to HIV prevention in the mid-eighties was a classic example of this. HIV was portrayed as a huge iceberg of death, slowly floating towards its viewers on the TV screen. Viewers were told to abstain from sex, be faithful, 'use condoms . . . or face the consequences'. Public reaction was to ignore the advert and switch channels. The message was too frightening to take in.

While such an approach may be described as an information process, adult educationalists make a distinction between information provision and behaviour change. For example, PRA trainers know only too well that information about the potential of PRA does not automatically lead to behaviour change in the field. Other fields of work, such as in erosion control (Pretty and Shah, 1994) have also shown how decades of lecturing at people is largely ineffective. The explosion of people-based approaches has highlighted the importance of beginning with and building on people's perceptions and experiences, and not imposing our own.

Why then have development workers avoided addressing HIV in their work, when there are now so many good theories about helping people to improve the quality of their lives? I think there are at least three main reasons: fear and scepticism; a disregard for psychological well-being; and excessive caution over the imposition of agendas.

Fear and scepticism

When HIV emerged, it was a new virus which we all feared and which touched our greatest taboos, those around sex and death. It has forced the development of people's communication skills in a manner way beyond what is ever normally expected, either personally or professionally. It demands, for instance, that women and men dare to discuss their sex lives and that parents overcome their embarrassment in talking about sex with their children. Few people find such things easy.

It is also inevitable that myths have grown up around HIV. Many people in Africa, for instance, believe that HIV is a scare story, created by

Europeans to stop Africans having many children. As one African bishop said: 'You Europeans came to Africa sixty years ago, telling us that all our sexual practices were wrong and that we should stop even talking about them. Now you're telling us that we should start talking about them again and in great detail . . .'. Confusion becomes understandable.

A disregard for psychological well-being

Development workers have often failed to recognize that quality of life is not just about material and physical well-being, but includes psychological well-being as well. Many development workers, brought up in the school of technical fixes, through agriculture, health or formal education, have been taught to consider that psychosocial issues have nothing to do with good, solid development. PRA has done little to dispel this belief.

Excessive caution over the imposition of agendas

What participatory development has helped many to realize, quite rightly, is that it is important to focus on people's needs and potential, instead of forcing them to do what we think is good for them. Since our own experience of HIV has so often been as recipients of top-down information, and since many parts of Africa are only now beginning to hear about HIV, development workers have been naturally reluctant to impose information about the virus on communities from outside. If army worm or cassava mosaic virus was likely to invade an area, however, or if a plague of locusts was forecast, it would be considered only natural to inform farmers about it and to help them to cope.

Personal fears of HIV and how to handle it has, perhaps, made many development professionals excessively cautious about not imposing their outsider agendas. Yet HIV affects every country in the world and every part of society, such as people's productivity, personal relationships, children, employment, legal rights and inheritance. This is only too plain to see in countries like Zimbabwe and Uganda, where the governments are open about the virus and its consequences. Where governments are less open to this discussion, the situation is often even worse. In Asia, too, the numbers of people infected are growing fast and India now has the greatest number of HIV-infected people in the world. Caution about addressing a real threat to personal lives and society at large is a luxury that few can afford.

Sadly, therefore, two groups can be distinguished. On the one hand, there is the work of those who are prepared to address issues around HIV but who often have a more top-down approach to their work (through their background in formal education, medicine or religious work). On the other hand, there are those who have developed a more grassroots approach to change through exposure to participatory methodologies, but who did not see or are too fearful to address the issues surrounding HIV in their own and others' lives. But, there are some significant exceptions to this (see IIED, 1995 and Williams, 1996). These describe the use of PRA with village women and men to explore their vulnerability to STDs and

HIV, and to develop some strategies for action. But these remain the exceptions rather than the rule.

But what has HIV got to do with gender and participation?

The most widespread route of transmission of HIV infection in Africa and Asia is through heterosexual penetrative sex.[2] Since heterosexual sex forms a natural part of the lives of most adults in these regions, negotiation of sex between men and women is a fundamental part of any discussion concerning HIV prevention.

The problems shown in these cartoons (Figure 12.1) are faced by millions of people around the world. They can only be confronted effectively by acknowledging that gender relations are about power, money, children, social status and now, through HIV, about life and death. Also, changing one's behaviour is extremely difficult for any man, and particularly any woman, without the support of others in their community. To achieve this means resisting peer pressure to conform to what is considered normal practice. Although the will to change can only be at an individual level, the force to make it happen needs to be supported by one's peers to make the change a lasting one. This implies that HIV must be tackled with a group, and ideally, a community focus. For instance, even though all medical evidence shows that smoking can kill people, it is much harder to give it up in societies and social groups where most people smoke, than where smoking is generally frowned upon. As with smoking or drinking, so with sex. It is much easier for us to change our behaviour when those around us have agreed to change theirs also, and are clearly doing so. But it is so much harder to verify this than with smoking or drinking!

"How can I suddenly suggest to my wife that we start using condoms? I want to be faithful now, but there are times in the last ten years when I haven't been. And I want to protect her from the risk of my past activities. What can I do?"

"What does my faithfulness matter if my husband has other sexual partners? Surely his sexual activities put us both at risk? He would throw me out if I suggested we abstain or that he stops seeing other women. And how can I suggest we use condoms when we both want children? What can I do?"

Figure 12.1: Problems arising from the spread of HIV (Welbourn, 1995)

The Stepping Stones process

These ideas formed the basis of the Stepping Stones-training approach and package. It is one way for development workers and facilitators who are familiar with participatory approaches to learning, to address gender, HIV/AIDS, communication and relationship skills with a community.[3]

A Stepping Stones workshop takes, as its starting-point, reflection on participants' own experiences in a peer group setting, and uses techniques which promote more open, dynamic and creative ways of reflection and action. The emphasis on role-plays and visualization techniques avoids any need for literacy. The process consists of 18 sessions,[4] with a suggested sequence of exercises. Each peer group carries out the same exercises during a particular session, but the specific issues with which each group deals are inevitably different, as participants are asked to 'think of a situation that someone like you has found themselves in, and develop a small role play about it . . .'.

The group structure and organization of the workshop are based on PRA experiences. In PRA, it is important to recognize the axes of difference within a community, to understand peer groups' perceptions of their own needs and potential. This approach was adopted also with Stepping Stones. So most of the sessions take place in separate peer groups of older women, younger women, older men, younger men. Each peer group is guided by a facilitator of similar age and gender. This enables individuals to explore safely their intimate sexual concerns and other sensitive issues. The peer group meetings are interspersed with mixed sessions, when each peer group presents its ideas to the other peer groups, and discussions about similarities, differences and solutions are encouraged.

This pattern of 'fission and fusion', of breaking into smaller, safer peer groups, then coming back to full workshop discussions, can be used very effectively, both in training sessions with community workers and with community members themselves. Besides livening up the training, it also allows the more difficult discussions to take place privately in preparation for more public discussions about the broader issues. The mixed sessions give equal time to each peer group, followed by discussion. This structure has often resulted in a heightened awareness of the needs and concerns of other members of the community. In PRA training sessions, for instance, it is not uncommon to hear older men declare: 'We did not know that our women knew so much about our village and they have drawn things on their map which we would like to add to ours'. The women, in turn, while initially often feeling apprehensive about presenting their ideas in public, have felt a growing sense of pride and self-respect through hearing praise for their achievements.

Participants, in their separate peer groups, have the time and space to work together and to decide for themselves the best solutions to the challenges they face. Earlier sessions develop peer-group identity and ground rules for cooperation. They also enable participants to start to discuss sexual health in general. No matter how uninterested people may be in HIV, older men, for instance, may well be concerned about declining sexual potency, and younger women may want to stop unwanted pregnancy.

Figure 12.2: Discussing topics relating to general sexual health can lead the way to discussions on HIV (Welbourn, 1995)

So talking about sexual health first, before moving on to HIV, is a way of beginning that everyone will find of interest and with which they can identify (see Figure 12.2).

The Stepping Stones process then moves on to more general life skills. Several sessions explore why we behave in the ways we do, and cover issues such as use and over-use of alcohol, the role of money in decisionmaking around sex, the hopes and fears of young men and women. The final sessions focus on assertiveness training, encouraging each peer group to consider and to apply ways in which they can change their behaviour and prepare for the future, even in the face of death. Thus the whole workshop enables individuals, peer groups and communities to explore their own social, sexual and psychological needs, to analyse the communication blocks they face and to practise different ways of addressing their relationships (see Figure 12.3).

Figure 12.3: Practising different ways of communicating in relationships (Welbourn, 1995)

First Steps with Stepping Stones

In reality, this process is only the beginning. In twelve weeks or so alone, no one can hope to achieve lasting change. So the facilitators then encourage each peer group to keep meeting regularly after the last session. The long-term development of such self-help groups has often been the key to sustained behaviour change, be it for credit collectives, water-user groups, ex-alcoholics or ex-drug users.

The Stepping Stones video was filmed in Buwenda, a community in southwest Uganda which is deeply affected by AIDS and where Redd Barna (Save the Children Norway) has worked for several years. Sixteen months after the filming, I returned to the community with Redd Barna staff to discuss subsequent changes. We spent several hours with each peer group, asking them to show us if and how they felt that the workshop had influenced their lives.[5] The preliminary results were very encouraging, suggesting that most participants have experienced a marked improvement in the quality of their lives as a direct result of the workshop. Table 12.1 summarizes the range of comments that were raised by different groups in the meetings.

Let us look more closely at some of these. The young women in Buwenda told us that they never used to bother going to public meetings, as they never felt there was anything there of interest to them and that no-one would listen to them anyway. But now they attend all such meetings. They said they are shown more respect by older people and have gained in self-esteem. They explained that they have realized now important it is to be self-reliant and not depend on a boyfriend for support. They also said that they have now made good friends with a number of the young men and that these relationships do not have a sexual basis.

Similarly, the young men's view have also changed. One said he used to think what did it matter if he caught HIV or not – he was unemployed and had no future anyway, so why not enjoy life while he had it? He said that he had now realized that life has much more to offer him, and that a number of friends have now formed a young men's income-generating group, in order to build a future for themselves. The young men also said that they used to blame girls for AIDS, but that they have now seen that it's no use blaming anyone; and that a number of the young women had now become their friends with whom they could discuss these things. In fact, they said, when it came to marriage, they would rather choose one of these young women who had gone through this workshop process than a young woman from elsewhere, as it would be easier for them to relate to each other.

Table 12.1: Changes in Buwenda after Stepping Stones process

Changes mentioned	Old men	Old women	Young women	Young men
less quarrelling between couples and more sharing of household costs	✓	✓	✓	
less wife-beating	✓	✓		
a respect for the wills of those who have died, regarding the rights of their spouses and children	✓	✓		
a greater sense of well-being and respect for others	✓	✓	✓	✓
greater mutual respect between young men and young women			✓	✓
greater ability of women to discuss sexual matters with their children		✓	✓	
greater self-esteem among young women	✓		✓	
a reduction of alcohol consumption, by older men especially	✓	✓		
a sustained increase in condom use by participants from all peer groups and others	✓	✓	✓	✓
continued peer group meetings		✓	✓	✓
wish to become economically self-sufficient			✓	✓
improved relations amongst others in the community who had learnt about the workshop from participants	✓	✓	✓	✓
development of care and support for HIV positive people and their carers within the community		✓		✓
enquiries from other communities about the workshop process		✓		✓

The comments in Table 12.1 suggest that it may be possible to help people change how they think about themselves, about others, and how they behave to each other. Acceptance of the technical fix (condoms)[6] alone would not be sufficient to persuade men, for instance, to share household decisionmaking or costs, or to write wills. There had to be a means introduced of encouraging people to want better communication, and then to undertake it. This appears to have worked. Stepping Stones can provide some first steps to take place in translating a gender- and age-based needs assessment into a meaningful and positive force for change.

Through developing and supporting self-help community peer groups, there is a hope that the burden on HIV counsellors of one-to-one counselling will be reduced. People become more able to share their fears and support one another's needs in their own communities. More work is clearly needed to sustain the older men's group, and Redd Barna has been working on this. Other personal experiences indicate that older men are often the hardest group to work with, but the continued enthusiasm of the younger men's group is, in contrast, particularly heartening.

Next there is a hope that HIV transmission rates will start to fall. People may be more prepared to care for and support those who are already sick, as people became more aware of the unfairness of ignoring or stigmatizing them. This will help them better to protect themselves and one another from infection. Finally, it is clear that there are knock-on effects for other aspects of people's lives. The younger women, for instance, decided they wanted to attend community meetings themselves, to find out what was going on, instead of feeling they had no place at such events. They decided that they wanted to form their own businesses, in order to break the cycle of economic, and sexual, dependence on men. Young men, instead of saying they had no future anyway so what did it matter if they got HIV or not, were now saying they wanted to work and build a life for themselves. Young men and young women alike realized that they can not blame each other for AIDS, but need to trust each other more and work together to overcome its threat to their lives.

Such statements are of deep significance in respect of their future roles as leaders of their society. There is a hope therefore that the material, physical and psychological well-being of people improves as they become more able to value themselves and respect each other. The coming months will see whether similar results can be obtained through use of this package elsewhere. The tragedy is that it has taken HIV to persuade people like me that such levels of communication have to be achieved. But perhaps the hope in this is that the younger people of Buwenda feel they have a future, one to which they are looking forward.

To Kim: In Memoriam.

References and Further Reading

AIDS Action newsletter, published and distributed by AHRTAG, 29–35 Farringdon Road, London EC1M 2JB, UK.

Berer, Marge with Sunanda Ray (1993) *Women and HIV/AIDS: an international resource book*, London: Pandora, available from AHRTAG, 29–35 Farringdon Road, London, EC1M 3JB, UK.

Gordon, Gill (1991) *Unmasking AIDS*, a video and two manuals, available from IPPF Distribution Unit, PO Box 759, Inner Circle, Regent's Park, London NW1 4LQ, UK; cost £20 in developing countries.

Guijt, Irene (1995) *Questions of Difference: PRA, gender and environment; a trainer's pack*, London: IIED.

IIED (1995) 'Participatory Approaches to HIV/AIDS Programmes', semi-special issue. *PLA Notes No. 23*.

Pretty, J.N., and P. Shah (1994) *Soil and Water Conservation in the 20th Century: a history of coercion and control*, Rural History Centre Research Series, No. 1, Reading: University of Reading.

Quaker Peace Centre (1992) *South African Handbook of Education for Peace*, QPC, available from them at 3 Rye Road, Mowbray, 7700, Cape Town, South Africa.

Sellers, Tilly and Martin Westerby (1996) 'Teenage Facilitators: barriers to improving adolescent sexual health', *PLA Notes* No. 23, pp. 77–80.

Welbourn, Alice (1991) 'RRA and the Analysis of Difference', *RRA Notes* 14: 14–23.

Welbourn, Alice (1995) *Stepping Stones, a training package on HIV/AIDS, communication and relationship skills*, Part of the Strategies for Hope series (see Williams, 1996, below) available from TALC, PO Box 49, St. Albans, Herts. AL1 5TX, UK.

Williams, G. (ed.) (1996) *Broadening the Front: AIDS as a development issue in India*, Booklet 11, Strategies for Hope Series of booklets and videos, available from TALC, PO Box 49, St Albans, Herts. AL1 5TX, UK.

Zeidenstein, Sondra and Kirsten Moore (1996) *Learning about Sexuality, a Practical Beginning*, Population Council, 1 Dag Hammarskjold Plaza, New York, NY 10017, USA.

13

Gendered Perceptions of Well-being and Social Change in Darko, Ghana[1]

MEERA KAUL SHAH

Recent years have seen significant reversals in the way rural development is approached and understood. Of particular significance is the realization that the criteria used by external development agents to make decisions and evaluate changes may not be the same as those used by rural people. Policy decisions must be made and development programmes designed only after people's own criteria are sought and their perspectives understood. In the case of measuring poverty and well-being, this therefore implies moving away from conventional, externally selected indicators, such as income and nutritional intake, towards seeking people's own indicators and analysis of well-being. In Jodha's words:

> These [people's] indicators of their economic status or poverty levels not only help in assessment of change but they also facilitate the understanding of the process of change. They tend to capture the existing situation as it operates rather than capture its formally quantifiable proxies (1988: 2422).

In order to value local people's criteria, it is essential to approach a rural community not as a homogeneous entity. There are many 'axes of difference' in communities (Welbourn, 1991), along social, political, economic and gender lines. While development practice, over the years, has taken account of economic, social and political divisions of society (perhaps in that order), gender-related issues are relatively overlooked.

Participatory rural appraisal (PRA) is one approach that has evolved to elicit people's perceptions, understand their priorities and plan for change together. Although it is best known for its visual methods, it is effective only when these are applied in an empowerment-oriented process. However, like many other development-planning approaches, it is weak in dealing with gender-based differences within a community. The growing literature on PRA shows a clear deficiency in how the approach can help understand gender relations and gendered-perceptions, not to mention the transformation of gender relations.

Chapter 13 looks at the scope of using PRA methods, in a research context, to understand gender differences related to three issues:

o perceptions of well-being and poverty;
o the differential impact that poverty may have on women and men; and
o the implications for economic and social change.

The fieldwork on which this is based was part of a training in PRA methods for Ghanaian researchers, in preparation for a World Bank

Participatory Poverty Assessment (PPA) in 1993.[2] We used a series of PRA methods, notably wealth ranking, to enable women and men to analyse their situation and define their perceptions of poverty, and economic and social change. This experience does not, therefore, provide an account of a full PRA process which leads to local change.

Laying the groundwork

The fieldwork took place in Darko, a small village in the Ashanti region, about 10kms from the market town of Kumasi. Darko was one of the two sites selected for the training fieldwork. The other was an urban site in Kumasi.[3] The World Bank had chosen a PRA-based methodology for the PPA, as it felt the need to supplement the statistical results from the conventional poverty assessments with some understanding of people's own definitions and analysis of poverty and well-being. Apart from providing such insights, a PPA also had the potential to elicit people's concerns and priorities for development priorities and, hence, to influence policy.

As PRA was hardly known in Ghana, it was necessary to train the researchers before they could undertake the fieldwork. A total of 16 participants attended the training, of which eight took part in the fieldwork in Darko. Four of the team members had visited the village earlier to seek permission for the study from the village chief and to inform community members about the poverty appraisal process.

The poverty appraisal process in Darko started with a meeting attended by about 100 women and men. Together they created a village resource map, showing village boundaries, residential areas, roads, rivers and ponds. The village was classified into family, or clan, lands. Preparing the map was a good ice-breaker, as general issues were discussed and person-specific information avoided.

Then, in separate groups, women and men prepared social maps of the village (see Figures 13.1 and 13.2). Both groups showed roads, houses, a church, school, borehole, children's playground and some key landmarks. However, there were some differences. For example, the men's map had 55 houses, whereas the women's final map had 73. Traditionally, a married couple does not share the same house, wives living in separate, smaller huts. The men had not included these dwellings on their map. However, as we found later, neither map showed all households, as nearly all the houses shown were compounds and each compound has more than one household.[4] Many compounds, as we found later, had more than ten households.

Moving on to well-being

The social maps formed the basis of subsequent wealth and well-being rankings by the two groups. Household categorization was an important aspect of the poverty assessment. It not only provided an insight into how community members categorized households, and distributed them amongst the household categories, but also explained the criteria on the basis of which the community sees internal differences. This community-based analysis also provided local definitions of wealth, poverty and well-being.

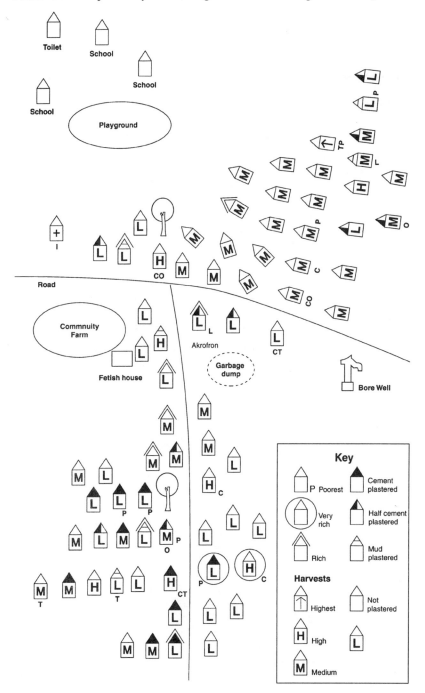

Figure 13.1: Social map prepared by women of Darko, Ashanti Region, Ghana

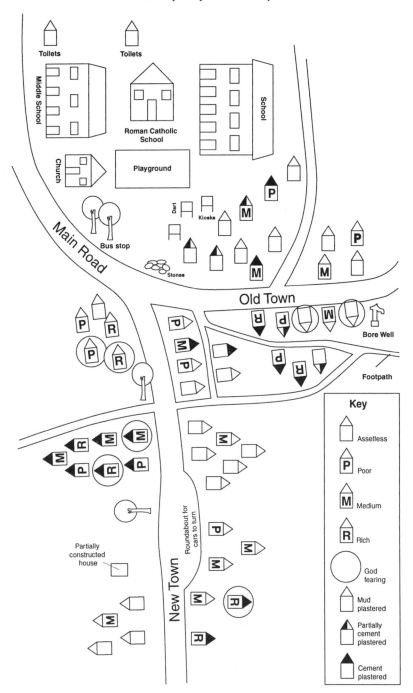

Figure 13.2: Social map prepared by men of Darko, Ashanti Region, Ghana

Men started the discussion by analysing the criteria for considering a household/individual as 'better-off'. A lively discussion took place on the relative merits of material wealth as compared to individual character. A consensus was reached that wealth did not necessarily mean being better-off economically. It was important to be 'god-fearing',[5] which was not conditional on having a cocoa farm or cash.

When we asked them to show the different categories of well-being on the map, the men ranked the houses according to wealth, or material well-being only. Although they had discussed well-being at length earlier, they found it easier first to categorize the households according to material well-being, since the criteria in this case were tangible and easily identifiable. They used three different kinds of seeds to show the rich, medium and poor[6] on the social map they had created earlier. The 'rich' were described as those who own houses, cars, farms, livestock, fish ponds, cocoa farms, and have other forms of wealth. The 'medium'-category households own smaller cocoa and maize farms, have some money but no car. The 'poor' were described as those who have maize but no cocoa farms. At the end of this analysis, some houses were left with no seeds. These had no assets or property, or had migrated. So a fourth wealth category, that of the poorest, was created. Then the men circled eight houses to show which were 'god-fearing', two of which belonged to the poorest group (see Table 13.1).

This descriptive economic stratification of Darko by the men led to a discussion about development opportunities, and whether it would be possible to get rich quickly. To do so, the men said they would need to cultivate more land which would require clearing the forest with chain saws that they did not own. Some people had migrated to the Côte d'Ivoire, Nigeria, Germany, Liberia and Japan, and had become better-off but opportunities to migrate no longer exist. Some people have become poorer as agricultural land had remained the same, yet the number of dependants and the cost of living had increased. Soil fertility had decreased over the years, and it was increasingly difficult to practise rotational cropping.

Meanwhile, the women had also discussed what defines well-being. They started with describing the 'rich' category, listing several criteria: ownership of assets (land, houses, livestock), ability to contribute money for community projects, having money, good health and good harvests. They differentiated between the 'very rich' and 'rich'. Defining poverty was more difficult, as the women equated it with going hungry, which they said

Table 13.1: Results from men's wealth- and well-being household ranking

Category	Number of households	'God-fearing' households
Rich	8	4
Medium	13	1
Poor	11	1
No assets	23	2
Total	55	8

did not occur in their village. However, they did identify three individuals, all women, who were unable to work due to ill health, old age or physical disability. Although they stressed that these women were not living in misery or going hungry, they were totally economically dependent on others. The women proceeded to identify the 'very rich', 'rich' and the 'poorest' household categories on the social map. The remaining 58 households were described as 'others', and as a category fell between the poorest and the rich.

However, after the categorization, the women appeared uncomfortable with focusing on material wealth. In further discussion, they explained that they wanted all houses to be ranked according to the size of the agricultural harvest, focusing in particular on the vegetable harvests. This also led to four categories but with a markedly different distribution (see Table 13.2). Table 13.2 shows that the women with the highest vegetable harvest do not belong to the highest wealth groups, and the richest have amongst the lowest vegetable harvests. While it may well be the case that women from richer households do not need to grow and sell vegetables, the group stressed that a woman can be considered happy when she can sell a lot of vegetables as 'then she does not have to depend on anyone'.

Several points emerged as the groups analysed their well-being results.

o Men's criteria of wealth centred around assets like a house, car, cattle and type of farm (cocoa or maize). They considered crops grown by men, and not women's crops. Initially, they left those with no assets out of the ranking altogether. They then moved on from wealth to a discussion of well-being, using 'god-fearing' as the main criterion

o Women started with indicators like a house, land and cattle but moved to analyse the basis of agricultural production. They considered only 'female' crops and did not mention cocoa or other crops grown by men. Contrary to common perceptions, women focused on marketed crops and not on subsistence food crops.

o Women's criteria for the 'poorest' were related to a state of destitution, and the lack of individual entitlements or health-related deprivation. Men focused on the absence of assets.

Table 13.2: Results from women's wealth and well-being household ranking

Wealth category	Number of households according to vegetable production				Total number of households
	Highest	*High*	*Medium*	*Low*	
Very Rich	0	1	0	1	2
Rich	0	0	5	5	10
Others	1	6	29	22	58
Poorest	0	0	1	0	3*
Total	1	7	35	28	73*

*Two of the poorest women were not farming.

o Both groups had different perceptions of well-being, focusing on their own group of women or men. Neither group looked at the household as a unit for analysing welfare.
o In both cases, being wealthy did not necessarily mean being better-off. In the men's analysis, none of the rich were 'god-fearing' and two houses with no assets had 'god-fearing' people. As for the women, the biggest vegetable producers were not in the richer categories.

Analysing people's perceptions of social change

The information generated from the wealth- and well-being ranking exercises was used to select sample households for more in-depth analysis of dimensions of poverty and how it affected different categories of households and individuals. First, we focused on livelihood analysis, with six households. We followed this with a focus group discussion with women, a time line with two older women, and individual case studies of two men and five women. While the livelihood analysis helped to understand the income and expenditure patterns of a household, along with the seasonality of stress in livelihoods and how the households cope, the individual case studies mapped the changes in an individual's life and the events that led to these changes (also see Chapter 16, this volume). We had used the results from the wealth and well-being analysis to create a sample to select households for follow-up discussions but local funerals led us to the next best choice of selecting households from all parts of the village.

Four of the six households selected for the livelihood analysis turned out to be units with only women. The menfolk had either migrated and not returned for long periods, had died or had abandoned the women. Some of the women were simply living without men. In one section of the village, four of the 12 compounds had no adult male member, and each of these compounds encompassed 7 to 12 households. All these households had been classified as 'average' in the wealth-ranking analysis. The phenomenon of women-headed and women-only households was apparently fairly widespread in Darko.

Household headship was discussed further with the women, revealing generation-specific differences. The older women still consider a man the head of the household, even if he no longer lives there or the woman is the only income earner. Only women with no husbands are considered heads of households, which is defined as such in the local term *osijani*. However, younger women disagreed. For them, if the woman is the main breadwinner, she is the head of the household, even if she has a male partner.

Discussions with two very old women, Maria and Mamiya, revealed further generation-specific changes. Previously, a woman and a man were considered a married couple only after formal marriage rites. This included the groom paying bride wealth, which was shared equally by the bride's parents. Nowadays, women are increasingly living with men and changing partners without the customary rituals, making them 'open prostitutes'. It was mentioned that 'earlier, girls used to sit down and wait, but not any more, because of economic pressures' (*Efia Safoa*). Maria and Mamiya said that younger generations are not interested in farming, refuse to help in the

---

Box 13.1: The impact of poverty on marital status

Ama Saa left her parents when they refused to give her money to buy clothes. She felt there was no other way out. Her partner did not have the money to pay the bride wealth (at least 25 000 Cedis; in 1997 US$1 = 2137 Cedi) which her father demanded. Her father forced her to return home after some time. She later had another partner with whom she lived in Kumasi, and has a child from that relationship. She returned to her mother's village when she got pregnant and her partner has not returned to take her back.

Regina did not want to get married when she was younger as she was scared of men. She has refused seven proposals for marriage. There came a point when she wanted to buy things for herself but had no money. On her parent's advice she accepted the next proposal. She left the village to live with her partner as he had promised a customary marriage, but later failed to pay the bride wealth. She too returned to her village when she was about to have her baby. Her partner had promised to take her back with him three weeks after the delivery but the next thing she heard was that he had migrated to the USA. The same sequence was repeated with her second partner. She is now hoping that her present partner, who lives in Kumasi, will come to Darko to take her back and marry her, now that her child from this relationship is born. In the meantime she is left with three children to raise.

Kokudia is an unmarried 28-year-old man. He wants to get married but has no assets with which to pay the bride wealth. He had to borrow 25 000 Cedis from a trader in Kumasi to grow tomatoes on 0.5 acre of land. He too admitted that he would probably take a partner in future when his economic condition is more stable, but getting married remains a distant dream.

---

fields, and in turn parents do not feed them. When their basic necessities are not met, the young women move out to live with a partner.

The effect of poverty on marital status was also discussed in focus groups and individual case studies with younger women. Two women, Ama Saa and Regina Gyamfi, had lived with their partners without getting married and would not have left home if it was not for their poverty (see Box 13.1). Everyone confirmed that, nowadays, marriages were rare. The relationship between the social institution of marriage, social behaviour among the youth, and poverty is clear. Changes in social norms and poverty are interlocked, one provoking the other and vice versa. Marriage as an institution is collapsing due to poverty and the migration of men to seek alternative livelihoods.[7]

Other changes in the social structure are appearing. Being a matrilineal society, property traditionally passed on to sisters and/or daughters after a woman's death. Now the general practice is for daughters to inherit their mother's property and the sons, that of their fathers. Under customary law, a father can publicly announce that the child is his shortly after birth, even without going through the marriage rites. This signals an acceptance of his responsibilities as a father and ensures the son's inheritance rights. But today this also rarely happens. While it is possible for women like Ama and Regina to claim their grandmother's and mother's properties, their present status as 'unmarried women' means that their sons have no right to their father's property. This could result in daughters and sons wanting to share their mother's property. With the changing household composition, women are not only experiencing less security and greater vulnerability, but their children are losing out on their customary rights. The collapse of marriage as an institution will have long-term repercussions on customary rights to property, especially for the descendants of female-headed households. This is of great concern for the poorest categories, and may lead to the further erosion of their already meagre agriculture-based livelihoods.

Even when women and men live together, they have separate income streams and expenditure patterns (see Box 13.2). Women and men also face different points of seasonal stress in terms of their livelihood. Thus basing a poverty reduction policy on the household, as an economic unit, would prove a futile exercise. The limited number of economic transactions between men and women means that they must be considered separately for livelihood and poverty analyses. Their inter-dependence stems only from women's responsibility to provide food for the household and men's responsibilities for construction work and agricultural land preparation.

Box 13.2: Women's and men's income and expenditure patterns

Men earn cash from cocoa and maize sales, seasonal employment in leatherwork, carpentry and masonry (to deal with pre-Christmas expenditure), and casual agricultural labour (to deal with Christmas excesses). Men experience economic stress in July, a period they refer to as *kitawansa*, or 'hold back your fist' (from spending).

Women's sources of cash income include vegetable and cassava sales and working as agricultural labour. Their incomes peak during April to June, with high vegetable sales and agricultural labour wages. Women spend most of their money in May/June and December, both related to Christmas. The mid-year expenditure is on clothes for themselves and children, and pots and pans, which they do not use until Christmas. Their rationale for making these purchases early in the year is because they cannot guarantee holding on to the cash until December and they feel secure if they buy immediately what they will need later. Women are hard up in January to March, after depleting their cash reserves and before the first income is available in April. This is also the period of illness, medical expenses and expenditure on land preparation. When they are desperate for cash, they work as labourers on other people's farms but generally do not ask their husbands for money.

Perceptions about what defines well-being were discussed further during the individual case studies and focus group discussions. Women mentioned that rich husbands are no guarantee for happiness, as they tend to have many wives and can make only one happy. Instead, women stressed the importance of:

○ having enough food from their own farms so they can feed the household;
○ having food surplus to sell for cash to buy other necessities;
○ not receiving any 'bad news', including children's illness or injury, as children's health is their responsibility, or illness or death of a relative;
○ maintaining good health so they can work and sustain their livelihoods;
○ living with a husband after getting married: 'Even with seven children to look after and few assets, a women will be very happy if her husband lives with her and cares for her'. (Regina Gyamfi)

Men mentioned that it had become important to acquire diverse skills, like carpentry, plumbing or mechanics. Farming alone did not provide enough, and they needed a supplement for periods of financial stress or to deal with poor harvests. Without these skills, a man is considered 'poor'. Agriculture holds the potential for increased income, despite limited land. With more access to credit, agricultural production and income would rise.

Women and men alike referred regularly to illness as a main cause of vulnerability and poverty. It makes work impossible and wipes out savings. Generally, women bear the expenses of ill-health, including increased work burdens. Although also expensive, funerals do not have the same impact as illness. Donations from relatives and neighbours generally more than cover expenses.

Learning from Darko

In Darko, household composition seems to be changing partly due to people's poverty. Shorter conjugal relationships, without customary rites, makes the future of women more insecure. The breakdown of marriage is triggering a cycle of vulnerability, as women take on greater responsibility for raising children who in turn are deprived of their customary rights. In these poverty-related changes, men are increasingly wanting to move out of the village in search of alternative livelihoods. Women find themselves returning to farming as their only option.

The use of participatory methods as described here demonstrate that gendered poverty analysis throws up essential differences between women and men that influence their development opportunities. The methods proved effective to understand people's own perceptions of intra-household relations and how poverty affects women and men. Women's and men's own analysis of poverty and well-being provided a far better understanding of the situation, and the changes that are taking place, than would have been possible merely by collecting data on externally deter-mined indicators. The use of participatory methods generated not only quantitative information on the distribution of households according to wealth and well-being, but also provided insights as to why and how the households differ.

The examples from Darko highlight only one aspect of the heterogeneity of concerns that a community can have. Ignoring the inherent stratification within a community and within households renders any appraisal and planning process incomplete and, therefore, wrong. Most literature on participatory approaches, not least of which the work with PRA, does not reflect such diverse community concerns. Households are generally assumed to be units, comprising members who share interests and priorities. This illusionary household image can lead to wrong conclusions and programmes being designed. Given the masculinist bias of most development agencies, be they state or non-governmental, the danger is that programmes are designed on the basis of livelihood profiles and seasonal patterns of economic stress and deprivation as experienced by men alone.

Studying the livelihood profiles, and their seasonal patterns, of women and men alike could enable more effective targeting of incentives and credit for development programmes. Enabling local men and women to target development programmes based on their own, diverse criteria and analysis of well-being and poverty should facilitate the development of locally supported systems of decisionmaking, resource allocation, planning and monitoring.

References

Jodha, N. S. (1988) 'Poverty Debate in India: a minority view', *Economic and Political Weekly of India*, special number, November.

Kabeer, N. (1989) 'Monitoring Poverty as if Gender Mattered: a methodology for Rural Bangladesh' *IDS Discussion Paper* No. 225, Brighton: IDS.

Welbourn, A. (1991) 'RRA and the Analysis of Difference', *RRA Notes* 14: 14–23.

14

Of Mothers and Men: Questioning gender and community myths in Bali

SARAH KINDON
based on work with Putu Hermawati

'Balinese women are passive like the eggs they produce, while men are active and dynamic because they are like their sperm.'

Perceptions or myths about gender differences like this one, expressed by a male district-level government official, abound in Bali. They are implicit in individual, indigenous/traditional, and official/government thought and practice with regard to community development. They also serve to maintain the status quo in which: 'Women and men learn to fulfil distinct, yet complementary, roles in a hierarchical relationship where men are organisers and women are organised' (Miller and Branson, 1984:8).

Moreover, these hierarchical gendered relationships and the myths on which they are often based, form the socio-economic, religious and cultural lives of Bali. They define notions of status and power as well as concepts of family, property, kinship, work and community. Gender myths are an integral part of myths about what constitutes 'community'. As myths about gender and community influence the nature of development thought and practice, they must be understood if development-induced change is to benefit all members of a community.

In this chapter, I describe my work with Putu Hermawati[1] in rural Bali, Indonesia, which focused on questioning commonly held gender myths. Our experiences highlight that the adaptation and application of participatory rural appraisal (PRA) methods within a framework of Gender and Development (GAD) is not enough to support empowering and equitable change. Instead, development practitioners must re-examine their ways of working with gender differences and power. This implies also reassessing their understanding of and interaction with a 'community' and the institutional frameworks within which their efforts are located.

Why GAD and PRA in Bali?

In 1991–92, I was employed as Gender and Development Coordinator for the Bali Sustainable Development Project (BSDP)[2] where I worked closely with Putu. Our primary responsibilities were to identify the community-development needs of village women and men, and to integrate these into the provincial planning process. The overall objective was to improve the implementation of government development programmes, particularly those aimed at women.

The use of a GAD framework was more appropriate to our tasks in Bali than the conventional and widespread approaches to Women in Development (WID) (Moser, 1989). GAD aims at understanding and transforming the mechanisms underlying dominant, male-dominated development paradigms rather than seeking to improve the integration of women into these paradigms. A GAD framework focuses on transforming unequal power relationships within, and between women and men rather than on women's roles themselves (CCIC, 1990) (see Chapter 3, this volume).

To date, in Indonesia, development targeting women has not reflected the principles of GAD. It has remained confined to the activities of a much-promoted, but rather marginalized, WID programme (Smyth, 1992) which works mainly through the PKK[3] (*Pembinaan Kesejahteraan Keluarga*, or Family Prosperity Guidance movement). The PKK views women primarily in their roles as mothers and wives (Suryakusuma, 1991), and by addressing these roles, its ten programmes aim to improve families' well-being and prosperity. Through other state-defined mechanisms, women (primarily young unmarried women) are targeted for skill-training programmes to enable them to overcome their limitation as an 'under-utilised economic resource'. These programmes supposedly enable them to support the country's economic development in what are considered 'appropriate' women's sectors, such as the garment industry, hotel services and catering (UPW, 1989).

One consequence of such institutionalized gender stereotypes is that most Government of Indonesia (GOI) development approaches involving women tend to be directed by men and implemented by women (Kindon, 1993). Furthermore, GOI approaches to community development are, in general, didactic and top-down. Programme priorities and funding are established at district level, mostly by male government officials. At the village level, official meetings are conducted in the state language of Bahasa Indonesia rather than a local language, and effective participation in programme activities by women and men is often only possible if they have a primary education.

Participation in the development context tends to mean women and men supplying their free time and labour in prescribed, stereotypical and gender-specific ways. For example, women prepare offerings, refreshments and decorations for visits by government officials. They are also targeted with income-generating projects which focus on sewing, embroidery or handicrafts, thus keeping them at home and in the domestic sphere in line with their perceived roles as wives and mothers. In contrast, men are often expected to provide free labour when temples, roads and irrigation systems are repaired. They are targeted for agricultural extension by government officials or are asked to participate in decision-making fora related to community development planning. These activities tend to involve them in the public sphere away from their homes, in line with their perceived roles as breadwinners and family representatives.

Such stereotypical prescriptions are reinforced by those in power and frequently undermine women's capabilities. One male government official summarized well what is a widespread perception about women's role in development: 'Women are vital to development for, without them, who would make the tea for the decision-makers in government meetings?'

Thus the characteristics of GOI development approaches effectively inhibit both the equity and participation of women in community change. They reinforce myths about gender roles and needs, as well as gender and community relations.

Given the above, PRA and GAD seemed to present attractive methodological and conceptual alternatives because of their emphasis on equity, participation and self-reliance. Moreover, it seemed that integrating the approaches would help overcome the inherent weaknesses of each (Kindon, 1993, 1995a; Humble, 1994, Chapter 3, this volume). GAD offers PRA a feminist framework with which gender differences in a community can be examined systematically and understood, in order to address the subordination of women. In turn, PRA offers GAD a series of empowering methods with which to share valuable information about gender perceptions/myths, relations and needs. Furthermore, the value placed upon participation in community development and the common belief in Balinese gender parity (see Myth 1, p. 157) meant that GAD and PRA seemed culturally appropriate to the communities with which we were working, and to the provincial government officials overseeing our work.

The use of PRA and GAD

Putu and I lived with local families in three villages. These were chosen by the BSDP to represent the province as a whole, thus allowing wide relevance to our final recommendations (BSDP, 1992). They encompassed the main geographic and socio-economic areas on the island: Desa Pualang in an upland, dry farming area; Desa Monasa in a central, wet-rice production area; and Desa Kesiman Kertalangu in a lowland, tourist peri-urban area.

We used the concepts and methods offered by PRA and GAD over several months in Desa Monasa and Desa Pualang.[4] I then lived alone in Desa Kesiman Kertalangu for a longer period of time while writing recommendations and training government officials in gender analysis. The approach we adopted was consciously informed by commitment to feminist conscious partiality (Mies, 1980),[5] and active involvement and respect for the women and men with whom we were interacting. Putu and I applied various PRA methods at each level of government, from *dusun* (the smallest administrative unit of a government village) to provincial level. Over 300 Balinese women and men were involved in the work. Their backgrounds ranged from pre-literate farmers and traders to academics and senior-level government officials.

In each village, Putu and I consulted with the village head to select the *dusuns* with which we could work and live. In these communities, we worked through the *Kepala Dusuns* (community leaders) and invited about 20 women and 20 men of various ages, castes, classes, occupations and education levels to participate in a series of discussion groups. In Desa Monasa, we met with three women's and three men's *dusun* groups, and in Desa Pualang with two women's and two men's groups. Groups met at a mutually agreed time each week, for about two hours and we provided refreshments. Women often brought their younger children along and the activities were frequently watched by older children.

At higher government levels, Putu and I interviewed key informants and held round-table discussions about gender-differentiated community needs. These discussions also involved male and female representatives from the *dusun* groups who made their own presentations to the government officials.

Methods old and new

Of the many methods recognised by PRA practitioners, we used those listed in Table 14.1 for village-based research to gather data on broad social, economic, cultural, environmental and political contexts. They were also used with villagers and village officials who were not involved in the *dusun* discussion groups. The short questionnaire was used only with female participants at a PKK Cadre Training Course we attended in Denpasar, and the secondary data analysis was conducted using village statistics, government records and university libraries.

We used another six methods only in the *dusun*-level discussion groups to facilitate more specific and in-depth discussions of gender roles, relations and needs (adapted from Kindervatter, 1983) (see Table 14.2). The information generated and analysed in these groups was then reinterpreted in light of the information generated from the methods used in Table 14.1.

We found all these methods relatively easy to adapt and apply within a GAD framework. As GAD requires critical and reflexive analysis of the gendered nature of how a community is organized, we adapted the methods to focus on questions of gender roles, relationships, needs, and access to, and control over, and resources (natural and institutional). Throughout, we used three central questions to help integrate the participatory methods within a GAD framework:

(1) Who, according to their gender, was participating and how?
(2) Who, according to their gender, was being talked about and how?
(3) Who, according to their gender, was affected by questions 1 and 2 above, and how were they affected?

Using PRA within a GAD framework meant that we paid greater attention to issues of power and control when organizing our activities, for example ensuring separate women's and men's discussion groups, and in

Table 14.1: Methods used in village living and contextual research

o Review of secondary data
o Small-group conversations
o Living with people
o Key probes and futures possible
o Learning-by-doing
o Short questionnaire
o Non-participant observation
o Self-correcting notes and diaries
o Semi-structured interviews
o Village-level (and above) discussions

Table 14.2: Methods used in *dusun* discussion groups

1. Daily activity role games
Participants (S) compete to identify all their daily roles and activities and discuss their likes, dislikes and ambitions. They discuss the myths around the appropriateness of different gender characteristics, roles and relations.

2. Picture-card stories
Participants (S) use pre-drawn picture cards to make stories about family life and environmental issues. They discuss how these stories relate to their own lives and the lives of others, both now and in the past.

3. Village-development picture discussion
Participants (S) discuss the development needs depicted in a picture of an imaginary village and then compare these needs to their own.

4. Needs assessment and priority selection
Participants (S) assess the needs they had identified collectively in Method 3. Each participant then selects her/his three priority needs by placing a coloured sticker next to drawings of those needs. Women's and men's needs are compared and contrasted in a joint meeting.

5. Community resource maps
Participants (S in a joint meeting) identify and locate human, natural and institutional resources on maps of their *dusun*. They discuss together how these can be used and managed better to address some of the priority needs identified.

6. Planning hand game
Participants (J) play a memory game using the 'planning hand' where fingers represent Why, How, Who, When and What. They use this to develop a plan for meeting one of their priority needs.

Note: S = women and men separately; J = women and men together

analysing the information. The gender-specific discussion groups, daily-activity profiles, key probes, interviews, non-participant observation and learning-by-doing techniques proved especially useful for the gender analysis and associated action promoted by GAD.

Questioning gender and community myths with PRA

In Bali, most gender perceptions are rooted in a culturally defined acceptance of biological determinism combined with the religious ideology of Balinese Hinduism. Together they create a dichotomy of gender myths that generally identify women and men with opposing characteristics and qualities (Kindon, 1993; 1995b; Ruddick, 1986). These myths are most frequently promoted by people in positions of power such as men, high-caste or powerful women, and urban, middle-class Javanese and Balinese government officials. However, talking with village women and men revealed much contradictory evidence which called into question many commonly held beliefs about gender, and community relations and organization. I will focus here on the five most common myths that we encountered and the evidence provided which questioned their validity.

Myth 1: Women and men have merged or shared gender roles, and are valued equally

When looking specifically at gender roles, it became clear that there is a certain 'blurring' of such roles and activities in some areas of Balinese life such as childcare. Such a blurring, may, in fact, have contributed to the notions of gender parity expressed by Geertz and Geertz (1975) in their earlier research in Bali, and by government officials and village men in interviews with us. Later research has shown, however, that women and men generally operate in distinct spheres of social, cultural and economic activity according to their gender (Kindon, 1993; Miller and Branson, 1984; Ruddick, 1986). For example, women make essential daily religious offerings which men consider to be 'women's work' and beneath their dignity. Generally, as elsewhere, women are primarily responsible for reproductive activities within the family and community, while men are primarily responsible for productive activities in the public domain (see also Myth 2, below).

Overall, the status accorded to women and men and the roles they fulfil is intimately related to religious symbolism and the ideological construction of gender through Balinese Hinduism. Men are symbolically associated with 'high', 'right' and 'day' which are superior and positive symbols. Women, conversely, are associated with 'low', 'left' and 'night'. In terms of their qualities, men are perceived to be rational, intelligent, productive and active. Women are perceived as emotional, less intelligent, less productive and passive (Kindon, 1993; Ruddick, 1986).

Therefore, the terms used to describe women and men highlight the distinct gendering of status, value and spheres of social and economic activity in Bali. The PRA methods we used, in *dusun* discussion groups particularly, often side-stepped the rhetoric of gender parity that abounds, to reveal the reality of separate gender roles and hierarchical gender relations based on men's perceived superior status.

Myth 2: Women are economically unproductive and have spare time in which to earn an income and/or participate in GOI development programmes

When asked directly by government officials whether they work, the women with whom we interacted often answered that they were 'just' housewives and their husbands were the primary earners. The casual or low paid nature of many women's jobs, combined with the undervaluing of women's reproductive work in the home, means that women often colluded with men's perceptions of themselves as economically unproductive.

Yet our discussions about family income and decision-making related to household purchases and money management revealed that many women support their families through multiple part-time or seasonal jobs such as trading, sewing or agricultural/industrial labouring. A comparative analysis of women's and men's daily activity profiles, generated through participant observation and discussion groups, visually challenged this myth. These portrayed women as working six hours longer than men and engaging in a more varied combination of productive, reproductive and community-related activities. In fact, many men are more likely to be economically unproductive and have spare time in which to earn and/or participate in GOI programmes than women.

Myth 3: Women are too shy, uneducated and/or unmotivated to participate fully in GOI community development programmes, therefore men are the best representatives of their families' and communities' needs

By working in Balinese, rather than Bahasa Indonesia, and using visually-based PRA methods, the assumption that women are *malu* (shy, embarrassed, lacking in confidence) was called into question. Women participating in discussion groups were generally out-going, knowledgeable and enthusiastic participants, with many insights about the development needs of their communities. They were simply inhibited by the conventional form of public participation.

Not surprisingly, women also generated different information to men about their community priorities. While both groups identified practical gender needs related to income generation, health, clean water and transport, only women identified strategic gender needs. These related to women's interest in receiving training in water-systems maintenance and their desire for men to share household tasks equally with them.

In general, village men were not convinced that women had different ideas from theirs until the joint meetings, when drawings depicting women's and men's priorities were compared, and women representatives discussed their conclusions with the men. Seeing women speak for themselves, and voice different opinions, provided an alternative image to community-held beliefs that women lack knowledge and/or confidence, and that men are adequately informed about the needs and interests of women.

Myth 4: Women and men participate equally in community development and decisionmaking

Balinese life is renowned for its communal spirit and *gotong royong* (mutual self-help), manifested through religious ceremonies and community work. In particular, the *banjar* (smallest administrative unit of a traditional, as opposed to a government village)[6] has been promoted as an effective model of participatory development. However, women and men participate in *banjar* affairs in gender-specific ways. Women are particularly valued as mothers and makers of ceremonial offerings, while men are perceived as the family head and representative.

Women and men alike participate visibly in essential areas of community life and development. Yet the discussion groups, participant observation and semi-structured interviews suggested that the locus of power and authority for decisionmaking rests with men in *banjar* meetings. Whenever we suggested this to men, they often denied it and argued that women (as mothers and/or wives) had the real power to influence their decisions through household discussions. But the women commented that their husbands or sons did not talk with them about *banjar* matters, and complained that men made decisions without consultation, many of which required women's labour and/or financial contribution.

Within the *dinas* structure, women have formal access to decisionmaking and credit, primarily through their involvement in PKK. PKK is, however, often marginalized from mainstream development by male officials if decisions or programmes do not directly involve family health and prosperity issues. As such, women have access only to decisionmaking in areas which clearly relate to, and reinforce, their roles and status as mothers and wives.

In neither the *adat* nor *dinas* structures are women and men equal. Women are subordinated through patrilineal and patriarchal systems which recognize their positions in society only as mothers and wives in relation to men who are expected to speak for them.

Myth 5: Balinese community life is based upon unity, harmony and cooperation

By including the less-educated, worse-off and lower-caste women and men in the *dusun* discussion groups, considerable tension, and sometimes conflict, arose. Different interests emerged, and various groups or individuals struggled for dominance. Such conflict contrasted sharply with the well-documented image of Balinese people's gentle and harmonious relationships. Divisions and use of power were particularly evident along caste and class lines.

The picture stories constructed by women and men in separate groups, and personal life histories shared with us in private conversations, revealed less than harmonious or unified families. Struggles were common around unhappy arranged marriages, historical kinship feuds over land and property, as well as around more recent problems associated with male gambling, alcoholism and sexual infidelity. When issues from women's and men's picture stories were compared and interviewed, the men in particular became defensive and accused women of lying. They argued that they did not want the idyllic image of their communities and culture to be tainted as tourists would stop coming to the island and they would all suffer economically.

The effectiveness of PRA and GAD

We noticed that when PRA methods were able to generate challenging visual information (such as the daily activity profiles of women and men) and/or action-based evidence (such as women presenting their needs assessment to a joint group of men and women), women and men alike took the points made seriously. However, when the methods generated only verbal challenges to more powerful individuals (such as women expressing the need to reduce male alcoholism and gambling), the information was perceived as rumour or opinion and dismissed. Such observations led me to reflect critically on the ability of PRA and GAD not only to challenge gender myths, but to use the evidence generated to support more empowering and equitable change.

Empowering or exposing women?

Using PRA methods in separate groups of women and men facilitated the construction of a unique emancipatory learning environment for the women we interacted with in Bali.[7] For example, Made Disini, a middle-aged farmer from Desa Monasa commented that it was the first time in her community that women's knowledge and opinions had been valued equally alongside those of men. She had benefited from the group discussions as they provided a safe space in which she could share her experiences, ideas and concerns, and where she could learn more about her community with other women.

Another younger woman, Ibu Desak, felt confident enough after four meetings to represent the needs and ideas of her discussion group to a joint meeting with men. She created a role play, spontaneously, with the village head to show how women and men need to communicate more openly and to understand their differing perspectives, if effective and equitable community development is to take place.

Elsewhere, some men in Desa Pualang re-evaluated their opinions about women's knowledge and needs after listening to women's presentations about their group's discussions and needs. While they did not always agree with women, and were sometimes quite domineering, they acknowledged publicly that more joint meetings would help them to make more representative decisions for their community.

Thus, in a relatively short time, there was a greater overall recognition of the gendered nature of knowledge, experiences and priorities. In addition, some women had gained confidence through their participation and some men had re-evaluated their ability to represent adequately women's interests to higher levels. Although such changes are clearly important, deeper shifts in behaviour and power relations remained unchanged, especially regarding ongoing male dominance of decision-making in community development. The gender-based conflict in joint meetings highlighted particularly men's efforts to maintain control of decision-making fora and culturally legitimated positions of authority.

In addition, the conflict and tension present in same-sex discussion groups indicated that far more complex systems of community relations and power structures exist which extend beyond the boundaries of gender. Tensions exist also around the use of power and authority related to caste, education, wealth, age and kinship, making gender analysis and conflict management particularly difficult.

PRA and GAD are both based on the assumption that raising awareness about issues of power and difference is vital for positive change and empowerment to occur. However, such issues cannot always be discussed safely in the group-based fora favoured by PRA methods. Highlighting differences or revealing private concerns in public may increase risks for the individuals involved. Women, in particular, may become more vulnerable, if they are empowered to speak and or act through the combined use of PRA and GAD. Care needs also to be taken to ensure that the use of group fora, which emphasize group consensus, do not mask intra-group differences. For example, at one men's *dusun* discussion group meeting, a high caste (Brahmin) man was present in a group of mid- to lower-caste men. No one would openly challenge anything the Brahmin had to say for fear of losing face, and the group's consensus to follow such status-related codes of conduct masked considerable disagreement with this particular man's views. Overall, the combined use of PRA and GAD should include the anticipation and facilitation of conflict management, in ways that ensure protection for, and representation of, less-powerful groups and individuals.

Questioning gender myths only to create methodological myths?

The process of participatory analysis of gender roles, relations and needs raised questions about many long-held gender myths within the broader political and institutional government context. As a result, government officials at various administrative levels became interested in the potential of PRA to improve their data collection and involvement of women in development programmes.

In particular, group-based visual analysis of women's and men's daily activity profiles with senior male officials in round-table discussions raised questions about the assumed gendered division of labour and its implications for women's participation in development programmes. Presentations on gender-differentiated needs by village women and men also highlighted the need to include women in decision-making fora if programmes were to be equitable and efficient. After providing officials with up-to-date information, several of the women's needs were met over the period 1993–94. For example, in Desa Monasa, a household water supply was installed and the road was tar-sealed. In Desa Pualang, a *dusun* water supply system was repaired, and a leadership programme in family and environmental health was organized for women.

Thus, PRA's integration with GAD effectively and rapidly facilitated the collection, analysis and dissemination of information related to gender-differentiated roles, relations and needs at the village level. This allowed practical gender needs to be met with relative efficiency, to the benefit of women and men alike.

In contrast, strategic gender needs, such as water-systems maintenance training identified by women in Desa Pualang, were not met.[8] In Desa Monasa, strategic needs related to curbing male alcoholism, gambling and infidelity were not dealt with. Officials were reluctant to discuss or address issues which they perceived to challenge cultural and behavioural norms about the family, or matters related to technical extension.

It was worrying indeed to note that government officials were mainly interested to learn more about PRA as a 'quick-fix' solution to support cost-effective programme implementation involving women. They were less interested in the potential of a gendered PRA to help them shift their own attitudes, behaviour, methods and power in support of equitable change.

Such attitudes are not surprising given the current political climate and highly centralized and authoritarian nature of the Indonesian bureaucracy. Consequently, there is a risk that PRA will be adopted by government departments with little or no change in power relations, or attention to quality assurance and self-critical reflection. The results of mythologizing the capacity of methods to affect social change could be particularly detrimental for women and other less-powerful individuals, if this simply maintains the status quo of their relative subordination.

Rapidly (and therefore inappropriately) analysing slow processes of change?

Perhaps the most promising methodological outcome was the adaptation of PRA techniques for gender analysis. This facilitated non-threatening and rapid access into the subtle realms of power relations between women and men, using their own terms. Moreover, the methodological process supported and enhanced GAD's theoretical emphases upon critical analysis, the participation of women and men, and ongoing reflexivity (Humble, 1994; Chapter 3, this volume).

The integration of PRA and GAD is also problematic. While it was able to provide mechanisms through which women and men questioned and evaluated the impacts of gender myths upon their relationships and needs, it also raised discontent among some women about their position and the limited opportunities for strategic change that were open to them. In addition, the rapidity of PRA's implementation[9] did not allow for a detailed social analysis of change in Desa Monasa and Desa Pualang. We felt quite limited in our ability to assess the relative magnitude or frequency of gender issues and conflicts. More gender-informed participatory methods are needed which access and assess political information relating to the history and distribution of power and authority in families and communities (cf. Mosse, 1995).

For this approach to have been more effective, Putu and I required longer residence time in each community, and deeper investigations into the longevity and relative severity of the various community problems we encountered. In addition, by using more standard social-science techniques, we could have identified social networks within which local-conflict management or development actions could have taken place more effectively (Mosse, 1995).

Fundamentally, the current tendency of PRA to consist of a relatively rapid process of analysis and facilitation of action is problematic when aiming to integrate it with the slow attitudinal and behavioural change associated with GAD. It is one thing to ask people to analyse the opportunities and constraints in their natural environment and to plan to change their practices. It is another to ask them to evaluate the strengths and limitations of their culture, social organization and power relations, and to plan to change those (Humble, 1994).

Implications for future practice

From these experiences in Bali, the adaptation and application of PRA methods and principles to fit a framework of GAD offer exciting possibilities for raising questions about debilitating gender and community myths. However, their methodological compatibility is currently inadequate to facilitate empowering and equitable change. At present, the relatively rapid use of PRA is incompatible with the longer time period needed for deeper social analysis to understand unequal gender relations and conflict. While some methods can access valuable information on gender quite easily, these do not yet provide satisfactory techniques for the management of gender-related conflict, or for the understanding of what constitutes 'community' in any given location.

PRA's and GAD's limitations have methodological and institutional implications: methodologically, more techniques must be developed with which to manage gender conflict, and protect vulnerable individuals and groups as they become more empowered; institutionally, support is needed to facilitate the training of development practitioners to use such methods in an open and creative manner.

There is also a need to combine more standard, non-participatory social-science techniques with participatory methods, if gender analysis is to be understood within the context of broader community structures and relationships. Failure to understand the context within which gender is socially constructed and maintained could place undue emphasis on gender as the key variable of difference within a community. It effectively underestimates the influence of other variables, such as caste, wealth, age, kinship, ethnicity and education, in perpetuating inequity. As such, using PRA for GAD without a wider understanding of the community context could lead to narrow, or misguided change.

Aiming for such deeper understanding of the community context brings major personal and institutional implications. Development practitioners need a wider range of professional research, facilitation and management skills, as well as the ethical commitment to use them critically and reflexively to challenge subordination and oppression. More time, resources and political commitment are needed from the institutions within which we work to facilitate the longer-term involvement required to support women and men as they work through analysis, conflict and change with each other.

The adaptation and application of PRA to a GAD framework has great potential to support long-term and empowering change that is gender-informed and clear about what constitutes 'the community'. However, unless the methodological and institutional implications highlighted above are addressed, there is a risk that gender and community myths will be questioned or, more seriously deconstructed, without the necessary reconstruction of alternatives for those most needing support.

References

BSDP (1992) *Sustainable Development Strategy for Bali*, Research Paper No. 40, University of Waterloo: University Consortium on the Environment.

CCIC (Canadian Council for International Cooperation) (1990) *Two Halves Make a Whole: balancing gender relations in development*, Ottawa: MATCH International Centre and Comité Quebecois Femmes et Developpement.

Geertz, H. and C. Geertz (1975) *Kinship in Bali*, Chicago: University of Chicago Press.

Gupta, A. (1994) *Rural Water Supplies in Indonesia: a case study of effective and sustainable development from Tengipis, Bali*, Student Paper No. 23, University Consortium on the Environment: University of Waterloo.

Humble, M. (1994) *Implementing Gender and Development Theory: assessing participatory rural appraisal as a GAD technique*, MA dissertation, Carleton University: Department of Political Science.

Kindervatter, S. (1983) *Women Working Together for Personal, Economic and Community Development*, Washington: Overseas Education Fund.

Kindon, S. (1993) *From Tea Makers to Decision Makers: applying participatory rural appraisal to gender and development in rural Bali, Indonesia*, Student Paper No. 16, University of Waterloo: University Consortium on the Environment.

Kindon, S. (1995a) 'Dynamics of Difference: exploring empowerment methodologies with women and men in Bali', *New Zealand Geographer*, 51(1): 10–12.

Kindon, S. (1995b) 'Balinese Gender Relations and the State: national transformation of a local system?' in J. DeBernardi, G. Forth and S. Niessen (eds) *Managing Change in Southeast Asia: local transformations, global connections*, CCSEAS XXI, Quality Color Press Inc: University of Alberta.

Mies, M. (1980) *Towards a Methodology of Women's Studies*, The Hague: Institute of Social Studies.

Miller, D. and Branson, J. (1984) *Pollution in Paradise: Hinduism and the subordination of women in Bali*, paper presented for the Asian Studies Association of Australia Fifth National conference, University of Adelaide, 13–18 May.

Moser, C. (1989) 'Gender Planning in the Third World: meeting practical and strategic gender needs, *World Development*, 17(11): 1799–825.

Mosse, D. (1995) 'Social Analysis in Participatory Rural Development', *PLA Notes* 24, London: IIED, pp 27–33.

Ruddick, A. (1986) *Charmed Lives: illness, healing, power and gender in a Balinese village*, PhD dissertation, Brown University: Department of Anthropology.

Smyth, I. (1992) *A Critical Look at the Indonesian Government's Policies for Women*, paper written for Indonesia Day, The Hague: Institute of Social Studies.

Suryakusuma, J. (1991) 'State Ibuism: the social construction of womanhood in the Indonesian new order, *New Asian Visions*, 6(2): 46–71.

UPW (1989) *The Changing Role of Women with Special Emphasis on their Economic Role: country report of Indonesia*, Jakarta: Office of the Minister of State for the Role of Women, Republic of Indonesia.

15

Video, Gender and Participatory Development

MARIA PROTZ

There is a popular belief that video offers many advantages as a communication medium and extension tool for sustainable rural development. And indeed, video does offer several benefits over other media. In the past 20 years or so of international rural development, it has been used extensively and has become increasingly popular (China and Longmead, 1985; Fabel, 1995; FAO, 1991; Fraser, 1980; Stuart, 1991; Thede and Ambrosi, 1991).

As with any technology, however, video must be used with awareness if it is to be an effective mechanism for long-term and equitable development. Otherwise it risks becoming a novelty for entertainment value only. If video is used in rural communities without assessing its usefulness and potential effectiveness for the expected purpose, it may, as Litwin (1984) has noted, cause far more harm than good.

Careful consideration of the potential pitfalls of video is particularly important when it is to be used for participatory development. Participatory development processes, such as those based on participatory rural appraisal (PRA), are concerned with the identification of problems and prioritization of solutions. This includes identifying, and possibly documenting, local knowledge and resources to identify priority solutions. The methods used in this process are often highly visual and oral, being based on diagrams, writing and discussions. Video offers further possibilities, particularly where literacy might limit the participation of some community members. It can only live up to this potential, however, if the implications of its use, particularly those concerning gender, are recognized and respected.

Chapter 15 reflects on a gender-sensitive use of video for participatory development. Following a definition of 'participatory video', I describe some of the more gender-neutral attributes of the medium. The chapter then discusses a Jamaican pilot project on communication, *Mekweseh*, which has used participatory video for soil-nutrient technology development with rural women.[1] I also explore other gender-related factors by drawing on other experiences in Jamaica and from Peru, India and St. Lucia. These suggest an initial set of considerations for those using or contemplating the use of video for participatory development.

Defining participatory video

As with 'participatory' work in general, the term 'participatory video' has been used to refer to very diverse experiences. These vary greatly in the extent to which local people are involved in the video production process.

There is, in fact, a continuum of experiences that could be defined as 'participatory video' (Protz, 1991).

The continuum is defined by local control. To live up to its claim of 'for the people, by the people' participatory video seeks community control of all decision-making involved in the production process. This process should also help develop analytical and negotiation skills among the participants.[2] It should include developing an awareness by the group of its indigenous knowledge and how this contributes to informing its decisions.

If these distinguishing features are accepted, then one end of the continuum relates to video experiences which see local people trained in video production skills. They research, shoot, edit and use their own video reports. The other end of the continuum includes experiences which give people final authority over what is to be said and shown but it does not involve them in any of the technological aspects of video production. Experiences with less participation of local people, such as documentaries, might be called 'alternative video' but cannot be considered 'participatory video'.

The appropriateness of one approach over another will depend on many factors. For instance, training local people in video-production skills is time-consuming and often expensive, both of which may preclude that approach. In some cases, it may also disrupt or detract from the main local development objective. For other purposes, however, it may be absolutely essential to develop these video skills in community members.

To understand better when video may be effective, it is important to consider the general advantages (see Box 15.1) and disadvantages of it as a medium.

The disadvantages of video

Despite video's advantages as a communication medium, it has significant drawbacks. These relate to the technology and to its association with entertainment and wealth. Video is an electricity-dependent technology. This is not always readily available in rural areas. Its appropriateness as a communication tool is often constrained due to this fact alone. However, recent advances in solar-powered equipment are changing this constraint, increasing its potential value and appropriateness.

Another technical drawback is the sensitivity of the equipment. Although video technology is becoming more compact and durable, it suffers under extreme temperatures. It is vulnerable to dusty or humid conditions and is sensitive to bumpy roads. Most rural settings entail one or more such conditions, and damage to equipment is always a risk.

Assuming that these drawbacks are overcome, then other disadvantages must also be considered. In most parts of the world, video is still associated with entertainment rather than with education. Viewers' expectations may, therefore, differ from those of development professionals, provoking two opposite effects. First, it may mean that the interest of the audience needs to be stimulated by including an entertaining dimension, such as through songs or creative framing,[3] etc. This does not have to detract from the video may mean that viewers do not take it seriously, but communities can learn to deal with video as a learning medium. In some cases, several videos

---

Box 15.1: Advantages of video

○ Unlike still photography or drawings, video can communicate movement. It is therefore a useful medium when it is necessary to show motion or changes over time.

○ Video is an audio-visual medium and can overcome literacy-related problems.

○ The electronic nature of video allows tapes to be used repeatedly, if needed.

○ Unlike film, processing is unnecessary and the video images can be played back immediately (although editing is often desirable).

○ Viewers can assess the credibility of persons in the video, since emotion and body language of the people filmed are clearly visible.

○ Unlike print, audio-visual testimonies on video can record indigenous knowledge. This can raise the status of that knowledge and leave no doubt as to the ownership of the knowledge and ideas presented.

○ Recent video technology is highly compact and relatively inexpensive, making it easier, more convenient and less conspicuous to use than previously.

○ Even surprisingly remote villages have access to video technology. People are becoming increasingly accustomed to moving images, thus reducing its reputation as a 'foreign' medium.

○ Video can be used alongside other media, such as drama or song and dance, and often more effectively. Sometimes, as in Jamaica, drama is far more successful at mobilizing people and sparking interest in a subject, while video is better at relaying technical information once interest exists.

○ When video is placed in the hands of local people for production of their own reports, the energy and enthusiasm that comes from handling such 'high-tech' equipment and producing what is considered a 'sophisticated' record can greatly motivate local development initiatives.

---

have been screened, some for entertainment and others for educational purposes, over a period of time before beginning to use video in its empowerment capacity.

A related constraint is determined by visual syntax. Viewer comprehension depends on the level of visual exposure within the community and their experience with video syntax. Although it is widely believed that 'seeing is believing', video is still subject to constraints related to visual literacy and cultural differences in visual syntax or style. A European or North American approach to video production may not be appropriate for audiences elsewhere, as visual styles and techniques differ. For example, different types and lengths of shots in a certain sequence are commonly used in western film to indicate a transition in time, such as from day to night, travel over distances, or 'before and after' shots. This represents a type of visual shorthand which avoids the need to show all the movement. However, western visual syntax is not necessarily natural, just like reading from left to right is not the practice in China or Japan (cf. Bellman and Jules-Rosette, 1977). People in non-western cultures may not understand or accept what is happening. Understanding a culture's own visual syntax is important for effective communication.

Another drawback that depends on people's exposure to video is related to the technical quality of images. Many people now expect considerable technical sophistication of all video productions, even those which are the result of participatory video efforts. Those that are rougher may lose in credibility, and achieving high technical quality in a participatory process is a challenge indeed!

Finally, despite decreasing prices, video is still too expensive for the vast majority of rural households. Hence it is commonly viewed as a high-status or 'rich' medium. This status is, in turn, bestowed on those featured on the videotape and those involved in the production process. While this can have positive effects, it can also cause jealousy and conflicts which can jeopardize the goals of participatory development. It is this aspect of video which has the greatest gender-related implications.

The transformatory potential of video

Given these strengths and limitations of video, then what is its potential to realize the goals of participatory development? Two main features of video have this potential: its capacity to show motion and change, and the portrayal of real people and actual locations. These features allow video to be used in four unique ways, each with gender-related issues that will be discussed later: (i) to document problems and priorities; (ii) to verify the process; (iii) to complement other methodologies; and (iv) to communicate between different knowledge systems.

Documenting problems and priorities

Just as some PRA methods can help elicit problems, sometimes in order of priority, so can video. Either the drawings or the actual objects and locations can be videotaped directly, and in the order of priority decided on by local people. Video may offer additional advantages. For example, video maps of communities can show significant local features, such as schools, places of worship, bore holes and collective gardens. Actual road conditions and slopes can be shown, as can soil conditions and colour, crop densities, pests and agricultural inputs.

In one Jamaican community, we asked men and women separately to videotape their agricultural problems, in order of decreasing importance. The two responses were very different. The women tended to identify and show that the distance between home and plots greatly impeded their ability to combine farm work and domestic responsibilities. Women with farms further away had less time to tend their fields, and greater difficulty and more expense in marketing crops. Men, by contrast, videotaped pest

problems and plant diseases as priorities. With fewer domestic responsibilities, they have more time to devote to their farm work.

If local video cassette-recorder playback facilities exist or can be organized in the community, then rough edits can be carried out and copies made
immediately for local use. These can be used to document the development
process, alongside whatever is recorded on paper. Less ideal but also possible is editing and making copies outside the community to be returned at a
later date. This can work only if those editing the video are trusted by the
community.

Verifying the participatory process

One of the hottest debates about participatory development revolves
around the concern that many approaches can be just as traditional as
research methods, despite claims to the contrary (Richards, 1995). Video
can be used to verify local findings as well as to assess how 'participatory' a
session may have been. The taped sessions can be played back in order to
assess group dynamics and see where unconscious domination or manipulation may have occurred. Facilitators and participants alike can be involved in a critical review of videotapes and use it to suggest
improvements.

Developing such video records at the beginning of a development intervention can help when reviewing and evaluating projects later on. Besides
checking progress, video offers people the opportunity to review themselves
critically, analysing what they were thinking and saying at various moments.
This is essential in long-term development efforts as people change their
minds and goals over time as a result of external factors or their participation
in the process. As people gain access to more information through a project
or learn from trying various solutions, they may need to revise decisions
made early on. Video reports made at the onset of a project can allow people
to compare what they expected would happen with reality.

Complementing other methodologies

Two experiences highlight how video can be used to great advantage in
combination with a survey approach and with drama.

First in our SNAP experience, a traditional baseline survey was mandatory at the beginning of the project. However, rather than conduct a more
conventional quantitative study, we (a small team of three) chose a more
qualitative approach, and videotaped as many of the interviews as possible.
The responses were then transcribed, coded and analysed using conventional methods. The process yielded several shorter video reports on key
themes that could be played back to all the respondents involved in the
research for further discussion.

This technique was not participatory as respondents did not help develop
the questionnaire or edit the short video reports. However, the experience
had several advantages that have enhanced other participatory project
activities:

o Unlike with most questionnaires, where responses are simply ticked or written, the interviewers were able to use the video to assess how their interviewing skills might have introduced biases and influences responses. In many cases, the responses that would have been recorded on the questionnaire were changed as a result of this video review process. This would have been impossible had only a questionnaire been used.

o Most respondents clearly enjoyed being interviewed on video. These interviews were initiated only after three months of close work and collaboration with the communities in which we worked on the women's farms, did laundry together and shared other tasks. This allowed for a certain level of trust and a personal relationship to develop. When the time came to conduct the baseline interviews, the women were keen to share their ideas as they felt that their opinions would be taken seriously.

o The videotaped interviews allowed a more objective interpretation of people's emotions. For instance, one of the questions dealt with the quality of extension services provided to the women farmers in the SNAP area. One way to deal with it is to use the statistics to show that only 6 per cent of the women were satisfied. The video reports, however, show exactly how the women felt – dissatisfied, disgruntled or downright irate! So besides numeric data, video investigations can record people's emotions about the choices they make and can carry far more significance that simple percentages. It is one thing to read that 90 per cent of women in a community do not know the name of their extension officer. It quite is another to see video testimony, one woman after another, saying exactly the same thing!

o By making shorter video reports, participants can review their own statements and verify the validity of what they said. Sometimes what we say in private is not what we would say in a group situation, and video reports of this nature can help clarify these points. For instance, when interviewed individually, women may respond differently than if debating the same question in a group video-interview. By comparing individual video testimonies with a group discussion, a community facilitator may understand better who may be influencing whom, who dominates and who stays quiet, and why. It may also indicate that what people want as individuals may not be what they feel is best for the community as a whole.

A second example highlights how other participatory methods can be used to verify video-based results. One issue we were trying to understand in SNAP was how the quality of gender relationships within the small farm family affects agriculture-related decision-making. Our video reports indicated that decision-making is largely held jointly within the home. But this seemed to contradict previous findings.

To check this, the project undertook a drama-based investigation with a community cultural group. The drama showed three sisters, all farmers, in a different relationship: an abandoned mother, one with an abusive husband, and the third with a supportive spouse. A comedy approach meant that potentially difficult gender-related issues could be raised without insulting anyone directly.

The play was a huge success in the three communities where it was shown. People were so excited about what it had to say that any critical discussion afterwards was impossible. Women's responses were: *'Dis no play! No drama dis! Dis real life! Dis my life a dat in dere.'*[4] Some women said later: *'So now me a know what a dis here project is about now!'* Fortunately each performance of the play was videotaped. We returned to the communities a week later and watched the video again. We stopped it, rewound it, and discussed those moments of the play that sparked the most interest. Much of the initial excitement had abated and we were able to analyse the contents of the play together. A second discussion with women only allowed us to focus on issues specifically of concern to them.

The discussion revealed several interesting issues. For one, the women were able to formulate alternative solutions to those chosen by the women in the drama. The discussions highlighted that there is much less joint decisionmaking than had been reported in the video interviews. Most of the women identified closely with the first two sisters, citing the third one as their ideal. Drama had exposed the deeper reality that women experienced. The process also offered women and men the chance to look at the quality of their own relationships without singling anyone out. Since then, women and men have referred often to the play, and some of the issues have been dealt with at other moments in more appropriate ways.

Communicating between indigenous and scientific knowledge

Video has also been used in Mekweseh's SNAP project to bring indigenous and scientific knowledge together for the design of appropriate soil-fertility technologies for rural households. Jiggins (1988) strongly recommends 'the need to develop methodologies for mutual communication of key concepts across the boundaries of researchers' and female producers' distinct knowledge systems' (pp. 52–3). Video is most helpful precisely at this juncture. It can be used to document women's indigenous knowledge about farming. It can then present this knowledge in an easily accessible manner to other farmers, and be used alongside the views of extension agents, researchers, and planners.

We used video for this purpose in two ways:

(1) The first started after the baseline survey and drama investigation. We developed a 'rough cut' video list of low-cost, low-labour soil-conservation and soil-fertility technologies for project participants to try on their own farms. Each community received several copies of the tape to review at their leisure (local playback facilities were available). One hundred and three women signed up to assess and comment on the suggested technologies. Together they discarded several and improved others using their own experiences.

(2) Several participants also received basic video training. They learned to conduct interviews and to record their own farming practices. As a result, a few sound, indigenous soil-fertility practices were documented and produced as short programmes for the benefit of other farmers'

experimentation. One of these was based on the use of *saila* (*clusia flava*), discovered by a woman to improve soil fertility and enhance crop development on her farm. Her authorship is undisputed as she is on tape discussing the findings. The project submitted the plant to chemical tests, which confirmed high nitrogen contents, thus providing scientific proof of her many years of experience.

SNAP is finalizing the video which documents these indigenous discoveries and women's assessments of the projects proposing soil-fertility technologies. The final video will involve those who were trained in video production. The end product will be broadcast on Jamaican TV and made available to other farmers throughout the island, thereby benefiting those not even directly involved in the work.

Gender and the camera

These examples show how gender is part and parcel of people's representation of their environment as expressed through video. But despite these potential benefits, video can be counterproductive if certain gender-related issues are not considered. Three issues are particularly significant:

(i)   the personal gender identities of those involved;
(ii)   household gender relations; and
(iii) gender relations within the community and society at large.

Gender identity

Gender identity, or how people define themselves as 'women' and 'men', has implications for the use of different media in rural development. Because gender identity is so often closely tied to self-esteem and personal aspirations, it is important to consider how a mediated participatory experience may influence these definitions of self.

In the Caribbean, for instance, many rural women are farmers in their own right, or farm in partnership with male household members for household economic survival. Yet when interviewed, few women call themselves farmers, defining themselves instead as 'housewives' (French, 1988). Farming is considered to be a masculine activity and a low-status one at that, yet when women begin to list their daily work, it is clear that many of their tasks are related to agriculture.

In some circles, including among academics and in official statistics, women's definition of themselves as housewives rather than farmers has been interpreted as a devaluation by women of their agricultural role. But this is not always the case. In the Caribbean, being a rural woman and a housewife means being a mother and taking care of all responsibilities associated with family life. Agricultural work is considered an extension of this private domain, whereas 'farming' in the masculine sense is considered primarily as public work for an eventual cash income. Women are, of course, involved in farming for income generation and are often head of the household. Yet this role is subsumed in the larger role of 'housewife', which has a more comprehensive meaning than 'farmer'. When asked by interviewers to choose a single definition to describe their work, it is of no surprise, then, that rural women choose housewife instead of farmer.

This does not pose a problem to their own self-identity, but it does create difficulties for official statistics, planners and academics who may not assign the same meaning to the term housewife, with all its complexities, as rural women do. In using video, especially with empowerment objectives, the meaning that rural women attach to their own roles must be addressed in ways that make sense for the women.

For example, during a workshop on participatory photography with 30 rural women, the complexity of gender identity became clear in an exercise that critiqued mainstream media and its neglect of rural women (Protz and Cebotarev, 1993). The exercise started with participants describing a 'typical day in the life of a rural woman', and listing the range of tasks. Then newspaper pictures were perused in search of images to illustrate those tasks. Not surprisingly, no pictures were found. Images were of professional urban women, beauty queens, fashion models, or were considered to be offensive and vulgar portrayals showing half-naked women or parts of female bodies. The group concluded that rural women were invisible within mainstream media.

Then one participant stated that, while the slog and grind of rural women's lives may be invisible, rural women were just as beautiful as the fashion models and beauty queens and were therefore not excluded after all. The others agreed with her. So while the daily routine exercise had managed to convey the harsher realities of the women's lives, it was not a complete portrayal of women's self-image as it did not include their aspirations.

As with photographs, video can sometimes reflect an all too grim reality, which may hinder a participatory process (see Box 15.2). For instance, efforts to educate against domestic violence that use posters, photographs or videos that actually show or illustrate acts of violence against women may have the unintended reverse effect of sensationalizing and sanctioning such behaviour. If such images are tolerated by the media, men may get the message that it is okay to hit women and women get the message that they have to accept it. How men and women's reality is engendered,

---

Box 15.2: Portraying reality or aspirations?

In an urban health education project in Peru, professional communicators were involved in producing visual materials to encourage basic hygiene such as washing hands before meals (Robson, 1991). A series of posters was developed, showing the neighbourhood in all its shades of dirt and glory. When the programme pretested the material in the community, the posters were totally revised. Homes were made prettier, with nice paint, flowers outside and clean, well-dressed children. These posters were considered more appropriate as they reflected local aspirations, instead of reinforcing the reality of poverty of which no community member needed reminding.

therefore has important implications for the use of visual media.

The extent to which the video may have to portray goals and aspirations, rather than realities, will also be influenced by the anticipated audience. Are women only going to view the video, or will their families, or the wider community also be watching, or even the entire nation?

In the Mekweseh experience, we fully expect gender aspirations to become an issue during the final taping of the SNAP video. To date, women have not felt uncomfortable being taped and shown as they are during training sessions. In their old clothes, dusted in soil after farm activities, the women knew that these tapes were for local consumption only. The final version will no doubt see women wanting their hair done and wearing their best clothes, even if they are speaking about the merits of cow manure for composting! This will require some clear discussions and careful negotiation. The desire to look one's best will need to be balanced with the need to make the video credible for other Jamaican audiences. The women's identities as farmers must be indisputable on camera.

Video, more than photography or drawings, reflects differences between the reality and aspirations of gender identities. People are not a static image on video. They move and speak, seeing and hearing themselves in action. When recording realities that could challenge gender identity and self-esteem, this must be dealt with sensitively. A programme dealing with participatory video production may need to include opportunities to discuss issues related to gender identities, particularly when documenting gender differences in indigenous knowledge.

Gender relations in the household

Using video to record women's work and knowledge may require dealing with conflicts related to household gender relations. There are many examples where men have had great difficulty accepting that the women in their lives are involved in video production. In some cases, this may be caused by religious or cultural taboos that prohibit women from showing their faces. In other cases, it is simply because women are not considered to have valuable opinions or ideas. Men may, therefore, feel that it is a waste of time and money.

Akhila Ghosh (1986) of CENDIT (Centre for Development of Instructional Technology) reports one comment from a male observer when using video with women in India: 'They are like a herd of cattle. What do you want to do, going about asking them questions? They don't know anything.' Elsewhere, CENDIT encountered outright hostility from men who felt threatened by the video production that their wives were involved with. Some women were beaten and not allowed to participate. The idea that women were important enough to be on video was beyond the comprehension of some of these men. What CENDIT also found was that women continued to participate, despite the abuse. They felt that speaking out on video and the subsequent status improvement was worth the pain at home.

Although this type of conflict will not always happen, it is important to be prepared for it. If it does occur, one should reconsider whether or not video is still the most appropriate or effective medium. If mechanisms to deal safely with such conflict cannot be implemented, then other, less personal, media may be more effective. One possible mechanism is to use video at a community-level, giving all a chance to familiarize themselves with this medium. Men's activities can also be documented to pave the way for working with video with women. Discussing concerns that the men might have about the involvement of women may also dissipate negative reactions.

Gender relations in the community

Conflicts similar to those at the household level may also surface at the community level. Video may reflect local power differences that some would prefer to keep below the surface.

Video was used in St Lucia by a group of rural women to improve local sanitation. The women were part of the community-sanitation committee in a community development project. Twice a month, they swept the streets and picked up garbage in an effort to keep the community clean. As a result, their community had won the Beautiful Village award three years running. The video project aimed to make a video to encourage the community to pick up its own litter. It was part of a six-month research project focusing on participatory communication with the whole community (Protz, 1987). Of the original group, only 12 women ended up being involved with planning, shooting and editing the video.

When it was time to initiate a discussion about rural sanitation, several obstacles arose. Although the video was a result of the efforts of 12 dedicated women, several community members felt these particular women were not important enough to be on video, this despite everyone having been invited to participate in the experience early on! The critics felt other community members were more important and that the video should be redone.

The strongest critic, who had the most difficulty with the women's success, was herself a woman. She was a strong community leader and, as the main spokesperson, was used to receiving most of the attention from outsiders who came to review the community's achievements. Despite knowing about the video, the shift of attention to other women posed a political problem for her. She was so disturbed by it that she actively sabotaged the screening of the video five times. When it was finally shown on the sixth occasion, no other community members spoke except her and she had nothing but negative things to say.

However, the women who had been involved in the video production process had gained self-confidence. They were undaunted by her reaction and recognized it as an expression of jealousy. When I asked them afterwards how her response made them feel about the video, they replied that although it might not help people clean up better, everyone now knew about their work and recognized that it was important for the community's well-being. If the video could stir up so much emotion, it had to be important! This gave them tremendous satisfaction and pride. The women also felt confident that they could and would handle this conflict in their own way and in their own time.

Conclusion

These examples show the tremendous scope for using video in participatory development.[5] It also highlights that, as with other methodologies and technologies, video is not gender-neutral. But while video can be as empowering or manipulative as other participatory approaches, it can rarely be as rapid. It involves too many stages of planning, shooting, editing and use to deal with a development process quickly.

If video is to make a positive contribution to development, consideration must be given to the potential impact that this media may have on existing gender relations and engendered perceptions of self and community. The effective and appropriate use of video will require supporting mechanisms to deal with some of the confrontations and conflicts that may arise.

References

Bellman, Beryl and Bennetta Jules-Rosette (1977) *A Paradigm for Looking: cross-cultural research with visual media*, New Jersey: Ablex Publishing Corporation.

China, Richard and Peter Longmead (1985) 'Using Video to Increase Farm Output,' *International Agricultural Development*, May/June.

Fabel, Elizabeth (1995) 'Video 1: developing a community project', in Rachel Slocum, Lori Wichart, Dianne Rocheleau and Barbara Thomas-Slayter (eds) *Power, Process and Participation: tools for change*, London: Intermediate Technology Publications.

FAO (1991) 'Using Video in the Field: guidelines for the use of video communication technology within FAO field projects', Development Support Communication Branch, Information Division, Rome: FAO.

Fraser, Colin (1980) 'Video in the Field – a novel approach to farming training', *Educational Broadcasting International*, September.

French, Joan (1988) *Women in Caribbean Agriculture Research*, Trinidad: Action Project Caribbean Association for Feminist Research and Action.

Ghosh, Akhila (1986) 'Demystifying Media with Rural Women,' in Akhila Ghosh, *Powerful Images: a women's guide to audiovisual resources*, Rome: Isis International.

Jiggins, Janice (1988) 'Problems of Understanding and Communication at the Interface of Knowledge Systems', in Susan Poats, Marianne Schmink and Anita Spring (eds) *Gender Issues in Farming Systems Research and Extension*, Boulder, Colarado: Westview Special Studies in Agriculture Science and Policy.

Jumani, Jyoti (1985) *Coordinating Video Sewa – A Personal Account*, Ahmedabad, India: Self-Employed Women's Association.

Litwin, Howard (1984) 'Video Work in Community Organization: boon or boondoggle?' *Community Development Journal*, Vol. 19, No. 3, Oxford University Press, July.

Protz, Maria (1987) *Visual Education Media for Rural Development: a comparison of professional and participatory materials in St Lucia*, unpublished MA thesis, University of Rural Planning and Development, University of Guelph, Canada.

Protz, Maria (1991) *Seeing and Showing Ourselves: a guide to using small-format videotape as a participatory tool for development*, New Delhi: CENDIT.

Protz, Maria (1991) 'Distinguishing between Alternative and Participatory Modes of Video Production', in Nancy Thede and Alain Ambrosi (eds) *Video the Changing World*, Montreal: Black Rose Books.

Protz, Maria and Eleanora Cebotarev (1993) *Seeing and Showing Ourselves in Print: a training module for participatory visual material production with rural women*, Ontario: University of Guelph.

Richards, Paul (1995) 'Participatory Rural Appraisal: a quick and dirty critique,' *PLA Notes* No. 24: 13–16.

Robson, Emma (1991) *Sketching a Better Life in Urban Peru*, UNDP Special Report, Division of Information, New York: UNDP, pp. 9–11.

Stuart, Sara (1989) 'Access to Media: placing video in the hands of the people,' *Media Development*, No. 4.

Stuart, Sara (1991) 'Training and Organisation for Change in India: video as a tool of the self-employed women's association, in Aruna Rao (ed.), *Women's Studies International: Nairobi and beyond*, New York: The Feminist Press, pp. 75–81.

Thede, Nancy and Alain Ambrosi (eds) (1991) *Video Changing the World*, Montreal: Black Rose Books.

16

Gendered Landscapes, Gendered Lives in Zambrana-Chacuey, Dominican Republic

DIANNE ROCHELEAU, LAURIE ROSS, JULIO MORROBEL
and RICARDO HERNANDEZ

In 1992–93 we[1] studied the past, present and potential effects of the Forest Enterprise Project on the land and people of Zambrana-Chacuey in the Dominican Republic. Timber had been introduced as a cash crop into the hilly patchwork of farms and forests in the region. Our research sought to understand the gendered changes[2] this had brought to local ecologies and economies. Together with the leaders and membership of the Rural Federation of Zambrana-Chacuey and the staff of ENDA-Caribe (an international NGO), we described the gendered knowledge, labour, space and resources in this frontier region that is home to over 10 000 people. Most inhabitants are smallholder farmers (with some traders and wage labourers) raising cocoa, coffee, tobacco, root crops and, most recently, timber.

Chapter 16 discusses our research methodology in that process, which mixed recent innovations in feminist ethnography and participatory mapping (Rocheleau, 1995; Slocum et al, 1995; Thomas-Slayter et al, 1993; Thomas-Slayter and Rocheleau, 1995) with the strengths of formal surveys over a four-month period. In particular, the combination of life histories, landscape mapping and a formal survey helped us formulate more comprehensive versions of local changes. We documented positive and negative effects of the forestry initiative on distinct social groups, based on gender, class, location and occupation. This enabled us to suggest changes in organization, technologies and tenure arrangements that would serve the interests of women and of near-landless households better (Rocheleau and Ross, 1995; Rocheleau et al., 1996).

The forest enterprise project

The federation has collaborated with ENDA-Caribe for over ten years in a forestry initiative involving nearly 90 per cent of the federation membership.[3] As of 1992 there were 87 community nurseries and more than 300 household nurseries for timber and fruit trees. *Acacia mangium* trees (from one tree to hundreds) were established on the farms of more than 85 per cent of the federation members (800 000 timber trees and 40 000 fruit trees on farms, and 250 000 seedlings in nurseries). At the time of our research, many of the acacia trees planted at the outset of the project were ready for harvesting and milling. Special accords between ENDA and the forestry service allowed the farmers to harvest the trees they had planted and permitted the newly formed Wood Producers' Association (WPA) to transport, process and market *A.mangium*. Seeing the widespread local adoption of acacia as a cash crop, ENDA and the WPA had constructed a cooperative sawmill in 1993.

The research methodology

To examine the successes and the failures of the forestry initiative, the study team traced the introduction of tree species and land use practices by the federation and ENDA to the household economies of its members. We focused on gendered interests in the introduction of new timber trees and their effect on livelihood systems and landscape patterns. To reveal the diversity of smallholders and the complexity of their livelihood strategies and landscapes, we also reviewed experiences of people in distinct classes. We used stories and maps of gendered space, resources, labour and knowledge to identify alternatives for smallholder forestry and agricultural production. With this approach we sought to make visible the many people, plants, and places that are engulfed by general statistics and the district maps of 'forestry-as-usual' (Rocheleau and Ross, 1995).

The cornerstones of our field study were personal life histories and landscape maps, combined with a questionnaire survey (see Box 16.1). The research led us to most of the 30 communities in the federation and to 31 of the 60 member associations.

Box 16.1: Data collection activities

- o Attendance at formal meetings
- o Walking and mapping tours of fields and forests
- o Group interviews
- o Focus groups
- o Key-informant interviews
- o Household histories, labour calendars and mapping exercises
- o Oral histories of communities, rural organizations and environmental change
- o Personal life histories
- o A formal questionnaire survey from a stratified random sample of the adult members of the federation.

We experimented with various combinations of oral history, personal life histories and gendered resource mapping. In some cases we had several long discussions with individuals about their lives. By creating an informal yet accurate colour sketch of their farm landscapes, joint mapping exercises became a surrogate for participant observation. This process also helped establish a shared visual and verbal vocabulary for further discussion of plants, livestock, landscape features and land use units.

Initial interviews focused on introducing ourselves and our research objectives. Later discussions dealt with many issues: local and personal histories, land use changes, previous and current practices in forestry and tree planting, and people's participation in projects. We also asked about the gender division of land, labour, knowledge, organization and decision-making in different domains of land use. The influence of family composition, land tenure, age and source of income on forestry practices and project participation was another research theme. We sought information and opinions about tree species, land use practices, project function and structure, and the role of ENDA, the federation and the Wood Producers' Association. Finally, we solicited suggestions for their future on the land.

Not all these topics were explored using the same methods. Specific methods leant themselves better to some topics than others. During this research process, we noted the complementarity of three methods in particular: life histories, landscape mapping, and the survey. Life stories in particular clarified for us the different influences of gender, life cycle and household differences based on class, family composition and occupation on women and men. Maps gave us a sense of local landscape features and their gendered uses and vocabulary. The survey tested, and confirmed, our findings. It also provided statistical validity to our research and revealed some social groups and important ecological information that we had missed previously.

The wealth of life histories

Early on in our group interviews, we began to identify men and women whose life experiences might shed light on past, present and future resource management and land use practices in the region. Besides the men leaders of the federation, the (mostly male) members of the affiliated WPA and male participants in the Forest Enterprise Project, we sought women leaders and heads of households. These women had challenged gendered norms of labour and authority, and had knowledge and contacts in men's and women's domains alike. Also important to understand the variety of situations that shape women's interests in land use change, were women who identified themselves as 'housewives'.

Several women and men recounted their lives to us in detail. Their own analysis of their life course and their future aspirations for themselves and their children allowed us to understand better the context for the many decisions made by individuals, households and organizations about the diverse dimensions of rural land use and resource management. These life stories helped explain how people's daily routines are linked to the community's economic and ecological well-being and how rural life is connected with national policies.

Through the life histories we learned about several contemporary processes and trends. One of the most dramatic insights was a deeper understanding of the gender division of labour, land and authority and its relevance to land use change and farm forestry. The stories of several women leaders in the federation clarified the linkages between herbal medicine and midwifery, religious leadership and political authority for women. Leadership status in women's established domains of authority were, it appeared, transferred and recognised within the federation hierarchy and in the larger community. This made it possible for some women to participate in the Forestry Enterprise Project, despite a strong bias toward male involvement in the formal scheme.

Not surprisingly, the division of labour at household level and regional constructs of gender identity also shape women's work in forestry. Unlike in other regions, the gender division of labour in Zambrana-Chacuey is flexible. It leaves considerable scope for choice, sometimes by women themselves and sometimes by their spouses, for women to identify and work as farmers, traders, artisans or housewives. The life histories provided many examples of specific options, and of the overall flexibility and degree of choice about occupational identity.

By comparing several women's histories, we saw the importance of family composition and life cycle in women's occupational training and development. For example, many women who were the eldest child or from a family with many daughters and few sons became apprentices to their fathers. These women were often more active in crop production and land management than those with older or many brothers. Fathers' and mothers' needs for assistance alike affected how girls were trained. Likewise, the women we met were affected in their occupational options and labour allocation decisions by the number and gender of their own children.

Many of the women were the main farmers and tree planters in their households. One woman, Ramona, had worked as a girl with her father in his coffee nurseries and plantations and was the main farmer in her own household, while her husband worked in a nearby mine. Yet she could not plant timber trees due to his reservations about regulation of tree harvesting and his lack of faith in the administrative and marketing assistance of the federation. Ramona's experience showed us that women's participation in forestry and land management was far more complex than simple gender equity or inequity, or a fixed norm for the gender division of labour. Two other women heads of households (one widowed and well-off, the other divorced and almost landless) planted their own timber lots. Others had relegated this activity to the men, had planted their own trees as well as their husband's plots, had helped with their husband's plantations or had chosen not to participate. Besides the gender division of labour, the life histories explained the complex gendered constraints and opportunities in forest enterprises based on gendered property, land-management authority and affiliation with the federation and ENDA.

From Julia's life we learned about the detailed workings of the land market and the pressure on smallholders to sell family lands to agribusiness corporations during times of financial stress. She recounted the story of her father-in-law's illness and the subsequent sale of all family lands to a citrus corporation to cover medical expenses. Julia also explained how she had come to be a health promoter for ENDA by drawing on three distinct kinds of knowledge: (i) the previously abandoned herbal medicine skills acquired from her mother; (ii) her formal schooling; and (iii) her recent experience with the formation of a housewives' association.

By including older and younger generations in the life histories, and later in the survey questions, we learned about broader issues such as migration and inter-generational education, caring and support. Family histories also clarified ideologies of gender identity, equity and authority and their effects on production, land use and management. For example, Rafaela told us about her daughter's abandonment by her husband at his family's farm. She helped her daughter acquire a milk cow, breeding sows and timber trees as independent sources of wealth. After the subsequent reconciliation of the couple, he and his family recognized the young woman's assets and enterprises as her own property. Rafaela explained: 'I taught my daughters how to say MINE'. This made clear that some women at least keep their own property and income sources within households headed by men, an ethic actively promoted by some members of the community. It also contrasted with initial responses of many groups, which referred to the ideal as household-level pooling of resources under the authority of men.

Through the life stories, we were introduced to the origins of the federation which lay in several prior peasant, democratic, religious and cooperative movements. There had been a long history of everyday conflicts and major confrontations between forestry officials and rural smallholders in the region over a tree-felling ban. The detailed accounts of arrest, imprisonment and pursuit by military forestry guards sharpened our understanding of the reservations of some farmers about tree planting. Yet the stories of participation in successful federation campaigns for land, justice, and political freedom[4] in the last two decades also offered a glimpse of the potential for successful negotiation between the federation tree planters and the forestry service.

The personal life histories, told without the constraint of our researchers' categories and preconceptions, helped us to grasp the meaning of our daily observations. Through the pattern in peoples' lives, we understood better the logic and spirit of the landscapes and livelihoods of individual smallholders, their households and their rural communities. In particular we saw the diversity of life experiences, choices and situations, not only between men and women but among women and among households normally lumped together as 'smallholders'. We gained insight also into the dynamism of peasant economies, ecologies and cultures, and the rapid and varied responses of rural households and individuals to the changing economic and political context.

Overall, the life histories taught us much more about gender identity and ideology than we could glean from quick, one-off group exercises, household or key-informant interviews. Other methods commonly used in participatory approaches, such as daily routines or seasonal calendars, usually reveal only the bare fact of these divisions. We gained precious insights about the 'why' and 'how' of the gender divisions of land/resources, labour, knowledge, organizations and power. Life stories clarified for us the distinctions between gender, life cycle and household differences based on class, family composition and occupation. They highlighted the flexibility and nature of peoples' choices of occupation, location and identity as farmers/housewives or farmers/workers, and showed how they affected participation in commercial forestry.

Limitations of life histories

While personal life histories substantially advanced and enriched our own work, they have several limitations. The first concern is time. One can ask about life histories in first encounters or in a single fairly long session, but researchers risk being intrusive and may fail to do justice to the person's story. If too little time is spent, the results are likely to be patchy and/or superficial. To get full stories, and not just chronologies, requires a careful introduction at the community level. We responded to this by recording two levels of life histories: the first group we interviewed in great detail and with substantial analysis and cross-checking; the second set of histories were more opportunistic and partial, based on one or two sessions, and would either confirm or supplement particular points of the detailed histories.

Another key consideration is the choice of participants and how their stories are documented. We combined life histories with group interviews, chains of key informants and a random sample to gain a better sense of where individuals fit within the community and how widely their experiences are shared. Our tendency to want to create an 'average' or representative life story, as is common in statistics, was balanced by using other methods. These helped clarify the difference between experiences which can shed light on some aspect of life and the incorrect presentation of individual life histories as representing an entire group of people.

The merits of landscape mapping

Landscape mapping and sketching was an invaluable component of almost every stage of our field work. We drew maps together with local people as part of the life history interviews, which allowed us to relate personal and environmental histories. We also used maps in initial key informant and household interviews and, later, in the random sample survey. Drawing maps during interviews made discussions more relaxed and allowed answers to flow visually. We compiled a local landscape dictionary with visual references, and more importantly, we gained a sense of the pattern as seen through the eyes of men and women who had shaped it. Just as in life histories, the participants narrated their account of the landscape in their own terms.

We usually worked in pairs, with a large poster paper and a large set of coloured felt pens, and drew while gathered around a small table or board with one or two participants. We often started with a walk through the person's farm or went to a lookout point to view the surrounding landscape. Then we settled into the telling-and-sketching exercise, usually in an open area just outside the house. One of us would pose questions and take notes while the other drew. This enabled us to record and draw in the midst of the running story and description of the farm.

We began most maps by asking people to help us to locate their house on paper and drew in boundary landmarks such as rivers, roads and fences, plus the house and other buildings. Next we discussed and drew in all land-use areas including the gardens, mixed croplands, annual cash-crop plots, multi-storey coffee and cocoa stands, fruit orchards, pastures, timber plots and riverine forest. Throughout the running narrative by the participants, we noted the tree, crop and medicinal species that grew in each place. We sometimes noted who planted and cared for them, as well as who harvested, processed, used and/or sold them. We also located all livestock, fences, wells and other water sources, and any other farm infrastructure. We asked the respondents to check the image and add to it if necessary.

In most participatory approaches, such as PRA, participants draw their own maps. These are then often, but not always, reinterpreted by outsiders at some stage of research and/or planning. However, we chose to do most of the drawing ourselves, responding to their descriptions and corrections. This placed our interpretation of the landscape in full view of the narrator, who could then question us and correct the image. Compared to questions about the same topics, the blank paper acted as a vacuum waiting to be filled with the complete image of the farm landscape.

Rather than reciting a list of species, the person speaking would talk about what was located in a particular part of the farm and would direct our sketching to reflect her mental image of the place. She would then refer back to the emerging picture to be sure that we had both gotten it right. This method allowed us to record the integrative knowledge of residents in a form that captured the complexity of landscape patterns, and the less visible elements of land use and management. It alerted us to relevant species, landscape patterns and land-use units. The sketch prompted more detailed accounts of species composition, use and management. It guided us to source areas of various resources (water, fuelwood, water, timber, medicine, food), and then to discuss gendered differences in resource control and access.

Drawing maps with individuals and small groups allowed us to understand better the multiple uses, biodiversity and economic diversity of landscape features at the farm and community level.

By working with women and men we were able to understand gender-specific priorities and practices in accepting new technologies on farm, and the gendered knowledge which shapes these decisions. The maps demonstrated concretely how the very space in which men and women work and live is gendered. The images set the stage for further discussion of ecological and social complexity by visually constructing what different groups of people know and do every day. By framing questions based on local everyday constructs, and not on predefined categories, we were able to avoid distortion of their realities.

By placing them in plain view, the maps allowed for a more transparent and reflective dialogue between the narrators' responses and our interpretation. In group contexts, the process of constructing the images provoked questions, comments and additions by other participants. We were also able to compare the maps and code some of the information, through the use of standard colours and shapes for particular species, supplemented by notes on a separate sheet. By linking information from the mapping exercise to the formal questionnaire survey, we achieved a more representative structure for the random sample. By doing the second round of maps within the survey, we enriched the data base on plant species, land use and landscape patterns, as well as the survey process itself.

The benefits of the survey

The life history interviews and sketch mapping with women and men generated rich information about complex social issues and ecological trends.

But to confirm our findings from these qualitative approaches, and to give our conclusions and recommendations legitimacy among natural scientists, we administered a formal questionnaire. We derived a stratified random sample from amongst the farmers' and women's associations of the federation. The formal survey mirrored the questions that we asked during earlier stages of research, including family migration history, changing roles in resource management, and opinions of the forestry project. The questions were also designed to gather bare 'facts' about the household (i.e. size of landholdings, species of trees, crops, medicinal plants, and animals present in different land-use units, and number of timber trees planted).

After a lively series of life history interviews, mapping sessions and small-group discussions, we tested a formal survey. The pilot surveys were dry for us and uninteresting for the respondents. In fact, the process was painfully boring and the responses sterile. To reintroduce life to the discussions, we decided to add the map and some life history questions to the survey interview. So after completing basic questions, we spent about an hour drawing the map, and then continued with questions on land tenure, employment, migration, organizational affiliation and the forestry initiative.

Besides confirming our earlier findings, the random sample survey revealed household situations that had previously been invisible to us and social categories that were under-represented in the Forestry Enterprise Project. We encountered a very high proportion of younger families who lived on small residential plots and depended on off-farm work or on family, rented or sharecropped land. We visited many young women who were the main farmers and whose families' contacts with the federation and the project came only through their membership of a women's club. The final sample also included several people (identified as 'not really farmers' by promoters) who made a living by regular trips to the capital to sell local produce. We also met federation members who farmed their own plots, and were caretakers of large holdings of absentee owners on which they had established large plantations of acacia. Each of these groups had some stake in the Forestry Enterprise Project, but were generally invisible to ENDA staff, federation leaders and, initially, to us.

Assessing the mix of methods

By combining qualitative, quantitative and visual field methods in our field research in Zambrana-Chacuey, we compensated for the shortcomings of relying on only one type. This allowed us to collect and synthesize a large amount of in-depth and gender-focused information in a relatively short amount of time. If we had relied only on oral histories to gather data, our understanding of the issues affecting the region would have been biased by the people with whom we spoke.

When we asked ENDA and federation staff who to speak with, they directed us to a certain group of people. Our own choice from amongst this group also carried a certain bias. This group was unusual in its special knowledge about the history of the federation and regional struggles against the state, and its experiences with ENDA and the forestry project.

It was also remarkably articulate. Certainly, without their insights we would not have been able to understand the diversity of impacts of the forestry project, and the flexible definitions of gender rights, roles and responsibilities within the federation.

Yet only through the random sample for the final survey did we discover the nature and distribution of distinct situations such as those of traders, caretakers, near-landless women farmers, and the male wage-labourers whose only connection to the federation was their wives' Women's Club membership. Without hearing these less heroic accounts, our conclusions would have been very different and our recommendations would not have suggested ways to transform the forestry project to serve them.

In turn, without the oral histories and the maps, we would have omitted survey questions that addressed what really mattered to local residents and federation members. Our experimentation with farm sketches during the early household and personal histories taught us ways to use them effectively in the survey. The oral histories also instructed us in local vocabulary, folklore and appropriate categories to apply to ecological, economic and social issues. This facilitated our entry into people's homes who had not met us in community or federation meetings. Without our ability to converse in a detailed and realistic way about the landscape, the federation, the project and other concerns of the residents of Zambrana-Chacuey, the survey would have been more difficult to implement and the responses less complete.

All field methods have weaknesses and shortcomings. In Zambrana-Chacuey, we learned that the sequence in which methods are implemented is crucial for two reasons: to compensate for weaknesses in individual data-gathering techniques and to build on knowledge systematically. If we could do the study in Zambrana-Chacuey again, we would plan more oral-history interviews with each respondent, include additional cases and be more systematic in our choice of questions about life cycle, livelihoods and skills acquisition, and environmental change at community level. In a second stage of study, we would use the findings from the survey to identify the less visible types of households for another set of life history interviews. This would provide a fuller understanding of how the project is affecting different people's land, livelihoods and political power. We would also return to some people to expand oral histories on specific themes, such as environmental change in the community. Finally, we would try to link mapping, oral history and survey updates to an on-going research activity inside the federation itself. We feel this would stimulate reflection and debate on the gender, class and other differences of interest in various development initiatives. It might then guide decisions to expand, reform or change specific programmes or policies.

Conclusion

Through this combination of methods, the research team and participating residents explored the possible futures of women and men within the gendered landscapes and livelihoods in the region. We gathered information on complex patterns of social and ecological interactions, in quantifiable form, from a representative sample of the federation membership. The methods helped us to understand and interpret the complex answers to such seemingly simple questions as: whose forests? whose trees? whose products? whose science? whose decisions? We found the answers to be embedded in finely patterned relations of gender, class, life cycle, family composition and life history, as well as the popular social movement which had spawned the federation.

Understanding the diversity amongst landscape and land-user groups alike proved valuable for the researchers, planners and resource managers involved with the Forest Enterprise Project. We were able to offer preliminary results and recommendations to the federation membership, the project management and the broader resource management community in the Dominican Republic. However, the detailed quantitative analysis of the survey required substantial time and effort beyond the original scope of the case study project. That part of the study may be useful to the academic and policy communities but may have little relevance to daily resource management and local-level planning by the time it is published. Overall, the life histories, maps and preliminary qualitative and quantitative summaries from the survey provided the information most useful for addressing gendered and class-divided interests in the future of the Forest Enterprise Project and land use change in Zambrana-Chacuey.

References

Rocheleau, D. (1995) 'Maps, Numbers, Text and Context: mixing methods in feminist political ecology', *Professional Geographer* 47 (4): 458–66.

Rocheleau, D. and L. Ross (1995) 'Trees as Tools, Trees as Text: struggles over resources in Zambrana-Chacuey, Dominican Republic,' *Antipode* 27 (4): 407–28.

Rocheleau, D., L. Ross, J. Morrobel and R. Hernandez (1996) *Forests, Gardens and Tree Farms: gender, class and community at work in the landscapes of Zambrana-Chacuey, Dominican Republic*, ECOGEN Case Study Series, Worcester, MA: Clark University.

Slocum, R., L. Wichart, D. Rocheleau and B. Thomas-Slayter (1995) *Power, Process and Participation: tools for change*, London: Intermediate Technology Publications.

Thomas-Slayter, B. *et al.* (1993) *Tools of Gender Analysis: a guide to field methods for bringing gender into sustainable resource management*, Clark University: ECOGEN.

Thomas-Slayter, B. and D. Rocheleau (1995) 'Research Frontiers at the Nexus of Gender, Environment and Development: linking household, community and ecosystem,' in R. Gallin and A. Ferguson (eds), *Women in Development Annual Review*, Boulder, CO: Westview Press.

17

Gender-blind or Gender-bright Targeting of Projects in Cambodia

SONJA VLAAR and RHODANTE AHLERS
with fieldwork by Tep Srey Pov, Sdoeng Van Youthea, Botum
Srey Neang, Tram Vutha and Em Khalavuth

The term 'gender-blind' is generally used in critiques of development policies and practices which appear neutral and which refer to target groups as generic categories, such as 'communities', 'the poor', 'the farmers'. To counteract this, development agencies have increasingly focused on 'women' as an important social category and have adopted this focus as their policy. However, an explicit focus on women as a disadvantaged group does not mean a 'gender-bright' policy and can even imply a gender-blind policy.

Simplistic use of blanket categories also occurs with 'female-headed households'. Various studies indicate that about 30 per cent of the households in Cambodia are female-headed households (Ledgerwood, 1992; Mehta, 1993; Sonnois, 1990). Many development interventions in Cambodia which aim to deal with poverty alleviation target their assistance at female-headed households. The underlying assumption is that these households are disproportionately represented among the poor, and providing them with benefits would promote both poverty alleviation and gender equity. Yet, in most cases, no convincing arguments for this assumption are provided. Although the sex of the household head certainly influences household circumstances, it cannot be considered the only, or even necessarily the most critical, criterion which determines the socio-economic status of the household.

Chapter 17 describes our involvement in a study on gender issues in irrigation in Cambodia that made us question the assumption that female headship of household is an economic (or poverty) indicator. The study involved wealth-ranking exercises as part of a gender-disaggregated socio-economic analysis of households and headship. The results show that female-headed households in rural Cambodia are very diverse and that their economic situation depends on the composition of the household in relation to the social and political context. We, therefore, challenge those who consider that female-headed households, by definition, are disadvantaged.

To understand better the relationship between gender and the socio-economic situation of a household, local perceptions of both gender and well-being are crucial. Using an externally derived, gender-analysis framework and categorization, such as female-headed households, may well obscure more significant local socio-economic differences.

Gender positions in Cambodian society

The division of labour in rural Cambodia before 1970 was relatively clear. Men and women performed certain clearly defined activities. Today, when asked who is responsible for certain tasks or decisions, men and women will describe these historical patterns. However, a closer look at who actually does the work reveals a different picture. Women carry out many of the activities for which men are said to be responsible.

As in other societies where political and economic reorganization has been caused by war or revolutionary forces, gender identities in Cambodia have been through radical changes (see Box 17.1). To undertake appropriate, effective and gender-sensitive development interventions, it is vital to understand current agricultural processes in the light of this dynamic history and the resulting confusion about the division of labour and gender identities. This confusion is apparent in several ways. First, although women are very active and have experience in most agricultural activities, they and their husbands refuse to acknowledge this. Therefore, what people say about the existing division of labour and decision-making is not necessarily what they do in practice. This means that statistics derived from surveys based on such statements need to be interpreted with utmost care if they are to be used in planning development interventions. Other forms of research must be used to seek more accurate accounts of gender issues in agricultural development.

Research methodology

In January 1994, at the request of several NGOs working in irrigated agriculture as a form of rural development,[1] the consultancy group SAWA undertook research on gender issues in irrigation in Cambodia (Ahlers and Vlaar, 1995). The objective of the study was to understand how gender relations are affected by, and in turn influence, changes brought about by irrigation development. Information was needed about the potential of irrigation interventions to support gender-balanced development.

A team of five Cambodian (two male and three female) and one Dutch researcher carried out the fieldwork in six villages in the provinces of Prey Veng and Takeo. The fieldwork consisted of two phases:

○ The first phase (April–June 1994) was used to compile a basis for assessing the potential impact of irrigation interventions. We focused first on gender issues in traditional rice-based agricultural systems where no recent irrigation interventions had occurred.
○ The second field phase allowed us to look at gender-related changes in two rice production systems with an irrigation-based intervention and compare that with the first four villages.

Our research methodology merged gender analysis with several participatory appraisal methods. We opted for a participatory research approach to allow villagers to analyse their own situation and identify relevant issues and priorities related to irrigated agriculture. Therefore, we chose research methods which would generate discussion and encourage village women

Box 17.1: Political upheaval and the impact of gender in Cambodia

Cambodia's agriculture has undergone three major transitions in the last 20 years. The first transition was the Khmer Rouge reorganization of society into a pure agricultural society. This period, from 1970 to 1975, was characterized by continuous fighting and a reorganization of agriculture in liberated areas. Villagers told us that their usual routines were completely disrupted. Men and women alike were involved in fighting, and society was restructured with labour divisions based on pragmatism rather than norms and values. The Khmer Rouge regime, installed in 1975, tried to optimize agrarian production in which labour needed to be productive. There was little use for a cumbersome gender division of labour.

After the overthrow of the Khmer Rouge in 1979, a second reorganization introduced a less rigorous form of rural collectivization than the Pol Pot era had known. Families were allowed to reunite and agriculture was organized in *krom samakis* (solidarity groups) of 10–15 households. A collective production process was encouraged in which men and women identified their own responsibilities. In most villages, widows were supported by the *kroms*. However, the ongoing civil war took the lives of many men, leaving women and children without husbands and fathers. The *krom samaki* system disappeared slowly and the agricultural production process was carried out primarily by women. One could no longer speak of a gender-based division of labour as such. Each village studied went through a different *krom samaki* process. Although most villages had abandoned the *krom samaki* system by 1986 some still use the *kroms* as labour pools for exchange labour.

The third transition started in 1989, when agricultural reforms took place, affecting land tenure policies, the organization of farm-level production, and the introduction of pricing, taxation and marketing. The state disengaged itself from production activities, subsidies were reduced, and state enterprises were privatized. This privatization affected social differentiation. Families with sufficient labour and capital were able to exploit the new possibilities, whereas it has put a greater strain on vulnerable households. The rural transition after 1991 is that from centralized state control to privatization and decentralization. The international recognition of Cambodia and the subsequent influx of multilateral aid, finds the country confronting structural adjustment programmes.

All three transitions affected the socio-economic situation of the communities at village and household level. In recent years, war has abated and more boys are reaching adulthood. The balance of the male and female population is stabilizing and returning slowly to normal, the female population now making up 53 per cent of the population, whereas the female labour force is 60 per cent. Until stability returns, this process will mean yet another reorganization of labour in agriculture. Although rice production is the main activity and priority of the rural population, this generates insufficient income for most households. Shortage of land and its limited quality, difficult water regimes, labour shortages and uncertain pricing are now determining rural livelihood strategies.

and men to share their ideas and knowledge. Box 17.2 gives an overview of the methods we used in the research process and the role of women and men in the research sequence. We also selected methods which could be managed by the fieldworkers and were feasible to use, given our time restrictions. The questionnaire was used to understand the perspectives of the heads of households on issues of rice production and irrigation. It provided quantitative information complementary to that from the other research methods.

Many of the methods we chose are associated with PRA. However, the study was clearly a research activity and was not directly linked to project implementation. We make no claim at having been involved in a PRA

Box 17.2: Methods used in the study

Method	Field phase	Number of participants							Gender-differentiated
		TS	PP	Kr	Sa	KK	PS	Total	
Mapping group	1 and 2	3	3	3	3	3	3	18	yes
Transect walks	1 and 2	2	2	1	1	1	1	8	no[a]
Seasonal calendars	1 and 2	3	3	2	2	2	2	14	yes
Well-being (group)[b]	1 and 2	3	3	4	4	3	4	21	no[a]
Semi-structured interviews	1 and 2	10	11	11	11	10	12	65	yes
Questionnaires[c]	1 and 2	50	31	46	29	37	46	239	yes
Life stories and time lines	1 and 2	2	2	2	2	2	2	12	yes
Venn diagrams	2	–	–	6	–	–	6	12	yes
Key-person interviews	1 and 2	3	2	5	2	3	4	19	no
Daily time lines	2	–	–	29	–	–	34	63	yes
Rice matrix (group)	1 and 2	1	1	1	1	1	1	6	no[d]

TS	– Toap Sdach, Prey Veng	Sa	– Samraong, Takeo
PP	– Po Pluk, Prey Veng	KK	– Kamplueng, Takeo
Kr	– Krang, Prey Veng	PS	– Prey Sambuo, Takeo

a. For the transect walks and the wealth-ranking exercises extra care was taken that women were represented. In several cases we spoke only to women as there were no men available and vice versa. Participation of mixed groups was encouraged.
b. The households for the wealth-ranking exercise were taken from a census list provided by the village leader. The maximum number of households ranked was determined during the field training days to be sixty. Village size varied from about 600 to 1200 inhabitants.
c. We used questionnaires to cover 25 per cent of the households in each village. Respondents were randomly selected.
d. Matrices on rice varieties were carried out only with the women as they are the ones who select the seeds.

Box 17.3: Participatory research in the Cambodian context

Even though the participatory approach was highly valued and put into practice as far as possible, certain factors limited its effectiveness. Unfortunately, the current Cambodia context does not allow for open and care-free discussions. Due to their recent history, many villagers were hesitant to share their ideas and opinions from fear of jealousy or malicious gossip. Both present membership of political parties and past participation in political movements determine consensus, or the lack of it. People do not trust others or confide in them easily. The wealth-ranking exercise was particularly sensitive. Being ranked 'poor' was associated with potential aid, thus biasing the discussions, but being ranked 'better off' was perceived as insulting and unjust. Nobody wanted to be identified as 'better-off' as it implied they were involved in exploitative debt relations or other activities of wealth accumulation. In one of the villages a big row erupted after the exercise, and the team was approached repeatedly by several households to be ranked again.

---

process that led to community-level action, and refer to our work as participatory assessment.

Research methodologies, be they participatory or not, must be appropriate to the context in which they are to be used. Our experience is that the political and social upheaval that Cambodians have been subjected to over the past two decades influenced the effectiveness of certain methods. Box 17.3 describes how participation in the wealth-ranking exercises was affected by local social and political history.

Unit of analysis

The conceptual challenge that we want to address in this chapter arose early in the research: how to disaggregate the community and understand gender-based differences better. Identification of the socio-economic situation of households or other groupings of individuals represents an analytical problem at the start of most socio-economic research. Although many attempts are made to define different types of households and to use these as a basis for development interventions, a typology of households remains an arbitrary classification. How should the community or the 'rural poor' be differentiated in terms of class, caste, ethnicity, religion, age and gender?

Instead of using gender-blind terms such as the 'better-off' and 'poorer' or 'farmers' or 'female-headed', we chose a more open-ended socio-economic and gender-disaggregated analysis of the household. We felt this would help us to identify which households have more chance of reaching their goals than others and why this is the case.

As our study focused on gender relations, differences and similarities, we explored irrigation-related issues with women and men alike. This focus should not be understood as denying other important social variables that also differentiate the users of irrigation facilities, notably class, ethnicity, religion and age. Such differences between women farmers, for example, may, in fact, be greater than any common interests they might share as women. The use of wealth ranking, in fact, led us to the challenge the very simplicity of 'women', and in particular female-headed households, as an all-determining category.

Although there may be strong policy reasons for targeting female-headed households and, therefore, a seeming practical urgency for classification prior to the fieldwork, this does not seem to lead to an accurate understanding of the diversity of livelihood strategies of distinct households. To put women in female-headed households in the right perspective, we also needed to understand the position of women in other types of households. We now know, for example, that women of young, recently married couples are a particularly vulnerable group.

Awareness of these debates amongst development planners, therefore, led us to identify two different approaches to data collection: one using pre-determined household types; the other with context-specific, locally determined household types.

The first set of data, which we will not discuss further here, was gathered using three pre-determined types of households:

(1) households that are female-headed and without any male support of a husband or partner throughout the year (widows/divorced women/ abandoned women/single women);

(2) households that are headed by a woman but receive some financial or material support from a husband or partner who has migrated temporarily; and

(3) couple-headed households where both husband and wife run the household.

For the second data set, we did not establish a classification of households in advance. We followed one of the guiding principles of the study: that it should reflect the views and perspectives of rural women and men. As it was their realities that we needed to discuss and understand, the obvious methodological choice was for a more participatory assessment of household well-being. To establish the relative position of households in the village and discover local criteria of socio-economic position and well-being, we conducted wealth-ranking exercises with about 60 households in each village. Box 17.4 shows the outcome of one such exercise in Toap Sdach.

Female-headed households in Cambodia

The study revealed that the female-headed households in the Cambodian villages we studied are not disadvantaged *per se*. They can be found throughout the strata of socio-economic classes. Female-headed households can be headed by a widow, an abandoned woman, a single woman or a divorcee. These differences influence significantly their status and access to resources. A widow might have far better access to entitlements by

193

Box 17.4:   Wealth ranking in Toap Sdach, a village in Prey Veng

A wealth-ranking exercise was carried out, identifying four groups in the village: rich, middle, 'next poor' and poor. The local criteria used to determine the socio-economic position of a household were:

○ access to cash or capital to invest;
○ draft animals in relation to labour availability;
○ rice produce; and
○ land ownership.

In Toap Sdach, the cash economy, and access to it, is increasingly important. Rice production is no longer structuring the economy. This is caused by a shortage of land and increased migration of labour, which brings large amounts of cash into the community. Draft animals are perceived as an essential capital good, a prerequisite for any agriculture.

Wealth is concentrated in one small group of people who have capital to invest in land or business ventures. A key source of capital for the better-off group is pre-Pol Pot wealth which has been invested, with high economic returns. The middle group is characterized by having access to a steady flow of cash. The next-poor group is composed primarily of farmers who grow just enough rice to last them until the next harvest. They earn some extra cash by selling pigs and their own labour to pay for hiring draught power. Those belonging to the poorest group experience a shortage of rice for 6 months or more and are usually dependent on others, as they must borrow rice from middle and rich households. They lack the means of cultivation. The lack of labour and draft animals proves to be particularly problematic. Several households in this group have sold their land to the better-off and middle households.

---

taking over the ownership rights of her husband, which in turn might allow her to participate more in irrigation organizations. The fact that she is a widow gives her a far higher status than a divorced, abandoned or single woman.

The following factors seem to influence the well-being of a female-headed household:

(i)   the age of the female head;
(ii)   the ratio of age and number of children;
(iii) the presence of married children;
(iv)   income sources from absent members; and
(v)   close and supportive relatives.

Several studies about the Cambodian context (Ledgerwood, 1992; Mehta, 1993) argue that it is access to male adult labour, in particular, which determines household well-being. Our study does not support this conclusion. Rather, availability of adult labour in general appears to be crucial for household well-being. If male adult labour is considered necessary for ploughing or other tasks allocated to men, this negates the fact that women will and do undertake these tasks in the absence of men or that they have alternative strategies for solving the problem, such as exchange labour or hiring labour. Wealthier female-headed households are able to arrange more access to male and/or female adult labour within and outside the household or through cash or payment. But it is the poor female-headed households which lack labour in general – the crucial determinant of well-being.

The research findings show that the five factors mentioned above are of more importance than the sex of the adult providing the labour. Only in one specific aspect are female-headed households at a general disadvantage. Women heads of households have no partner to support them in their domestic concerns. Being solely responsible for managing household problems and finding solutions presents a relative psychological burden that is not insignificant in determining the development potential of that household.

The implications for development interventions

The underlying assumption of many development interventions in Cambodia that female-headed households are poor households is incorrect. Female-headed households, as a category within gender analysis, are not a homogeneous category and need further disaggregation if they are to be used to focus development interventions. Female-headed households do, however, comprise a vulnerable category if they have little access to adult labour, many mouths to feed and few relatives to fall back on. This clearly has implications for development interventions which aim to work towards poverty alleviation and gender equity.

'Gender-bright' targeting of development interventions in Cambodia must consider the positions of different types of women and avoid targeting female-headed households blindly. Poverty-oriented development interventions must be based on a local analysis of poverty and gender relations in order to have a better insight into the vulnerability of different groups of people.

Understanding household diversity and how household characteristics determine well-being cannot be determined accurately using externally derived criteria. Participatory assessment of well-being using wealth ranking is an invaluable approach which can contribute to a sharper socio-economic analysis.

References

Ahlers, R. and S. Vlaar (1995) *Up to the Sky: a study on gender issues in irrigation in the Cambodian provinces of Takeo and Prey Veng*, Ede: SAWA.

Ledgerwood, J. (1992) *Analysis of the Situation of Women in Cambodia: research on women in Khmer society*, Cambodia: UNICEF.

Mehta, M. (1993) *Gender Dimensions of Poverty in Cambodia: a survey report*, Cambodia: OXFAM.

Sonnois, B. (1990) *Women in Cambodia: an overview of the situation and suggestions for development programs*, Cambodia: Redd Barna.

18

From Crops to Gender Relations: Transforming extension in Zambia[1]

CHRISTIANE FRISCHMUTH

based on work with the Siavonga District staff of the Ministry of Agriculture, Food and Fisheries, Zambia, especially Mss Jester Cheelo, Lillian Hamusiya and Edna Maluma, Gossner Mission, Sinazeze

'Our husbands have to join us for our next meeting'. 'We have to plan together as a household and share information'. 'We should discuss all aspects concerning our family together, as a family'. 'Our husbands and the other men in our village should learn what we are learning and we should learn what they are learning'.

The women behind these statements were initially part of a village extension group in Siavonga District in Zambia. But some years earlier, they had formed a women's group to undertake income-generating activities and keep any profit they made.

At group meetings, the women discussed freely topics that would not have been possible in mixed groups: the difficulty of not being allowed to travel, budget their own income or determine which crop to grow. Even in the group, they could not extricate themselves entirely from the need to seek men's cooperation. Vegetable growing, a collective money earner, needed the men's cooperation to obtain poles and to solve conflicts with the cattle owners whose livestock ransacked the gardens. The women also felt unhappy about their husbands' opposition to the group and about not being able to share what they had learned with them. Over time, the women started realizing that they could not hide in their groups but had to address certain issues publicly.

The women soon realized that the basis of their problems lay in traditional divisions of labour, the stereotypes of men and women, traditional roles, views and values. Change would be possible only if men were included in these discussions. The women wanted to talk about their work overload, men's sole decision-making power, and the lack of communication in the family which aggravated undernourishment, illiteracy, poor harvests, low income, illness, insecurity and jealousy.

Although the women in Siavonga District did not mention the word 'gender', their discussions were clearly about gender relations, gender roles and gender needs. They saw that women and men alike had to change their attitudes, behaviour and values. The growth in women's self-confidence to tackle traditional barriers did not happen overnight. It was a long process in which the women were supported by agricultural extension officers. Chapter 18 describes that process.

Background

The people in Siavonga District are primarily farmers and fisherfolk. The main linkage between them and the government is the extension services of various ministries, the Department of Agriculture being the most prominent. The district is divided into 15 agricultural 'camps', with one Camp Officer responsible for providing technical advice to farmers. A Block Officer supervises four camp officers. A Subject Matter Specialist develops technical messages, and monitors, evaluates and assists the field staff in their daily work. Most extension staff are male. The few female staff are mostly Subject Matter Specialists. An Assistant and a District Agricultural Officer manage the extension system from Siavonga, the district capital. These managers also represent the agricultural sector in the District Development Coordination Committee, which is responsible for the overall development of the district.

Village extension groups vary in size (10 to 30 people) and are open to all, men and women. Although each group has a list of members, and office bearers are elected, membership and attendance is always open. Before the recent changes described in this chapter, field staff received technical messages to pass to farmers in the village extension groups. Theoretical sessions, practical demonstrations and individual farm visits were used to pass on scientific knowledge from research and via the Subject Matter Specialists. While the extension officers had a good relationship with the farmers, attendance at group meetings was low and messages were adopted by few farmers and with varying success. The process of knowledge transfer was one way.

From knowledge transfer to joint learning

Since 1992, the agricultural extension staff in Siavonga District has been developing a gender-oriented participatory extension approach (PEA). In this venture, they are supported by the German–Zambian Siavonga Agricultural Development Project (SADP). An initial impulse came in the form of a group of students from Germany. Together with the extension staff, they tested a range of PRA methods to make the existing extension approach more participatory. Staff got a first glimpse at how participatory methods could help create agricultural extension based on farmers' needs. Subsequently, the district staff received national-level support to develop this into a more comprehensive participatory extension approach with GTZ[2] financial support and technical advisers.

In the intense process that followed, the perceptions and behaviour of all those involved changed, facilitation skills of extension staff and villagers improved, and the understanding of extension as a whole shifted away from a process of giving technical advice. The staff came to see themselves as facilitators who guide villagers through a process of self-discovery, of finding solutions themselves, of providing information and linkages to other services, of identifying causes, effects and linkages of their problems and needs. Income-generating activities, self-help, village-development plans, food-for-work initiatives, and stronger community spirit grew out of this process-oriented extension approach.

By using their training in facilitation skills, gender and participatory methods in their fieldwork, the extension staff realized that technical problems are often not the main concern, that they can learn from the farmers, and motivate the farmers for action. They lost their fear of not knowing all the answers, instead trusting their role of asking questions so that farmers could find answers themselves. This was no small transformation for staff trained in technical knowledge and the passing on of technical messages.

The role of participatory methods

Participatory methods are used to initiate and guide the process of joint learning. They help people to visualize the analytical process of identifying causes and effects and their linkages, serve as common points of reference, and help to mobilize communities for action. As illiteracy is very high, especially amongst women, symbols, whether actual objects or drawn on the ground or on paper, help to visualize discussions and to record final plans and agreements reached. Original documents remain in the village and copies are passed to the extension office. Meetings are always held in the villages, usually under a big tree or sometimes in a school room which is not in use.

The two key methodological points are flexible use of the methods and continual adaptation. Whatever the topic, combinations of participatory methods are used for needs' identification, planning, message development, research trials in farmers' fields, monitoring and evaluation. Role plays, poems, songs and stories are particularly effective. During one meeting, a role play might be followed by a problem census and end with a song. By working with other NGOs active in the area, methods as well as facilitators are interchanged and practised together.

Participatory extension in Siavonga

The extension cycle starts in the dry season, a good time to meet with farmers for a problem census and preference ranking to determine priority needs for the coming season. Farmers raise all their needs. When these relate to non-agricultural problems, extension staff either link the group with other sectoral specialists or assist the farmers in developing their own solutions. Agricultural activities are discussed further, maybe with another, more detailed problem census and preference ranking. However, as agricultural and non-agricultural needs are closely linked, in practice they cannot be dealt with entirely separately.

The next step involves creating a seasonal calendar, to plan the timing of activities, the kind of activities, the interested parties, and requirements. The calendar remains with the village extension group, and can be referred to and modified when necessary during the season. The farmers use it as a monitoring tool, to see if their needs are really taken into consideration and plans adhered to. Field staff pass the village plans to senior management, which incorporate them into district-level plans and budgets.

During the season, technical messages are developed and trial plots on farmers' fields are operated jointly. Technical messages might be based on a general identified need. These are developed from an analysis of the local situation and discussion of the required changes, possible benefits and existing local solutions. For example, the need 'hunger' might be taken as the starting-point to identify agricultural income-generating activities. These might then form the basis for the Subject Matter Specialists to develop their own messages about improved livestock husbandry, legumes, crops, etc. They will use role plays, diagramming methods, field visits and demonstrations to do this.

Monitoring is carried out jointly by field staff and farmers, either individually or as a group. During harvesting time, a participatory evaluation takes place, focusing on the field trials, the benefits derived from new messages and the extension service, and recommendations for future research and extension. Inter-community visits are also useful for exchanging ideas and experiences between groups. Recommendations from the participatory evaluation sometimes serve to start planning the next season's work.

The missing link: gender

However, despite using participatory methods and improving facilitation skills, the extension staff became aware that not everybody took part and benefited from the extension activities, and that certain fundamental needs were not being addressed. Some agricultural trials failed, and messages were not adopted because women, though active farmers, did not attend the extension sessions. Husbands did not repay the loans given for seed purchases because they spent the money on other things and had discussed neither the loan nor the seed purchase with their wives. Women's groups failed to market their produce because their husbands did not allow them to travel. Children remained malnourished because men, who choose which crop to cultivate the following year, did not attend the health and nutrition meetings attended by women, and favoured cash crops over food crops.

Evaluation of seasonal extension messages clearly showed that men benefited more from extension than women. Men usually attended extension sessions, were elected as office-bearers and received specialized training such as record-keeping. They also received information about such matters as loans and where to buy seeds. Women did most of the work in the field and at home but were either not allowed to attend the meetings or had too much work to do. Women received valuable information only in women's groups, as was the case for hands-on experience in leadership positions and training in accounting and budgeting.

A major turning-point was a district-wide participatory evaluation held in September and October 1994 (GTZ/SADP, 1994). Extension staff from the field, management and national levels discussed some of the problems separately with male and female group members. The outcome was simple and incisive. Basically, the conclusion was that the practical procedures of the extension system were not conducive to allowing all groups of farmers, and especially women, to participate in extension activities. Meetings were called by extension officers rather than village headmen. If male officers announced meetings, it was difficult for women to attend, in the case of female officers, village men were uninterested. The distance of the meeting place and the time of the meetings were important. However, even if officers catered to their wishes, women still had too little time to attend meetings. The formal registration of the members meant that only the male head of household was registered. Female heads were often not acknowledged, and illiterate participants, the majority of whom were women, became automatically excluded. Women felt neglected, while men felt chided when they failed to attend a meeting and were asked about their absence. Men preferred to cease attending rather than lose face.

It became clear that the notion of a 'village extension group' needed a radical overhaul. The group had to be seen as an opportunity to discuss community and individual concerns, to improve village and personal lives, and to learn about new possibilities. It had to change from a fixed group where attendance is mandatory. In some cases, women clearly wanted to meet on their own with female extension staff. In other cases, they wanted to remain in a mixed group. While some problems were general, others were group-specific. The message was clear: the extension service had to become more flexible, less formal, and more in tune with local structures of authority.

The evaluation also highlighted an essential issue which had been emerging during the transformation: the extension staff accepted that their target body consists of a variety of interest groups with different needs, roles, resources, and options. These groups are linked through power relationships which are mostly unequal. Without ensuring the participation of all these groups and addressing these relationships, message adoption and motivation to engage in a learning process would remain poor and the extension service would be less effective. Although these fundamental conflicts seemed to go beyond the official mandate of the extension service, they could not be avoided. The basic power relationship which affected all spheres of the farmers' lives was that of gender relationships.

Initial changes

Following the evaluation, the entire project made a concerted effort to involve women more. For every field trip, every extension meeting, every demonstration in the field, couples were asked to attend together. Through role plays, extension staff stimulated discussion about the impact of not sharing information and not participating together in development activities. For these meetings farmers were asked to prepare role plays on different village scenarios, e.g. the husband gets sick, gets drunk, dies, and the wife has not attended meetings. Women's demands for more women's groups, leadership training, and more legume crops were taken up. More female store-keepers were sought for the decentralized seed and plough spare-parts sale centres,[3] to increase accessibility for women and to give women the benefit of training in store-keeping and accounting.

During problem-census and preference ranking, men and women either worked in separate groups or visualized their needs and preferences with different colour symbols. In each exercise, men's and women's varied interests, needs and preferences emerged clearly. The villagers themselves started to discuss whose preference was more important, why there were differences, and how to deal with the various demands on the extension service. This led to heated discussions about gender roles and needs. For example, in some villages extension officers were told that, traditionally, men decided these things and that's how it is and will be. The facilitators, nevertheless, grew confident over time in dealing with this difficult task and offering further meetings about these issues.

When drawing up a seasonal calendar to plan the extension work, men and women worked separately, or named or drew their activities in different colours. Extension staff often had to encourage women to also list their daily chores, such as firewood collecting and cooking. These calendars highlighted that although women were much busier than men, their daily activities were not considered as 'work' by the men and even by many of the women. They revealed that men were often unclear about women's activities or the correct timing of certain agricultural tasks. The location and timing of extension meetings were changed, based on analysis of the calendars, to suit the women's preferences. Finally, women wanted to include topics such as land-use planning, transport for water, nutrition and leadership training in the calendar of general extension activities, even though men felt these topics were more appropriate for women's meetings.

The facilitators' task was to probe further about causes and effects and offer the possibility of more discussions at another time. Usually, a discussion lasted up to four hours. When topics were not completed satisfactorily, they were later pursued further at an agreed time.

Gender is not sensitive

The extension staff initiated, guided and were themselves part of a process of self-discovery, and changing perceptions and behaviour about gender. Their initial fear was that gender is simply too sensitive to be addressed. In their eyes, gender had meant traditions, taboos, an issue which is foreign to villagers and will not be understood. Gender for them meant: women, liberating women, changing traditions, setting the men up against the extension staff who initiated the 'women's revolt'. The Camp Officers, who depend on good personal relationships with the farmers, feared conflicts and animosity for being too provocative. They reasoned that it really wasn't their business to talk about gender.

However, extension staff gained great confidence from the response of villagers who addressed gender issues at most meetings without naming them as such. Extension officers learned, through the responses of village men, and the analysis of cause and consequences, that gender meant men and women and their relationship. They saw that gender affects all aspects of village life and had to be addressed to effect sustainable change. Gender became a substitute for participation,[4] as addressing gender would empower men and women, enabling all to participate and benefit. As facilitation skills improved and methods were developed, the extension officers became more confident about the questions to ask and how to guide discussions and deal with conflicts. They switched from seeing their role as purely technical advisors to facilitators of a more intense, and broader, process of change.

Observing the sub-groups and conflict during group meetings, extension staff soon noted that gender relationships were not the only power relationship within the community. Old and young, rich and poor, livestock owners and farmers, etc., all presented different power hierarchies which they had to be aware of to allow for broad participation. Yet awareness was not enough. The relationships had to be addressed and methods designed to compensate for power differences. For example, voting procedures had to allow everyone to express themselves freely. During sub-group work, extension staff had to join certain groups to facilitate an open exchange of opinions. To make this easier, they sometimes had to predetermine the composition of sub-groups.

The extension staff also started to think about the participation of children. They were the farmers of tomorrow, but during meetings they were always chased away. What could be done to incorporate them? This insight completed the picture of the complexity of village-level relationships. Extension staff needed to develop skills and methods to circumvent the relationships of power and subordination, at least during the meetings, and to initiate changes.

Activities to address women's subordination

Activities to deal with topics raised, such as women's work overload, women being forbidden to attend the extension meetings and not receiving information, were developed by extension staff and advisors for use in group discussions.

Generally the meetings follow a similar pattern. The event is opened with a role play by the farmers about a typical day in the life of an overworked woman and her husband. In the ensuing discussion, extension staff ask women and men separately to illustrate their daily activities. Comparing the visualized work loads has an amazing effect on farmers. Men try to justify that traditions dictate the workload of women and discussion follows on bride price, the role of women, how husbands see their wives and women's reactions to those views. Then the group starts to analyse the effects of these workloads and to explore solutions. Sometimes, men see the benefit of contributing to the education and care of their children, to free up time for their wives, to keep them healthy (and beautiful!) and allow time for other, often supplementary income-generating activities. Some men are stunned when the work overload of their wives is visualized. Quite often, they discuss ideas about how to assist in collecting firewood and water, conserving trees, etc. The men add these new extra tasks to their activity profile, for the benefit of the whole family and community.

Some changes observed in some families are: assisting each other with child care; attending meetings jointly or taking turns; and husbands or fathers training some women in previously male tasks such as brick-laying. The real changes which are taking place within the family and their impact are, however, so intimate, the information too private for access, and often incremental, as to be beyond the monitoring capacity of the extension workers. The challenge is to devise a system of providing long-term self monitoring data and holding regular follow-up meetings with the same participants, as well as involving the immediate community to discuss their observations. To date, these activities have not yet taken place in the project area.

A big problem is how to persuade husbands to attend general extension activities together with their wives. The extension staff again use role plays as openers and then create a division-of-labour chart with the whole group. For each activity they identify who does it and who is responsible for decisions. The picture which emerges is that women and children do most of the work, even concerning livestock, which is considered a predominantly male responsibility. Discussion then follows on questions such as: 'Why do only men attend extension meetings?' 'Should not those who do the work also learn how to do it better?' 'And what happens if they don't learn about innovations?' Decision-making and transparency of the family budget are also debated, including who has power to earn, to spend and to decide about money.[5]

An eye-opener for the community and the extension staff is when, sooner or later, discussions focus around men's cooperation in health, nutrition and child care issues. The men regularly complain that efforts to assist their wives are blocked by the women themselves. Their own wives laugh about them, even call their friends over or gossip about their husbands who 'work in the kitchen'. The women foster the image of a strong man who beats his wife to show his dominance. One of the men took his daughter to the village clinic for a check-up and was laughed at publicly by the women there. Once, the men suggested starting a men's group to support each other in initiating changes in their households but the women mocked the idea. This represents a learning process for the women. It shows the women that they influence the process of change as much as their husbands. These experiences show the extension staff that gender is an issue about and for men and women alike.

One result of this gender-sensitization process has been an increase in requests by women for leadership workshops. Training in management, budgeting, household planning, good leadership and official positions were key demands. The women also wanted to generate their own income, to learn without the interference and dominance of men, to practise assertiveness and speaking freely in public meetings, and to gain self-confidence. The activities they planned were often for the benefit of the whole village. While some women's groups have dissolved, mostly due to internal and personal conflict and mistrust between members and the leadership, others undertake increasingly complex and independent projects and have more confidence in their dealings with non-village institutions and during public village meetings. The members are also respected by men as leaders in village development. Some women have even decided not to meet separately from the mixed village extension group any more.

Leadership workshops

The women's leadership workshops last for one to two days and take place in their village, to minimize the inconvenience. The women provide lunch and drinks and have to organize child care and someone to prepare lunch for their husbands at home.

The facilitator opens a discussion intended to identify local conflicts requiring solutions. The group is asked to prepare role plays about these conflict situations. If the group is new, it is asked to think of conflict situations which other nearby groups have or which they have at home or in the village in general.

When a role play is performed, it is stopped at the height of the conflict. The group is asked to describe what happened, if it is a real situation, and why it happened. The women discuss possible solutions in sub-groups. The solutions are then either discussed or re-enacted.

Another part of the workshop also involves role plays, this time showing good and bad leaders. In follow-up discussions, participants identify the qualities of a leader. In some cases, the women then chose their office bearers, based on the qualities they have identified. The role plays might continue to demonstrate how a good leader behaves in conflict situations.

Discussions follow concerning the tasks and responsibilities of office bearers. The final stage is the detailed planning of the activities, roles and responsibilities of each member of the group. If the group is unsure about its activities, the women discuss its goal and how to interact with the rest of the village. They explore ways of dealing with curious husbands and with those who are suspicious about their wives' involvement in a women's group. The facilitators guide the discussions, and offer advice on training topics and how to invite technical advisors.

Gender-awareness workshops

At different stages during the learning process, groups reach the point when they either demand a separate meeting to deal with gender issues or take up the offer of the extension staff to provide one. In all cases, the groups become motivated enough to deal with gender relations and see a real need to change. This point can be reached during discussion on the division of labour, or during land use planning or monitoring meetings. Sometimes this point is reached when the women become confident enough to invite their men to women's group meetings to deal together with fundamental changes.

The extension staff use these entry points to offer a gender-awareness workshop. There are three conditions: (i) couples must attend together; (ii) they must set aside two to three days of their time; and (iii) they must provide their own lunch. The extension staff work as a mixed gender team of field staff, Block Officers and Subject Matter Specialists. The workshops are held in local school rooms. Paper is stuck onto the walls or blackboards and everything is written in the local language.

After introductions, men and women are asked to split into single-sex groups and discuss 'What I like about being a woman/man' and 'What I do not like about being a woman/man'. Relatives of the same sex, e.g. a mother and daughter, are separated, as this encourages a more open discussion. Key points are written or symbolized on paper by the groups. The plenary presentations then usually provoke fierce debate. Facilitators must often ensure that women are given a chance to speak up, but, by the afternoon of the first day, the women have usually warmed up and participate freely.

These discussions form the basis for identifying key issues of concern for women and men. Usually, the issues are: oppression, lack of freedom, sole responsibility for the children, no control over resources, bride price, heavy workload, being seen as the men's slave, and the burden of being responsible for the extended family. To limit discussion and to highlight the importance of these issues in everyday life, groups are asked to select issues and depict them in role plays. Here, the guidance of the facilitators is important to ensure that the role plays are short (3 to 5 minutes) and clear.

The role plays provoke many emotions. To help women and men process the issues that are raised, they are asked to analyse each sketch in terms of the causes, consequences and solutions portrayed. If the group has difficulty thinking about solutions, it undertakes another exercise. The groups are asked to list traditional views and roles of men and women. Then they discuss the causes and effects of traditional roles and how these contribute to the oppression of men and women. Although this is time consuming, it helps enormously in making people think about what they take for granted and think is unchangeable.

Women's heavy workload usually provokes heated discussion as men refuse to admit it and women defend it. Seeking solutions for domestic responsibilities also meets with much resistance. The facilitators ask the group to enact the present conflict-situation and then an ideal situation, for example with the husband playing with the children and gathering firewood. At first, everybody laughs but inevitably they agree that this is the best solution.

The workshop ends with couples discussing how they can change their behaviour and attitude in their family and community. Seeing couples sitting together in public, which they traditionally do not do, discussing their relationships, is a powerful experience. As this is quite sensitive, the couples are given as much time as they need and can go wherever they want to talk. They are then asked to share whatever they wish about these discussions.

The workshop is evaluated either publicly or anonymously and the results are shared and considered. Everything which is written down during the workshop is copied and translated into the local language. The report is given to field staff, their supervisors, management and the villagers. As there is always someone in the women's group or in the family who can read, the participants have not yet considered a written workshop document to be problematic.

Each evaluation inevitably includes a request for a follow-up workshop. The participants want to meet again to continue certain discussions and to check which of the proposed changes and initiatives have been implemented. The women, in particular, value this support for the changes they are trying to effect from the community and extension staff. To date, these follow-up workshops have not yet taken place, as the time between initial and follow-up workshops was requested to be 6 to 12 months, depending on the season and the workload. It will be important to ensure that the same participants attend the follow-up workshop, in order to generate more support at a community level for this process of transformation.

These workshops are constantly modified, as facilitators gain experience and experiment with various methods. Evening feedback sessions amongst the facilitators are essential to assess the day and plan the next steps. Since the team sleeps in the village, villagers usually stop by the fire at night and discussions about gender issues continue long into the early hours. Workshop participants also spread information about the discussions in their community, and extension officers are often approached by others for more workshops. Schools are also expressing interest in both the topic and the approach.

One aspect has been of particular interest to the facilitation teams: village men seem to have thought about gender issues and can offer more solutions more readily than women. It is far more common to hear from the men: 'We could help with child care, we should allow our women to travel, our girls should also go to school, we should budget together, etc.' than to hear women propose: 'We should support our husbands to change and not laugh about them, we should be more open with our feelings at home, we should support other women more during public meetings, we should ask our husbands more questions for more information'. It may be that men are more used to and more courageous about expressing their ideas in public or are more used to changes due to greater involvement outside the village. But this observation needs to be understood better. At present, extension staff are still speculating about it and are starting to raise the issue with the farmers.

The institutionalization of gender-oriented participation

Several factors were significant for the institutionalization of gender-oriented participation in the extension system in Siavonga District:

o teamwork;
o interactive method development;
o training; and
o changing the terms of reference for extension staff.

A supportive system for teamwork and feedback

Feedback from the field staff was actively sought by management and the extension system responded to their needs with training, technical messages, field-level support in the field, feedback and innovative methods. One of the main support structures established was teamwork. Rather than working alone or being joined occasionally by supervisors or Subject Matter Specialists who then took over village meetings, staff members formed teams, supporting each other, sharing roles and responsibilities, and providing one another with feedback. Especially when testing new methods or in difficult village sessions, the team setting gave a sense of support. Sometimes members of other sector departments or NGOs join in, which is also effective. Generally, the field staff responsible for the village extension group carry out most of the facilitation to improve her/his skills, but in tricky situations, colleagues can be counted on to help out.

Interactive method development

The project supported extension staff in changing their attitudes, behaviour and facilitation skills with intensive backstopping in the field. Methods were first practised, safely, on themselves at meetings and training sessions, then mixed gender teams applied the methods in the villages, provided one another with feedback about the facilitation itself and discussed necessary methodological adaptations. Longer workshops were organized and conducted by teams of supervisors, field staff and Subject Matter Specialists. During monthly block meetings, field staff, their supervisors and management discussed problems with methods, facilitation or specific conflicts.

The need for different or new methods is identified by field staff at block meetings. Then Subject Matter Specialists, together with the advisors, begin the process of developing or searching for these. These are presented to the field staff, who are also trained in their use, then tried in a village setting and adapted, either on the spot or following a feedback session.

Close cooperation with NGOs in the area, such as support with training extension officers, co-facilitating village meetings or attending each other's training, stimulates inter-organizational learning. Farmers who attend NGO training sessions become village animators and assist extension staff as village facilitators in local extension group activities. Field trips to other projects and NGOs are also successful catalysts for change.

Training

To change perceptions and behaviour, training must touch the personal level (see Chapter 5, this volume). Therefore, each training starts with the personal experiences of each staff member and includes much reflection about themselves, their work and the target group. Past behaviour and situations are discussed, methods and skills proferred and future activities planned. During one of the workshops, the staff were asked to show a situation, either as a live sculpture[6] or a role play, where they had negative experiences because of their gender. Discussion followed on changes in gender roles and relationships at school, at home, in public, at church and at work. The exercises show that women and men have very emotional experiences, as children with their mothers and fathers, as students, as spouses. Men and women alike have felt oppressed and limited because of existing gender roles. It is these exercises which drive home the point that gender is relevant for women and men, is emotional and touches everyone. They highlight that changes are slow, often painful and require efforts at all levels (personal, family, community and society).

Changed terms of reference for extension staff

As part of the transformation, the role of Subject Matter Specialists who used to deal only with home economics had changed. Rather than being responsible only for women's groups and traditional women's-group activities, the female staff member was trained and assumed primary responsibility for participation, facilitation and gender. At the same time, gender issues and awareness workshops became part of the mandate of all staff. The terms of reference of Block Supervisors and Subject Matter Specialists included giving feedback and support to the field staff on facilitation skills, method development and conflict resolution.

With provincial- and national-level support, extension staff expanded their role from that of a technical advisor in the field of agriculture to a more general facilitator. They now provide linkages to other sector departments and give advice on a variety of topics: water-point development committees, adult literacy groups, school agricultural programmes, nature conservation clubs, land use planning activities.

The resulting increase in workload presented few problems. Hardly ever did staff complain about having to attend or arrange more meetings. The predominant issues were of increased fuel rations for their motorbikes due to more village visits, and the only slowly overcome resistance to working in areas which were perceived as responsibilities of other sector departments. 'Why should we do the job that should be done by the water department?' was an often-discussed question until the staff accepted that to act in the interest of the villagers meant assisting them in establishing linkages and going beyond narrowly defined sectoral technical advice.

While more meetings had to be attended and preparations for trainings which included role plays took up more time, the meetings themselves were more fun, efficient and effective, and drew a large crowd of participants. The staff were increasingly sought out as advisors and perceived as beneficial. This in turn increased the staff's standing in the village, their self-worth, sense of achievement and motivation. Since the meetings and preparations for training were also social events, it was more the increased report writing, monitoring and administrative meetings which were perceived as work overload, and silently sabotaged. Work as such was perceived as too time-consuming only when the financial situation required extensive private activities to ensure survival, a fairly frequent situation as the government coffers ran dry at regular intervals. At those times, the extension staff regulated the scale of their activities themselves and were learning to plan only those tasks for which they had adequate preparation and follow-up time.

Participation must be institutionalized if it is to be effective. Extension staff who practise participation demand appropriate management styles. They claim support structures which follow up activities and processes initiated in the villages, and planning which takes into consideration their village plans. They want a more multi-sectoral approach because the farmers' needs are not divided into categories according to government departments and cannot be solved in isolation. These demands strengthen as staff feel increasingly accountable for the processes which they generate in villages.

Conclusions

The process of institutionalizing a gender-oriented participatory extension approach described here is not complete. It has not yet taken hold in all 80 active village extension groups with which the programme works. As staff leave, new ones must be trained. Not all staff members are confident about being a facilitator nor are they all gender sensitive. It is still easier to talk only to male farmers and invite only them to meetings, than to go that extra step, do that extra bit of work, to ensure women's participation. Poor conditions of service affect motivation and job satisfaction. When another drought hits, frustration levels are high. For no matter how great participation is, if there are no results in the form of improved harvests or higher income, what difference does the approach make? How can farmers continue to be enthusiastic? The goal of the approach is human well-being, and if that is not in sight, why bother? Challenges remain.

The perspective of extension has, however, changed. The self-image of the staff, how they view their roles and those of the farmers have all changed. Many are saying that they could not and would not revert to their old work styles even if they were to be transferred to another district. Village extension groups have many more female members who speak up. The groups also expect less free assistance from the outside and are more willing to help themselves.

For now, up to this point, the work in Siavonga District offers these lessons:

○ Gender is not the sensitive topic some claim it to be. With the right methods, attitudes and approaches, it is welcomed by local people and extension staff alike.

○ Gender can be demystified. It is not a foreign, theoretical concept, can not be addressed only by women and is not only about women. If handled appropriately, gender is not a 'hot' issue that will cause problems for the facilitators. Before embarking on gender discussions, however, facilitators must feel comfortable about dealing with potential conflicts.

○ Gender affects all aspects of life and determines the success of extension work and development. At the same time, gender is inherent in the notion of participatory development, but not automatically addressed.

○ The extension staff must challenge themselves and change their views and attitudes. They need to pursue and allow change at a personal level in order to become sensitive facilitators.

○ Methods must be adapted constantly and used flexibly. They must promote change of attitudes and behaviour, and help see causal linkages between perceived needs, causes and consequences.

○ Visual PRA methods serve to accompany discussions in the process of change. However, these are only one group of methods which must be supplemented by others. In the Siavonga context, role plays have proved to be particularly useful.

○ Institutionalization must be a participatory process itself, responding to demands for change and inputs from the actors and participants concerned, and following the pace of change and development that the actors and participants in the process set and undergo.

References

Frischmuth, C (1995) *The Siavonga Experience: Integration of gender-oriented participatory approaches into the agricultural extension system – the gender-oriented participatory extension approach (GPEA)* 1993–1995. Unpublished report.
GTZ/SADP (1994) *Evaluation Report*. Zambia: GTZ–SADP.

19

Gender, Participation and Institutional Organization in Bhutanese Refugee Camps

JUSTIN GREENE-ROESEL and RACHEL HINTON
based on fieldwork with Rita Dhakal, Gita Rai and Jamuna Nepal

In the last three decades, the sum of money disbursed by donor-aid countries (DACs) to developing nations more than quadrupled.[1] Simultaneously, the philosophies and methods underpinning much assistance has been challenged by two trends: (i) non-government organizations (NGOs) are increasingly perceived as the most effective agents of micro-development;[2] and (ii) many organizations are trying to incorporate issues of gender and power (or 'empowerment') into their programmes.

One popular mechanism to achieve both these transformations has been the promotion of women's participation, and of their communities, in local development initiatives. Participation, however, is a highly variable concept. It can be encouraged in many ways, each producing a unique outcome for gender relations, empowerment and project efficacy.

The assumption is often made that a greater degree of participation will produce more effective projects and contribute to the empowerment of participants. However, it is as yet unclear whether the widespread confidence in this connection is justified. Chapter 19 examines three non-governmental organizations,[3] which operate in Bhutanese refugee camps in Nepal, to analyse the different approaches to incorporating women and refugees into organizational structural hierarchies, and the impact this has had on programme activities and on women. In so doing, it probes the multi-faceted relationship between the structure of development organizations, women's participation, and empowerment.

Background

Between 1990 and 1995, 106 600[4] men, women and children fled Bhutan in fear of political and ethnic persecution. Over 91 000 of the refugees settled in Nepal in camps such as those at Beldangi, Khundunabari and Timai.[5] As their numbers grew, eight NGOs[6] established operations in the camps, including the Refugee Development Programme (RDP), the Union of National Societies for Investment in Development (UNSID) and the Links in Service Fund (LSF).[7] They fall under the general jurisdiction of the United Nations High Commissioner for Refugees (UNHCR), which also funds a substantial part of their refugee work.

Each of these three organizations is responsible for a specific, bounded aspect of the refugees' essential needs. RDP is charged with providing facilities for formal education, in response to a request for support from young refugee teachers. LSF organizes income-generating projects, and adult education for adults or children with no previous formal schooling. UNSID, one of the first organizations on the scene, was particularly concerned about the immediate health hazards posed by the rapid settlement of a quickly growing population on a riverbank. It focuses on sanitation facilities, clean-water provision and the construction of durable shelters.

The ways in which each of these NGOs pursues its goals in the camps reflects a divergent set of assumptions about the nature of its work. For some, development means primarily the effective provision of services, with the process of that provision generally being a secondary consideration. For others, development lies not only in the material changes in the camps but also in fostering democratic[8] social relationships and shaping expectations about when, how and by whom power should be shared. These latter NGOs uphold the principle that the pursuit of empowerment is particularly important for refugees, who constitute a distinctively vulnerable group, with women warranting special attention. They believe that increased power grows from greater involvement of project beneficiaries. Thus, the participation of women, and refugees in general, is pursued as a highly effective methodology.

These different assumptions about the purposes and methods of development are forcefully reflected in the organization and distribution of power in RDP, UNSID and LSF, both in the managerial structures of the local office and in the execution of projects in the camps. The following case studies examine how women participate in the NGOs and their projects, both in the office and in the field.

The structure of organizations and the distribution of power

The Refugee Development Programme

The most notable feature of RDP's organizational structure is its relative flatness (see Figure 19.1). With the exception of the director, power is distributed evenly between employees, and both information and authority flow horizontally rather than down the hierarchies. RDP's political framework is highly egalitarian. Employees share power and responsibility for making decisions. Women are employed at every level of operation, from senior management to camp-based staff. These women occupy positions and hold responsibilities with equal voice in decision-making as men and expatriates. Similarly, many of these women are refugees, who hold considerable managerial authority and are incorporated into the political structure of the organization. The distribution of authority between partners at RDP partially reflects the organizational philosophy of its director, who champions equality and the sharing of power and decision-making. This atmosphere of communication and cooperation is discernible to employees of RDP, whose diagrams of the organization point to the absence of hierarchy (see Figure 19.4).

Women, whether refugee, Nepali or expatriate, are decision-makers at the office level, and pass on plans that are developed together to field-based employees who implement them. They are confident about their

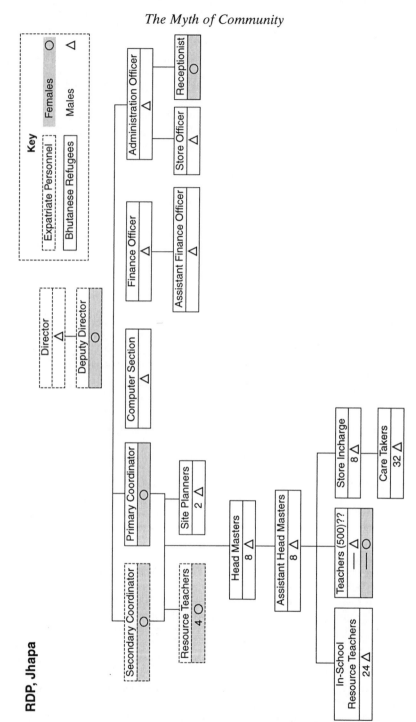

Figure 19.1: The organizational structure of the RDP office

management and teaching skills, which, with the high standards of education that are prevalent in Bhutan, encourage their participation.

In the field, the horizontal structure of power virtually duplicates that of the office. Even the entrance of RDP into the camps followed a request made by young refugee teachers for a supporting agency. The UNHCR, with whom the request was lodged, worked more with international organizations than indigenous ones to limit the potential for internal conflict and the politicization of issues. RDP, however, offered the young teachers its services, a gesture which was welcomed. Women refugees held particularly great authority in the RDP for two reasons: (i) most of the available teachers in the camps were female, and (ii) the lack of Nepali teaching staff in the host country made Bhutanese women much more eligible for teaching and project staff jobs than Nepali women or men. These factors facilitated the incorporation of refugee women into RDP's organizational structure, and allowed the refugee teachers' group to retain control over its own educational programme.

Links in Service Fund

Like the RDP, the Links in Service Fund (LSF) has a political commitment to encouraging participation in decision-making and implementation as a means to empowerment. But it is organized more hierarchically (see Figures 19.2 and 19.4), with structural and cultural constraints that, at times, impede the full participation of female employees and project beneficiaries. As in RDP, women are employed at LSF in every capacity, from managers to fieldworker. Although most of its employees are women, they are noticeably absent from senior management. Women hold only two senior managerial positions in the organization. One of these is the head of LSF, who, being an educated expatriate from a western culture, finds social integration with men easier than do the refugee women. The second post held by a woman is the income generation officer (IGO). This position, while intended to be managerial, has been relegated to one of implementer because of patterns of gender relations prevalent in Bhutan and Nepal. The postholder was contracted to join the senior management team as a decision-maker who passes decisions along to her subordinates. However, the woman who took this role was supervised by a man who was unable to delegate authority effectively, nor support the woman socialized into a culture which rendered her less confident about claiming this decisionmaking power.

The income generation officer's situation is a clear example of how, despite a commitment to the reciprocal and equal sharing of information and authority, a range of barriers (structural or cultural) may impede organizational structures from empowering women and refugees (see Chapter 22, this volume). The IGO expressed her frustration, lamenting: 'As a woman I cannot speak out against him [my supervisor]. I must request permission before taking decisions. I have ideas but if they are not made his, there will be no action.'

The flow of power and decision-making at LSF was nearly always directed from men to women, despite having two women in senior management positions. Elsewhere in the organization, women occupied capacities

213

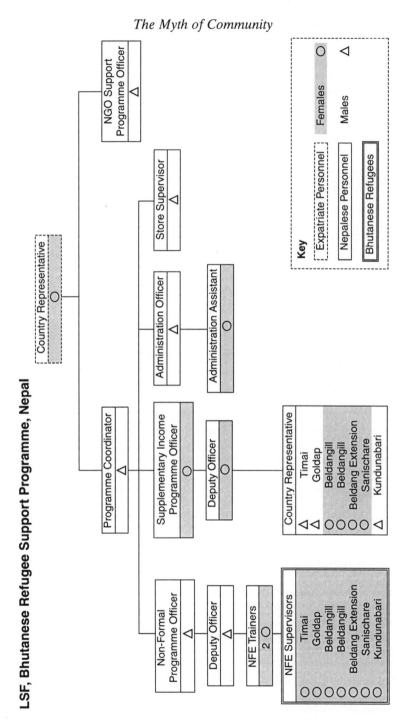

Figure 19.2: The organizational structure of the LSF office

that are culturally more traditional (e.g. teachers), and operated generally in all-female fora, with meeting places typically located on the camp's outskirts. Furthermore, the women employed by LSF were rarely refugee women. Refugees were typically employed only at the very bottom of the organizational hierarchy, and were virtually always supervised by Nepali staff.

One Nepali project officer at LSF explained the reluctance to hire refugees as follows:

> The Asian culture is different. They [the refugees] do not have the capacity to participate fully. Outside they are honest and say what they think but they do not have the courage to talk in front of the others. Participation should only be for operational stages; for planning and organizational issues it is too difficult for their involvement (Fieldnotes, 1994).

In fact, LSF focuses explicitly on Nepali candidates to fill staffing positions, virtually excluding refugee women from its employment in any official capacity. As the Nepali Programme Coordinator claimed: 'It is not good to have refugees at the office level, as all kinds of problems may arise'. LSF's agenda aims to empower local people as an important component of its operations, but it gears its 'local' capacity building, management training and skill development specifically towards Nepali people, rather than the many women who are its project beneficiaries.

In a broader sense, however, LSF International's commitment to women is clear. Though women are not typically 'decisionmakers' in the field, they account for approximately 98 per cent of its 'employees'.[9] These women are paid teachers or adult education (AE) supervisors, and thousands of them receive incentives to produce a variety of crafts in LSF's income-generating projects. At the field level, LSF is eager to encourage multi-directional flows of information and decision-making, from and between the women who are project beneficiaries. Women empower themselves by earning an income, by participating in action-oriented literacy programmes, and by helping plan and manage projects (such as an adult education school) sponsored by the LSF. But cultural constraints impede, at times, the 'empowerment' of women through participation, as in the office setting. The LSF directs its Nepali field supervisors to share the implementation and decision-making tasks of building the school with the women. Often, however, the rigidly hierarchical gender relations typical of Nepal makes this transfer of power difficult to achieve.

Union of National Societies for Investment in Development

Of the three NGOs described here, the organizational structure of UNSID is the most obviously hierarchical (see Figures 19.3 and 19.4) and is virtually exclusively male.[10] In 1994, male managers at UNSID recognized the considerable gender imbalance in their organization and created a supervisory post to be occupied by a woman, to whom eight camp-based women would report in their capacity as community mobilizers. Although, strictly speaking, authority flowed to these women from a female

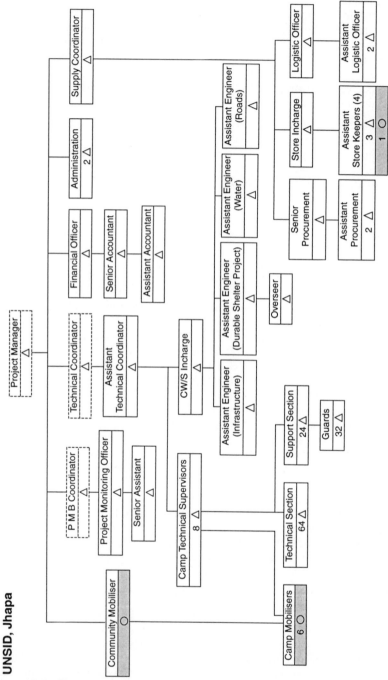

Figure 19.3: The organizational structure of the UNSID office

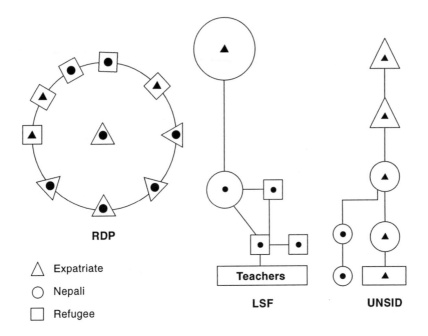

Figure 19.4: Employees' representations of the organizational structures of three NGOs

superior, in reality, the male administrators of UNSID camp-based activities directed their work. These nine new posts were conceived quickly and were poorly planned, designed specifically to resolve perceptions of inequality in the institution's management. This tokenistic treatment of women's absence from decision-making produced artificial roles and few responsibilities for the women, leaving them largely unoccupied and subordinate to male authority. Yashodha, one of the camp mobilizers, explained: 'I just have to sit here. They do not tell me what to do. I must mobilize the community . . . so I speak with the women in the committee.'

Fieldnotes describe her predicament:

Yashodha is becoming very despondent, and sits in her room for hours on end. When she is bored she wanders into our research room to observe the activity. She knows the overall goals of her post, yet has not been equipped with the skills and does not command the authority to approach the community.

Despite intentions to the contrary, authority at UNSID flows routinely from men to women who implement decisions, and from expatriates to Nepalis to refugees. Simply placing women in high positions of authority and inviting their participation in decision-making and initiating action does not negate other, structural factors that may prevent them from filling prescribed roles and, in the end, from being empowered.

During the initial emergency phase of the camps, UNSID projects were typically and understandably reactive to crisis, such as the outbreak of cholera or a dearth of potable water. In fact, most of the needs addressed by UNSID were identified by international monitoring organizations, such as the World Health Organization (WHO) or the UNHCR. This stands in marked contrast to the LSF and RDP projects, which were either initiated by or focused on refugee women. UNSID's goal was to provide critical health and sanitation services in a timely and efficient manner. Refugee capacity building and 'empowerment' were not its priority and, moreover, were not seen as feasible in an emergency situation.[11] As a result, Bhutanese women (and male refugees also) appear at the bottom of UNSID's hierarchy. They may implement policy but are seldom given the opportunity to design it themselves. Unlike with RDP and LSF, women are not specifically targeted as project beneficiaries. Their participation is not coordinated in any deliberate manner, and the empowerment of women, especially in the crisis phase, is not identified as a key objective. Only after the emergency phase in the camps had passed, did UNSID attempt to redress the absence of women on its staff but without an explicit focus on the needs and empowerment of women.

Employees' views of the organizations

The diagrammatic representations in Figure 19.4 are from Beldangi camp. They were produced in discussion with a group of four to six refugee women employees from each organization. In RDP they were teachers, in LSF they were income generation instructors and in UNSID they were the women community mobilizers. The equivalent request was made of each level of management, and differing perceptions of the management structure were produced.[12] The higher up the management structure the employees were, the closer they came to producing a replica of the official 'organigram'.

In diagramming the structures, the refugees used people's names and, without exception, noted when they were 'outsiders' (Nepalis rather than refugees). This was more prominent in the discussion than the gender issue which was the central topic of debate where the local head of the organization was male and exerted great control over the programme officers. In many respects, the structure of UNSID seemed to be the least problematic for the refugees. The clear hierarchical staffing was recognized, accepted and represented in discussion and on paper. Power was located in those at the top of the organization, who also happened to be male. This was not seen as problematic, as when the refugees seemed confused about the lines of responsibility and control as in the case of LSF. Interestingly, discussion about RDP mentioned the head of the organization as a 'central' coordinator, rather than a director controlling from 'above'. The links between these different organizational structures and impact will be assessed in the next section.

218

A closer look at 'participation', empowerment and conflict

The key factor which we have discussed so far is the general inclusion, or 'participation', of women in NGO activities in the camps. Advocates believe that greater participation is both possible and desirable, whether for greater project sustainability, or the empowerment of women and the transformation of their lives.

Despite its widespread emphasis, the purpose and characteristics of participation are rarely differentiated or clarified. It may be understood to be a means to an end (a strategy to reduce costs[13] or improve project quality and maintenance) and/or as an end in itself (as a mechanism promoting empowerment and democratic social relationships)[14] (Nelson and Wright, 1994). For an example that appears to combine these perspectives, Rifkin (1986: 933) defines participation as 'a social process whereby specific groups with shared needs living in a defined geographic area actively pursue the identification of their needs, take decisions and establish mechanisms to meet these needs'.[15]

Paul (1987) provides one typology of participation, breaking down project development and execution into four types, which may exist simultaneously: information sharing, consultation, decision-making and initiating action (see Box 19.1). Each of these types affords project beneficiaries (as opposed to implementing agencies or other non-beneficiaries) an increasing degree of control over project objectives and procedures. This sort of analysis has been criticized for several reasons, particularly on the grounds that participation is not linear or bounded in simple ways.[16] Despite its weaknesses, Paul's classification offers a basis for comparing the inclusion of certain groups and communities in development processes. It also allows a basis for deciding if other forms of participation that devolve more power to beneficiaries are desirable and feasible.

As with other typologies, Paul's framework for assessing the nature of community participation assumes that a greater degree of participation (in ascending order from types 1 to 4 in Box 19.1) will produce more effective projects and contribute to the empowerment of participants. This is a common, but rarely stated assumption. It is as yet unclear whether the widespread confidence in this connection is justified, as there are few studies that have looked explicitly at the impact of participation (see Winkler and Finsterbusch, 1989; Narayan, 1993; and IIED, forthcoming).

Certainly, participation can have a marked impact on the timing of project completion, the quality and maintenance of construction and the comparative costs of the projects. In building projects sponsored by each of the three NGOs, work was completed approximately on time, though with participatory projects (for example of LSF and RDP) this was probably because they allotted a much longer period of time for completion. Non-participatory efforts (such as those undertaken by UNSID's contractors) produced a higher quality of construction. Yet a lack of a feeling of ownership led to little maintenance of the building following its completion. While participation in the form of labour contributions can reduce daily financial inputs into a project, work must be funded over a longer period of time and may eventually be more costly.

Box 19.1:   Paul's four types of participation

(1) *Information sharing* refers to a process in which agencies inform intended beneficiaries about a project they plan to conduct. Although beneficiaries may contribute labour and local resources, all information and authority emanate from the organization.

(2) A relationship characterized by *consultation* similarly distributes power and information from the top down.[17] However, the implementing agencies employ local knowledge in formulating their plans. In such a relationship, participation is a means to improving project effectiveness. It may also enable the NGO to reach a larger group of people and to identify more accurately its target population.

(3) A *decision-making model* is pursued by some NGOs which emphasize information flows to and from communities and, specifically, women as an essential component of their activities. Beneficiaries actively discuss needs, identify solutions and plan intended projects. However, a fair degree of responsibility and control is retained by the external agency.

(4) *Initiating action* is characterized by the upward flow of both information and control, though these are often limited by the constraints of donor agencies and project procedures.[18] Participation at this level is encouraged by ensuring local responsibility and ownership of a project. This form of participation represents the ideal for many agencies but remains an elusive goal as it usually requires fundamental changes in organizational cultures and skills.

More critical to this discussion, however, is the emphasis of participation as a means to empowerment. Using the case studies presented above, together with Paul's classification, the remainder of this chapter will examine the relationship between women's participation and empowerment.[19]

Assessing participation

Women employed at various levels of each of the organizations were requested to rate the extent to which they had a voice in programme design and implementation. The results are represented in the form of affirming involvement, partial involvement or no involvement. The comparisons highlight a correlation between vertical structures and levels of participation, and reflect interesting cultural differences between the NGO and beneficiary population. Women's relatively high degree of participation was apparent at each level in the RDP and LSF, which stood in contrast to the reported situation for UNSID (see Tables 19.1 and 19.2).

At RDP, women were integrated at all levels of the organization, were project initiators and administrators. They reported active involvement at

Table 19.1: Women's participation at office level

Participation type	RDP	LSF	UNSID
Consultation	+	+	+
Information sharing	+	%	−
Decision-making	+	−	−
Initiating action	+	−	−

Note: + yes   % partially   − not at all

Table 19.2: Women's participation in camp-based projects

Participation type	RDP	LSF	UNSID
Consultation	+	+	+
Information sharing	+	+	−
Decision-making	+	−	−
Initiating action	+	+	−

Note: + yes   % partially   − not at all

each stage of the project cycle from initiating action to decision-making and consultation. Women comprised half of the population targeted by the RDP's education projects. This contrasts with LSF and UNSID.

Women at LSF reported differential inclusion in its organizational structure at the office and camp levels. Surprisingly it was at camp level, where the majority of 'cultural barriers' were reported to lie, that the highest levels of participation were seen. At the office level, participation occurred primarily in the form of consultation. The new positions that LSF established did not challenge the traditional gender hierarchy. The differences between camp and office also reflected the less rigid gender hierarchies in Bhutanese society and leadership from high-caste Nepalis, respectively. At the project level, women requested, initiated and were largely responsible for the adult schools project, though they participated less in the income generating programme. Women were also targeted exclusively as beneficiaries of these projects, with LSF classifying '99 per cent' of its employees (i.e. beneficiaries) as women.

Finally, UNSID did not include women as decision-makers or action initiators in either its organizational structure or in its projects. Partly, women were not the primary targets of project activities (although this was also true for RDP); more significantly, the realm of work was considered to lie in the male domain. The existence of poor male:female employee ratios reinforced this belief. UNSID's ability to mobilize women's support in the camp was lacking. Both in the office and in the field, women, like other refugees, were simply 'informed' of the organization's goals, despite management's attempts to do otherwise and the employment of women camp mobilizers.

221

Assessing the claims to empowerment

Having established the levels at which women participated in the organizational structures and activities of these three NGOs, we can turn to the relationship of women's participation to their empowerment. Is the empowerment of women intended? Is it achieved? How are the two linked?

One definition of empowerment, on which this analysis will rely, points to its goal of changing the social relationships of men and women in Bhutanese society (see Chapter 2, this volume). Empowerment, according to this definition, is expressed when 'women and men themselves are involved in the articulation of goals, the allocation of resources and the execution of programmes and projects, which should ultimately lead to the goal of autonomy in decision-making about matters affecting their lives' (Overseas Division Strategic Plan, 1993). It thus refers to the appropriation of power by groups of people who previously lacked it, both in the acquisition of skills and tools of taking action (e.g. language and literacy), and of confidence and experience in self-determination.[20] As promoted by development organizations, empowerment is fundamentally a democratic process which implies that women should be able to 'participate positively in social changes, in terms of both personal growth and public action' (Rifkin, 1986:13). In the case of refugee camps, however, this goal is often elusive, because the 'empowered' person's state of dislocation as a refugee renders him or her much more vulnerable.[21]

What, then, are the links between participation and empowerment? Clearly, participation at a high level (as in Paul's classification) stimulates a greater sense of autonomy and a demonstrable capacity to be decision-makers. Yet we challenge the assumption of a linear, causal link between the two processes.

In the RDP project, women are empowered as decision-makers and action initiators both at the office and project levels. Though they are not exclusively the targets of the projects themselves, the development of literacy among young women certainly promotes their capacity for creative analysis and decision-making. Women, in this context, are empowered within the organization, within each project and by the project activity itself. The pursuit of women's empowerment is thus thoroughly integrated into the RDP's programmes.

At LSF, women are exclusively the targets of the adult education programme and the income generating projects, and define themselves positively in relation to these schemes. These women remark readily on the confidence and valuable new skills they have acquired in the process:

We are building the classrooms, so that we can learn more and come up to the level of the men. Many women want to learn, [so] we all help with the building. (Sabitra, refugee woman)

I feel very happy [to be a part of LSF's programme] because women have got the opportunity to work equally and together with the men. This will help the women to develop more confidence and work together. (Prova, refugee woman)

The LSF classroom was requested by the women themselves and they participated in the project in all four ways identified by Paul. The camp's female coordinator explains:

> All the materials from the contractors are handled by the women. Sometimes even the women returned the goods, for example if they didn't meet the quality . . . All the carpenters' requirements, the receipts, the money, they are handled by the [women] . . . I do not take full authority. I asked the [women's group] secretary to sign the papers for the building. That has made her also take more responsibility. It's made [the women's group] feel that LSF's programmes are theirs. The women participate . . . I could employ the guard myself, but I involve the [women]. They employ them. The [women] take responsibility.'

While the literature on development assumes that greater degrees of participation are required to achieve women's (or community) empowerment, the case studies challenge that linear correlation. The LSF's income generation project is a prime example. Women are, by Paul's standards, participating in consultation and initiating action but not in the important level of decision-making. Their practical gender needs were being addressed without affecting their strategic needs. Women requested the project but are otherwise only implementers, receiving and carrying out the decisions of the NGO's management. Women are placed at the bottom of LSF's structural hierarchy.

Yet the 300 women who work as LSF's knitting and weaving instructors considered the programme empowering. They say it is the first time they have been able to develop the skills of community leadership. As a body of women, they have formed alliances and supported one another collectively. In 1994 alone, over 7000 women increased their personal autonomy through activities which gave them independent access to cash. Yet the women make no decisions with regard to the project, and acquire few skills which enhance their capacity to occupy positions of greater power within local structures of authority. In this example, participation and empowerment are largely unrelated to the acquisition of power in a public domain.

Another example supports the absence of a linear, causal link between participation and empowerment. In contrast to its income generating activities, LSF's adult education project in 1994 gave 6409 women greater access to participation in decision-making:

> When in Mai [the original refugee site], we had opened schools amongst ourselves. We founding members wrote an application to the LSF. We put forward the proposal for an education programme.

As teachers and students, they gain confidence and fortify their voice. Yet they had achieved this in a private, female space. It is the nature of the activity rather than the structure of authority, decision-making or the acquisition of personal income which has empowered the camp's women. As Tulsha, a refugee woman, described: 'We feel a sense of respect from other community members. I feel proud'. Another confirmed: 'We can say that we have started this LSF programme by ourselves and now it is running well' (Devika). The adult education project cultivates in the women the

223

skills that they perceive as necessary for entry into the male domain of decision-making, of language and literacy or, as Sita said, the confidence to 'speak out'. The proficiency in verbal expression that they gain is then applied in other areas of camp life.[22]

Education and literacy promoted careful, capable decision-making, and the income-generating projects expanded women's abilities to transform their decisions into the material reality of their family lives. But women are not involved at Paul's highest levels in the LSF office, and at only one of the highest levels in only one of its two main projects. Women's empowerment is not achieved in these contexts, despite being one of the organization's foremost goals.

Finally, at UNSID, women's empowerment is not sought in the organization's structure, in its project design and implementation, or in the actual activities each project initiated (see Table 19.3).

Particularly with respect to UNSID, excluding women from participation in the decisions which affect their lives breeds a strong sense of disempowerment. One refugee noted the feeling of being a notional participant in the NGO's schemes: 'With UNSID, we just do as they direct'. Project beneficiaries are fully aware of the implications of their exclusion from the decision-making and action-initiating processes, and expressed resentment and cynicism. One refugee leader articulated this sentiment, noting at a UNHCR meeting that: 'We are the children; when we cry, we are fed'. This statement conveys the sense of dependency and disempowerment that a lack of significant participation stimulates, in which people expect their every need to be provided for, as though they were children. Simultaneously, it is a tool by which the refugees also elicit sympathy and support, a mechanism used pragmatically by the 'disempowered'.

These examples make it clear that empowerment can be achieved at several levels, whether in the organizational structure of the NGOs, in the design and implementation of the projects, or in the outcomes of the project activities themselves (e.g., income-generating schemes or literacy projects). But in only one of these three organizations, in RDP, is the goal of women's empowerment integrated at each of these levels. At LSF, empowerment is only partially integrated, and at UNSID, it does not appear as a priority at any level.

Conflict and change

Inequalities of participation are more readily examined within the beneficiary community and, ironically, may be left unaddressed within the very

Table 19.3: Women's involvement in different aspects of the NGO programme

Women's empowerment	RDP	LSF	UNSID
Structure – NGO organization	+	%	–
Process – skill development	+	%	–
Project – activity	%	+	–

Note: + yes   % partially   – not at all

organizations promoting gender equality. Organizations differ in their willingness to include women in their structure and individual managers feel threatened to different degrees by the power they may adopt. Often the desire for women's empowerment at the local level is driven by the NGO leaders motivated by western feminist ideals, rather than change being due to underlying indigenous initiatives.

As an increasing number of NGOs incorporate participation and empowerment into their organization and project paradigms, the examples above testify to the changes that can transpire in women's lives. They may lead to community members themselves exposing inequalities since they are more likely to see themselves as decision-makers and hold authority in their families and communities. But what many fail to recognize is that these very shifts in women's relationships frequently breed conflict in societies which have not yet, as a whole, integrated the values associated with women's empowerment. What remains unclear is the intensity of hostility where the community, rather than an outsider, itself exposes inequalities.

The empowerment of women is particularly complex with respect to the domestic conflicts it engenders, for the hierarchical and male-dominated structures of Nepalese society are generally hostile to elevating women's status. LSF's work in promoting the position of women in the camps was noted to have caused family tensions. Many of the women's husbands, for example, resented the manifestations of 'empowerment' in their daily lives, especially the women's new found access to spending power through the income generating projects, or their growing tendency to assert themselves as decision-makers at home. Husbands' frustrations with shifting domestic power relations was, at times, expressed aggressively, or by restricting women's activities and behaviours. One refugee woman described, for example, how:

> When my third daughter fell sick the remedies did not work so I called for a *puja*. These days I have the money to decide what remedies to take. Birkha does not agree that women should be involved in that way. He wants me to be in the hut. But here there is nothing to do and it is hot. Sometimes he becomes angry that I am free to roam but all night he is drinking in the bazaar.

Participatory projects may also breed discord at a community level (Rifkin, 1986) or trigger existing latent conflicts. For example, women active in NGO projects are often envied for their income or are held accountable to their neighbours for unpopular organizational decisions. One refugee explained, for example, that because she was employed by the refugee NGO and had to call upon her friends and neighbours to provide volunteer labour she felt guilty about her privilege: 'Sometimes I feel embarrassed about the money I receive'. Others protested at what they saw as RDP's unfair selection of certain women (and men) for paid positions.

Conflict in the camps as a result of women's participation and greater access to power and decision-making was described by another woman. She recalled the refugees' response to the decreasing standards of plastic issued by the UNHCR. While once they were given high-grade plastics stamped with a UNHCR insignia:

Now we just get plain plastic, and the community thinks the original good ones were sold [by refugee employees] in collaboration with the agencies. So there is much mistrust [among us].

When problems arise, community members are suspicious of those most closely connected with the NGOs, blame them and accuse them of corruption.

Conclusions

With the burgeoning of spending by donors and non-government organizations in recent years, self-reflection by agencies into their development philosophies and strategies has led to an overwhelming emphasis on community participation. This chapter has examined how three organizations have sought to increase the participation of women and of refugees in their activities in Bhutanese refugee camps in Nepal. It has presented a framework for the assessment of the level of participation, and analysed the implications of increased participation in office- and field-based activities. Each case has illustrated several factors which may influence the achievement of empowerment through participation in local development processes.

What is clear is that empowerment and participation are not necessarily linearly or causally linked. Women may be empowered by a project activity, despite having little or no participation in its design or administration. But empowerment without women's participation in the highest ranks of an organization, and at every stage of project design and implementation, fails to establish even the most minimal commitment to the very goal the NGOs intend to pursue.

Two of the NGOs discussed here achieved their objective of enhancing women's autonomy in decision-making about matters affecting their lives. Such autonomy is particularly pertinent in women's relationships with men and with their communities. Yet the NGOs' objective must be translated into one final relationship: that of the relationship of women with the NGOs themselves.

Failure to include women in organizational and project administration renders the pursuit of women's empowerment an empty and imperialistic goal. It attempts to initiate change in hierarchical, male-dominated societies but neglects to take responsibility for the same objectives within the organization itself.

The pursuit of such an ideal is not without problems. Conflicts occur where positions of power are threatened and NGOs would do well to recognize that change usually involves confrontation between interests. Whilst the agencies may act as the catalysts for intervention, for sustainable change women have to be the initiators and take on the responsibility and consequences of empowerment for themselves. NGOs need to be sensitive to the pace of change and the level of support required. A clash of interests is fundamental to the democratic participation they are trying to encourage. Yet conflict often remains invisible, disguised as a negative event by NGOs keen to portray an image of project harmony. Until its existence is recognized and addressed, both within and outside the organizations, the real process of change will remain undocumented.

References

Adnan, S., A. Barrett, S.M. Nurul Alam and A. Brustinow (1992) *People's Particip-ation, NGOs, and the Flood Action Plan*. Dhaka: Research and Advisory Services.

Buvinic, M., (1986) 'Projects for Women in the Third World: explaining their mis-behaviour', *World Development*, Vol. 14, No. 5.

Cornwall, A. (1996) 'Towards Participatory Practice: Participatory Rural Appraisal (PRA) and the Participatory Process', in Koning, K. de and M. Martin (eds), *Participatory Research in Health: Issues and Experiences*. London: Zed Books.

Cuny, Frederick (1987) 'Refugee Participation in Emergency Relief Operations', Washington, DC: Refugee Policy Group.

Esman, M. and N. Uphoff (1984) 'Local Organizations: intermediaries in rural development', in A. Fowler, Non-governmental Organizations in Africa: achiev-ing comparative advantage in relief and micro-development, *IDS Discussion Paper* No. 249, August.

Finsterbusch, K. and W.A. van Wicklin III (1989) 'Beneficiary Participation in Development Projects: empirical tests of popular theories', *Economic Develop-ment and Cultural Change*, 37(3): 573–93.

Galjart, B. and D. Buijs, (1982) *Participation of the Poor in Development*, Leiden: Leiden Development Studies.

van Giffen, D. Flud (1982) 'Problematics of Participation: a post-facto contribu-tion', in B. Galjart and Buijs, D. (1982).

Guijt, I. (1998) 'Assessing the Merits of Participatory Development of Sustainable Agriculture: experiences from Brazil and Central America', in: J. Blauert and S. Zadek (eds), *Mediating Sustainability*, Hartford, Conn: Kumarian Press.

Hart, R. (1992) *Children's Participation: From Tokenism to Citizenship*, UNICEF: Florence.

Hayward, Fred (1981) 'Political Participation and Its Role in Development: some observations drawn from the African context'.

IIED, (forthcoming) *Fertile Ground: The impacts of participatory watershed man-agement*, London: Intermediate Technology Publications.

Moser, Caroline (1989) 'Gender Planning in the Third World: meeting practical and strategic gender needs', *World Development*, Vol. 17, No. 11.

Narayan, D. (1993) *Focus on participation: evidence from 121 rural water-supply projects*, UNDP World Bank Water Supply and Sanitation Program, Washington DC: World Bank.

Nelson, N. and S. Wright (eds) (1995) *Power and Participatory Development: theory and practice*, London: Intermediate Technology Publications.

OECD (1988) *Voluntary Aid for Development: The Role of Non-Governmental Organizations*, Paris: OECD.

OECD (1997) *Major Recipients of Individual Members' Aid – Total DAC*, Www.oecd.org., Table 42.

Paul, S. (1987) 'Community Participation in Development Projects', *World Bank Discussion Paper*, No. 6.

Pretty, J. (1994) 'Alternative systems of inquiry for sustainable agriculture', *IDS Bulletin* 25 (2).

Rifkin, S. B. (1986) 'Lessons from Community Participation in Health Pro-grammes', *Health Policy and Planning*, Vol. 1, No. 3.

Stone, L. (1992) 'Cultural Differences in Community Participation in Health', *Social Science and Medicine*, Vol. 35, No. 4.

20

Agreeing to Disagree: Dealing with gender and age in Redd Barna Uganda

IRENE GUIJT, TONY KISADHA and GRACE MUKASA[1]

with fieldwork by Geoffrey Mugisha, Simon Okalebo, Richard Ochen, Joanita Sewagudde and Benon Webare

After many years of civil war, Uganda is undergoing an intense process of national reconstruction. Planning for more equitable development plays a central role in ensuring that resources are allocated to benefit all parts of the country and all social groups. Redd Barna Uganda (RBU), a non-governmental organization (NGO),[2] is providing support to government agencies and other NGOs in planning efforts that will benefit Uganda's children. This means building planning capacities at both the district and national levels, and also with communities.

In 1994, Redd Barna Uganda turned to participatory rural appraisal (PRA) as a methodology with great potential for community-based planning. The principle of 'community participation' seemed to fulfil its need for a methodology that could deal with gender and age differences, or 'intra-communal difference'. However, RBU found a surprising lack of information about two fundamental aspects: (i) how intra-communal differences can be addressed systematically; and (ii) how communities can be involved in planning and not just appraisal. The legacy of quick analysis, inherited from the rapid rural appraisal tradition, had persisted in much of the initial PRA work in the early 1990s. This fostered a belief that successful PRA could be identified by the existence of a 'Community Action Plan'. Yet such plans are often developed over too short a time frame, and wrongly claim to reflect 'the community's opinion', while commonly ignoring the needs of younger women and children.

Redd Barna Uganda set out to modify participatory planning to ensure inclusion of women and children, and emphasize the building of local planning skills. Two main features now guide its community-based work: (i) it encourages a slower and more adaptive planning process, based on understanding and negotiating differences within the community; and (ii) it encourages planning with smaller groups of community members, alongside community-wide plans, to enable gender- and age-specific needs to be expressed and resolved. Through this process, community members learn to 'agree to disagree' about priorities, while not losing the benefits of collective action at the community level.

Chapter 20 discusses the context in which RBU is aiming to make a positive difference and how it evolved its particular approach to participatory planning that involves five social groups: younger and older men and women, and children. It describes the steps that Redd Barna Uganda takes to ensure the participation, in particular, of women and children in community-based planning.

Development challenges in Uganda

Just over ten years ago, Uganda was in the throes of a traumatic and drawn-out civil war. Today it is engaged in an intense effort of national reconstruction. This is taking place at many levels: physically, with the repair of roads and health infrastructure; socially, notably with the reintegration of soldiers into peacetime professions and the reconciling of many ethnic differences; and politically, with open national elections and decentralization of government roles and responsibilities (c.f. Hansen and Twaddle, 1991; RBU, 1996). Uganda with its current rate of 8 per cent growth is widely recognized as a success, particularly in comparison to neighbouring countries and its own recent past.[3]

Yet Ugandans still face many severe social challenges. Although the infant mortality rate has improved since the late 1960s, it still stands at 98[4] (Fuglesang and Chandler, 1996). HIV infection is rampant, up to 30 per cent in some areas, with 80 per cent of infections found in the economically and reproductively active ages of 15 and 45. HIV infection affects girls from about 10 years old, much younger than for boys, and infection rates among women are generally higher than those of men (Barnett and Blaikie, 1995). AIDS is the leading cause of death in adults in Uganda (Barton and Wamai, 1994), and over 8 per cent of the total AIDS cases are children.[5]

Not only does great human tragedy lie behind such statistics; the data also indicate problems for the agricultural sector on which Uganda depends. Almost 90 per cent of the population live in rural areas and most are active in agricultural production. Subsistence agriculture, based on human labour, is the main source of food for most Ugandans. Agricultural productivity is likely to be seriously threatened as people fall ill and die, and labour decreases. With fewer adults, dependency ratios of children on adults will rise, exacerbating this problem.

RBU's response

For Redd Barna Uganda, the way forward lies with child-centred planning. Its strategy is one of supporting planning efforts at different levels (from groups within communities to the national level) with the aim of increasing resource allocation to address better the needs of children. Instead of funding and implementing on-ground works, it facilitates these planning processes. Therefore, as a non-operational organization, it relies heavily on strong partnerships with other NGOs, community-based organizations, and government agencies. Central to its work are its district-level staff, the Child Advocacy Project Officers.

The focus on children and planning

Three factors underpin RBU's approach:

(1) Strong national development is possible only with a healthy, educated and committed population, of which Uganda's 8.5 million rural children are the foundation. While children are generally warmly welcomed in

Ugandan society, they lack basic needs and are thus hampered in their mental and physical development (Barton and Wamai, 1994).

(2) Uganda is decentralizing, shifting responsibility and power to the districts and sub-counties.[6] While new powers to plan, budget and implement provide new opportunities, it has also created problems as there is a weak planning tradition, insufficient capacity to fulfil the new responsibilities and much opportunity for corruption. These problems are exacerbated in the case of child-oriented planning, which requires integration across the agricultural, education, health, and social-welfare sectors. This situation has created greater awareness amongst district and sub-county officials of the need for increasing their planning capacity.

(3) Pervasive social differences hinder child-centred development, by neglecting their needs and those of their main carers, younger women. As elsewhere in the world, differences in status and power maintain disparities between the old and young, the better-off and worse-off, and, of course, between women and men. Such differences make collective planning difficult and require careful thought as to how marginal groups can be included safely and effectively.

How RBU works

Redd Barna Uganda works simultaneously at the national, district, sub-county and community levels. At the national level, it is supporting the recently established National Council for Children by advocating child-friendly legislation and the implementation of a National Plan of Action for Children. At the district and sub-county levels, it is working with government planners, supporting the collection of essential statistics and helping them write Sub-county and District Plans of Action for Children. At the community level, it works mainly through partner organizations, playing a coordinating, facilitating and training role, rather than a direct operational one. In particular, it trains community members, government extension workers, district heads of departments, and staff of NGOs and community-based organizations in participatory planning.

Key to these activities are the Child Advocacy Project Officers (CAPOs),[7] who work in teams of two in the district capitals. They facilitate the district and sub-county level planning, establish relationships with partner organizations, facilitate training related to child-centred planning and advocate for children's rights in all fora. On recruitment, each CAPO is trained in planning-related methodologies, including: basic communications skills (BCS), mediated learning experience (MLE),[8] the logical framework approach (LFA), and participatory rural appraisal and planning (PRAP). In recognition of the many roles CAPOs are expected to fulfil, training has recently expanded to build skills in facilitation techniques, conflict resolution and the Child-to-Child[9] methodology.

Learning about participatory planning

In the three years since the work started, RBU's approach has developed around 'five crucial stages of the journey of child-centred development which recognizes intra-communal differences' (Sewagudde *et al.*, 1997). This section describes how RBU evolved its approach from the first steps with community-based planning.

First steps

RBU's first experience with PRAP took place in March 1994 in the community of Kyakatebe (Masaka District) and involved a training facilitated by IIED. It was the first exposure to participatory appraisal and planning for the newly recruited CAPOs. Five groups of community members were involved in the week-long analysis: children (mainly school-going), younger unmarried women, married women, younger men and older men. Initial results seemed positive. Within a few months, a community action plan was finalized,[10] and implementation started. Changes after six months included several new women's income-generation groups, improved agricultural plots, and extensive home improvements. Two years later, two schools had been (re)built by employing and training local unemployed youth.

However, about 18 months later, despite the initial positive impacts, the community planning and action process seemed to fizzle out. A community meeting in Kyakatebe, on 29 September 1995, identified the lack of determination, patience, trust, pleasure in the work and confidence in their own capability as reasons for the apparent collapse of the planning process. Furthermore, not everyone had benefited. In particular, the needs of children (other than improved classrooms) and younger women had been neglected.

Three main lessons stood out:

(1) RBU concluded that the process of developing the community plan had been too quick and had assumed that planning by a community was easy. It was now clear that planning collectively was a complex skill that required as much attention as and more time than the collective appraisal on which PRAP focused.

(2) RBU saw that creating greater understanding of and respect for differing needs was essential to ensure that everyone's interests could be included in the planning process. When the younger women in Kyakatebe had voiced their needs in the planning meeting, they had been ridiculed. Community consensus about priorities had not been built and efforts to include younger women, children and the worst-off in the planning process had proven inadequate.

(3) It had also proved difficult to involve local extension agents in helping the community implement its plan. RBU felt that there could have been greater commitment if they had been included from the beginning.

Subsequent work

Six months later, the second step was taken with participatory planning. IIED trained a small group of CAPOs in how to train others in participatory

The Myth of Community

planning. The CAPOs immediately applied their new skills, by guiding a new group of CAPOs and several local-extension agents through a field-based workshop in Akoboi (Soroti District). The training included sessions about the lessons learnt from the planning process in Kyakatebe.

An intense period of further analysis followed, with groups of younger and older women and men discussing local problems and possible solutions in meetings facilitated by the responsible CAPOs. The aim was to agree on one priority that could be pursued in a community-wide action plan. Unlike Kyakatebe, which included a long list of activities, this process aimed to identify only one with which to start. To deal with the planning and implementation, community members from Akoboi established and registered their own community-based organization, AKOCODA. It has started rebuilding and extending the local school, and has found external funding to complement local contributions.

Reflection on this process helped RBU to make further changes to its planning approach (Guijt, 1995):

(1) In sharp contrast with the hasty process in Kyakatebe, the villagers of Akoboi felt that the process had been too slow and too time-consuming. The subsequent drop in participation was exacerbated by the second issue.
(2) By focusing on only one community priority, many people had become disinterested as their priorities remained unresolved. RBU decided to encourage developing smaller group plans, alongside a community plan.
(3) The CAPOs had great difficulty in guiding AKOCODA through the planning process, as their capacity in the practical application of LFA at the community level was inadequate. They started rethinking how to deal with the practical planning of priorities.
(4) Although local extension agents had been included from the beginning, they had insufficient resources to attend to the many new requests for support, and no partner organization had been involved. This meant that the CAPOs were responsible for the whole process, keeping them from their duties related to sub-county and district planning. RBU formulated guidelines for working better through partners and government agencies.

A third key experience started in March 1995 in Bulende-Bugosere, a village in Iganga District. The CAPOs facilitated a workshop on participatory appraisal and planning with a local partner organization. CAPOs were only marginally involved in the follow-up, leaving most to local extension agents and the partner organization. Over the following year, the changes were impressive.[11] Many homes were cleaner, diseases decreased, school attendance increased from 60 to 360 children, gender relations improved with some men returning to the families they had abandoned, incomes rose due to improved agricultural productivity and income generation activities increased greatly. Local extension workers were in hot demand and expressed greater job satisfaction. A village management committee was established to deal with community-wide interests. Pride in their progress led the villagers to organize a PRA festival to celebrate the improvements realized with local efforts and resources!

However, it has proven difficult for the committee to develop a community action plan and to monitor its progress. Unlike in Kyakatebe and Akoboi, here all the changes had occurred through independent, small group activities. Also, the partner organization had insufficient capacity to provide the strong guidance that the villagers wanted in the early stages. Children's participation in the committee was limited to one boy representative. These problems were recognized and are being redressed by RBU, by providing training on facilitation skills to the partner organization and planning skills to the village management committee (Mukasa, 1996).

Main lessons

In 1996, those involved in these first experiences[12] met to analyse what had worked, what had not succeeded, and why this was the case. It was clear that specific action was needed at different moments to include women and children in what was, after all, meant to be a participatory planning process. Four key areas of improvement were identified and incorporated in the guidelines which describe RBU's approach to participatory rural appraisal and planning (Guijt, 1996).[13]

1. First contacts with the community tended to focus on the, mainly male, local council members and elders, to the detriment of women and children. Women must be deliberately sought out and invited to participate in the planning process. Sensitizing men to the importance of women's involvement is essential to gain their overall support. Also, for children's input to be possible later on, it is essential to undertake some child sensitization activities with women and men.
2. Although community interest was generally quite high in the initial analysis, this tended to exclude the younger women whose confidence must be built first so that the community takes them seriously. More attention must be paid to ensuring that meeting times and places suit them because they are always busy with child care and domestic chores. Time must be spent discussing how they can best benefit from the process.
3. Working with children means adapting appraisal methods to keep them interested and make their input meaningful. Children have a shorter concentration span and generally more limited analytical skills than adults, so cannot be expected to undertake a full-scale appraisal. The very young children (under about 6 or 7 years of age) are particularly difficult to involve and are perhaps best included in community action via other routes, notably the schools.
4. During the slow process of analysis and planning, community participation is likely to drop, as it has few immediate tangible benefits. Younger women's and non-school-going children's involvement reduced to virtually nil, as CAPOs were unclear how to motivate and seek to include them. By focusing on less ambitious, smaller-group priorities, women and even children can develop their own plans alongside community-wide plans.

Dealing with gender and age differences

Several subsequent experiences with PRAP (e.g. Kisadha and Bitikerezo, 1995; Chandler and Kisadha, 1996), and continuous reflection, have helped RBU make the planning process more participatory. This section discusses the shifting focus from community- to group-action plans, and the five stages of the planning approach. It explains how RBU, with its partner organizations, guides communities through the process of understanding their internal differences.

The relative merits of community and smaller-group plans

A common feature of PRA processes is that the organizations involved claim that they lead to viable community action plans (CAPs), often after less than one week of analysis and planning. It is, of course, nonsense to assume that community consensus on development priorities, with equitable benefits, is possible in a short time span. A plan that aims to encompass concerns of the whole community has two main problems: lack of representativeness and excessive complexity.

A CAP, in theory, embraces the ideas and priorities of all community members. Rarely, if ever, has every community member had a say in what the plan is to include. Even if most people have been involved, the resulting community plans are more likely to deal with less contentious concerns, and can easily ignore burning issues of marginalized groups. For example, in Kyatakebe the younger women were concerned mostly about family planning, yet this did not appear in the community plan. Smaller group plans allow such priorities to be addressed.

The second problem occurs when many activities are squeezed into a community plan, as is common. The more comprehensive the list of issues to be included, the more difficult will be the planning and implementation. This is problematic when communities are not used to planning as a larger collective. The Community Action Plan in Kyakatebe is one such example, with many different activities happening simultaneously. The CAP in Akoboi is more modest, reflecting a community action *priority* (school improvement). Starting small, with one defined activity, is a safer way for a community to learn about collective planning, is more likely to succeed, can generate a more concrete sense of achievement, and is more likely to stimulate subsequent planning, than an ambitious plan which disappoints everyone (see Box 20.1).

RBU has attempted to recognize these realities of community planning by encouraging smaller group plans. The group plans can involve mixed groups such as younger and older women together, or younger men and women together, or a group on its own.

Yet community plans remain essential. Development problems that relate to shared resources and structure (such as water wells, the school or village forests) are best resolved through a community-wide initiative. This corresponds with traditional local community activities referred to as '*bulungi bwansi*' ('for the good of the community'). At such occasions, all able-bodied women and men come together and work on a shared structure or area. To do it in a formal manner means identifying a locally

---

Box 20.1: Community or group plans?

When asked to compare the merits of developing a community versus a group action plan, the men of Akoboi (Soroti District) favoured the community plan, as funding it would be easier. However, the women felt that a group plan would work better as it is much easier to implement something with fewer different opinions. They say that making and implementing one large plan keeps failing. Nevertheless, the women agreed that some collective activities could join all groups in the community

Source: Guijt, 1996.

---

catalytic, and not just an important, issue. Such an issue is perceived by all groups as bringing collective and individual benefits alike, and therefore is sufficiently high on most people's agendas to encourage collective action. It is not necessarily, and unlikely to be, the first priority of any single group (unless the community is collectively experiencing extreme stress, as in times of environmental disaster or war).

RBU's planning process

To deal well with gender and age differences, therefore, RBU sees great potential in pursuing community and group plans alike. But plans do not happen overnight. The experiences to date have led RBU to conceive of its PRAP approach as a five stage process: preparation, initial immersion, analysis of intra-communal difference, planning, and implementation with monitoring/evaluation. To facilitate this process well, the CAPOs and partner organization staff need specific skills at each stage (see Table 20.1).

Stage 1 Preparation begins by carefully selecting an appropriate partner organization,[14] one which has enough basic resources and capacities to pursue the follow-up and above all is committed to working with women, children and the poorest. Together, the community or communities are identified, one that is interested in the process, not embroiled in excessive internal conflict, not overrun by too many other NGOs etc. Participants are selected, usually a mixed group of NGOs/community organization staff, government extension workers, local leaders and villagers. They will be trained in participatory planning and will pursue the work through all the stages.[15] Much negotiation is needed: with the partner organization to clarify roles and responsibilities; with government agencies to release staff for training and follow-up; and with the community to ensure its interest and commitment. This stage includes various training sessions, especially for new partner organizations, such as on basic communications skills and child rights.

Stage 2 Initial immersion involves the use of the well-known PRA diagramming methods over 5 to 6 days with five groups of community

Table 20.1: RBU's stages of participatory planning

Stage	Main activities	Methodologies and skills used
1. Preparation (1 to 3 months)	o identifying stakeholders o negotiating with stakeholders to clarify roles and responsibilities o clear communication to avoid raising expectations or suspicion o reaching as many local people as possible, particularly the poorest, aged, disabled children, and women	o Basic communication skills o Mediated learning experience o gender and development o children rights and responsibilities
2. Initial immersion (2 to 3 weeks)	o facilitating initial situation analysis that represents gender and age differences o explaining the role of outsiders in the planning process o advocating inclusion of children's values, capacities in analysis o creating opportunities for women, especially the younger ones, to be involved	o PRA, with the child-focused adaptation called 'Giving voice to children' o conflict resolution o Mediated learning experience o dealing with group dynamics
3. Analysis of intra-communal difference (2 to 6 months)	o facilitating group-based analysis to identify shared or group-specific concerns and possible solutions o building understanding between groups of acceptability of gender-and-age-based differences in priorities	o PRA, especially the issues matrix o Basic communication skills o conflict resolution o Child-to-child o Mediated learning experience o dealing with group dynamics
4. Planning community/ group action plans (less than 1 month)	o facilitating the planning and training in planning o resolving conflicts o negotiating group responsibilities and consensus on timing/level of inputs	o conflict resolution o Logical framework analysis o Mediated learning experience
5. Implementing and sustaining plans (varies per plan)	o helping to structure implementation committee o facilitating the adjusting of plans o monitoring progress o linking community to external resources	o monitoring o Child-to-child o Logical framework analysis (for reviewing plans) o leadership skills o basic book-keeping skills

members (younger and older women and men, and children). Many other organizations would describe this as 'PRA', but RBU sees it simply as the first steps in community analysis. This stage also includes the final logistical preparations, conducting the classroom-based orientation (for those who are new to participatory planning), and documenting the initial outcomes of the community analysis. An initial 'issues matrix' is one important output of this stage.

Stage 3   Analysis of intra-communal difference is the focus of immediate follow-up. It is the stage about which almost no PRA documentation exists, yet which is essential to any organization sincere about including marginalized groups. It involves group-based analysis of the initial fieldwork, identification of shared concerns and group-specific concerns, and the prioritization of possible solutions. RBU uses the 'issues matrix' to guide this stage. Meeting with and motivating community members requires much time on the part of RBU, the partner organization, and/or extension agents. At this stage, efforts are made to include those who were not involved in the initial analysis, and who are often the poorest. This stage is marked by high drop-out rates and requires careful thought about how to sustain motivation.

Stage 4   Planning involves working out the details of how the selected priorities will be implemented. Final decisions are made about the priority for the community action plan, and those for the group action plans. There is much negotiation about group responsibilities and the sources of funding and other inputs. It is also the phase when some form of village management committee is likely to be formalized, with clear objectives and activities. The output of this stage are the final plans and the monitoring system.

Stage 5   Implementation and monitoring/evaluation involves carrying out the community-level and group plans, and monitoring their progress. RBU links the community to government agencies and other non-government organizations that can help implement the plans. The issues matrix developed in Stage 3 is used to monitor progress and develop the next community and group plans.

Although, the five stages are sequential, there is often some implementation immediately after the initial analysis. Community members might be motivated to tackle an urgent need or relatively simple issue on their own, such as clearing the community footpaths or making drying racks for dishes. Local extension agents are often galvanized into action, responding to the issues that have been raised without waiting for formal plans and requests for support.

A closer look at negotiating difference

PRA practitioners generally experience great difficulty with what happens after the exciting and inspiring initial analysis that often produces mountains of diagrams and pages of notes. RBU's field staff were no exception. While 'including the marginalized groups' in follow-up is always promised, how this is best carried out remains a mystery to most. The poorest often have difficulty in participating because of the urgency of resolving immediate material needs, such as food and clothes to appear in public. For groups that are marginalized in other ways, such as women, the challenge is no simpler. RBU has struggled to make sense of this stage in particular, as it lays the basis for equitable benefits later on. Its approach aims to encourage different social groups to accept the value of differing priorities, while still pursuing opportunities that require collective action from all groups.

The 'issues matrix' has guided RBU, the partner organization, and villagers through the analysis of gender- and age-differences (see Table 20.2). It is a composite list of all the issues initially identified by the different groups[16] in Stage 2. It helps to examine systematically which issues matter for which people in a community and why. The remainder of this section discusses in general terms how this learning tool guides the discussions and planning in subsequent stages. In each community, of course, variations in its use will occur.

Immediately after the initial immersion, whoever is facilitating the process (CAPOs, partner organization staff, and/or local extension agents) arrange meetings with the different groups to discuss their issues in more detail. At its first meeting, each group develops a common understanding of what an issue is. This helps to avoid the tendency that RBU has noted of villagers describing issues in general terms, such as 'water'. The more specific the issue, the easier it becomes to identify possible solutions later on.

Two other tasks usually occur at the first meeting. First, the group issue list is revised. Any ambiguously worded or vague issues are clarified. Repetitive and unimportant issues are deleted. Second, the group decides who else could or should join in their group, and how this is best done. A social map produced during the initial fieldwork helps identify where they live and house-to-house visits are planned.

Table 20.2: Extract from the issues matrix of Kyakatebe

Issues raised initially	C	YW	YM	OW	OM
Lack of clean water	X	X	X	X	X
Orphans	X	X	X	X	X
High level of school drop-outs	X	X	X	X	
HIV/AIDS		X	X	X	X
Land shortage/fragmentation	X	X	X		X
Lack of fuelwood		X	X		X
Environmental degradation		X	X		X
Lack of local organization		X	X	X	
Situation of single mothers	X	X			
Punishment at school	X	X			
High rate of teenage pregnancies		X		X	
Taxation					X
Drunken teachers	X				

Notes: C = children; YW = younger women; YM = younger men; OW = older women; OM = older men; X = an issue raised in group discussions

Source: Guijt *et al.*, 1995

The group also compares its issues with others in the issues matrix, a key step in fostering greater understanding of the specific position of others in the community and more tolerance of their needs. By discussing the issues of other groups, new concerns may be identified and others refined. The facilitator[17] can also ask them to analyse why others might have different concerns.

Subsequent meetings focus on analysing the causes and impacts of each issue, which are clustered into themes, such as health, agriculture, water, education, income generation and environment. New concerns will probably arise and some will disappear. Once the list is clear, the issues are prioritized per theme.[18] A start is made with the identification of possible solutions for each issue, but the main task is to agree on the priority issues, or concerns.

Then the lists of priority concerns are shared amongst all the groups. This step is essential to increase understanding about why different people in the same community might have different needs that are equally important. Ideally, each issue of each group is discussed, using questions such as: 'Do you think this is a valid concern?', 'Why or why not?', 'What can your group do to help resolve it?'.

After discussing the priority lists of the other groups, each group then has the opportunity to revise its original list before discussing possible solutions. Each solution is assessed in terms of its feasibility.[19] When possible solutions have been clarified, the group members also decide to identify those action points that can and perhaps must be tackled at a community level, i.e. in a community action plan, and those that are best addressed in smaller group plans.

Up to this point, groups will not have met in a community-wide forum to discuss their priorities. To prepare for this, each group prioritizes the community action points it has identified. It also decides if it wants to focus initially on a community or a group action plan, or if it wants to invest time in developing both. Then, for the first time after the initial fieldwork started, the groups meet to share their prioritized issues and solutions in public, and to negotiate which action points will, in the end, be carried out collectively and which by smaller community groups. This lays the basis for Stage 4, the practical planning.

The issues matrix has recently started taking on an important role in monitoring and evaluation (Mukasa, 1996). A review by the village management committee in Bulende-Bugosere led the committee members to regroup the issues that had first been identified two years earlier as follows:

o issues which the community has fully addressed, and deleting them;
o issues which the community has started addressing, explaining what action had been undertaken;
o issues which have been addressed, but need continuous implementation (e.g. road maintenance);
o issues which still exist unchanged and require action;
o issues which are completely new; and
o controversial issues, such as polygamy and its effects.

This helped them see the participatory planning process as a never-ending cycle, which needs to respond to new needs if development is to continue.

Implementation, monitoring and evaluation

RBU is steadily streamlining its approach to implementation, monitoring and evaluation. Although not the focus of this chapter, two aspects are relevant for sustaining equity in development: the role of the village management committee (VMC) and the evolution of the interest groups.

The end of Stage 3 usually marks the birth of VMCs, as the sub-groups cannot and will not continue meeting so often. RBU and/or the partner organization facilitate a community-wide meeting in which decisions are made about the number and type of committee members, and its roles and powers. Care is taken to clarify that a VMC is not a replacement of the formal local authorities, Local Council I, which are represented on the committee to avoid tensions. Also represented are the different age and sex groups, religious groups (especially in multi-religious communities), and government extension workers. Various criteria used to select members include: commitment; willingness to sacrifice time/effort for the community; honesty and trustworthiness; and ability to work without pay. After this, the VMC is trained in the different skills they need to enable them to handle their various roles: developing the community plan; coordinating and ensuring implementation; conflict mediation and resolution (but not arbitration which is the role of the LC courts); resource mobilization for implementation; regular feedback to the community on the PRA process/progress; and monitoring of change using the PRAP log book (one per community), as an accountability tool, to record key events, when what takes place, by whom, how, etc. Children on the VMC participate in the planning workshops, as do the women. Sometimes a VMC strengthens to such an extent that it wants to register formally as a CBO, as in the case of AKOCODA.

The initial age and gender groups that are helpful for analysis in stages 2 and 3 are not necessarily sustained. Smaller groups emerge, crystalling out of the original group, and based on a concrete activity (e.g. agricultural production, livestock raising, brick-making, and health improvement). As the main motivation for a group is a common interest, they sometimes mix ages and women/men. In general, the groups need considerable support with group formation and management, and with conflict management. This is being addressed via training for the VMC and group members but RBU staff still want to refine their approach to group dynamics considerably.

Remaining challenges

The learning curve for Redd Barna Uganda has been steep, beginning with its first quick attempt at a community plan in Kyakatebe, to the long drawn-out process in Akoboi, and the subsequent search for the middle ground. The commitment to include women and children in participatory development has led it to pursue group action plans alongside community plans. Furthermore, RBU is focusing on local people's capacity to plan, and not just to analyse.

RBU intentionally kept its initial experiences with participatory planning small scale, as it knew adaptation was inevitable. Over the past three years, the process of community-based participatory planning has expanded slowly to twenty communities in seven districts. In all cases, local women and men have noted improvements in school attendance, income levels, agricultural yields, incidence of diseases and social relations. Less tangible yet essential changes include recognition by women and men of the value of collective action, of existing resources and skills, of the capacities of children to contribute to their own development if given support by adults. These villages are showing a high level of organization, mobilization and a sense of direction, and are taking on the stature of a 'model village' in the sub-county. They have started accessing sub-county development funds and are causing sub-county officials to engage more actively in local development. For example, Bulende-Bugosere received iron-sheets and cement to support the construction of the school which they had started on their own. These examples are inspiring other villages: 'If Bulende-Bugosere, which used to be one of the worst-off villages can achieve so much within such a short time, why not us. . .?'

To other organizations seeking participatory development that includes women and children, RBU's experiences offer the following lessons:

o Change cannot be rushed, particularly when traditional power hierarchies are being challenged. Participatory development which includes, rather than ignores, women and children needs a firm management decision to give field staff the time required for the slow pace of social change.[20]
o Time and effort must be invested in developing more appropriate methodologies and methods that allow women, and especially children, to take a more active part in local development. It is essential to find ways that encourage greater understanding within communities of the validity of different needs.
o As each context is unique, locally appropriate methodological variations must be allowed to evolve. Senior management must provide incentives for field-based experimentation and give the staff much freedom to pursue this.
o A balance must be found between giving freedom for innovation and providing guidance. Regular collective analysis with the field staff and villagers involved are a critical source of ideas for staff guidelines.
o To keep better track of where gaps and problems lie, field staff must be involved in developing a monitoring system that also fulfils accountability needs. This must be complemented with community-based monitoring that stimulates continual local reflection on progress and acts as a catalyst for ongoing local development.
o Staff training must be continual. In RBU's case, this extends beyond the CAPOs to include partner organizations, villagers and local extension agents.

The work is far from over. Perhaps Redd Barna Uganda's biggest challenge is, ironically, related to another aspect of social difference: that of class. From its first internal review and discussions with villagers in Kyakatebe, RBU has been painfully aware that its work to date has tended to benefit the slightly better-off rather than the poorest, despite its many efforts. As Fuglesang wrote 'It cannot be stressed often enough how those who are a little better off understand better how to reap the benefits offered by a development project' (in Guijt, 1996). Despite their efforts, it is proving exceedingly difficult to reach the poorest, who are often the disabled, the aged and the ill. 'The fact is that we rarely reach the poorest. [But] we do not yet quite know how to.' (Fuglesang and Chandler, 1996). Redd Barna Uganda is continuing to evolve participatory planning to include not only gender and age as important areas of social difference, but also economic class.

References

Barnett, T. and P. Blaikie (1995) 'On Ignoring the Wider Picture: AIDS research and the jobbing social scientist', in David Booth (ed.), *Rethinking Social Development: theory, research and practice*, pp. 226–50 Harlow: Longman Scientific and Technical.

Barton, T. and G. Wamai, (1994) *Equity and Vulnerability: a situation analysis of women, adolescents and children in Uganda.* Kampala: NCC.

Chandler, D. and T. Kisadha (eds) (1995) *Breaking the Gourd. Aibwang Etuo*, A report of a PRA Training Workshop in PRA, Kampala: RBU.

Fuglesang, A. and D. Chandler (1997) *Youth with an eye for the future. Child advocacy Norway Uganda Report*, Kampala: RBU.

Guijt, I. (1995) *Moving Slowly and Reaching Far. Institutionalising participatory planning for child-centred community development. An interim analysis for Redd Barna.* Kampala: Redd Barna Uganda and London: IIED.

Guijt, I. (1996) *Participatory Planning in Redd Barna Uganda: reflections and guidelines*, Kampala: Redd Barna Uganda and London: IIED.

Guijt, I., T. Kisadha, and A. Fuglesang (eds) (1994) *It is the Young Trees that Make a Thick Forest*, London: IIED and Kampala: RBU.

Hansen, H.B. and M. Twaddle (eds) (1991) *Changing Uganda. The dilemmas of structural adjustment and revolutionary change*, London: James Currey Ltd.

Jamal, Vali (1991) 'The Agrarian Context of the Ugandan Crisis', in Hansen and Twaddle (eds) (1991), pp. 78–97.

Kisadha, T. and M. Bitikerezo (eds) (1995) *Wild Flowers Instead of Food*, Report on a PRA Training Workshop, Kampala: RBU.

Mukasa, G. (1996) *Progress Report on the PRAP Process in Bulende-Bugosere, Iganga*, internal memo, Kampala: RBU.

RBU (Redd Barna Uganda) (1995) *Draft Country Strategy for Uganda*, Kampala: RBU.

RBU (Redd Barna Uganda) (1996) *New Uganda. A partnership development programme 1990–1996*, Kampala: RBU.

Sewagudde, J., Geoffrey Mugisha, Richard Ochen and Grace Mukasa (1997) 'Mixing and Matching Methodologies in Redd Barna Uganda', *PLA Notes* 28: 79–83.

21

'Salt and Spices': Gender issues in participatory programme implementation in AKRSP, India[1]

MEERA KAUL SHAH[2]

A participatory development process, by definition, implies that all sections of a community have equal access to, and take part in equal measure in, the decisionmaking process. In most contexts, however, especially in India, it is not socially acceptable for men and women to share a common public space and women are usually left on the periphery or are not allowed to take an active part in public fora. Given this social constraint, a participatory process implies adopting one or both of the following strategies: (i) changing the existing gender relations, so that men and women can participate equally; and/or (ii) seeking ways within existing gender relations to enable men and women alike to have an equal say.

For most development programmes, changing the existing gender relations is not the primary objective (see Chapter 7, this volume). While some projects state their intentions to ensure that there is no negative impact on the women, and that men and women are able to take part in the development process equally, they rarely have an explicit strategy that describes how the internalized oppression of women will be handled. Several factors contribute to the lip-service towards 'gender issues'. It is primarily affected by the lack of a working model, which goes beyond the theory of gender and provides ways in which gendered concerns, as dictated by existing context-specific gender relations, can be addressed in implementation (see Chapter 22, this volume). Developing such a working model requires experimenting with new ideas and approaches (see Chapter 20, this volume). It also requires an organizational recognition of its merits, and commitment to provide the opportunities for experimentation. Gender-sensitivity on the part of field staff, who usually need training in appropriate concepts and analytical tools, is crucial. This is a slow process, and management and field staff alike need determination to pursue it, despite the lack of quick and tangible results.

Chapter 21 describes the efforts of and problems encountered by an NGO, Aga Khan Rural Support Programme (AKRSP), India, in its attempts to integrate the concerns of men and women, while supporting local village institutions in managing their natural resources. The organization supports a variety of natural-resources management projects including: small-scale irrigation, soil and water conservation in micro-watersheds, community forestry, agriculture development, credit (linked to savings), marketing, animal husbandry and biogas. In 1992, AKRSP was working in three districts of Gujarat state: Bharuch, Junagadh and Surendranagar. This chapter focuses mainly on the experiences from Bharuch district.

AKRSP objectives and approach

AKRSP was established in 1984 with the objective of providing an enabling environment for rural communities to manage and develop their natural resources in a productive and sustainable manner. From the outset, the organization had outlined a strategy of supporting participatory development processes in villages. The programmes were based on several principles: participation, equity, cost-effectiveness, and transfer of skills to villagers to equip them to take over the planning and management of the programmes. Technical and financial support to local village institutions and extension volunteers is a central strategy.

The village institutions (VIs) supported by AKRSP are membership organizations. While some are registered as cooperatives, especially those undertaking irrigation projects, others are informal, common interest groups. In Bharuch District, VI membership usually encompasses the entire village. All VIs have elected representatives, including a management committee which is headed by a chairman. In 1992, all the elected representatives of VIs in Bharuch District were men.

Extension volunteers (EV) play a pivotal role. They are selected by the village people to take up special responsibilities for planning and implementing the different activities decided on by the village institutions. EVs are trained by AKRSP staff. Apart from supervisory and monitoring responsibilities, EVs also act as facilitators of participatory appraisal and planning exercises in their own, and sometimes other, villages. EVs are paid performance-related incentives. By 1992, this payment was shared equally by the recipient clients (VI members) and AKRSP for some of the programmes, such as watershed management. For other programmes, for example, credit and marketing, this payment was completely borne by the VI members availing these services.

The early efforts at involving women

From its first efforts, AKRSP had tried to involve women and men equally in the projects it supported. It assumed that 'gender equity' could be attained by 'mainstreaming women', i.e. having village institutions with membership open to both sexes. To ensure that women joined these VIs, AKRSP staff stressed that two members per household, one woman and one man, were eligible for membership. Furthermore, each member would have an individual savings account with the village institution. And indeed, some women did join, with as many women members as men in many villages. Equal numbers of women and men could also be seen participating in activities such as tree planting and tank construction.

However, participating in such employment generating activities did not automatically give women a role in decision-making. Meetings of VIs remained largely a male reserve. In Bharuch District, it is not socially acceptable for the women to share a common platform with the men of their village, nor are women expected to speak in a public gathering where men are present. When AKRSP staff encouraged women to attend meetings, some would turn up and sit right at the back, but they would rarely express their opinions.

244

The village men had a simple explanation for women's limited participation: women are not supposed to make important decisions related to the village as they have inadequate information. According to the men, there was little point in wasting time asking the women to share their views as they were not used to taking part in such discussions and their menfolk would speak for them. Initially, this was also an easy way out for the predominantly male staff of AKRSP.[3] For them, initiating discussions with separate groups of women was difficult and time consuming. Particularly in new villages, talking directly with women could be seen as suspicious by the men.

Realizing that more was needed besides open VI membership, AKRSP decided that some of the activities it supported could be reserved for women. As a result, it was decided that animal husbandry and raising plant nurseries (for plantations) could be implemented as 'women's programmes'. Since women take most of the responsibility for rearing milch animals in Bharuch and nurseries can be conveniently close to their homes, it was felt that these activities would fall naturally in the women's domain. As a result, it was the women who received the improved cows in their names, on credit, and plant nursery-raising has by and large been women's activity.

Although slow, these initiatives eventually yielded some positive results. For example, men attended the nursery-raising training programmes, despite the nurseries operating in women's names. The problem was quite simply one of geography: the training took place far from the villages, making it difficult for women to attend. So when training venues were decentralized, the women nursery raisers started attending. Another example was that of payments for the nursery raising. Initially, the VI secretary would make payments only to the man of the household. Later when payments were routed through banks, each female nursery raiser had to open and operate her individual bank account, thus travelling several kilometres to the bank to cash her cheque. This enabled the women to interact with the outside formal sector, giving them confidence in handling their own earnings (Shah and Shah, 1995). Despite some positive impact on the existing gender roles and relations in the villages, it was clear, however, that the women were still not very active in the functioning of the local village institution.

In March 1991, AKRSP organized an internal workshop for all staff to review women's participation in the programmes it was supporting and to prepare a strategy to improve this. The workshop also served as an opportunity to sensitize the staff to gender-related issues and to discuss their concerns on the subject. There was general agreement that special efforts were needed to involve village women more and better. The strategy decided on was one of separate discussions and participatory appraisals with the women, to understand how they could play a more active role in the VIs.

Participatory appraisals with women

Since late 1988, AKRSP's focus on PRA as a process had led to considerable progress in 'handing over the stick' to the village community. It appraised its own situation and problems related to its natural resources, and prepared action plans. In most cases village men have been the main participants in these appraisals.

Subsequent to the internal workshop, two types of appraisals with women were conducted in Bharuch District: (i) in new villages, the micro-planning exercises were carried out simultaneously with groups of men and women; (ii) in some of the older project villages, appraisals were carried out only with women. The response from the village women was overwhelming. Large numbers of women took part in these appraisals, and slowly it became accepted for them to present their analysis and plans in meetings with village men. This helped boost women's confidence (see Box 21.1). Village men were able to see the value of women's appraisal, as the issues the women raised tended to be different from their own.

Box 21.1: Where did the confidence come from?

While carrying out the village micro-planning exercise in Samarpada, the women analysed their problems and priorities separately from the men. Even among the men, there were separate groups, based on the size of their landholding. When it came presenting their proposals in a village meeting, the women presented their analysis first. The next presentation was by the group of smallholder farmers (men). They explained their priority of soil and water conservation and some community wells, that could irrigate farms belonging to most of the poorer households.

The big landowners, who also held the social and political power in the village, immediately rejected the proposal and loudly proclaimed that this was not the best alternative for developing the village. They asserted that the village needed a bore hole, located near the river, that would irrigate much of the most fertile land.

There was a hushed silence at this retort. The fertile lands near the river, as everyone knew, belonged to two of the richest households and the bore hole would benefit these most, besides giving them ownership over the water as the bore would be located on their land. The poorer men became silent at this outburst. The social hierarchy forbade them openly to refute the rich and powerful.

Just when the AKRSP facilitators were wondering how to handle the delicate situation, they were surprised to see some of the women get up and speak. One woman told the rich men, 'When we were carrying out our analysis, we evaluated each of the options by comparing the cost of the activity and how many households would benefit. We should look at your suggestion the same way. A bore hole would be very expensive and would benefit only two households, even if the land covered would be significant. This can't be a priority solution for the village'. The whole village and the facilitators looked at the women in amazement. They had quietly stood up to challenge the most powerful village men. And the rich men knew that they had just lost their argument.

'Salt and Spices'

While participatory planning exercises had already been carried out in the older programme villages, with every effort made to ensure that the interests of the rich and the poor had been considered, AKRSP staff had invariably assumed that women's priorities would be the same as those of their menfolk. New appraisals carried out in these villages revealed several issues:

○ in projects like the community protection of forest lands, women's interests had been completely overlooked by the village men, resulting in a negative impact on the women (see Box 21.2);

Box 21.2: Whose forests. . .?

The Pingot VI stands out as an example of successful efforts by the community in protecting their common forest lands. Large tracts of hillsides which had previously been heavily deforested have been reforested and the VI has devised a system of protection, whereby one man from every household takes turns, in groups, to patrol the protected area. These guards walk the forest day and night, every day of the year. Heavy fines and penalties are imposed by the VI on defaulting members. The regenerated forests provide a spectacular sight. The VI has won a national award in recognition of its environmental conservation efforts.

When the women were asked how they felt about the reforested land and the national recognition, the reply was sarcastic, 'What forest? We don't know anything about it now. We used to go to the forest to pick fuelwood but ever since the men have started protecting it they don't even allow us to look at it!'

So what were the implication of their isolation? They drew a map on the ground showing what they meant. Since most of the 'forest' land in Pingot had been reforested and was being protected by the VI, there were only two small plots left at the two extreme corners of the village where they could collect fuelwood. Since Pingot had a vast expanse of 'forest' land, there had been no dearth of dead wood earlier and women were able to collect enough fuelwood to meet their requirements without too much effort. They were now forced to take their daughters with them, spending more than six hours a day and walking five times further than they used to, to collect the same quantity of fuelwood. A walk with the women to both sites revealed that there was virtually nothing left on the plot closer to the village and women were forced to dig the root stock.

The lessons from this experience were clear. The appearance of cohesive community participation, where men from nearly all the households had participated in protecting their forests, was, in fact, extremely deceptive. While local men had guarded the forests enthusiastically, the women emerged as absolute losers. The undermining of women's concerns and their limited bargaining power with men proved to be more harmful to the long-term sustainability of the forests, and caused them much frustration and personal hardship.

Source: Shah and Shah, 1995.

---

o in projects like soil and water conservation, women's homestead lands[4] had been ignored by the male village EVs, and none of the conservation measures were being carried out on them; and

o wherever women's homestead lands had been included in the project activities, such as that of lift irrigation, women' lands were the lowest priority and were very often ignored, in favour of the main fields.

Clearly, while the participatory planning and programme implementation processes had achieved equity by dealing with differences based on wealth categories, the interests of women were rarely considered separately from those of men. Although women mentioned that in most of the cases the overall well-being of the households had improved considerably after the VIs started functioning, they felt that additional activities could be taken up by the women separately.[5]

Mainstreaming or separating women's concerns?

Interestingly, when the negative impact of some of the activities on the women began emerging, it became easier to stress gender equity within AKRSP. Clearly community-level equity could not be achieved by ignoring women. As the strategy of mixed VIs was insufficient for ensuring women's involvement in decisionmaking, it became necessary to establish a norm of separate appraisals with the women, allowing them to take up activities separately from men. While most of the activities suggested by women were in line with men's priorities, they tended to focus more on assets they owned or used themselves.

In the case of their steep homestead plots, women wanted to carry out soil-and-water conservation measures. They were keen to grow more vegetables on these small plots. The appraisals also brought out that, while the men had been able to use their savings as collateral to obtain group credit to purchase agricultural inputs for their farms, the women continued to purchase vegetable seeds from traders on credit at exorbitant interest rates. Their needs were small, but as they had no access to cash, they relied on these traders, despite having large savings in their accounts. The male EVs, responsible for savings and credit activities, had simply not taken account of women's small-scale needs. Almost all the women's groups also discussed the need for introducing labour- and time-saving devices that could ease their work burdens and also release more time for productive activities (Shah, 1993; see Chapter 8, this volume).

Although women's groups began to have to their own identities and separate plans, it was necessary to integrate their efforts into the VI to ensure acceptance from the village men. Hence women presented their plans in the village meetings, and links were established with the activities being undertaken by the men. The male EVs started to take responsibilities for supporting women's activities (see Box 21.3).

For activities that were not being implemented directly by the men, like the biogas programme, women EVs were selected and trained. It proved to be easier to 'mainstream' women in the VI decision-making process by first giving them a separate space and a chance to develop their own separate

---

Box 21.3: 'We want to do it differently. . .'

During discussions in the Bilothi Group Panchayat (comprising four villages), the women analysed that the only productive asset they controlled fully was their homestead land. During a transect, the women pointed out the fields that had been treated with soil and water conservation measures, commenting on the increased productivity. They then asked why their homestead lands had been left out of the treatment plans. The male EV responsible for soil and water conservation activities was present and replied casually 'because this is the village residential area and not the agricultural lands!'. The women retorted, 'But we grow crops on these lands, and they are so undulating that hardly any rain water is retained'. They turned to the AKRSP staff and asked whether their homesteads could also be considered for treatment. When asked how they would organize the activity, they explained, 'we will cover all the homestead lands. If the EV gives us the layouts for the bunds, we will organize the rest ourselves. We have worked on the bunds in the fields, and know how to do it. The EV can guide us for quality control'.

Within three weeks, women from six villages had completed the soil and water conservation treatment on all the homestead lands in their villages. Although the area covered in each case was small, it required strong organizational capacity and a resolve to complete the task. Later, they explained: 'If we had arranged to do it the way the men did it elsewhere, it would have taken us forever. Instead we decided to divide the village in zones. Women from each zone formed a team. The team worked together on a woman's plot till the work was over. The owner of the plot had to provide lunch. We did not worry about whether the plot was big or small. If a woman was not well, or too old to work, we still covered her plot. Some of them provided a better lunch!' Having completed the treatment of their plots in no time, the women had further plans. Collectively they prepared the list of improved vegetable seeds they wanted to buy, collected the cash from the women and gave the responsibility of purchasing the certified seeds, with help from AKRSP staff, to several women from each village.

Having benefited from the vegetable production that season, they wanted to obtain good quality fruit-tree saplings so they could maximize the benefits from the increased moisture retention in their homesteads. They were also planning to select some women for training on preparing grafts on the existing trees, and further improving productivity.

The male EVs, the other men in the village and the AKRSP staff, were overwhelmed by this enthusiastic response of the women. The EVs commented, 'We have to persuade the men to take up new activities. These women are persuading us to provide more and more support.' To show their appreciation for the efforts put in by the women in their villages, the male EVs in Bilothi did not take any payments from the women for the services they had provided.

identity. It was easier for the women to talk and make presentations in front of the men, when they had their own analysis, rather than expect them to contribute to a predominantly male conversation.

Monitoring and other organizational procedures

To institutionalize a gender-positive approach in the AKRSP programme, it became important to modify the monitoring systems accordingly. At the village level, this meant involving women and men in deciding the indicators for monitoring different activities, and holding separate review sessions with them periodically. Invariably there were some differences in the way men and women analysed change and the impact of VI activities on their lives (Shah, 1995).

Apart from monitoring the activities, it was also important to include women's role and participation as indicators to assess the effectiveness of the VIs. This was discussed in a workshop with village representatives in early 1992 (see Box 21.4).

Preconditions for institutionalizing gender concerns in a participatory process

The process described here took several years during which we learnt much from our mistakes and the new challenges that surfaced with each step. The process was still evolving in 1992, needing further phases to sustain the efforts being made by the women in these villages. Our experiences indicate certain preconditions that enable the participation of women in the development process.

(1) Ensure commitment of the support organization to gender equity in the programmes it supports. This commitment must be shared by all staff at the field and management levels.

(2) Allow time for experimentation and developing an appropriate field methodology to integrate gender concerns in the programme-implementation process. Being a slow process, where there are no 'ready-made models' to follow, results can be seen only after a period of time.

(3) Train field staff in gender analysis skills. Simple classroom-based conceptual training is not enough. Training must be field-based, with clear guidance on how concepts can be applied in practice. Such support is required on a long-term basis, at least in the initial stages, when results are slow and problems inevitably arise. Field staff also need training in negotiation and in conflict resolution.

(4) Discuss separately with the women, if it is socially unacceptable for them to discuss in the presence of men. Participatory appraisals must be carried out with separate groups of men and women so the latter can voice their concerns without gender taboos. It is important to allow both groups to analyse their situations separately and interpret the reality for themselves.

'Salt and Spices'

Box 21.4: 'You need both salt and spices. . .'

A one day workshop on 'The future of Village Institutions' was organized in Netrang in February, 1992. Representatives from about 50 VIs attended. Since all the representatives were men, it was decided to also invite some women. The intention was that these women could at least hear the discussions and later inform other women about the process. The main objective was to discuss indicators for monitoring the progress of their VIs, and to plan ahead. The workshop started with a brainstorming session on the features of a 'good VI'.

While the list of indicators was fast expanding, one man mentioned 'participation of women' as a criteria for a good VI. Immediately another man reacted, 'This is not an indicator for a good VI. Even if they [women] are not there, it will do.' We, the facilitators, looked at each other, wondering how we could resolve this issue, when to our utmost surprise two women stood up to respond. One nearly yelled, 'What do you mean – will do? How will it do when there are no women in a VI? Will you call a household good if there are no women? It is the same with a VI. You can't cook a good curry if either salt or spices is missing. You need both salt and spices.' Having said this the woman sat down.

There was a definite impact on the men present. The man with reservations about women's participation hid his face, and other men pressurized him to take back his words. 'Active participation of women' became a criterion for assessing the performance of a good VI.

The final list included about 36 criteria. Participants later selected and ranked the seven most important criteria, with 'participation of women' in third place. The entire process was carried out by the village representatives with no prompting or support from the AKRSP facilitators.

Afterwards, reflecting on the process, we felt that having some women present at the workshop, even in a very small number, made all the difference to the process. Although they did not speak much, their courageous outburst in front of the men was highly effective, far more than any discussions that we could have facilitated. Most of all it was the confidence with which the women had reacted in front of about 130 men that took us all by surprise.

---

(5) Encourage women and men to share the findings from their separate analyses in a joint gathering. This increases the public acceptance of women's initiatives by men.

(6) Support women to undertake their activities separately from men, if they plan different events. Similarly, women's and men's groups can arrive at different procedures or norms for carrying out the same activities, so support such differences.

(7) Consider women's and men's indicators separately in the monitoring process, even if the activities are being undertaken jointly by both groups.
(8) Ensure that activities are reviewed separately with men and women in order to understand the situation from both perspectives and to gauge whether the project is having a gender-differentiated impact within the community.
(9) Record and store all data in a gender-segregated way.
(10) Modify organizational procedures and staff evaluation to take account of the efforts required to work separately with men and women. Provide incentives for gender-sensitive facilitation at the field level.

Conclusion

I have often been told that it was possible to integrate women in the AKRSP projects in Bharuch District because I, as the programme coordinator, happened to be a woman. While there may be some truth to this argument, I feel that having a female coordinator is not a necessary condition to ensure women's participation. Men with the right kind of committed sensitivity can achieve the same results, as was proven by several of my male colleagues. Given a situation such as ours at AKRSP, where it is extremely difficult to find women field staff, it is not possible to wait until the right women staff appear. It is essential instead to re-orient existing male and female personnel in the necessary skills to identify gender concerns and to work equally with village women and men. All that the process requires is appropriate training, guidance and back-up support in the field, particularly in the initial stages.

AKRSP did not start with the objective of changing the gender relations in the villages where it worked. However, involving women in the decision-making process for local development activities meant that these village women were stepping outside the social norm. The approach adopted by AKRSP was based on understanding women's concerns and then to support the meeting of basic gender needs. In this process, the women were encouraged to analyse their own problems and to design their own development activities. While some of the initiatives undertaken by the women matched those of their male counterparts, there were others which had no precedent in their villages.

Giving women a chance to share their plans and the progress of their activities in meetings attended by village men boosted their confidence. This helped change their image from one of silent spectators of male decisionmaking to that of groups with their own identities and plans. Although slow, this represents the transformatory potential of participatory development to challenge the norm of women's subordinate positions in their communities.

References

Shah, Meera Kaul (1993) 'Impact of Technological Change in Agriculture: women's voices from a tribal village in South Gujarat, India', unpublished paper, Brighton: IDS.

Shah, Meera Kaul and Parmesh Shah (1995) 'Gender, Environment and Livelihood Security: an alternative viewpoint from India', *IDS Bulletin*, Vol. 26, No. 1: 75–82.

Shah, Meera Kaul (1995) 'Participatory Monitoring: some reflections', paper presented at the ODA Social Development Colloquium, London, December.

22

Institutionalization of Gender through Participatory Practice[1]

CAREN LEVY

Many would argue that the process of making gender issues a regular part of development practice necessarily contains within it a commitment to participation, not only as a means but as an end in itself.[2] Making women's as well as men's voices heard and counted in planned interventions implies their active involvement in decision-making in issues which affect their lives. Similarly, many would argue that participatory development is necessarily socially inclusive, incorporating gender issues along with other social relations like class, ethnicity and age. Yet practice shows that neither contention can be supported.

There is already a critique in the relatively 'young life' of the Gender and Development (GAD) approach[3] that it is sometimes being applied in a technocratic manner, disconnected from the critical political processes surrounding gender relations. Similarly, much of the research and planned intervention professing to be 'participatory' excludes women and other subordinate social groups. Both perspectives challenge power relations. However, while power relations linked to gender and power relations linked to participation are overlapping and intersecting, they are not neatly congruent. This has implications for any process aimed at making gendered participatory practices a regular part of planned intervention.

Chapter 22 describes a diagnostic and operational framework for the institutionalization of a gender perspective in development policy, planning and practice.[4] The framework stresses more than the basic compatibility of gender and participatory perspectives: they are essential and mutually reinforcing partners on any agenda for change. This chapter seeks to respond to two related questions: (i) under what conditions can a gender perspective, which reflects more equitable power relations between women and men than exists in most development practice, be taken on to the point that it can be said to be institutionalized? and (ii) how can a gender perspective be promoted and sustained to the point that it can be said to be institutionalized, while remaining responsive to the variety of women's and men's experiences and their interpretation of reality? Here I propose an operational definition of how to institutionalize gender within the participatory practices of organizations such as those described in this volume.

Defining institutionalization

Institutionalization is defined as 'the process whereby social practices become sufficiently regular and continuous to be described as institutions', that is, 'social practices that are regularly and continuously repeated, are sanctioned and maintained by social norms, and have a major significance in the social structure' (Abercrombie *et al.*, 1988:124). The term encompasses two important concepts: that of the *room for manoeuvre* which individuals and their organizations have to generate change, and that of the notion of *sustained change.*[5] Both concepts challenge the possible rigidity and lack of responsiveness that could be associated with the term 'institutionalization', which might be viewed as reflecting predetermined and fixed practices. Moreover, the concept of 'sustained change' recognizes the tension that all organizations continually confront, between their regular practices (which inevitably reflect particular interests), and their responsiveness to participatory change (which reflects other power relations and interests).

The term 'institutionalization' has been widely used in relation to integrating women or gender[6] into regular development practices. Yet, while WID has managed to institutionalize itself since the mid-1970s, it has not institutionalized women in the practices of development organizations. To avoid GAD and participatory development suffering a similar fate, it is essential to explore the process of institutionalization more explicitly.

The notion of a 'web of institutionalization'

To institutionalize a gender perspective requires action related to at least 13 elements, as shown in Figure 22.1. Each element represents a site of power. Gender relations, and their intersection with other social relations, operate within each site of power in any institutional context and its organizational landscape.[7] When collective action is undertaken to change a particular element, the underlying power relations will offer opportunities as well as resistance to change. Power is expressed in each element not only in the visible products and practices of organizations, but also in the invisible values and motivations which influence these outputs. Therefore, underlying each element is a series of 'organizational cultures', which are gendered. Organizational culture, for Newman, is the: 'shared symbols, language, practices. . . and deeply embedded beliefs and values. Each of these domains has to be understood as gendered, and together they constitute an important field in which gendered meanings, identities, practices and power relations are sustained' (Newman, 1995:11).

The 13 web elements provide a means not only for systematically guiding a diagnosis of an existing situation.[8] Once assessed, they also help identify what options for change exist, thus directing action to promote institutionalization of gender and participation. Moreover, these elements are not just a list of variables: they are linked and interrelated like a 'web'. Sustained institutionalization of gender issues within participatory development requires that all the elements are present, reinforcing each other. Changing only one or several elements will almost certainly be unable to sustain gendered participation as part of development practice.

Three further characteristics of the web are critical to understand its potential use:

(1) The substantive content of the elements is context-specific, thus will differ according to political and socio-economic conditions, and will

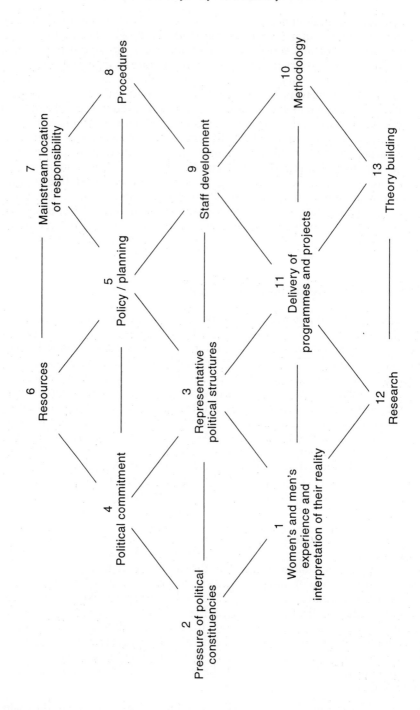

Figure 22.1: The 'web' of institutionalization

change over time. Each web will be unique. Therefore, strategies for institutionalizing gender in different contexts may also differ. In this sense, the replicability of the use of the web lies only in its potential as a methodological tool.

(2) The web, and its elements, can be applied to different groups acting at different levels: international, national and local. As each group at each level will have a different perspective on gender and participation, the 'webs' that result will identify group-specific and level-specific interpretations of the opportunities for and resistances to change.

(3) These elements are influenced by different (groups of) people in many interrelated spheres of activity (Levy, 1991). The critical point here is that, as an individual, one can usually influence only some elements in the web, depending on one's role, position and power. Putting all the elements in the web in place requires collective action through conflict resolution, cooperation, consultation and negotiation at different levels (local, national and international) between the relevant actors.

The importance of a number of these 'web elements' have been highlighted in the past. Eloquent and sophisticated research and writing can be found on individual or sets of elements.[9] This chapter attempts to present these elements in a particular relation to each other, in the form of a 'web'. The discussion will therefore touch only on relevant literature that it is pertinent to the 'web' and its linkages.

The elements in the web of institutionalization

The sequence of presentation of these elements here does not represent a universal sequence for applying the 'web'. Each context will indicate what element is the most appropriate starting point.[10] The sequence presented here is particularly relevant to those engaged in participatory development, which bases itself on listening to local voices. My intention is to take the 'voices' of women and men as the starting point, and trace them through a series of elements that require focused attention, if gender is indeed to become part and parcel of participatory development.

Women and men's experience and their interpretation of reality

For practitioners of participatory development, it is common sense to start with local perspectives or 'communities',[11] that is, women and men's experience and their interpretation of reality (see Figure 22.1). The choice of words here is important. It is not about planners or development experts interpreting women's and men's reality, but their own interpretations of their lives. Over the last 25 years, a range of theoretical gendered perspectives has emerged on how to understand and interpret local realities.[12] Despite their many merits, these approaches do not always recognize the principle of enabling women and men in communities and organizations to define and interpret their own realities, and the role of power relations in this process of interpretation. It is clear that the current developments with participatory methodologies can offer significant help, although they, in turn, rarely pursue gender-specific interpretations of reality (see Chapter 1, volume).

To promote the institutionalization of a gender perspective, the expression of gender interests related to women's and men's gender roles, access to and control over resources and felt gender needs,[13] must go beyond the level of random and reductionistic discussion. It must be expressed at the level of collective action in the political arena, the heart of any participatory process,[14] and thus link to two more elements in the web.

Pressure of political constituencies

Through mobilization and consciousness-raising,[15] women and men can initiate or get involved in collective action around particular gender interests, forming new political constituencies or joining existing ones. In this process of acting in their constituency-politics roles,[16] women and men face specific gender, class, age and/or ethnic constraints (cf. Levy, 1991; Moser, 1989a). Understanding these constraints on the constituency-politics roles of women and men is crucial if development efforts are to reinforce this element of the web.

In the 1980s and 1990s, community-based organizations and non-government organizations (NGOs) with advocacy agendas are amongst the political constituencies that are strengthening with the opening up of civil society. Such organizations clearly do not automatically operate in gender-aware ways. Neither are they automatically participatory or directly accountable to women and men in communities.

Institutionalizing gender within participation-oriented efforts will need to include the fostering of women's as well as men's capacities to exert pressure through political constituencies, and not just to describe their situation (see element 1 of the web). The distinction made by Molyneux (1985) between practical and strategic gender interests is very useful here to identify the different constituencies around gender issues, making it possible to identify competing or complementary interests at work which may affect the strength of the pressure of these political constituencies. The implications of this element of the web is that many organizations dealing with gender and participation need to address their relations with more representative political consituencies.

Representative political structures

For sustained gender institutionalization, women and men must be able to elect and/or actively engage with representative political structures within the formal political system. Otherwise they risk having their interests ignored by formal politics. Representation is used here in two distinct senses (which are often confused):

○ in terms of equal numbers of women and men on the basis not only of gender, but also of class, ethnicity, religion and age, as appropriate to the context; and
○ in terms of reflecting the practical and strategic gender interests of women and men.

It seems obvious to point out that having women in positions of power does not automatically lead to gender interests coming through in formal political arenas. Nor are all male politicians unable to represent the gender interests of women or men. Gender interests can be taken on by either elected women or men. The point here is to stress that gendered representation in political structures must encompass equal numbers and attention to gender interests alike.

The reinforcing triangle (see Figure 22.1) between the three elements is critical for sustained change. Women and men's experience and interpretation of reality, the element on which many participatory approaches pride themselves, can create pressure from political constituencies for social change through mobilization (see Chapters 8, 18 and 20, this volume). While increased awareness of gender issues is a first step, transforming this perception into collective action in the political arena is crucial for sustained improvements in gender relations. Through lobbying, the pressure of political constituencies can be brought to bear on the representative political structures. Clearly in countries with little political accountability and intolerance of the pressure of political constituencies, political struggles are waged on a broader front than merely gender issues, but one in which the latter may be a pawn in or a victim of political compromises and change.[17]

Political commitment

This first triangle links into another triangle of elements in the political sphere (see Figure 22.1). Through the influence of political consituencies and representative political structures, gender issues can be translated into political commitment. Political commitment, though mentioned often as key to any societal change, is a 'slippery' concept. I refer to it here as the public articulation of a political intent or stand. For example, Nelson Mandela, in his inaugural speech, made direct reference to the need to address gender issues in the new South Africa,[18] indicating the success of 'gendered' political constituencies in the country.

Such statements set the tone for action from which women and men in communities, as well as in development organizations, take their cue, either for or against. Political commitment to integrate gender issues is, therefore, a critical element in institutionalization.

Policy

One test of political commitment is its translation into policy (see Figure 22.1). Policymakers have two broad, complementary options: integrating gender into ongoing sectoral and cross-sectoral policy (gendered policy), and formulating gender-specific policy (gender policy). Separate policies on women or gender on their own have shown to be unsuccessful in directing gender integration into mainstream policy. They have usually ended up as a separate chapter at the end of national development plans or in a completely separate plan.[19] Gender policies can be seen, therefore, to be a necessary but insufficient condition for gender integration.

Participatory channels are crucial in the development of gendered and gender policies alike. The inputs from members of representative political structures are one key element in the making of both types of policy (see Figure 22.1). There is a range of analytical tools available to assess the content and implications of policy on gender roles, resources, and the gender needs and interests of women and men, and the extent to which it is participatory.[20]

New terms like 'enablement' and 'partnerships', which are increasingly part of current policy debates,[21] appear sympathetic to issues like participation and gender. Certain questions are not, however, automatically addressed from a gender and participatory perspective. For example, who is 'being enabled' by whom to do what and how? How representative are the 'partners' of the interests and needs of women and men?

Resources

Political commitment also needs to be translated into resources to support policy. For example, many governments signed the UN Women's Decade agreement in the 1970s, illustrating a certain degree of political commitment. Just what this was worth became apparent when looking at the resources allocated to WID in many countries – the financial amounts were minuscule in relation to budgets for other policy areas.

However, the growing focus on mainstreaming gender has shifted the resource question to one of making existing policy and programme budgets more gender aware. At the same time, increasing emphasis on the principle of cost recovery in partnerships between public, private and community sectors raises worries about equity in the use of existing budgets. This includes concerns about how decisions are made about the contribution of money and labour at community level to supplement state resources, and their gender and class implications. In reaction to this, exciting new initiatives in some parts of the world illustrate how communities raise and control their own resources, entering into negotiation with public-sector agencies from more equal and less exploited positions.[22] Nevertheless, new and sustained resources for the promotion and maintenance of gender integration remain critical. To achieve the involvement of women and men in decisions about the use of existing and new resources, the three elements of political commitment, policy and resources are a crucial reinforcing triangle in the web, throwing up many challenges for organizations pursuing the agenda of participatory development.

Mainstream location of responsibility

Resource allocation and policy formulation for gender integration depend fundamentally on the mainstream location of responsibility for gender issues. The experience of the UN Decade has highlighted how easily WID, and now potentially GAD, can be marginalized from mainstream development when a WID/GAD specific institution is created to deal with half the population, as if women were not participants in activities related to other ministries.

A key element in successful institutionalization is clarifying that the responsibility for taking on a gender perspective lies with each ministry or division, and not only with the WID or GAD ministry or department.[23] This involves creating a culture that accepts responsibility for integrating gender as part of 'good' practice, no matter what the focus of the ministry or the organization. Integral to this culture is sharing learning and decision-making with women and men alike at the community level. This notion of broad gender responsibility can be promoted through gender-integrated policies and shared decisions about allocating resources to 'gendered inter-ventions.'[24] As the triangle shows (see Figure 22.1), clarity about the main-stream responsibility for gender issues will reinforce and support gender integrated policy-making and resource allocation.

Procedures

No matter how clear policies and responsibilities might be, without gen-dered procedures, the 'paraphernalia' of bureaucracy can undermine the institutionalization of gendered interventions. This is also a common expe-rience for those organizations making the transition to participatory development. Procedures are the 'routinized' daily activities of an organ-ization's programme or project cycle, or the rules governing actions within or between organizations and individuals. For example, terms of reference and memorandum formats, have long been identified as 'entry points' for integrating a gender perspective.[25] Such gender-supportive procedures often remain hidden, however, in WID manuals rather than in mainstream guidelines.

Staff development

The implementation of policy and the interpretation of procedures will be limited without appropriate staff development. This refers to training in gender policy and planning skills for all professionals (women and men alike) and equal opportunities for male and female staff.[26]

Training in many organizations tends to be issue based, without a recog-nition of the conceptual and practical intersection between issues.[27] For example, many organizations organize separate training on gender and participatory techniques. The gender trainer does not always impart par-ticipatory principles or techniques, while the training in participatory re-search and development often treats gender randomly, or not at all.

As has been the case for institutionalizing participation, many develop-ment agencies have emphasized training as a means of promoting gender integration. Although skills are essential to translate gender awareness into practice, the last 10 to 15 years have indicated that training on its own does not change practice in a sustained way.[28] One clear recipe for wasted training is women and men returning to their organizations after gender training, without the support of a clear gendered policy framework and/or gender-aware procedures. If new skills are not used, they will soon be forgotten.

As has been widely recognized, staff development is also related to the progress of women and men workers through their organization and their participation in decision-making about work practices. This has less to do with the content of policy and planning which governs the organization's external practices, and more to do with conditions of work within development organizations, though the two are often confused. For example, despite the long recognition of the sex imbalances in most public, private and non-government organizations, and the acceptance of equal opportunity or affirmative-action policies, these sex inequalities persist.[29] The treatment and involvement of women on an equal basis to men in organizations is clearly influenced by appropriate policy and procedures. Together, these three elements of the web reflect much about organizational culture.[30]

Methodology

Effective staff development, particularly training, requires a clear methodology (see Figure 22.1). Yet this element has been strangely neglected in many development organizations. This partly reflects a lack of clarity about the organizational implications of taking on new cross-cutting issues like gender (or the environment)[31] or new techniques like the now ubiquitous, logical framework analysis.[32]

A 'clear' methodology comprises a clear rationale for integrating gender into development practice plus participatory and other techniques for operationalizing gender issues. Some interesting examples have emerged recently, including those discussed in this book.[33] Without both characteristics (rationale and techniques), a methodology will not be able to sustain change in the staff development of organizations. For those bodies working with participatory methodologies, integrating gender often means a more radical overhaul of their approach than simply tacking on another variable or including a new method.

Delivery of programmes and projects

The proof of staff development through an appropriate methodology is when the 'delivery' of programmes and projects meets the needs of women and men. Without this, the institutionalization of a gender perspective in development activities will certainly fail. This element is a pivotal point in relation to a number of reinforcing triangles in the web (see Figure 22.1). In addition to appropriate methodology and staff development, a supportive policy environment is critical to the formulation, implementation and management of gender-aware intervention

For effective institutionalization, groups involved in the 'delivery' of programmes and projects must include women and men from communities. Within the context of participatory development, their involvement is, moreover, not just in terms of carrying out the plans of male-dominated decision-making structures.[34] If programmes and projects are to relate to 'women and men's experience and their interpretation of reality' (see first element discussed, pp. 257–58), their needs and interests must be reflected in representative political structures. These include not just formal structures at a national level, but also those at local and programme/project levels. Within these structures, gendered participation would mean shared

262

decision-making in the formulation, implementation and management of interventions. For example, in Sri Lanka, women were observed as being largely silent participants in important meetings, thus biasing participation (see also Chapters 16, 18 and 19, this volume)[35]

Moreover, a gendered approach to 'delivery' also means that the decision to have women-specific, men-specific or integrated programmes is one of strategic choice based on the views of women and men involved (and the objectives of the intervention). Too many gendered interventions are being translated automatically into women's projects, often without consultation.

Research

For institutionalization to signify 'sustained change', rather than entrenched practices, 'public learning' is critical.[36] Effective 'delivery' of programmes and projects must be able to respond to the dynamic reality of women and men's experience and interpretation of that changing reality. 'Applied' research is the element in the web that allows for this learning to take place. Gender-sensitive participatory research techniques[37] have much to offer, given their potential to empower women and men in communities and organizations. They also help strengthen monitoring and feedback mechanisms to improve the delivery of programmes and projects.

Theory

Finally, 'applied' research, in its critical examination of practice, also contributes to the accumulation of knowledge about integrating gender into policy and planning practice. It contributes to building new theories around gender as a variable in development policy and planning, which, in turn, help develop better methodologies. Clearly, theory-building takes place within and between different disciplines.[38] It reinforces the elements of methodology and 'applied' research in the web, as well as the 'delivery' of programmes and projects. This includes the education of the next generation of women, men, girls and boys, which is essential to sustainable institutionalization.

Using the web as a diagnostic and operational tool

The 13 elements of the 'web of institutionalization' can help assess the extent of gender institutionalization at a country level or in one organization. It can be used in the context of many of the experiences described in this book, to reveal how far participation has become part and parcel of a development NGO or government agency. And ultimately, the hope is that the 'web' can be used to determine to what extent *gendered participation* has occurred. On the basis of such an assessment, actions can then be identified to strengthen the weaker elements in the institutionalization process. In this sense, the web can act as both a diagnostic and an operational tool.[39]

When using the web as a diagnostic tool,[40] the user's needs will define how to start. One important question that users must consider is the level at which institutionalization is being assessed. Is it at the level of one organization or that of a sector, for example, education? Or is it an entire country? Each level represents a different layer of the web, with different groups operating in many possible ways with respect to each element of the web.

A second important question to consider when identifying the starting-point is whether the web is being used to assess the impact on the institutionalization of gendered participation of a particular set of actions. This will determine with which elements the diagnosis starts. It might be most appropriate to begin with staff development if, for example, you want to assess to what extent gender training in an organization using Participatory Rural Appraisal has had an impact on institutionalizing gender throughout the PRA work, or is the user trying to assess the impact of their own sphere of influence, for example, policy or delivery of programmes and projects?

The extent to which each element is in place is, of course, context specific. However, in every context, a set of questions relating to each element can be asked in order to assess the extent to which a gender perspective is present in it performance (see Levy, 1996). Answering the questions can help identify critical areas where gender institutionalization is not working, as well as opportunities for change. Both can be identified through participatory techniques.

This then leads to the use of the web as an operational tool. The web can be used to identify which actions can be taken for each element, in order to strengthen the web and promote the institutionalization of gender. Not only will the form of each element be unique in each context, but the courses of action will differ.

Confronted by the web and a list of problems and possible improvements relating to each element, the obvious question is where does one begin to implement the possible changes? Who 'one' is, is clearly important, as it defines the power of that entity to influence the elements. Few individuals, groups or organizations can influence every part of the web. For example, some bodies may be involved in politics and advocacy work, as well as development activities, and are thus able to influence two critical areas of the web. From a diagnostic perspective it is, therefore, important to understand what is going on with respect to each element, while operationally it is then essential to define clearly the appropriate sphere of influence.

The configuration of the web is not a cause-and-effect hierarchy. Some form of prioritization of problems and potentials is necessary.[41] Based on this prioritization, particular elements and the linkages between them are targeted for action, and entry strategies can be developed for implementation.[42]

The framework of the web can then be used to monitor the success, or not, of the actions that are undertaken to strengthen particular elements. Similarly, changes brought about by 'external' influences can also be monitored, ensuring that the gender diagnosis is kept up to date and that responsiveness to new problems and potentials is maintained. In this way change can be sustained.[43]

Who is weaving the web?

In presenting the web to different audiences or workshop participants, one recurring question is: 'Where is the spider?' This question should be of particular interest to those involved in participatory development, as the 'weaver of the web' is closely related to discussions about 'who participates'. While the location and form of 'the spider' depends on the context, it is highly unlikely that 'the spider' will be one person. It is almost always likely to be a group of people operating within some organizational structure. Thus, to orchestrate strategically the strengthening of the different elements requires a level of conscious collective action by women and men in different parts of the organizational landscape. Such collective action also needs to take place at different levels: locally, nationally, regionally and internationally. Among the major actors of this orchestration should surely be women or gender-focused organizations inside and outside government.

For the many individuals and organizations pursuing participatory forms of research and development intervention, there is a need to ensure that the work benefits women and men alike, as urged by the contributions in this book and elsewhere. Community participation, in its current forms, has clearly not provided the means to achieve this development aim. Few organizations have been successful at institutionalizing gender, as is evident from the inequitable impact of many programmes and projects. An increasing number of organizations and individuals recognize this fundamental contradiction in participatory development, and are struggling to find ways to remedy the situation. The web of institutionalization offers a clear framework to start assessing the critical gaps and possible opportunities for change. The web's 13 elements can be analysed with, for example, women and men in local communities, in political groups, and with male and female staff within the development organization. The more this is carried out with those who are to live with the changes, the more consistent it will be with the principles of participatory development. Successful gender institutionalization in development organizations can be said to have happened when the incorporation of a gender perspective in a participatory way becomes a regular part of the practice of all development practitioners.

References

Abercrombie, N., S. Hill and B. Turner (1988) *Dictionary of Sociology*, Harmondsworth: Penguin. (2nd ed.).

Afshar, H. (ed) (1992) *Women and Adjustment Policies in the Third World*, London: Macmillan.

Bailyn, L. and R. Rapoport (1996) 'Re-Linking Life and Work: Report from a Collaborative Project with Business Supported by the Ford Foundation', Working Paper, Boston, MA: MIT.

Bakker, I. (ed) (1994) *The Strategic Silence: Gender and Economic Policy*, London: Zed Books.

Buvinic, M. (1983) 'Women's Issues in Third World Poverty: a policy analysis', in M. Buvinic, M. Lycette and W. McGreevey, *Women and Poverty in the Third World*, Baltimore: The Johns Hopkins Press.

Feldstein, H. and J. Jiggins (eds) (1994) *Tools for the Field: methodologies handbook for gender analysis in agriculture*, London: Intermediate Technology Publications.

Fernando, M. (1985) 'Women's Participation in the Housing Process: the case study of Kirillapone, Sri Lanka', Working Paper No 46, University College, London: Development Planning Unit.

Goetz, A M. (1995) 'Institutionalizing Women's Interests and Gender-Sensitive Accountability in Development', *IDS Bulletin*, Vol. 26, No. 3, July.

Guijt, I. (1995) *Questions of Difference: PRA, gender and environment*, London: IIED.

Hannan-Andersson, C. (1992) 'Institutionalizing and Operationalizing a Gender Approach in Development Co-operation Organizations', in *Gender Planning Methodology*, three papers on incorporating the gender approach in development co-operation programmes, Institutionen fur kulturgeografi och ekonomisk geografi vid Lund Universitet, Rapporter Och Notiser 109, Lund.

IDS (1995) 'Getting Institutions Right for Women in Development', *IDS Bulletin*, Vol. 26, No. 3, July.

Itzin, C. and J. Newman (eds) (1995) *Gender, Culture and Organizational Change: putting theory into practice*, London: Routledge.

Jahan, R. (1995) *The Elusive Agenda: mainstreaming women in development*, Dakar: University Press Ltd and London & New Jersey: Zed Books.

Levy C. (1991) 'Critical Issues in Translating Gender Concerns into Planning Competence in the 1990s', paper presented at the Joint ACSP and AESOP International Congress, Planning TransAtlantic: Global Change and Local Problems, Oxford, UK, 8–12 July.

Levy, C. (1992) 'Gender and the Environment: the challenge of cross-cutting issues in development policy and planning', *Environment and Urbanization* 4 (1): 134–149.

Levy, C. (1996) 'The Process of Institutionalizing Gender in Policy and Planning: the "web" of institutionalization', DPU Working Paper No. 74 University College London: Development Planning Unit.

Levy, C. (forthcoming) 'The Operational Components of Gender Policy and Planning', Working Paper, University College London: Development Planning Unit.

Maia, M. (1996) 'NGOs as Mediators: their role in expertise, language and institutional exemption in urban development planning in Recife, Brazil', PhD thesis, University College London: Development Planning Unit.

Molyneux, M. (1985) 'Mobilization Without Emancipation? Women's interests, states and revolution in Nicaragua', *Feminist Studies* ll (20).

Molyneux, M. (1994) 'Women's Organizations in the Face of Post-Communist Reconstruction', lecture given at the DPU, 17 May.

Moser, C. (1989a) 'Approaches to Community Participation in Urban Development: programmes in Third World cities', *Progress in Planning*, Vol. 32, Part 2.

Moser, C. (1989b) 'Gender Planning in the Third World: meeting practical and strategic gender needs', *World Development*, Vol. 17, No. 11.

Moser, C. (1993) *Gender Planning and Development: Theory, Practice and Training*, London and New York: Routledge.

Nelson, N. and S. Wright (eds) (1995) *Power and Participatory Development: theory and practice*, London: Intermediate Technology Publications.

Newman, J. (1995) 'Gender and Cultural Change' in C. Itzin and J. Newman (eds) *Gender, Culture and Organizational Change: putting theory into practice*, London and New York: Routledge.

Patel, S. (1996) 'A Case Study of SPARC and its work with the National Slum Dwellers Federation and Mahila Milan, India', a paper presented at a workshop on Poverty Reduction in Urban Areas, co-ordinated by IIED, Bangkok, 8–10 October 1996.

Safier, M. (1993) 'Organizational Landscapes, Institutional Innovations and Shifting "Terms of Trade" in the Roles and Capacities of Public, Private and Social-Sector Agencies', *Technical Notes*, No. 6.

Schon, D. (1971) *Beyond the Stable State*, Harmondsworth: Pelican.

Sen, G. and C. Grown (1987) *Development, Crises and Alternative Visions*, New York: Monthly Review Press.

Slocum, R., L. Wichart, D. Rocheleau and B. Thomas-Slayter (1995) *Power, Process and Participation: tools for change*, London: Intermediate Technology Publications.

Taher, N. (1994) 'Impact Study of Gender Planning Training in ODA Projects: Nepal', A Report Presented to South East Asian Development Division, ODA.

Taher, N. (1992) 'Monitoring the Programme of Strengthening the Development System of Namibia Through Gender Planning', ODA.

UNDP (1991) 'Cities, People and Poverty: urban development co-operation for the 1990s', A UNDP Strategy Paper, New York: UNDP.

Whitehead, A . (1979) 'Some preliminary notes on the subordination of women', *IDS Bulletin* 10 (3).

World Bank (1991) 'Urban Policy and Economic Development', a World Bank policy paper, Washington DC: World Bank.

World Bank (1993) 'Housing: enabling markets to work, a World Bank policy paper, Washington DC: World Bank.

Young, K. (1993) *Planning Development with Women: Making a World of Difference*, London: Macmillan.

Notes

Chapter 1

1. Marginalized refers to those groups (and individuals) that have less access to and therefore exert less influence over decisions that are made on behalf of the collective good. This type of development is less likely to benefit them.
2. They have even developed very similar methods, such as the 24-hour day (Moser, 1993) and the daily routines that are common in PRA-based work.
3. Where chapters only are cited, these refer to contributions in this volume.
4. Despite its limitations, the term 'community' is used widely in this book. It refers to a geographic collective (as compared to a generic use of community such as in 'the global community', 'the gay community', etc.): a group of people who live (full and/or part-time) in a locality and are connected by a web of emotional, economic and/or relational bonds and a culture, and share a set of values, norms, and meanings. Within the community, there are, of course, social sub-groups who share sub-sets of values, norms and meanings.
5. The contribution of anthropology to development practice has been limited by the chasm between the worlds of academics and practitioners, although this situation is improving slightly.
6. AEA: Agroecosystems Analysis; BA: Beneficiary Assessment; DELTA: Development Education Leadership Teams; D&D: Diagnosis and Design; DRP: Diagnóstico Rural Participativo; DRPA: Diagnóstico Rural Participativo de Agroecosistemas; GRAAP: Groupe de Recherche et d'Appui pour l'Auto-Promotion Paysanne; LLAP: Local Level Adaptive Planning; MARP: Methode Active de Recherche et de Planification Participatif; PALM: Participatory Learning Methods; PAR: Participatory Action Research; PIDA: Participatory Integrated Development Approach; PR: Participatory Research; PRM: Participatory Research Methodology/Participatory Resource Management; PRA: Participatory Rural Appraisal; PRAP: Participatory Rural Appraisal and Planning; PTD: Participatory Technology Development; PUA: Participatory Urban Appraisal; Planning for Real; RAAKS: Rapid Assessment of Agricultural Knowledge Systems; RAP: Rapid Assessment Procedure; RAT: Rapid Assessment Techniques; RCA: Rapid Catchment Analysis; REA: Rapid Ethnographic Assessment; REFLECT: Regenerated Freirean Literacy through Empowering Community Techniques; RFSA: Rapid Food Security Assessment; RMA: Rapid Multi-Perspective Appraisal; ROA: Rapid Organizational Analysis; RRA: Rapid Rural Appraisal; Samuhik Brahman (joint trek); SSM: Soft Systems Methodology; Theatre for Development; Training for Transformation; VIPP: Visualization in Participatory Programmes; OOPP: Objective-Oriented Participatory Planning.
7. Only recently have more applied gender analysis and planning approaches been developed for sectors, in particular irrigation, forestry, agriculture and health.
8. During a 1993 Gender Training of Trainers workshop, participants from Latin America, Asia, and Africa berated the gender trainers from Europe and North America, for failing to call on local gender knowledge when flying in for consultancies and research.
9. Though this criticism is by no means exclusive to PRA.

10. Clearly, difference between women and between men are equally significant (see Chapters 4, 11 and 20).
11. Nelson and Wright (Chapter 1, 1995) provide an excellent introduction into the development of diverse interpretations of participation and the links to empowerment.
12. F. Thompson (as cited in Bryson and Mowbray, 1981:257) expresses a rather cynical view, by saying that community is a convenient panacea that supplants the need for revolution or reform.
13. See Guijt and Kaul Shah, 1993. Several of the chapters (6, 7 and 8) in this volume were presented there.

Chapter 2

1. As Lukes (1986:5) suggests, concepts of power reveal hidden assumptions and unanswered questions. Is power the actual production of intended effects or the capacity to produce them? Is it necessary that the effects be intended? Is the presence of conflict and resistance endemic to power? Although he concludes that the very search for a definition may be a mistake, he does suggest in general terms that 'to have power is to be able to make a difference to the world'. Friedmann (1992), by contrast, distinguishes between three types of power: social, concerned with access to certain 'bases' of household production; political, concerned with the access of individual household members to the processes by which decisions, particularly those that affect their own future are made; and psychological. Meanwhile Deutchman (1991) notes that some feminist theory argues not only that power is gendered but that women define and use it differently than men. Therefore, whilst men see 'empowerment' as 'power over', women define 'empowerment' as 'power to'.
2. Kabeer (1990: 11) argues that what is most striking as specific about the power dimension in gender relations, is the extent to which ideologies about gender difference and gender inequalities are internalized as a natural state of affairs by women as much as men.
3. 'Empowerment' is similarly defined by Bystydzienski (1992:3) as 'a process by which oppressed persons gain some control over their lives by taking part with others in the development of activities and structures that allow people increased involvement in matters which affect them directly.'
4. Bystydzienski (1992) suggests that small consciousness-raising groups can raise awareness among women of their personal and immediate circumstances and thus are an important strategy. This is the equivalent of what Friedmann (1992) describes as 'psychological empowerment'.
5. There are clearly examples where the use of PRA has not only validated women's knowledge but has also created a sense of collective awareness. Grady et al. (1991) have, for example, described the use of participatory research to initiate a process of consciousness-raising and confidence-building among women in Gaza. Krishnamurthy's (1994) case study of self-reflection on gender stereotypes in Tamil Nadu, India illustrates the potential for collective recognition and understanding of some of the forces and different institutions which perpetuate gender stereotypes, in turn raising issues surrounding the extent to which women have control over their bodies, sexuality and fertility. Devaraj (1993) suggests that this can have real implications for women's lives. As a result of a gender PRA training workshop, women, through sharing their personal problems, 'developed a strong bond and solidarity which later led to the formation of a Women's Co-ordination Committee'.
6. Cornwall (1992b) suggests that although PRA techniques can give some insights into the effects and processes of gendering, strategies and techniques for

addressing wider issues of power and social complexity are yet to be developed fully.

7. Welbourn (1991) notes, referring to her use of PRA techniques with women in Sierra Leone, that some women commented: 'The changes we need cannot be drawn' when asked to draw improvements they would like. They were referring specifically to issues such as the breakdown of co-wife relationships and violence from husbands. See also 6 above.

8. This refers to conflict in the broadest possible sense.

Chapter 3

1. As Kabeer (1994: 227) notes: 'Power relations are kept in place because the actors involved – both dominant and subordinate – subscribe to accounts of social reality which deny that such inequalities exist or else assert that they are due to individual misfortune rather than social injustice'. GAD does not assume women have perfect knowledge of the world around them or have some greater intuitive power than men, and are therefore unaffected by ideology. Because of this, providing space for women to discuss their condition and unravel the images of ideology from the reality of interest is a crucial GAD strategy (see Young, 1993).

2. 'Critical' derives, in this sense from the roots of critical social theory as developed by members of the Institute of Social Research in Frankfurt (commonly known as the Frankfurt School) in the 1930s. Critical theory is seen as having two roles: one negative and one positive or creative. The negative role is essentially to critique ideology: criticism should illuminate the systems of domination and the ideologies which conceal and legitimate the social and economic structures of oppression and unequal power relations. However, critical theory also has a practical intent which is the basis for its positive or creative role: it aims to improve radically improve human existence (see Held, 1980).

3. In this regard, not only is the personal political, so too is the organizational. As Kabeer (1994: 36–7) notes, advocacy for gender equity has wider implications than advocacy for other forms of institutional change, as it directly concerns the personal as well as the professional lives and relationships, beliefs and values of those who are required to devise and implement change.

4. Tools such as seasonal calendars or daily activity diagrams and focus group discussions provide excellent means for determining what women and men actually do, their different areas of responsibility and their respective contributions to the well-being of households and communities. This is particularly important, since women's contribution is often overlooked or undervalued by outside planners, men and even women themselves. (Flora, 1994). Social structures, power relations and networks of support can be investigated through social mapping and wealth ranking, which can be adapted to ensure information is gender-disaggregated.

5. An excellent example is provided by Welbourn (1991: 14–23). Welbourn asked men and women to draw 'mental maps' of the kinds of improvements they would like to see in their villages. Women's maps reflected their responsibilities for health care, education and water collection, while men's maps were grounded in their role as community decision-makers. In another village, women undertaking the same exercise suggested that they could not draw the changes they needed in their village, as these related to overwork, isolation and domestic violence, more structural and strategic issues. Many other practitioners emphasise the importance of repeating exercises with separate groups to show the diversity of opinion and decision-making processes in a community (see Theis and Grady (1991: 77).

6. Chambers (1992) discusses the centrality of attitudinal change on the part of 'outsiders', which includes recognising the knowledge and capacity of local people even when they do not have 'formal' or 'western' learning. Welbourn (1991) discusses the need to look beyond the apparent homogeneity in communities or households and to recognise the power differences inherent in many social relations.

7. This section is based on a wide range of sources including personal communication with Aga Khan Foundation staff in London and project staff in India. Written sources include: AKRSP Annual Progress Report (Ahmedabad: AKRSP) 1991, 1992, 1993; and photocopies of unpublished reports from Meena Bilgi: 'Need for promotion of separate women's groups and AKRSP's view on women in development' (nd), 'Strategy for WID programme' (nd), 'Visit to village Jambhar, Netrang' (nd), 'Entering the Women's World: PRA exercise with women in Village Nana Kandhasar' (1991) 'PRA in Village Chingharia, 3–4 January' (1992) and 'Entering Women's World through Men's Eyes: a participatory rural appraisal at Boripitha, Netrang' (1992).

8. Given their particular focus on natural resource management, AKRSP may not have been able to respond to women's social sector needs. AKRSP has recognised this problem, and has begun discussing ways of expanding or cooperating with other groups on health and education issues (see AKRSP, 1994).

9. This section is based on a wide range of sources including personal communication with individuals associated with the BSDP project. Written sources include: Putu Hermawati and Sara Kindon (1993) 'Gender Roles, Relations and Needs in the Balinese Development Process', University Consortium on the Environment Student Paper No: 14 (Waterloo: University of Waterloo); Bala Hyma (1991) 'Sustainable Development from Gender Perspectives', BSDP Working Paper (photocopy); Bala Hyma and Sara Kindon (1992) 'A Review of the Bali Sustainable Development Project Village Surveys from a Gender Perspective', University Consortium on the Environment Research Paper No: 29 (Waterloo: University of Waterloo); Sara Kindon (1993) 'From Tea Makers to Decision Makers: Applying Participatory Rural Appraisal to Gender and Development in Rural Bali, Indonesia', MA thesis (University of Waterloo, Waterloo); Bali Sustainable Development Project (1992), 'Report on the Fourth Workshop: a sustainable development strategy for Bali', University Consortium on the Environment Research Report No: 43 (Yogyakarta and Waterloo: Gadjah Mada University and University of Waterloo); and BSDP (1992) 'Sustainable Development Strategy for Bali', University Consortium on the Environment Research Paper No: 40 (Yogyakarta and Waterloo: Gadjah Mada University and University of Waterloo).

10. This is speculative, however, as the overall influence of a culture which expects women to be deferential to men in decision-making may have as great a negative effect on women's equal participation as the positive effect of their greater exposure to and confidence in planning with PRA.

11. 'Optimal ignorance' and 'appropriate imprecision' mean that practitioners should only gather as much information as necessary for appropriate action at each stage of analysis, and should determine what is not worth knowing and justify their choices.

Chapter 4

1. Recent exceptions include Guijt, 1995; Thomas-Slayter *et al.*, 1991; Rocheleau *et al.*, 1991; Buenavista and Flora, 1993; and Srinavasan and Narayan, 1994.

Chapter 5

1. SARAR stands for: **S**elf-esteem – **A**ssociative strength – **R**esourcefulness – **A**ction – **R**esponsibility. This concept was developed by Lyra Srinavasan (1990, 1992).
2. And feelings should be seen as facts in development!
3. The other two facilitators, with whom I shared this learning process, were Colleen Crawford Cousins and Michelle Friedmann.
4. This was the first occasion at which the term PRA was used, although many other workshops on participatory approaches had been held under different names and acronyms.
5. For the fieldwork stage of workshops, participants are divided into smaller groups, or teams, which work together in a specific geographic area of the community, with a specific group or on a specific issue. The teams then come together to link their analysis.
6. It is quite common for facilitators to designate, secretly, one or the other participant as a 'saboteur' and to ignore the lessons that these people offer.

Chapter 6

1. Editors' note: The extent to which it was necessary and/or ethical to manipulate some people, in order to support others in an empowerment strategy issue, was strongly debated during the 1993 PRA and gender workshop.
2. As described, apparently unconsciously, by a facilitator in a paper to the 1993 workshop.
3. This lack of familiarity would apply much less forcefully, if at all, for example, to Filipino urban trade union members.
4. Health is gender-conscious up to a point but is usually neither very participatory nor empowering beyond the narrowly functional.
5. Although the exchanges and cross-obligations are by no means usually fully equitable, they are rarely outright slavery.
6. While all are known, no general picture has been researched.

Chapter 7

1. The author would like to thank the *dais* (midwives), ADITHI and BMK staff for giving her an opportunity to be part of the process of sharing, analysing and learning.
2. The term 'survey method' as used here refers to simple procedures by which surveys are carried out, while the term 'survey methodology' refers to the conceptual framework underpinning it and the social relations through which it is carried out.
3. However, independent inquiries revealed that the practice had spread to these communities as well, from the fourth daughter onwards.
4. BMK staff noted that official census data is not sex-disaggregated.
5. Purdah is the practice of secluding women from public spaces.

Chapter 8

1. We were a small team of myself, the Programme Executive for Gender at AKRSP, and several other of AKRSP's community organisers.
2. An extension volunteer is a local person who is trained to take on the responsibility of extension work in their own community.

Notes

Chapter 9

1. Agricultural Extension Department of the Ministry of Agriculture.

Chapter 10

1. The authors wish to acknowledge the contributions of the following people in the field research and on-going adolescent sexual and reproductive health programme development in Chawama Compound. From Chawama Clinic, Christine Matabini, Mary Chikwanda, Corina Zulu and Lilian Zulu. From the Chawama Neighbourhood Health Committee: Freeboy Chilala, Sophie Chipanda, M. Lungu, Kelvin Munengo, and Febby Sinyenga. From CARE: Tabitha Chikunga, Rose Zambezi, Pene Ward, Fortune Chibamba, Doras Chirwa, Dorothy Khombe, Roy Mwilu, Carlton Sulwe, Elizabeth Mbewe, Burton Munkomba, and Mary Simasiku. The authors also gratefully acknowledge the participation of the adolescent community residing in Chawama, too numerous to mention individually, for sharing personal and sensitive information with the team and for stimulating us to continue with the design of an adolescent programme. This study would not have been possible without the generous support of The United States Agency for International Development (USAID) who provided funding under its Grant 011–6234 to CARE. Special thanks to Paul Hartenberger, Chief of the Population, Health and Nutrition Unit of USAID/ Zambia, for his continued support of community-generated programming, and to Greg Duly, Aben Ngay, and Michael Drinkwater at CARE for their critical review of the manuscript.
2. CARE International in Zambia is a country office of CARE International, a non-governmental organization which undertakes development and relief activities around the world. CARE Zambia started in January 1992 and is currently implementing activities which include micro-credit, urban livelihood security, population control, and community health.
3. CARE Zambia received funding for its adolescent health programme in Lusaka from the United States Agency for International Development through its MotherCare Project (John Snow, Inc) and through the Population Council, Nairobi. Funding has also come from the Overseas Development Authority (now Department for International Development) to mount similar programmes in urban centres in the Southern Province and Copperbelt.
4. If Chawama conforms to the national profile, many children, up to 50 per cent of the school-going age population, never enrol in primary school (UNDP, 1995).
5. 'Core poor' is a phrase used by the World Bank to define those people whose 'mean per adult equivalent expenditure' is 50 per cent. In Zambia, 54 per cent of the population has been defined as 'core poor' (World Bank, 1994).
6. This methodology is also known as participatory rural appraisal (PRA) (Pretty *et al.*, 1995) and participatory urban appraisal (PUA).
7. Although this helped the appraisal process considerably, we later realized that boys felt equally comfortable talking with male and female facilitators alike. Girls, by comparison, preferred speaking with women only.
8. Chawama has a copy of the report with all recorded visuals and outputs. The original copies are still with CARE. Members of the field team kept their own notebooks, so what they recorded has remained with them.
9. Facilitators probed into the issue of sexual activity among pre-pubescent adolescents in an effort to distinguish between 'playing at sex' and 'penetrative sex'. While there is an element among younger adolescents to imitate adult behaviour, there is also evidence of penetrative sex within this age group. This finding was confirmed during two subsequent PLA studies.

273

10. Data from CARE's Livelihood Monitoring Survey which is conducted regularly in four compounds by staff of the Peri-Urban Self-Help Project-Phase II indicate that households within the lowest socio-economic strata are experiencing more frequent shocks than in previous years.
11. *Tuntemba* stands, small cardboard or wooden stalls stocked with common household items such as candles, matches, and soap, are usually run by adolescent boys who have been given seed money (10000 to 20000 kwacha, or US$8–10) by their families, and are then expected to earn their pocket money through vending.
12. Pair-wise ranking is used to compare several options. In this case, the different reasons for early initiation of sexual activity for girls were listed and compared two at a time. Each pair in the table was compared, and one of the two was selected as more important. The results show the frequency with which options are chosen. In this analysis, boys think that 'money' is the most important reason why girls have sex, followed by 'enjoyment'.
13. One group of adolescents provided a free score of 152 for poor girls versus 40 for better-off girls.
14. Girls initiate sex earlier than boys, around the age of 12 according to adolescents in Chawama, while boys initiate sex at around 14 years.
15. We wish to acknowledge the financial and programme support of the Population Council for organizing this workshop.
16. It was useful that we had also collected more detailed quantitative date during household interviews and as part a social mapping exercise, thus confirming the PLA-derived findings.
17. In the Dambwa PLA in Livingstone, the most important landmark on the adolescents' social map on one section was the local bar which featured a male striptease artist called a *chosa* dancer.

Chapter 11

1. JFM is now approved by 17 state governments.
2. 'Handing over the stick' has become a symbol in PRA training of the importance of devolving speaking power to local people. It originated during discussions related to large diagrams on the ground. These discussions often require a stick to point out the key features that were being debated. As the person holding the stick tends to determine the focus of the discussion, many PRA trainers focus attention on the importance of outsiders not to dominate discussions and to 'hand over the stick'.
3. Social Action for Rural and Tribal Inhabitants of India.
4. SARTHI had not used what has come to be called 'PRA' although its staff was sensitive to facilitating women's and men's participation, in fact, far more than many PRA practitioners.
5. It was again difficult to know which women and which men were absent, and why they were not present.

Chapter 12

1. With thanks to all the donors who made Stepping Stones possible: ACTIONAID, Charity Projects, OXFAM UK/I, Redd Barna (Norway), Swiss Development Cooperation, UNDP, WHO-GPA; and the UK Overseas Development Administration (now Department for International Development) who have kindly agreed to fund French versions of the manual and video, and a Swahili version of the video. Redd Barna gave us enormous support in Uganda. Professor Rose Mbowa of Makerere University Department of Music, Dance

and Drama, acted as workshop coordinator as well as giving much invaluable advice. Germine Sebuwufu, Baron Oron and Milton Bakebwa were marvellous facilitators. Finally, the people of Buwenda, in south west Uganda, generously agreed to take part in the first Stepping Stones workshop. Drawings in this chapter are by Petra Röhr–Rouendaal, in Welbourn 1995.

2. Mother-to-child transmission, transmission through infected blood or un-cleaned knives, blades or syringes, and penetrative sex between men are also routes of transmission, but will not be discussed further here.

3. The package consists of a manual, which describes how to run a workshop with community members, and a workshop video, which is made up of fifteen 5-min-ute clips, designed for viewing at separate stages of the workshop, as a spring-board for the viewers' discussion about issues in their own community.

4. Sessions, each about 3 hours long, are spread over 9–12 weeks. Some would say that asking for twelve weeks' commitment to a workshop is asking too much. Yet the few days between each session allow individuals to reflect on what they have been confronting.

5. Flow diagrams proved to be a very effective way to guide these discussions.

6. Nonetheless it is encouraging to note that young women mentioned that they no longer have unplanned pregnancies and that married women are only be-coming pregnant as planned.

Chapter 13

1. I wish to thank all the residents of village Darko for their enthusiastic participa-tion in this assessment. I also thank all the members of the PPA team with whom I worked in Darko.

2. I was involved in the PPA as a trainer in PRA methodology.

3. Darko was especially suited for the research as one of the local NGOs participating in the PPA was working in the area and could follow-up the research with appropriate development initiatives in the village.

4. Household here refers to a set of people residing together and sharing their economic resources. A compound consists of varying number of such units, who are usually related by kin, but have separate cooking arrangements.

5. Explained as those who do no steal, who help the community and do not think evil of others.

6. Note that the categories 'rich' and 'poor' are relative assessments. No one might be either rich or poor if compared to other communities, regions or countries.

7. Kabeer (1989: 9) also observes, '[Women] can become poorer along with the rest of the family-based household through a deterioration in its total package of entitlements in which case, women's interests are interdependent with the collective interests of the rest of the household membership. Alternatively, they can become poorer with the breakdown of the family unit itself and with it the system of rights and obligations on which they critically rely'.

Chapter 14

1. At the time of our work together, Putu had a BSc in Civil Engineering from Universitas Udayana. While she had some previous village research experience this was her first exposure to GAD, PRA, and working with a foreigner. She is now lecturing in Engineering at the Technical Institute and Polytechnic associated with Udayan University in Denspasar, Bali.

2. The BSDP was established in 1989 and is a collaborative research endeavour between the Faculty of Environmental Studies, University of Waterloo (Canada) and Gadjah Mada University in Yogyakarta with assistance from the

Udayana University in Bali. The BSDP is part of an initiative funded by the Canadian International Development Agency (CIDA). Its main objective has been the creation of a Sustainable Development Strategy (SDS) to contribute to Bali's five year governmental planning process.

3. The PKK is the principal mediating body between the state and households.
4. For purposes of confidentiality, I have given these two villages pseudonyms.
5. Conscious partiality aims to move away from the myth of value-free research. The researchers/facilitators take the side of a certain group, partly identify with its members and their causes, and then consciously set up a process of dialogue between it and other groups.
6. A traditional village or *desa adat* consists of a number of small hamlets and temples based on kinship, genealogy and land ownership. A government or official village (*desa dinas*) is a conglomeration of households and associated land into one unit for government administrative purposes. In some cases, a *desa dinas* may overlap with a *desa adat*, in others several *desa adat* may be incorporated into one *desa dinas*.
7. This was also the case for pre-literate women and men, and less confident men.
8. A Canadian BSDP colleague later facilitated training in water-systems maintenance for women in Desa Pualang to address this strategic need (Gupta, 1994).
9. The problems with rapid PRA processes are partially addressed by factoring in more time, but other issues also need addressing to make effective use of this time (see Chapter 20, this volume).

Chapter 15

1. 'Participatory Communication for Fertilizer Technology Transfer: a gender approach' is a sub-project executed by *Mekweseh* for Soil Nutrients for Agricultural productivity (SNAP), a joint project of the governments of Jamaica and Canada in St Ann, Jamaica.
2. This is the case for any participatory communication process, whether with video or another medium.
3. Creative framing has to do with the different ways in which various cultures may compose their shots. For instance, the style of an action-packed hindi movie or a Kung Fu film (which might have many top-down shots at a quick pace) would be very different from that of an English film of a Jane Austen novel. Creative framing requires knowledge about the genre and visual style used in entertainment films in the culture in which one is working. This style may then be adapted to make educational videos more entertaining and, therefore, more effective.
4. 'This isn't a play! This is no drama! This is real life! And this is my life in there . . . So now I know what this project is about.'
5. These reflections have not dealt with technical aspects, such as those related to the training of rural women, as these have been documented elsewhere (Jumani, 1985; Protz, 1991; Stuart, 1989).

Chapter 16

1. The team consisted of two women geographers from the ECOGEN (Ecology, Community Organization, and Gender) project at Clark University in the United States, and one male forester and one male historian from the Forestry Department at the Instituto Superior de Agricultura (ISA), Dominican Republic.
2. Gendered changes are gender-specific changes, while gendered interests are those interests as shaped by gender identities. Gendered space and knowledge

are, similarly, space and knowledge as experienced and used by different gender groups.

3. Membership stands at nearly 700 people in 500 households.
4. This included land struggles, school and transportation strikes, and protests over forest-service abuses.

Chapter 17

1. The NGOs were NOVIB, PSO, AFSC, CAA, CIDSE, LWS, MCC and Oxfam UK/I.

Chapter 18

1. This article draws on Frischmuth 1995.
2. Gesellschaft für Technische Zusammenarbeit.
3. In villages with female store-keepers, these ideas were accepted readily. The women themselves, however, were reluctant to accept the responsibility of keeping the money at home. They were afraid that it would be stolen or that their husbands would claim it, which the women would then be unable to refuse. As gender sensitization and leadership training continues, it is hoped that these issues will become less of an obstacle to women accepting leadership roles. In villages, where the store-keepers were women's club chairwomen, they had a high level of self-confidence and felt they could deal with their husbands should problems arise.
4. And not the other way around, which so often leads to the neglect of gender issues in the name of participation!
5. Such discussions occur in many villages but not all and not at the same time. It depends on the camp officer, on the seasonal programme, and on the willingness of the community to take up the issues. However, the discussions are becoming a more integrated part of the extension programme, and an increasing number of villages and camp officers are taking up these issues.
6. In live sculptures, participants are 'sculpted' into fixed positions to portray a situation. Unlike role plays there is no dialogue or changing of positions. The scene is shown briefly and then analyzed.

Chapter 19

1. Total disbursements from DAC countries, which were US$0.9 billion in 1970 (OECD, 1988: 19), grew to $22.6 billion in 1980–81, and to $66 billion in 1994–95 (OECD, 1997) (not discounting for inflation).
2. For example: 'Of 24 (of 150) 'successful' projects . . . only four were established under government auspices. . .' (Esman and Uphoff, 1984: 15).
3. Based on 12 months of fieldwork conducted in 1993/94. Research was carried out by Rachel Hinton, Rita Dhakal, Gita Rai, Jamuna Nepal and many refugee women.
4. This is an approximate figure up to October 1995. Though in very small numbers, refugees continue to trickle into the camps.
5. The remaining 15 000 settled outside the camps.
6. The term NGO refers to implementing agencies recognized by UNHCR, which are usually international NGOs. Numerous other local NGOs operate in the camps but are not officially recognized.
7. The names of the NGOs and informants have been changed throughout the text.
8. See, for example, the Refugee Policy Group's discussion about western liberal concepts of democratic participation (Cuny, 1987: 2).

9. This number includes project beneficiaries.
10. Like LSF, UNSID sponsors staff training on gender issues.
11. UNSID argues that crisis situations require speed and reliability, and participation is considered time-consuming and unreliable.
12. The exercise was repeated across five camps for comparative purposes and similar patterns emerged.
13. The Refugee Policy Group (Cuny, 1987: 13–14) adds that participation has a powerful psychological capacity to build self-esteem, self-confidence, reduce isolation, lethargy and depression. It helps reduce costs, promotes protection of projects, and encourages self-sufficiency.
14. Because of its potential for dual use, philosophers of language describe participation as an example of process-product ambiguity (Galjart and Buijs, 1982). The same distinction between process and product is also discussed in van Giffen (1982) and Moser (1989).
15. Other definitions of participation are presented in Cornwall, 1996; Pretty, 1994; Hart, 1992; Adnan et al, 1994.
16. Moser (1989), for example, emphasizes the multi-textured quality of participation, rejecting the use of dualistic dichotomies in its analysis. Korten (1990) too acknowledges the complexity of development goals, noting that within a single agency, several approaches and methodologies may be used. Buvinic (1986) points to progressive phases within project cycles, in which organizations such as UNSID move from low initial participation (in crisis management) to higher participation once the state of emergency has resolved. Guijt (1996) summarizes the problems with typologies of participation as: assuming erroneously its static nature over time, failing to identify clearly who is participating in what way at what moment, and feeding the illusion of a linear process of participation culminating in one single ideal form for all situations.
17. For a discussion of top-down and bottom-up approaches to participation see Moser (1989).
18. The Refugee Policy Group (Cuny, 1987: 9–10) offers an examination of several constraints to participation.
19. Hayward (1981) notes that participation is both argued to foster 'a sense of efficacy, understanding and responsibility without which development is difficult if not impossible' and to raise 'expectations, create disorder [which] results in popular cynicism and leads to instability which is detrimental if not fatal to development'.
20. According to Stone (1992:415) 'perhaps the time has come to see participation as a common sense development strategy, but not as a goal in itself, nor as a powerful tool of democratic reform, since in the latter cases the concept always seems to carry more significance for outsiders than for the poor'.
21. LSF's income-generating project with women challenged this assumption for emergency situations. It is generally assumed that as women are at home and not equal actors in a political or economic sense, they are most vulnerable. Their husbands are thought to be relatively empowered through their 'work'. Women involved in the LSF project indicated the opposite, however. As their husbands are accustomed to working, the sudden lack of purpose and occupation in the camp made them more vulnerable than the women.
22. For example, women gained a markedly greater voice in camp committees, and expressed grievances and solidarity in the Camp Counselling Board.

Chapter 20

1. Irene Guijt from IIED was involved as the PRA trainer and outside reviewer throughout this process. Tony Kisadha is Director of Programme Development.

278

Grace Mukasa was amongst the first group of recruited field staff and, after acting as a regional CAPO supervisor, is now Programme Officer based in Kampala.

2. Redd Barna Uganda is one of the country programmes of Redd Barna, the Norwegian Save the Children organization.
3. According to the World Bank, it had the worst growth performance of all sub-Saharan countries between 1961 and 1989 (Jamal, 1991).
4. Infant mortality rate represents deaths under one year of age per 1000 live births.
5. Anyone under the age of 18 is technically a child so, legally speaking, the number of children is higher. However, as many children in Uganda between 15 and 18 carry responsibilities commonly equated with adulthood, including for girls the bearing of their own children, 15 is commonly used as a cut-off point for childhood.
6. Decentralization is being implemented at various levels, through the local councils (LCs) that operate at district, county, sub-county, parish and village levels (LC5 to LC1).
7. Again, the Masaka Project is different, operating with a range of other staff besides CAPOs.
8. A methodology that improves adults' interaction with children.
9. A UNICEF-sponsored methodology that encourages children to teach other children in basic health care.
10. With support from the CAPO who organized and facilitated a series of community-level meetings.
11. As analysed by villagers and extension agents in Bulende-Bugosere.
12. The review included the CAPOs, senior management of Redd Barna Uganda, several groups of villagers in the communities, local extension agents, the partner organizations and IIED.
13. These are now being used by all the CAPOs to scale up their efforts with community-based work.
14. This is particularly the case in the districts where CAPOs are just beginning to facilitate community-level work. In the districts where this is already occurring through partner organizations, new partners do not necessarily need to be sought.
15. To avoid problems with follow-up, RBU has developed a series of criteria to help identify appropriate partner organizations and trainees.
16. Its use is based on the assumption that field staff work with distinct social groups, in this case: younger women, older women, older men, younger men and children. This would and will differ from one context to another, and could be constructed for any groups that have different needs, e.g. pastoralists, agriculturalists, small landholders, larger farmers, etc.
17. A CAPO and/or a staff member of the partner organization.
18. The use of PRA methods continues, with pair-wise ranking helping at this step.
19. Matrix ranking of possible solutions per problem area can be effective. The group will need to generate its own criteria, such as social acceptability, needs much money, high level of technical complexity, etc.
20. Credit for giving RBU this time to experiment and learn goes to Andreas Fuglesang and Dale Chandler. They acted as a buffer towards the Norwegian funding agencies, repeatedly explaining the need for extra time.

Chapter 21

1. Chapter 21 is based on work with men and women in about 50 villages in Bharuch district of Gujarat. This collective learning process has been enriched

by the active participation of several thousand men and women from these villages, to whom I am indebted. I would like to express special thanks to four women, Raiben and Shardaben of Samarpada, and Lakshmiben and Sumitraben of Sakwa, who were always willing to take new initiatives, despite the problems and challenges they so often faced, and without whom the learning process would have been far more difficult. I want to thank the male village extension volunteers, who broke so many conventions while attempting to involve women from their villages in the projects. The process described in this chapter is based on the collective efforts of the AKRSP Spearhead Team in Bharuch District. I want to thank my colleagues Ranjit Ambastha, Haribhai Mori, Natwar Virani, Ashok Sojitra, Bhadresh Rawal, Dilip Dave Jaimati Desai, Parmesh Shah and Anil Shah for their enthusiastic involvement and efforts in trying to integrate the concerns of women in the programmes we were supporting.

2. I worked for AKRSP during 1987–92, first as Programme Executive, Monitoring (with additional responsibilities for Animal Husbandry, Marketing, WID and production of training materials), and later as the Coordinator of the Spearhead Team in Bharuch District of Gujarat. Chapter 21 is based on the organization's experiences during this period.

3. In 1992, the AKRSP Spearhead Team in Bharuch comprised 18 professionals. Only two of these were women.

4. Homestead lands, or *wadas* as they are called in the local language, are the small parcels of land around a house. These *wadas* are controlled and used mainly by the women. During the rainy season they grow some cereals and vegetables on these lands, and some women also grow fruit trees. The decisions of what to grow and how to use the produce are taken by the women, unlike in the case of the main agricultural fields. Women obtain seeds and other inputs from the traders on cash or credit, and are able to sell some of the vegetables they grow in their *wadas*.

5. Women's analysis of impact and the indicators they selected are discussed in Shah (1993).

Chapter 22

1. Chapter 21 draws directly from my original paper: 'The Process of Institutionalizing Gender in Policy and Planning: the 'web' of institutionalization', DPU Working Paper No 74, Development Planning Unit, University College, London (1996).

2. See Moser (1989a) for a discussion of the different purposes of participation.

3. While a concern with gender relations in development can be traced back to the late 1970s, particularly in the debates of feminist academics, e.g. Whitehead (1979), it was only in 1988 that SIDA (Swedish International Development Cooperation Agency), the first development organization to start the process of the institutionalization of a gender perspective, began the process.

4. This framework evolved out of my involvement in the teaching, training and advisory work of the Gender Policy and Planning Programme at the Development Planning Unit (DPU), and a review of the practice of others, covering a range of international agencies, government agencies and NGOs.

5. The importance of the notion of 'sustained change' was emphasized for me in discussion with Rona Rapoport in relation to ongoing action research in large US corporations (cf. Bailyn and Rapoport, 1996).

6. In this chapter when I use the phrase 'women and gender' I am not using these words interchangeably, but rather acknowledging that some work has a women focus while other efforts have a gender focus.

Notes

7. The term 'organizational landscape' is borrowed from the work of Safier (1993), who uses it to describe the configuration of the public, private and community sectors in any particular context.
8. Gender diagnosis is used here as a component of the gender policy and planning methodology advanced by DPU, and as distinct from 'gender analysis', the approach associated with the Harvard School, which comprises different components and techniques.
9. For example, Hannan-Andersson (1992), Jahan (1995), Goetz (1995), IDS (1995).
10. Since the elements are part of a web one could, in principle, start anywhere.
11. 'Community' is used here not as an undifferentiated unit of social organization but with the recognition of their heterogeneity and diversity on the basis of class, ethnicity, religion, age as well as gender.
12. For example, the concepts which form the basis of 'gender analysis' as associated with the Harvard School, 'social relations analysis' as associated with IDS, and gender policy and planning as developed in the first instance by the DPU.
13. While Molyneux (1985) talks about gender interests, Moser (1989a) talks of gender needs.
14. This is certainly the case for participation as an end. Some would argue that this is also the case for participation as a means, if implementing this aim is to avoid the exploitation of women and men.
15. This can happen through a range of processes internal and/or external to women and men in communities and organizations.
16. 'Constituency-based politics role' is defined as political activities undertaken at community, local, national and/or sometimes international levels by or on behalf of interest-based constituencies, within the framework of traditional/customary structures, party politics and/or lobbying/campaigning groups (DPU Gender Policy and Planning team, Training materials for training in gender planning, 1992–93). While this term includes Moser's definition of 'community politics' (1993), it encompasses political activities beyond the community level.
17. For example, in Palestine some women's groups feel their interests are being compromised to pacify more extremist religious and political bodies. In Eastern Europe, social services which provided support for women in their reproductive roles and enabled them to participate in the productive and constituency-based-politics roles are being swept aside in the new political climate because they are being conflated with the communist era (see Molyneux, 1994).
18. Political commitment can also be reflected in public acts and images.
19. These chapters or plans often conflate issues related to women, with those of children/youth, the disabled and, in some cases, ethnic minorities.
20. For example, Buvinic (1983), Molyneux (1985), Moser (1989a) and (1993), Sen and Grown (1987), Young (1993) and recent work on macro-economic policy on the impacts of globalization and structural adjustment, for example Afshar (1992), Bakker (1994).
21. For example, see UNDP (1991) and World Bank (1991 and 1993).
22. See for example, the joint activities of SPARC, Mahila Milan (Women Working Together) and the National Slum Dwellers Association in India (Patel, 1996).
23. There are striking parallels with participation being marginalized in one unit of an organization or a certain ministry.
24. This is in addition to any 'gender-specific' policy or any 'gender-specific' allocations that are agreed.
25. For example SIDA, EU, UNIDO all have guidelines or reference manuals which highlight the integration of gender into terms of reference.
26. For example, recruitment, access to training and promotion.
27. For example, this is the case in training around gender and environment issues respectively.
28. For example, the experience of the regular gender-training programmes started in the mid 1980s started by ODA in 1987 and SIDA in 1988.

29. With men in top positions, women in lower positions in organizations; or with a majority of women or men in sex-segregated activities. Although some believe that the situation with respect to the former is different in NGOs, evidence would suggest that this is a myth, as for example in Maia (1996).
30. See, for example, Itzin and Newman (1995).
31. See Levy (1992).
32. Logical framework analysis has been widely introduced in a variety of forms in international agencies, for example, GTZ, NORAD, ODA and the EU. Gender is either absent as an issue, or as in the case of the EU, is categorized as a social issue. There is ongoing work on the integration of gender into the various forms of logical-framework analysis in GTZ and in the EU (with DPU).
33. See for example, Nelson and Wright (1995) and Slocum *et al.* (1995), for the use of participatory techniques in understanding and working with communities, and Bailyn and Rapoport (1996) for their use in understanding organizational culture.
34. This highlights the usefulness of the distinction between community-managing and constituency-based politics roles, and the relegation so often of women to community-management roles.
35. See Fernando (1985).
36. See Schon (1971) for a discussion of 'public learning'.
37. See for example, Nelson and Wright (1995), Guijt (1995), Feldstein and Jiggins (1995) on PRA, and Taher (1992 and 1994) on other techniques of monitoring gendered and gender strategies.
38. The dialogue between disciplines has been critical in advancing theoretical work on gender, not only in subject areas like economics, sociology and anthropology, but also in applied disciplines like planning and policy analysis. Similarly, theoretical work on participation and gender has greatly enriched each other.
39. The web has been used by the DPU at organizational level (for example, in DG VIII of the EU, IBIS (a large Danish organization) and Plan International (an international NGO); at sectoral and country levels (for example, in Namibia working with the National Planning Commission with SIDA support); and to assess the impact of a programme (for example, in Nepal).
40. The web is one of the key gender diagnosis tools in the gender policy and planning methodology developed at the DPU. For a more detailed discussion of this methodology and the role of the web in it, see Levy (forthcoming).
41. For prioritization techniques used in DPU's gender policy and planning methodology, see Levy (forthcoming).
42. This process is described in more detail elsewhere, including a discussion of other key planning concepts in the gender policy and planning methodology (for example, working objectives, constraints and assets). See Levy (op. cit).
43. This process also highlights the false separation of diagnosis and action in any policy and planning endeavour.

Index